What is a Romance language? How is one Roma[n]
to others? How did they all evolve? And what c[a]
language in general? In this comprehensive surv[e]
distinguished Romance specialist, examines this g[roup]
from a wide variety of perspectives. Her analysis combines philological expertise with insights drawn from modern theoretical linguistics,
both synchronic and diachronic. She relates linguistic features to historical and sociological factors, and teases out those elements which
can be attributed to divergence from a common source and those
which indicate convergence towards a common aim. Her discussion is
extensively illustrated with new and original data, and an up-to-date
and comprehensive bibliography is included. This volume will be an
invaluable and authoritative guide for students and specialists alike.

THE ROMANCE LANGUAGES

Cambridge Language Surveys

General editors: B. Comrie, C. Ewen, R. Huddleston, R. Lass, D. Lightfoot, J. Lyons, P.H. Matthews, R. Posner, S. Romaine, N.V. Smith, N. Vincent

This series offers general accounts of all the major language families of the world. Some volumes are organised on a purely genetic basis, others on a geographical basis, whichever yields the most convenient and intelligible grouping in each case. Sometimes, as with the Australian volume, the two in any case coincide.

Each volume compares and contrasts the typological features of the languages it deals with. It also treats the relevant genetic relationships, historical development and sociolinguistic issues arising from their role and use in the world today. The intended readership is the student of linguistics or general linguist, but no special knowledge of the languages under consideration is assumed. Some volumes also have a wider appeal, like that on Australia, where the future of the languages and their speakers raises important social and political issues.

Already published:
The languages of Australia *R.M.W. Dixon*
The languages of the Soviet Union *Bernard Comrie*
The Mesoamerican Indian languages *Jorge A. Suárez*
The Papuan languages of New Guinea *William A. Foley*
Chinese *Jerry Norman*
Languages of Japan *M. Shibatani*
Pidgins and Creoles (Volume I: Theory and structure; Volume II: Reference survey) *John H. Holm*
The Indo-Aryan languages *Colin Masica*

Forthcoming titles include:
Korean *Ho-Min Sohn*
The languages of South-East Asia *J.A. Matisoff*
The Austronesian languages *R. Blust*
The Slavonic languages *R. Sussex*
The Germanic languages *R. Lass*

THE ROMANCE LANGUAGES

REBECCA POSNER

University of Oxford

CAMBRIDGE
UNIVERSITY PRESS

PUBLISHED BY THE PRESS SYNDICATE OF THE UNIVERSITY OF CAMBRIDGE
The Pitt Building, Trumpington Street, Cambridge, United Kingdom

CAMBRIDGE UNIVERSITY PRESS
The Edinburgh Building, Cambridge CB2 2RU, UK
40 West 20th Street, New York, NY 10011–4211, USA
477 Williamstown Road, Port Melbourne, VIC 3207, Australia
Ruiz de Alarcón 13, 28014 Madrid, Spain
Dock House, The Waterfront, Cape Town 8001, South Africa

http://www.cambridge.org

First published 1996
Reprinted 2002

Printed in Great Britain at the University Press, Cambridge

A catalogue record for this book is available from the British Library

Library of Congress cataloguing in publication data
Posner, Rebecca.
The Romance Languages / Rebecca Posner.
   p.   cm. – (Cambridge Language Surveys)
Includes bibliographical references and index.
ISBN 0 521 23654 1 (hardcover). – ISBN 0 521 28139 3 (paperback)
1. Romance languages.   I. Title.   II. Series.
PC43.P595   1996
440–dc20   95-42167 CIP

ISBN 0 521 23654 1
ISBN 0 521 28139 3

TAG

CONTENTS

Preface   *page*   xi
List of language names   xv
List of abbreviations   xvii
Maps   xviii

INTRODUCTION

Why the Romance languages?   1
What do Romanists worry about?   7
What do Romanists argue about?   10
What contribution can Romance studies make to
synchronic and diachronic linguistics?   11
Conclusion   30
Further reading   30

PART I   THE SIMILARITIES

1   What is a Romance language? Part 1

1.1   What is a Romance language?   35
1.2   Person markers   39
1.3   Noun gender   55
1.4   In place of a partial conclusion   69
      Further reading   70

2   What is a Romance language? Part 2

2.1   Romance 'family' and Romance 'type'   71
2.2   Romance functional morphemes   71
2.3   Word formation   80
2.4   Shared lexicon   87

2.5	Loanwords	93
2.6	How close are Romance lexicons?	94
2.7	Romanceness as a continuum?	94
	Further reading	96

3   Latin and Romance

3.1	Derivation	97
3.2	Proto-Romance or Vulgar Latin	98
3.3	Differences between Latin and Romance	104
3.4	Latin influence	139
3.5	Who killed Latin?	152
	Further reading	154

4   Convergence, interinfluence and parallel development

4.1	Drift and metarules	155
4.2	Diphthongization	157
4.3	The infinitive	163
4.4	Object clitics	167
4.5	Periphrastic aspectual forms	175
4.6	The future	177
4.7	The passive	179
4.8	Lexicon	181
4.9	Conclusion	184
	Further reading	186

PART II   THE DIFFERENCES

5   How many Romance languages?

5.1	How many Romance languages are there?	189
5.2	Genetic classification	196
5.3	Typology	200
5.4	Dialectometry	202
5.5	Standardology	206
5.6	Language and dialect	217
5.7	Creole and dialect	219
5.8	Creolization as creation, or as catastrophic change?	224
5.9	Conclusion	225
	Further reading	226

6 When did the Romance languages differentiate?

6.1	Introduction	227
6.2	Early dialectalization?	227
6.3	Spread of Roman rule	231
6.4	Breakup of the Roman Empire – superstratum	245
6.5	Syntactic differentiation in the early modern period	254
6.6	Conclusion	280
	Further reading	281

7 How did the Romance languages differentiate?

7.1	Processes of change	282
7.2	Phonological changes	285
7.3	Morphological changes	296
7.4	Syntactic changes	302
7.5	Hypercharacterization, simplification and exaptation	310
7.6	Lexical and semantic differentiation	319
7.7	Conservatism in Romance	326
	Further reading	328

8 Sociolinguistic factors

8.1	Social aspects of Romance	329
8.2	Sociolinguistic variation	329
8.3	Language conflict	332
8.4	Romance–Romance bilingualism and diglossia	335
8.5	Romance interlects	338
8.6	Contact with other languages	339
8.7	Romance overseas	340
8.8	Language attitudes: in place of a conclusion	343
	Further reading	345

References	346
Index of names	356
Index of languages	359
Subject index	367

PREFACE

This is an extraordinarily difficult book to fit into the Language Surveys series, which was originally intended to provide a means for those who are more or less proficient in linguistics to have access to knowledge about languages they are not familiar with. The volumes in the series that have so far appeared differ considerably among themselves, sometimes concerned with diverse languages within one geographical area, sometimes with genetically related languages, sometimes – like the two volumes on *Pidgins and Creoles* – with languages grouped together because of their social function and historical development. They are perhaps most successful when they provide the sole authoritative account of the languages they describe. The types of exposition adopted are as diverse as the subject matter. Some examine each language or sub-group of languages separately, some treat chosen themes by adducing comparative data; some adopt a strictly synchronic approach, while others introduce diachronic considerations.

One problem with writing about the Romance languages is that so much has already been written on them: I shall survey the history of Romance linguistics in my introductory chapter. Elementary introductions for the layman abound – my own paperback written some thirty years ago (Posner 1966) is apparently still going strong. 'State of the art' surveys are also readily available – the one in four volumes I edited (1980–4) with my colleague John Green (Posner & Green eds.) was in 1993 supplemented by a fifth volume, perhaps not the last. Comprehensive reference works are also readily available, the latest being the massive project from Niemeyer (Holtus, Metzeltin & Schmitt 1988–) that is still in the process of publication.

The task of keeping this book down to a single volume has meant that much interesting material has had to be omitted or merely touched on. For phonology and morphology especially reference will still have to be made to the comprehensive manuals, some of which date back more than a hundred years. Specialist monographs have since then flooded into libraries and now seem to be increasing in number, especially on syntactic and lexical questions. Adherents of virtually every school of linguistics have used Romance data to validate their ideas. Generativists' interest in Romance largely postdates my comments in Iordan, Orr & Posner (1970), when there were comparatively few Romanist generativists. The 'Principles-and-Parameters' model, in particular, has attracted linguists with Romance mother tongues, who initially were led to contrast their own languages with English and so to recognize that the Romance languages have much in common. A result is that examples from the Romance languages are now commonplace in the works of non-Romanists.

Yet, in preparing the book I have often been frustrated by the lack of solid information in many problematic areas of Romance linguistics. The abundant studies on the standard languages are often slanted towards the theoretical predilections and social prejudices of their authors; the body of material on non-standard languages is huge but patchy, both in geographical and social coverage and in exemplification. Transcriptions of texts are inconsistent and sometimes uninterpretable. I have tried to transcribe as accurately as I can into the IPA alphabet whenever the phonetic detail is relevant to the argument. In other cases, though, more traditional orthography suffices for the purposes of exposition. Similarly, morph-by-morph translation sometimes seems helpful, if laborious, but more often I have made do with general indication of the sense.

In citing examples (which are usually fairly randomly chosen samples of the material available) I have tried to avoid tendentious classification of 'languages' and 'dialects', using, as far as is feasible, geographical nomenclature. Thus, for instance an Italian dialect (Ital. dial.) is a non-standard variety spoken in Italy, and where relevant the locality in which it has been attested is cited.

Judgements about usage are sometimes unreliable, not only because of the inherent difficulties of collecting such material, but also because of the ideological viewpoint of some of the speakers and investigators. I have frequently found that, when I had expected merely to summarize the work of others, I have had to embark on my own detailed examination of a particular topic. Much work remains to be done, and some Romance varieties are near to extinction, so there is a degree of urgency. All too often, though, new work that promises to be exciting turns out to be little more than a reformulation of findings that were already well known to readers of older works. It is tempting to cite works hot off the press, but it is difficult coolly to assess their lasting worth until the novelty has worn off.

I have had, of course, to rely very much on others, not only in their published work, but also for comments on, and corrections of, my own drafts and for the sight of unpublished fieldwork, lecture notes and the like. There is no way in which I could have first-hand knowledge of all currently used Romance varieties: although quite widely travelled, I could not possibly even have visited every locality within the Romance-speaking world. Similarly, I cannot be personally familiar with the vast amount of published historical documentation, including high-quality literary works, in the languages, let alone the yet-untapped resources that still lie untouched in archives and attics. Most recent works on Romance (like Posner & Green 1980–93, Harris & Vincent 1988, Holtus, Metzeltin & Schmitt 1988–) are collaborative enterprises, accepting that no one individual can have sufficient expertise to cover all the field. The result must be, however tough the editorial control, a certain lack of cohesion and consistency.

The problem of which works to cite in the bibliography was daunting. I therefore decided to rely heavily on reference to previous surveys and bibliographies, rather than to attempt a comprehensive coverage, which in itself would fill up several massive tomes. I have for each chapter given an indication of further reading, but this can be only a preliminary guide, which the serious student would have to follow through further. Regretfully, I have had normally to limit my references to monograph-length works published during the 1980s and 1990s. Important periodical articles will normally be cited in these works and in the bibliographical surveys.

To undertake my task required a greal deal of *hubris*: mine has threatened to desert me several times during the preparation of the book. What I have tried to do, however unsuccessfully, is something a little different from what has been done before, aiming at a theoretical coverage of topics that I believe to be of interest to all linguists, combining both synchronic and diachronic material, drawn from a wide variety of Romance varieties, and not merely standard languages. I have chosen not to give a language-by-language account, trying to treat every topic with a wide range of comparative material, both ancient and modern. Some friends and colleagues have urged more exemplification from more languages, others have suggested that I indulge too much in 'philological' detail. Because I believe that there will be a body of readers who take pleasure in the actual examples, as well as those who have a more theoretical interest in language, I have tried to illustrate from actual language material as much as possible, avoiding, as far as I can, the standard examples found in most handbooks.

Some of my consultants complain that I often am hesitant in my judgements, over-using such hedges as 'perhaps', 'apparently', 'allegedly' and so on. I do not apologize for this: even in those areas in which I count myself an expert, I have frequently found that new material has radically changed my view of linguistic reality. My ignorance remains almost bottomless, even though I have spent my life in the study of Romance languages. I am very conscious that anything I say too firmly may very soon be demonstrated to be nonsense. I should like to think that this book will not be outdated before it reaches the shelves of its readers: I therefore leave some questions open for further research, while presenting my own current views. I have nevertheless tried to present a reasonably coherent case for writing a book on 'The Romance Languages' as a unit, rather than on each individual language. I know how assailable my stand is, but I am prepared to defend it against anticipated attacks.

It remains for me to thank all the people who have given me advice and help while I have been preparing this book – some of them at considerable cost of time and patience. Most of all I wish to thank Roger Lass for reading a draft of the whole book and giving me the benefit of his inspiring insights from the point of view of a Germanist and theorist, especially in phonology and historical linguistics. Many others have read part of the book and supplied material: in particular I should like to mention John Green, Valerio Lucchesi, Yakov Malkiel, Ed Tuttle, Max Wheeler, Roger Wright, as well as many of my pupils who have suffered, though not silently, imposition of my views. I should also like to thank Judith Ayling at the Press for her patient help. My thanks also to Christopher Posner for preparing the Indices, and to Michael Posner for his patience and for giving me the time required to complete this task. Needless to say, I have only myself to blame for errors and shortcomings: I only hope that these are not so numerous that they spoil the reader's enjoyment.

Rebecca Posner
Oxford

LANGUAGE NAMES

For convenience language data are cited according to geographical area; for more detailed information see chapter 5. The following abbreviations are used.

dial. a non-standard regional variety within a geographical area ('dialect').
ns.: non-standard usage that is not necessarily regionally based.

Otherwise reference is made, where appropriate, to a standard variety, using the following general classification.

Cat. (Catalan): the Barcelona standard, but also used to refer to varieties spoken in Catalonia, Roussillon (France), the Balearics, Valencia and Alghero (Sardinia).

Dalmatian: the Romance language once spoken along the Dalmatian coast (former Yugoslavia). The variety for which we have most evidence is from the island of Veglia (Krk), off the Istrian peninsula.

Francoprovençal: varieties used in the south-east of the French-speaking area, including part of Switzerland and the Val d'Aosta in Italy (see chapter 5).

French (includes non-standard varieties of northern France, usually cited according to locality).

Galician: spoken in north-west Spain, closely related to Portuguese.

Ital. (Italian): the standard and also regional varieties (dialects) of Italy.

Occ. (Occitan): used for the standard and non-standard varieties spoken in southern France, cited according to locality.

Ptg. (Portuguese): used for the European and Brazilian standards, and for non-standard varieties, cited according to locality.

R-R (Rhaeto-Romance): a cover term for some Romance varieties spoken in Switzerland' (Grisons) and northern Italy (Dolomites and Friuli). Forms are cited according to locality (see chapter 5).

Rum. (Rumanian): Daco-Rumanian is the standard language of Romania; for Arumanian, Megleno-Rumanian and Istro-Rumanian see chapter 5.

Sard: varieties spoken in central and southern Sardinia.

Span. (Spanish): used for European and Latin-American standards, and for non-standard varieties cited according to locality.

NOTES ON CONVENTIONS USED

Phonetic transcription is in the IPA alphabet. Foreign citations in traditional orthography are italicized. Latin words are cited in small capitals; except where inappropriate the traditional convention is followed of citation of nouns in the accusative form without a final consonant (e.g. LUPU for LUPUS, LUPUM, etc.). Terminological keywords are in boldface, usually at their first appearance.

ABBREVIATIONS

acc.	accusative case
C	consonant
dat.	dative case
f.	feminine gender
gen.	genitive case
m.	masculine gender
n.	neuter gender
nom.	nominative case
p.1–6	verb persons 1–6 (1st, 2nd, 3rd sg./pl.)
pl.	plural
pres.	present tense
pret.	preterite
sg.	singular
subj.	subjunctive
SVO etc.	subject–verb–object etc. word order.
V	vowel
V1/V2	verb-first/verb-second word order

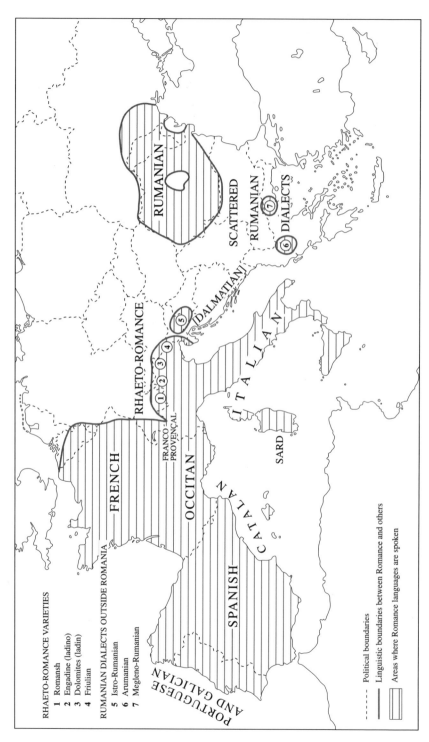

RHAETO-ROMANCE VARIETIES
1 Romansh
2 Engadine (ladino)
3 Dolomites (ladin)
4 Friulian

RUMANIAN DIALECTS OUTSIDE ROMANIA
5 Istro-Rumanian
6 Arumanian
7 Megleno-Rumanian

- - - - Political boundaries

— Linguistic boundaries between Romance and others

Areas where Romance languages are spoken

Map 1   The distribution of Romance languages in Europe

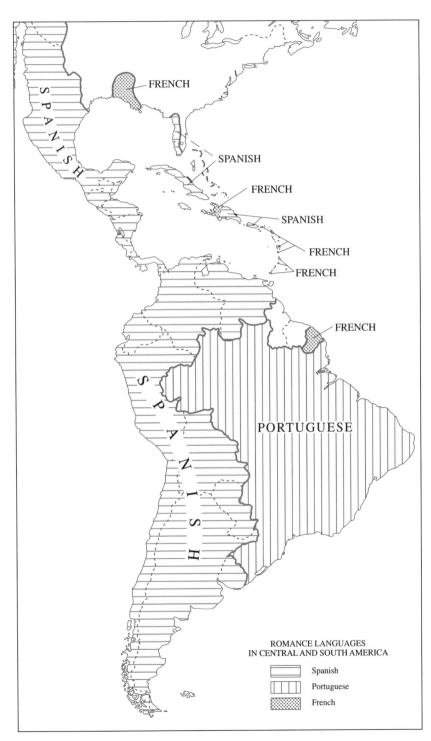

Map 2   Romance languages in Central and South America

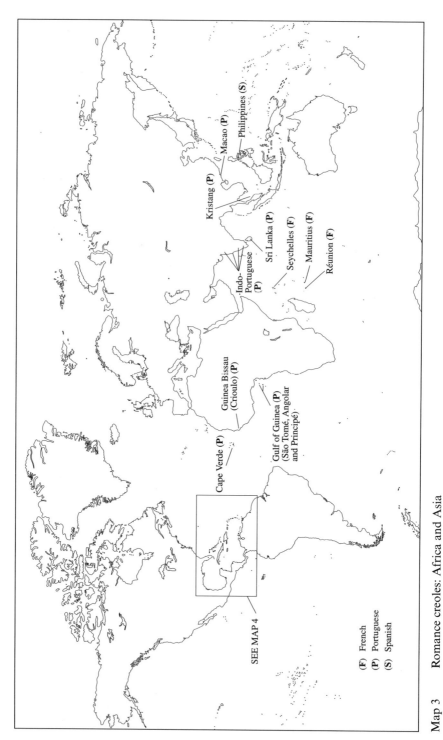

Map 3   Romance creoles: Africa and Asia

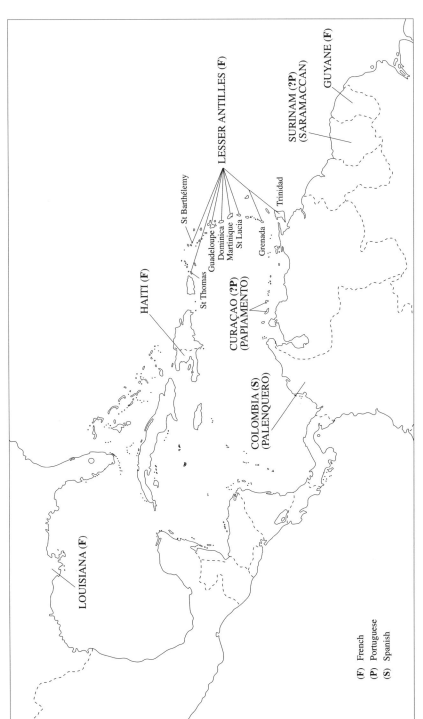

Map 4 Romance creoles: the Caribbean

LOUISIANA (**F**)

HAITI (**F**)

St Thomas

St Barthélemy

Guadeloupe
Dominica
Martinique
St Lucia

Grenada

Trinidad

LESSER ANTILLES (**F**)

SURINAM (**?P**)
(SARAMACCAN)

GUYANE (**F**)

CURAÇAO (**?P**)
(PAPIAMENTO)

COLOMBIA (**S**)
(PALENQUERO)

(**F**) French
(**P**) Portuguese
(**S**) Spanish

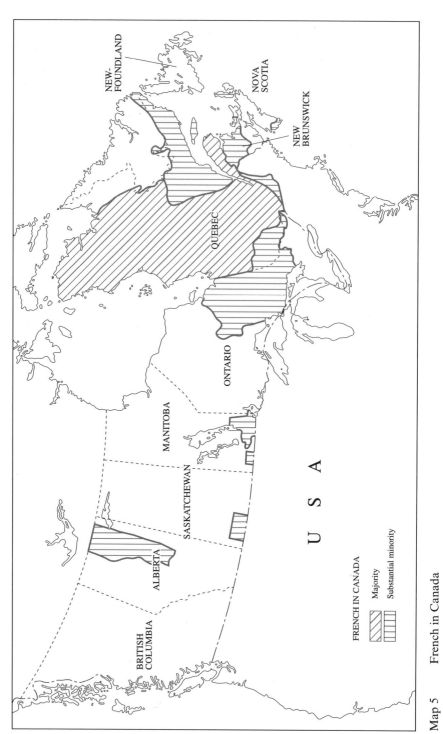

Map 5   French in Canada

FRENCH IN CANADA

Majority

Substantial minority

Introduction

WHY THE ROMANCE LANGUAGES?

Why write about the Romance languages? Perhaps just because, like Everest, 'they are there'. But are they – as an entity, that is? Is there anything about the Romance languages that makes them susceptible to treatment as a single unit? That is a question I shall be addressing all through this book, and to which I believe the answer is 'Yes!' Others, however, deny that synchronically they have more in common than any arbitrarily chosen collection of languages. The only reason why we treat them together is, then, because they are related historically, and are all derived from Latin, or, conceivably, a near-relative to Latin. In this view the features shared by the Romance languages would form the common heritage, or be a consequence of borrowing, or result from a common process of 'drift', or be merely coincidental (or any combination of these).

This must, surely, be true. What I would contest is the next step in the argument: that synchronic comparison of the languages would yield no linguistically interesting insights, and that only a historical approach is possible or desirable. I shall maintain that, although there are many differences of detail between the Romance languages that cannot be accounted for except in terms of history (social as well as linguistic), there are many cases in which description of the synchronic state of one language loses an important dimension if no comparison is made with the other languages.

This is so not only of the standard languages, which have both influenced each other and recoiled from each other, but also of the non-standard languages, which often preserve, or innovate, parallel features that are spurned by their prestigious counterparts. Thus, what appears a puzzling anomaly in one language may, when it appears in another, become intelligible because the conditioning is more transparent.

Whether there is such a thing as a 'Romance type' – a guiding principle which governs how the language mechanism ticks – is something I shall discuss at length. How this may relate to a postulated 'Eurotype', which would presumably owe much to the common history and aspirations of European peoples, is also worth considering.

Of one thing I am certain: it is misguided to attempt to account for every feature of the Romance languages without recourse to historical explanation. On the other hand, some mechanisms in the languages can be illuminatingly described in synchronic terms, by concentrating on the often minute ways in which the mechanism differs from language to language, and taking for granted that in a broad sense it works in much the same way in all.

Nevertheless it is still true that any comparative study of the Romance languages will cast most light on the workings of linguistic history. In a sense, as linguistic geographers were quick to notice in the past, historical development of the language can be mirrored by the geographical distribution of variants, with some regions appearing to be more innovative, whereas others resist change. Thus with synchronic variation it is possible to factor out the time parameter of historical linguistics, substituting for it geographical or social space.

Time, however, must come back into the picture when we are faced with the introduction or the loss of a variant in any one language: here we shall be concerned primarily with changes in the socially acceptable 'norm' of a speech community, and only secondarily with system or type changes. How far changes in the norm feed into the language acquisition process (perhaps via a change in **parameter setting**) is a burning question.

History of Romance comparative grammar

Most comparative studies of Romance have, until very recently, been historical in their orientation. Romance philology is often said to have started with Dante's unfinished Latin treatise *De vulgari eloquentia* (written after 1304), in which he divides the Romance languages into three groups, according to their word for 'yes', *si*, *oc*, *oui*, contrasting them with other European languages. It is far from clear, however, whether Dante had a view on their relationship with each other and with Latin. His aim was to devise an 'illustrious vulgar tongue' that would rival Latin as the language of serious discourse, and in so doing he disparaged the claims of contemporary spoken Italian varieties. It is likely that in the early Middle Ages the Romance languages had been viewed as fluctuating spoken versions of Latin, which remained the main vehicle for writing. Separate names for the vernaculars, based on their geographical spread, began to be used regularly only from the late twelfth century (see 3.3), and there is evidence of multilingual usage within the Romance area, not only between Latin and vernacular, but also between the different vernaculars.

It was only later, from the sixteenth century on, when vernaculars were ready to take over completely from Latin, that the question of the Romance–Latin affiliation was hotly debated: some even claimed that Romans had always used Italian varieties in colloquial speech and that the Latin of texts had never been other than a literary convention. The other Romance languages would in this view reflect adulteration from the barbarian tongues with which they were in contact from the time of Roman colonization (see 6.4). For the French their language stood somewhat apart, as incorporating Germanic (Frankish) elements, or, even, as being derived from Greek or Celtic, rather than from Latin.

During the eighteenth century, when the regularity of phonological change began to be perceived, treatises on the origins of Romance languages began to appear in profusion, but the title of 'father' of Romance philology is usually bestowed on François-Juste Raynouard (1761–1836), writing in the post-Napoleonic period. He discerned in the Romance languages common features that could not all be ascribed to Latin heritage, and therefore postulated a common ancestor, *la langue romane*, that he believed replaced Latin before AD 1000, and which most nearly resembled the language of the troubadours (now called Old Occitan, or Old Provençal).

Raynouard's hypothesis received short shrift from the more professional German comparative philologists, in particular August Wilhelm von Schlegel, who viewed Romance as the spontaneous outcome of the decomposition of Latin, after the disappearance of the normative pressures exerted by a stable cultural environment.

The first systematic treatise on Romance was published in 1831 by Lorenz Diefenbach, who maintained that the Romance languages derived from a popular form of Latin, further adulterated by contact with other languages, especially in the case of French, which he characterized as 'very creolized'. Diefenbach's fellow-student at Giessen, Friedrich Diez, was to become the first specialist in Romance Philology, at Bonn. His

Grammatik der romanischen Sprachen in three volumes, which went into three editions and two further reprints, began to appear in 1836. He too believed that popular Latin was at the origin of the Romance languages which developed by phonological processes and functional adjustments dictated by the 'spirit' of the people, originating from speakers' negligence in the absence of a normative standard. For him Rumanian ('Wallachian') was only a semi-Romance language, and French was more influenced by German than by Celtic.

> The French translation of the Grammar, under the direction of his illustrious pupil Gaston Paris, appeared in 1869.

For half a century Diez's Grammar remained the Bible of Romance philology. Meanwhile numerous treatises on individual languages, especially on medieval texts, and essays on the question of the origin of one of the languages, were appearing. We should mention especially the contributions of Hugo Schuchardt, who battled against the idea of sound-laws and traced the origin of Romance phonological features to archaic popular ('Vulgar') Latin, and of Graziado Isaia Ascoli, whose work mainly concerned dialectal usage.

After Diez's death in 1876 a new wave of German Romance philologists came on the scene, associated with Neogrammarian views about linguistic change, as stemming from mechanical and exceptionless phonological shifts, limited in time and space. Gustav Gröber, who became professor at the new University in Strasburg after the Prussian annexation of Alsace, had launched the tone-setting *Zeitschrift für romanische Philologie* in 1877 and in 1888 edited the first edition of the *Grundriß der romanischen Philologie*, a 'state-of-the-art' survey of the discipline.

Regularist and reconstructionist views were dominant, especially in the contribution of Wilhelm Meyer (later Meyer-Lübke), whose own *Grammatik der romanischen Sprachen* (1890–1902), translated immediately into French, was to replace that of Diez, for phonology and morphology, at any rate, and to remain the standard work. For Meyer-Lübke the pivot of grammatical study was phonetics: change is a physiological process not controlled by meaning, which causes disintegration, which may then be patched up by analogical change, dictated by functional needs. He was able to improve on Diez, not only in phonological methodology, but also in his coverage of language data, drawn from both literary languages and from dialect material.

> On syntax, however, he is on less firm ground, hampered by a lack of
> methodology and by the multiplicity and heterogeneity of this material,
> mostly drawn from older texts. Comparative Romance syntax remained a
> stumbling-block for later scholars, many of whom hesitate to plunge into that
> murky pond, or refuse to isolate syntax, preferring to treat morphosyntax as
> a composite functional level. It is only recently that new ground has been bro-
> ken in the study of Romance syntax, both synchronic and diachronic.

The Franco-Prussian war is held by some to have occasioned the often bit-
ter divorce between French and German linguistic thought. Certainly, by
the end of the nineteenth century the French were turning away from regularist and reconstructionist Romance philology and concentrating more
on dialectology and on sociological and pragmatic approaches to the
individual languages. 'Idealist' linguistics, with its emphasis on the conscious creativity of linguistic processes and on the communicative functions of language, became the hallmark of Romanist work within the
Romance-speaking countries. The standard French work on Romance
philology, Edouard Bourciez's *Eléments de linguistique romane*, which first
appeared in 1910, considers each language separately and adopts a functionalist view of change as resulting from a tension between economy of
effort and desire for effective communication.

In spite of Saussure's remarks, in the Introduction to his *Cours de linguistique générale*, on the importance of Romance philology, there were
no important additions to comparative Romance linguistics between the
world wars, except for the idealistically slanted methodological survey by
Iorgu Iordan, especially in its 1937 English version prepared by John Orr,
Introduction to Romance linguistics: its schools and its scholars. New versions of this influential work appeared in a variety of languages after the
Second World War, when there was an upsurge in interest in comparative
Romance studies.

The most successful of the immediate postwar works was Carlo
Tagliavini's *Le origini delle lingue neolatine: introduzione alla filologia romanza*, first appearing in 1949, which concentrated on the early stages of the languages, juxtaposing rather than comparing them. Similarly juxtapositional
of literary languages, except for a 'Common Romance' chapter, is Walter
Elcock's popular *The Romance languages*, which first appeared in 1960.

Heinrich Lausberg's three-volume *Romanische Sprachwissenschaft*,
beginning publication in 1956, is concerned with the genesis, rather than
the evolution, of the languages. As a functionalist, influenced by the ide-

alist stance of Eugenio Coseriu, Lausberg sees language structure as in unstable equilibrium, ready to topple if undermined at its weak points, and insists on social factors and speakers' consciousness of their language as a community possession.

One of his innovations, stemming from his own expertise in dialectal morphophonology, is to distinguish the classic **Vulgar Latin** phonological system from the 'archaic' one of Sardinia, Lucania and Africa and the 'compromise' one of Balkan Romance and Eastern Lucania. Another is his introduction of the concept of 'mechanization', a phenomenon that permits repetition and reproduction of a chance innovation, enhancing social intercourse by reducing the effort required to formulate expression. This is related, it seems, to what is often called **grammaticalization**, by which linguistic items are impoverished ('bleached') of lexical content and come to serve as grammatical items, and perhaps to **morphologization**, by which hitherto general phonological rules are restricted to marking certain morphological functions.

Whereas Lausberg's work is representative of European structuralism, Bloomfieldian structuralism, in its comparativist guise, is exemplified by the work of the Cornell Romanists, Robert A. Hall Jr and Frederick B. Agard. Hall has long defended the regularist and reconstructionist stance in Romance linguistics, especially against 'idealism' and generative approaches: three volumes of his comparative work on the Romance languages appeared between 1974 and 1983. Agard's 1984 *A course in Romance linguistics* has both a diachronic and a synchronic volume: the latter provides a contrastive grammar of five standard languages (French, Spanish, Portuguese, Italian, Rumanian) using an eclectic grammatical model – a hierarchical phrase-structure grammar, with some relational concepts and simple transformations, not unlike traditional grammar.

Maria Manoliu-Manea, a Californian Romanist of Rumanian origin, was perhaps the first systematically to essay the application of Chomskyan 'standard theory' to comparative Romance problems, in her 1971 *Gramatica comparată al limbilor romanice*. Her later work (1977; see Manoliu-Manea 1985) on Romance typology leans more towards case grammar and generative semantics, though grounded in European structuralism.

Recent years have seen a great increase in research into comparative Romance linguistics. Even within the generative camp, where interest is focused on language universals and cognitive structures, rather than on languages as such, Romance languages have become a centre of attention. Assuming that language is organized according to restrictive principles, it is suggested that nevertheless specific parameters of variation can account for some differences between languages. The language learner is thought to determine the value of these parameters through exposure to language data.

The interest of Romance languages to the theorist is that they provide abundant material from systems that are closely similar but which differ interestingly in some features, which may be attributable to parametric differences. By minute examination of variation within Romance it is believed that **parameters**, which account for a cluster of seemingly unrelated differences, can be pinpointed. Such Romance features as use or non-use of clitic pronouns, order of elements, the status of inflections or of auxiliaries, causative constructions and so on have been discussed from this angle.

The range of language material used has widened to cover not only standard languages, but also regional dialects, so that our knowledge of some areas of Romance syntax has improved immensely as a result of these studies. On the diachronic plane, the question has also been addressed of how, over time, the **parameter setting** of a language can change: what are the characteristics of language input that persuade the language learner to decide that a different value should be attributed to the parameters of variation?

> Although there is as yet no general work on comparative Romance syntax within this framework, there are several that tackle specific questions within Romance: the names of Richard Kayne, Luigi Rizzi, Luigi Burzio, María Luisa Rivero, Oswaldo Jaeggli, Hagit Borer, Jean-Yves Pollock, Jean-Roger Vergnaud are among the many that can be mentioned.

WHAT DO ROMANISTS WORRY ABOUT?

It is, however, probably true that these generativists would not regard themselves primarily as Romanists, but as linguistic theorists who, often, are native speakers of a Romance language and for whom the Romance data provide a stimulus to refinement of conceptual argumentation.

Many others who may indeed call themselves Romanists concentrate on one Romance language, or on the transition from Latin to Romance. They will usually have rather different interests from the Principles-and-Parameters brigade, in that they do not limit themselves to study of individual manifestations of a hypothetical core grammar, but also, and perhaps principally, to what Chomskyans call the 'periphery' and regard as accidental–historical residue, chance idiosyncrasies, features arising from language contact, dialect mixture, social or pragmatic factors or conscious seeking for stylistic effect – but what others regard as the fascinating mysteries of language that await elucidation. Not all are convinced that one Romance language can cast light on another: in some cases national pride is at stake, in others the promotion of elegance in language use is more important than the investigation of causes.

Comparative Romance linguistics as such is still, as in the past, mainly fostered outside the Romance-speaking area – especially in German-speaking countries – though Romania (Rumania) has a long and respected tradition in this field. German interest in Romance may be a result of historical accident, as a spin-off from the nineteenth-century popularity of comparative philology, with roots in the search for a Germanic identity, but in the postwar period it has gained momentum, embracing all manifestations of both modern and medieval Romance.

(a)   Classification

Among the topics that most preoccupy comparative Romance linguists is the classic one of the relationship of Romance to Latin and of the Romance languages to one another. Classification of the languages is traditionally discussed in 'family tree' terms, with branching determined on the basis of **common innovations** – nearly always phonological – but several other schemata, including synchronic typologies, are used (see chapter 5).

(b)   Dialectology and sociolinguistics

Of particular interest to Romanists are the social functions of language and the relationship of non-standard varieties (especially regional dialects) to standard languages, of spoken to written usage (see chapter 8).

(c)   Stylistics and pragmatics

Given that several of the languages are vehicles for literary discourse of undisputed high quality, it is not surprising that Romanists are particularly concerned too with stylistic and pragmatic study.

(d)   Phonology

Phonology has been at the centre of historical Romance linguistics, certainly since the Neogrammarian era, with particular emphasis laid on shared developments, like **palatalization** and **diphthongization**, as well as on processes that affected only some languages, like **nasalization**. From a strictly synchronic point of view there is no particular reason why phonetics or phonology should be treated in a pan-Romance perspective, though certain topics that relate to morpheme structure, like accent placement and **sandhi** phenomena, can profitably be examined cross-linguistically. However, some synchronic phonological treatments do mirror quite closely diachronic analyses, and past phonological processes not infrequently can be viewed as ongoing in contemporary varieties. Morphology is frequently closely linked to phonology, especially through morphologization processes, but many Romanists concentrate more on the semantic and grammatical functions of 'morphosyntax', as well as on grammaticalization of lexical elements.

(e)   Lexicon

The lexicon has most attracted Romanist attention. This most idiosyncratic and least systematic aspect of language is also, by that very token, the most diagnostic for Romanceness, as the lexical similarity between the languages could not have arisen by accident or through common cognitive requirements. Some historical link must therefore be assumed – either common origin or close interaction.

For Romance both conditions obtain and are well attested. The common origin or proto-language is obviously seen, on the basis of both linguistic and historical evidence, as a form of Latin; so tracing the trajectory of Latin words into Romance, or reconstructing the origin of Romance words, is an activity particularly beloved by Romanists, as is the unravelling of the history of borrowing and new creations. From this perspective, not only form but also meaning, and change of meaning, can be examined, and linked with social and ideological changes in the speech communities. Word formation from native sources is also much studied, lying as it does between the idiosyncratic and the systematic levels of language, and allowing comparison of the mechanisms used by the different languages, and of the functions they fill.

(f)   Syntax

As I have already pointed out, until recently Romance syntax was rarely studied, except in terms of semantics and style, partly because of the difficulty of obtaining reliable comparative data, except from literary languages which interact considerably, but also because methodology was insufficiently developed to permit plausible extrapolation from the multifarious material. The 'parametric' approach has, however, given a new boost to this aspect of Romance linguistics, even among those who are doubtful about its validity.

(g)   Historiography

A mention should be made of the interest shown by Romanists in the history of the discipline and its relationship to social and ideological history. As we have already glimpsed, speculation about the origin of the languages and analysis of their structures and social functions dates far back, even into the 'prelinguistic' era, and much conscious manipulation of language use as a social tool is evident in all the standard varieties.

WHAT DO ROMANISTS ARGUE ABOUT?

I have already hinted strongly that Romanists are far from unanimous about the way the languages should be studied. Conflict has often arisen between those who see the discipline as part of the humanities or of social studies and those who seek a more 'scientific' approach, between those who believe that historical factors must be taken into consideration and those who attempt to keep to a strictly synchronic line, and between those who view language as the property of a community and those for whom it is a part of individual cognitive makeup. Indeed, as in other linguistic enterprises, we not infrequently find a *dialogue des sourds*, in which interlocutors follow their own line of thought completely oblivious of what others are saying. A consequence is that the wheel is constantly being re-invented – as the history of Romance linguistics demonstrates – while the metalanguage that describes its form and function undergoes frequent radical transformations.

Classical Romance philology tended to concentrate on the chronologically earlier stages of the languages, seeking to unravel the testimony of medieval texts and to reconstruct the linguistic past. The interests of medievalists and students of modern Romance varieties are not always identical, though they can be complementary. The differences between students of dialects and other non-standard varieties and those who limit themselves to the literary languages, as between comparativists and experts in a single language, can be extreme. However, it seems that Romanists feel they have enough in common regularly to gather in congresses and symposia, seeing themselves as a coherent group within linguistics.

WHAT CONTRIBUTION CAN ROMANCE STUDIES MAKE TO SYNCHRONIC AND DIACHRONIC LINGUISTICS?

At one time Romance linguistics was seen as at the forefront of linguistics, especially of diachronic linguistics, because of its wealth of primary material in an unbroken chronological record. Later the very abundance of material, both primary and secondary, was to deter neophytes who would find richer pickings in less exploited linguistic seams. Romance philology came to be seen as a backwater, rather than part of the mainstream, especially when synchronic linguistic theory became more highly esteemed than language history. The rehabilitation of diachronic, or panchronic, linguistics, and the use made of Romance data by linguistic theorists, has changed the picture. I shall give three examples of the contribution that Romance linguistics has made or is making to more general study of language – in the realms of lexical reconstruction, of morphosyntax, and of phonology. I shall go into more detail than I can in later discussion, in order to give some picture of the richness of the data and the complexity of the argumentation. Ancillary information not essential to the main thrust of the discussion will appear in small type.

(a)   Lexical reconstruction

The greatest contribution of Romance studies must surely be to comparative philology reconstructionist techniques, as Romance is the only extended 'family' with a well-attested 'mother' (*Ursprache* or **proto-language**), so that reconstructed forms can be matched with attested equivalents. Take, for instance, the word for 'sweet', which has cognates in all the Romance languages:

(1)   Rum. *dulce*, Dalmatian (Veglia) *dolk*, Ital. *dolce*, Sard (Logudorian) *dulke*,
                 R-R (Engadine) *duc*, (Friuli) *dolts*, French *doux*, Occ. *dous*, Cat. *dolç*, Span.
                 dulce (Old *duz*), Ptg. *doce*.

Most of the differences between these forms are regularly found in
parallel correspondences, like the presence or absence of a final -*e*, of
preconsonantal *l* (replaced by *u* in some of the graphical forms), or of the
following consonant which may be a voiceless velar (as in Sard and
Dalmatian), a palato-alveolar (as in Italian, Rumanian and Engadine
Rhaeto-Romance), a dental sibilant or affricate (as in most other
languages). The correspondence between *o* and *u* for the stressed vowel is
also regular, except in the case of Spanish, where we should expect *o*.
Classic reconstruction from the Romance forms would end up with
/dulke/: the Latin word for 'sweet' is DŬLCEM in the accusative, the case
form which most often closely matches Romance forms (see 3.3).

> Latin final -m almost never is reflected in Romance, and we have ample evi-
> dence that it was not pronounced as a consonantal segment in later Latin.

(i)   Inheritance or borrowing?

We can therefore be confident that our reconstruction matches exactly the
phonemic structure of the form attested in texts. The slight discrepancy in
Spanish is usually explained away as influenced by, or borrowed from, the
learned Latin form. Sometimes it is hard to detect whether the Romance
forms are inherited or borrowed from Latin, and we are usually suspicious
when resemblances between Romance and Latin are too obvious. Take,
for instance, the word for 'sad', which also has cognates in all the
Romance languages:

(2)   Ital. *triste*, *tristo*, Occ. *tritz*, Span., Ptg. *triste*, Rum. *trist*, Sard (Logudorian)
                 tristu, Cat. *trist*, R-R (Engadine, Friuli) *trist*, French *triste*.

The Latin accusative form is TRISTEM, but some of the Romance forms
require a reconstruction with final -*u*, which is attested in a valuable text,
known as the *Appendix Probi*.

(3)   TRISTIS NON TRISTUS.

A nuance of 'morally reprehensible' is sometimes attached to the -U versions in Romance.

The modern French form could conceivably represent a feminine /trista/, which would have replaced the attested form *trist* (also *tristre*). In any case the preconsonantal s should regularly have disappeared in central French by the modern period (see 7.2): there is an Old French nominative form *triz* (/trits/) and the spelling *trite* is attested until the fourteenth century, while *triste* can rhyme with *ermite*, and *tristre* with *traître*. So to explain the presence of -*s* in the modern French word, we have to postulate a spelling pronunciation probably from the sixteenth century (as in *registre*).

(ii)   Vowel length

There is no doubt, however, about the reconstruction of /tri:st-/ with a long vowel, compared for instance with CRĬSTA 'coxcomb, crest', which has the following reflexes in Romance, dictating the reconstruction of a short vowel:

(4)   Rum. *creastă*, Ital. *cresta*, R-R (Engadine) *krasta*, (Friuli) *kreste*, French *crête*, Occ., Span., Cat. *cresta*. (Ptg. *crista* and Sard *krista* would allow reconstruction of either a long or a short vowel.)

The problem here is that we do not know whether Latin TRISTIS had a long vowel 'by nature', as it represents a case of 'hidden quantity' – for metrical scansion purposes, as it occurs in a 'heavy' medial consonant-final syllable, it is counted as long 'by position' (see 3.3). The Romance forms seem to provide the main evidence for a long vowel in this word, although some Latinists mention, without citing, epigraphical evidence: the etymology of the word is obscure, and graphy provides no clue to the vowel quantity. Elsewhere in Latin an *s+consonant cluster* is usually preceded by a short vowel, but here influence from the near synonym MAESTUS (with a long diphthong) has been suggested. Some commentators prefer to discard the Romance evidence in this case, regarding the forms as early borrowings rather than as inherited.

A similar niggling worry about vowel length spoils enjoyment of the anecdotally amusing history of Romance words for 'liver'. The Latin word IECUR has not survived, but the following (near) cognates are representative of the normal words for the 'liver', found in a range of Romance languages:

(5)   Rum. *ficat*, R-R (Friuli) *fiât*, Sard (Campidanian) *figau*, (Logudorian) *fikatu*, Span. *hígado*, Old French (Norman) *firie*, French *foie*, Ital. *fegato*, Ital. dial. (Emilia, Lombardy) *fidak*, (Abbruzzo) *fétteche*, French dial. (Walloon) *feute*, Occ., Cat. *fetge*.

These words can be linked with the Greek word *sykotón*, which literally means 'figged' (Latin FICATUS, attested from the fourth century). It refers to the habit of feeding animals, especially geese and pigs, with figs, to fatten the liver for culinary purposes. The Latin word for 'fig' is (fourth declension) FĪCUS, the long vowel of which can be reconstructed from the Romance forms:

(6)   Ital. *fico*, Old French *fi*, Span. *higo*, Ptg. *figo*

as well as from the related feminine forms, like Occ. *figa*, from which French *figue* was borrowed in the twelfth century (masculine *fi*, *fic* survives in dialects, meaning 'wart'). There is also indirect evidence for a long vowel in Germanic borrowings, like German *Feig*, Dutch *vijg*.

In the word for 'liver', however, the modern French and Italian forms point to a short Latin ĭ (or perhaps a long *e* taken from a Latin pronunciation of Greek upsilon). Moreover, these forms, like those of Old French, Spanish and Logudorian Sard, are accented on the Latin first syllable, and not, as we would expect and as happens in Rumanian, Friulian Rhaeto-Romance and Campidanian Sard, on the penultimate. A Latin distortion of the oxytonic Greek word is blamed for this latter anomaly.

> To make things more complicated there must have been metathesis (giving *FITACUS, *FETACUS) to account for some Italian dialects (Emilia, Lombardy, Abruzzo), and Occitan and Catalan forms.

(iii)   Proto-Romance lexicon

Although it is rare for there to be no snags in identifying the reconstructed with the Latin forms, in the main the textual attestations confirm reconstruction techniques, and Romanists are justified to some extent in taking the short cut, 'peeping in the back of the book', by working down from the Latin form, rather than up from the Romance reflexes. Sometimes, however, reconstruction gives us information about the proto-language that the texts do not unambiguously provide. For instance, the word for 'fire' in Romance corresponds not to IGNIS but to FOCUS 'fireplace, hearth':

(7)   Rum. *foc*, Dalmatian (Veglia) *fuk*, Ital. *fuoco*, Sard (Logudorian) *fogu*, R-R (Engadine) *fög*, (Friuli) *fug*, French *feu*, Occ. *fuec*, Cat. *foc*, Span. *fuego*, Ptg. *fogo*.

Similarly a 'cultivated field' is not from AGER, but from CAMPUS, 'plain, level ground' (especially a sports field):

(8)   Rum. *cîmp*, Ital., Span., Ptg. *campo*, Occ., Cat. *camp*, French *champ*.

Occasionally texts provide us with confirmation of our phonological reconstructions. For instance, the word for 'old' is not VĔTUS (which gives words for 'rancid, musty', like Ital. *vieto*), but apparently /veklu/, with palatalization of the medial cluster identical to that found in the words for 'eye' /oklu/, in which there is amply attested **syncope** (see chapter 3) of the short atonic Ŭ of OCŬLUS:

(9)   Rum. *vechi* (the near synonym *batrîn* < VETERANUS is a little less common) /
             ochi, Ital. *vecchio/occhio*, French *vieil/oeil*, Span. *viejo/ojo*, Ptg. *velho/olho*,
             Cat. *vell/ull*, R-R (Engadine) *vegl/ögl*, (Friuli) *viéli/vóli* (note also Dolomite
             vedl/ödl – here velars in such clusters regularly become dentals).

Again the *Appendix Probi* provides us with a clue:

(10)   V&ULUS NON VECLUS

(where & is an abbreviation for ET) confirms our deduction that in the diminutive VETULUS, syncopated to /vetlus/, the un-Latin cluster /tl/ was replaced by /kl/, which subsequently regularly palatalized in most of the languages.

(b)   Auxiliary selection

A morphosyntactic question that has not ceased to arouse the curiosity of Romanists, who have thereby contributed to wider linguistic discussion, is that of 'auxiliary selection' in the Romance compound tenses with the past participle. Later (see 3.3) we shall return to the Romance **compound perfect**; here I look in some detail at only the auxiliary selection question, as it raises general questions in syntactic analysis. Though normally a HABĒRE (or TENĒRE) 'have' auxiliary is used in the compound tenses, sometimes an ESSE 'be' auxiliary is chosen. Some commentators have implausibly attributed the use of the ESSE auxiliary with some intransitive verbs to the influence of German, where the distribution of *haben* and *sein* auxiliaries is similar, but others have linked it to stative and passive uses of the ESSE auxiliary. Most regard the choice as determined lexically, with some degree of semantic cohesion, and some believe that it is revelatory of a syntactic distinction.

(i)   Which languages?

Not all the modern Romance languages can choose a *BE* auxiliary in the active perfect. Spanish and Portuguese ceased to do so by the seventeenth century, though some Catalan and Aragonese varieties still can do so, marginally:

(11)   Cat. (Balearics) *som anat* 'I have [am] gone'.

In 'unreal conditional' clauses, *BE* (*ser*) auxiliary forms were also attested during the 1970s in the speech of elderly illiterate Spanish speakers in Colombia:

(12)   *si mayo fuera sido invierno* 'if May had been winter' (for . . . *hubiera sido* . . .).

The tenuous evidence we have for Dalmatian shows that the Veglia variety in the nineteenth century made no use of a *BE* auxiliary:

(13)   *Ju ai venut* 'I have come', *Jai sait* 'I have gone out', *Se jai martuot* 'I have got
        married'.

In Daco-Rumanian, on the other hand, *fi* 'be' (usually in the infinitival form < FIERI?) is consistently used in some of the active compound tenses, though *avea* 'have' is required for the most frequent past form, the perfect:

(14)   perfect indicative *Am jurat* (or *jurát-am*) 'I have sworn, I swore'; but perfect
        subjunctive [*Să*] *fi jurat*, future perfect *Voi fi jurat* 'I shall have sworn', past
        conditional *Aş fi jurat* 'I should have [be] sworn'.

        The past participial form, *fost*, is also used in the popular *surcomposé* plu-
        perfect (*Am fost jurat* 'I had sworn', literally 'I have been sworn'; see 3.2).
        This has supplanted an older type with the imperfect of 'have' (*Aveam jurat*)
        still found in dialects south of the Danube, alongside the (infrequent) syn-
        thetic standard form *jurásem*.

There is some trace of use of *fi* with some intransitive verbs:

(15)   *Este plecat* 'He is arrived', for *A plecat* 'He has arrived'; in
        dialects south of the Danube, *Sam vinit* 'I am come', for stan-
        dard *Am venit* 'I have come'.

If Old Daco-Rumanian did resemble Old Spanish in its use of a *BE* auxiliary in the perfect tense, however, the usage had virtually disappeared by the time of the first Rumanian texts in the sixteenth century.

Slavonic (specifically Bulgarian) influence is plausibly invoked to explain the current usage, which can lead to ambiguity in some tenses:

(16)   *voi / aş fi chemat* 'I shall/should have called' or 'I shall / should have been called'.

In the perfect subjunctive, on the other hand, *fi* is conjugated in the passive whereas it is invariable in the active:

(17)   *să fiu chemat* 'that I have been called' / *să fi chemat* 'that I have [be] called'.

In standard French the auxiliary *être* is selected by some score of intransitive verbs, most of which are used with *avoir* in non-standard varieties. There is resistance to the switch to *avoir* with some motion verbs, like *venir* 'to come' (*Il est allé* 'He has [is] gone' commonly being supplanted by *Il a été* 'He has been'). This is so too with crucial 'change-of-state' verbs, *mourir* 'to die' and *naître* 'to be born'. Earlier in history, the choice was not so clearly lexical and examples like *a alé*, 'he has gone', compared with modern *Il est allé*, are found.

Occitan on the whole follows the same sort of pattern as French, though the range of ESSE verbs is slightly wider. Rhaeto-Romance varieties show a similar distribution, though generalization of HABĒRE is not so evident in Surselvan as in other varieties, perhaps because of the German influence in this dialect.

Standard Italian makes the greatest and most consistent use of *essere* as a perfect auxiliary. So, as a more clear-cut case, it receives most attention from linguists. In standard Italian *essere* may be selected even when the verb is proceded by a modal, unlike in French (where similar constructions are found in Middle French, there may have been Italian influence):

(18)   Ital. *È andato, È dovuto andare* / French *Il est allé, Il a dû aller* 'He has gone', He has had to go'.

Italian modal verbs are called *servili*, with 'servile' adoption of the auxiliary associated with the lexical verb. Central Italian varieties are similar to the standard in this respect. In North Italy HABĒRE is traditionally used with modals, but perhaps through Tuscan influence, ESSE is found, especially in Piedmont, Lombardy, Emilia-Romagna and Liguria:

(19)   Romagna *A jo vlò partí* 'I have [am] wanted to go off' / Venice *Go volú partir*, Milan *U vursü parti* 'I have wanted to go off'.

Non-standard Italian varieties adopt a host of different solutions in auxiliary selection. In the south HABĒRE tends to be generalized, with variation in some areas:

(20)   Naples *Aggio venuto* / *So bbenuto*, 'I have/am come', *A muorto* / *È mmuorto*
          'He has died / is dead'; Calabria *Annu venutu* 'They have come'; Sicily *A*
          murutu 'He has died'.

In the north most dialects use ESSE with rather fewer verbs than the standard, but some use only HABĒRE:

(21)   Liguria *A ndèt* 'He has gone', East Veneto *El ga torná* 'He has come back'.

In several Central and in a few Northern and Southern dialects ESSE is consistently used for transitive as well as for intransitive verbs, though sometimes the auxiliary may vary according to the person of the verb (often the third and sixth persons select HABĒRE):

(22)   Genoa *Son dormì* 'They have [are] slept'; Carpignano *Sun krumpá* 'I have
          [am] bought'; Novara *Mi i son mangià* / *Lü l'à mangià* 'I have [am] eaten' /
          'He has eaten'; Marche (Servigliano, Ascoli Piceno) *Sò mazzato lu porcu* /
          Issu ha magnato / *Issu è vvinutu* 'I have [am] killed the pig'/ 'He has eaten' /
          'He has [is] come'; Latium (Cori) *Nù simo magnato* / *Issi èo magnato* 'We
          have [are] eaten' / 'They have eaten'.

One consequence is that the *BE* passive tends to be avoided in these dialects. Similar generalization of ESSE is recorded for some Catalan varieties, apparently with verbs that do not passivize:

(23)   Capcir *Sun tingut* 'I have [am] had'; Gerona *Sò bist* 'I have [am] seen'.

(ii)   Semantic factors

The particular aptitude for ESSE and HABĒRE to grammaticalize as auxiliaries, bleaching further their rather colourless lexical content, has long been recognized. Some have claimed that in essence they represent grammatically predicative and transitive complementary versions of the same functional entity. In a few Romance languages (some Francoprovençal dialects, for instance) they merge into one set of forms; elsewhere they may influence one another morphologically.

> One curious feature of some Eastern French and Francoprovençal dialects,
> also found in Old Italian texts and in Swiss Italian varieties, is that forms

cognate with **être eu* 'be had' replace *avoir été* 'have been' (compare standard Italian *essere stato* 'be been').

Some semantic coherence among the intransitive verbs that select an ESSE auxiliary in the compound tenses is readily discernible. The distinguished French linguist, Benveniste, for instance, saw *être* as signalling a resulting 'situation', and *avoir* an 'operation'. No single semantic criterion, however, seems to predict which verbs require an ESSE auxiliary, although state or change of state seems often to be involved. Most centrally, and historically most durably, it is used with verbs of motion or lack of motion, especially when the type of motion is not lexically specified:

(24)   French *Il est allé* 'He has [is] gone', *Il est resté* 'He has [is] stayed'.

In some examples a distinction can be made between stative or telic uses of a motion verb and those that place more emphasis on the action itself:

(25)   Ital. *Maria è corsa a casa di Gianni* 'Mary ran [is run] to John's house' / *Maria ha corso più velocemente di Gianni* 'Mary ran [has run] quicker than John'.

(iii)   Unaccusativity

In recent discussion the relationship of the grammatical ('surface') subject to the verb has emerged as an important determinant of auxiliary choice. In the framework of Relational Grammar, Perlmutter (apparently following up a suggestion of Postal) put forward the hypothesis that the single argument of some intransitive verbs is a derived subject which underlyingly is a direct object – functionally a **theme**, or **experiencer,** rather than an **agent**.

Because such objects do not acquire accusative case, these verbs are labelled **unaccusative**, while other intransitives are (rather confusingly) called unergatives.

> Generativists use the term **ergative** for 'unaccusatives', following Burzio, who describes them in configurational terms (as having a D-structure frame [e] *V NP*, with the subject base-generated in postverbal position), and who suggests they assign a theta role to the direct object position and not to the subject position. However the 'ergative' cannot assign accusative case to the underlying object NP which assumes the status of a subject, acquiring nominative case via an agreement relationship with the verb.

Just as in passive constructions in most of the Romance languages, in which the surface subject is also underlyingly a direct object, the *BE* auxiliary is associated with promotion of the underlying object to subject status. Indeed choice of auxiliary ESSE has been proposed as one of the criteria used for identifying unaccusative or ergative verbs.

Romance languages, however, provide some instances of the *BE* auxiliary being used only when promotion to subject has been effected, whereas the 'theme' can remain in postverbal position with a *HAVE* auxiliary:

(26)   Occ. (Foix) *Qualqus es bengut* / *A bengut qualqus* 'Someone is come' / 'There
            has come someone'; Sard (Lula) *Tres pitzinnas sun arrivatas* 'Three girls have
            [are] come' / *B'at arrivatu tres pitzinnas* 'There has arrived three girls'.

            It has been claimed that the choice between *BE* and *HAVE* auxiliaries for
            intransitive verbs is determined by parametrized principles which can also
            account naturally for **subject inversion** and use of the adverbial clitic, Ital. *ne*,
            French *en*, in Romance.

(iv)   Pronominals

German bears many resemblances to Romance in the matter of auxiliary selection in the compound tenses. However, one important difference is that in Italian and French reflexive (or better, **pronominal**) constructions require a *BE* auxiliary, whereas in German *haben* is used in parallel constructions. In Romance a pronominal structure (with a reflexive clitic) is used not only for true reflexives and reciprocals:

(27)   French *Il se tue* / *Ils se tuent* 'He kills himself' / 'They kill each other':

but also as a **middle** for passives (see 4.7):

(28)   *Cela se fait*/ *La branche se casse* 'That is (usually) done' / 'The branch breaks'.

There are also **lexicalized** ('inherent') pronominals:

(29)   *Il s'évanouit* 'He faints'.

In some languages, too, the third person reflexive (< SE) plays the role of non-specific human agent (the so-called 'impersonal' use, see 6.5).

            Under the 'unaccusative'/'ergative' hypothesis, as it applies to Romance, the
            identity of subject and direct object calls for reflexives to be treated in the
            same way as unaccusative intransitives – but this applies only when the
            reflexive element is a clitic pronoun:

(30)   Ital. *Si è lavato* / *Sé ha lavato, ha lavato sé stesso* 'He got washed' / 'He
            washed **himself**'.

Generalization of ESSE in pronominals is fairly recent and may indeed be connected chronologically with **cliticization** of object pronouns. It has not spread to most non-standard varieties in either Italy or France. It is to be noted too that in Italian ESSE is selected by reflexives through a modal only when there is **clitic climbing** (see 6.5):

(31)   Ital. *Ho voluto levarmi* / *Mi son voluto levare* 'I have wanted to get (myself) up'.

The precise structural effect of cliticization of the reflexive element is much discussed, and related to non-reflexive pronominal constructions like:

(32)   Ital. *Si è sbagliato* 'He has made a mistake' (inherent); *Si è comprato un rega-lo* 'He bought a present for himself'(with dative *si*); *Il regalo si è comprato ieri* 'The present was bought yesterday' ('passive').

> On semantic grounds one would think that passive and inherent pronominals should be more prone to act like unaccusatives than true reflexives and recipro-cals, which are transitive constructions. That these latter should opt for ESSE causes much puzzlement. Early commentators suggested that the usage derives from a Latin impersonal passive construction, like LODATUS EST SIBI 'it was praised to him', in which the dative pronoun (SIBI) was reanalysed as a reflexive.

Certainly the evidence is that before the modern period French and Italian pronominal constructions (whether reflexive or 'inherent') selected HABĒRE as often as, or more often than, ESSE:

(33)   Old French *Conan s'a bien defendu* 'Conan has defended himself'; *S'a pasmé* 'He has fainted'; Old Ital. *S'a segrolato* 'He has ruined himself'; *Se l'ha sposata* 'He has married her'.

This still happens in non-standard usage and in dialects nearly every-where, even where ESSE is used for unaccusatives. In all the following examples a *HAVE* auxiliary is used:

(34)   Ital. dial. (Asolano, Veneto) *Se on lavà e man* 'We have washed our hands'; *Me a ò godestà* 'I have enjoyed it'; *I se géa intosegà* 'They have got angry'; *Me ò marida* 'I (female) have got married' / *È nato* 'He has gone'.

> Quite often there is hesitation about which auxiliary to use, though some-times this may be due to influence from the standard, which sometimes dic-tates the use of ESSE when popular usage prefers HABĒRE :

(35)   R-R (Friuli) *Mi soi vistide* / *Mi ai vistît* 'I got dressed' / 'I have dressed myself'; (Surselvan) *Jeu sun sescaldaus* / *Jeu hai sescaldau* 'I have been scald-ed' / 'I have scalded myself'.

It is possible here, as my translations hint, that true reflexives prefer HABĒRE, whereas inherent pronominals select ESSE, and that a semantic difference is signalled by the choice of auxiliary. However, hard evidence is not usually available for the modern non-standard varieties. A turn-of-the-century description of the Lower Engadine Rhaeto-Romance dialect does suggest, though, that true reflexives may be treated differently from inherent pronominals, which act like unaccusatives:

(36)   *No eschan schtats, tuornats,* 'We have [are] been, returned' (unaccusative) / *E m a müdá* 'I have changed (myself)'; *Tü t asch lavá* 'You have washed (yourself)' (reflexive) / *Tü t esch schbagliá* 'You have made a mistake (are mistaken)'; *El s esch arabiá* 'He has [is] got (himself) annoyed' (inherent).

Surselvan also provides some examples that point in the same direction (but here the invariable reflexive marker is agglutinated to the past participle, and it can be claimed that the forms are lexicalized as unaccusative or transitive respectively):

(37)   *Il giuven ei sepladius* 'The young man was hired out (has [is] contracted himself as a labourer)'; *La plaga ei s'aviarta* 'The wound has [is] opened [itself]'; *La madregna veva sevistgiu de femna veglia* 'The godmother had dressed herself up as an old woman'; *Quella ha sedostau* 'That one [female] has resisted (defended herself)'.

Evidence from other Rhaeto-Romance varieties points to the opposite conclusion, however:

(38)   Friuli *Lor e son lâs* 'They have [are] gone' (unaccusative) / *Si sin sentâz* 'We have [are] sat ourselves down' (reflexive) / *Jâ si a mitût a vaî* 'She has begun to cry' (inherent).

Similarly, though Friulian optionally uses *jessi* 'be' with true reflexives, in the 'impersonal' construction *vê* 'have' is normal:

(39)   *Si a balat tude la gnot* 'There has been dancing [it has danced itself] all night'.

Sometimes auxiliary choice with pronominals is sensitive to the person of the verb, as we saw was the case with unaccusatives in some Italian varieties. In the Francoprovençal dialect of Vermes in the Jura, for instance, ESSE is used only in first person singular forms:

(40)   *L car s'è raté* 'The bus has stopped (itself)'; *I m sé di* 'I have [am] said to myself'.

It has been suggested that agreement of the past participle with the subject in pronominals using HABĒRE in some dialects is a relic of original use of ESSE:

(41)   Ital. dial. (San Tommaso, Abruzzo) *Ci auamme erreuéte* 'We have arrived' /
         S'a rrauate 'He has arrived'; R-R (Engadine) *Mieus ögls s'han avierts* 'My
         eyes have opened', (Lower Engadine) *Ela s'a lavada il ceu* 'She has washed
         her hair'.

         However, it is possible that here we have examples of agreement with the
         direct object, as in transitive verbs (see 6.5).

The traditional view is that the use of ESSE in true reflexives results from
a contamination with unaccusative use, through the middle or passive
pronominals which share some syntactic and semantic characteristics
with unaccusatives. The spread may have been more marked in the standard languages as a reaction to the more popular tendency to abandon
distinction between HABĒRE and ESSE perfects in general.

There is clearly some connection between the ESSE choice and the use of
pronominals with passive value (see 4.7). One as yet unexplored possibility
is that there is also a connection with the spread in some Romance languages
of the compound perfect into the territory of the **preterite** inherited from the
Latin perfect (see 3.3, 7.3), and with the development of two distinct *BE* auxiliaries in some languages that have not retained auxiliary selection (see 7.5).

(v)   Weather verbs

One question that has been raised with respect to the unaccusative
hypothesis concerns the status of weather verbs in Romance. In Italian,
but not in French, such verbs can select ESSE in the compound tenses:

(42)   Ital. *È piovuto, Ha piovuto* / French *Il a plu* 'It has rained'.

In some contexts the *essere* option seems to be the preferred one in standard Italian:

(43)   *È piovuta una pioggerella fina* 'It has rained a fine drizzle'; *Mi è piovuto addosso*
         'It has rained on me'.

But where the action is emphasized *avere* is used:

(44)   *Ha piovuto tutta la notte* 'It has rained all night'.

Elsewhere, too, although HABĒRE is more frequent, ESSE is possible, apparently emphasizing the result of the phenomenon:

(45)   R-R (Surselvan) *Id a ploü tuotta di a tschèl ruot* 'It's [has] poured in bucket-
         fuls all day' / *Vara, vara id e ploü* 'Look, look, it's [is] rained'.

In Italy regional dialects vary in their usage. In the north both auxiliaries are possible, but in most places HABĒRE is more frequent:

(46)   Milan *L'è fiukà*, Bormio *L'e flokà* / *L'a flokà* 'It has [is] snowed' / Piedmont *A l'a fiukà*, Venice *El ga nevegà*.

Whereas Central dialects use ESSE, in the south, Sicily and Sardinia we find only HABĒRE :

(47)   Sard *A probiu*, Abruzzo *Ha piovute* 'it has rained'.

Usually the dialectal treatment of weather verbs is similar to that of other impersonals:

(48)   Tuscany *È bastato* / Venice *Ga bastà* 'It has been enough'; Milan *M'é piasú* / Venice *El me ga piasú* 'It has pleased me'.

Interestingly, however, Tuscan uses HABĒRE in constructions like:

(49)   *Ha fatto piogga* 'There's been rain'.

One possible explanation is that weather verbs have as their only argument an implicit cognate object (that can become a derived subject, somewhat as in 'The rain, it raineth every day'), and that they should be counted as unaccusative. Certainly in French there is a parallel with indisputably unaccusative verbs in the impersonal construction:

(50)   *Il est arrivé plusieurs personnes* 'There arrived several people' / *Il a plu toute la journée une petite pluie fine* 'There rained all day a very fine drizzle'.

If weather verbs are unaccusative in French, then obviously choice of the *être* auxiliary is not coterminous with unaccusativity. One problem in discussing the whole question of auxiliary selection is that in French, as in most of the modern Romance languages, the ESSE option is obsolescent and frozen into its place by normative grammar. Older texts, and usage in some conservative varieties, hint at more flexibility, perhaps dictated by pragmatic requirements.

(c)   Nasalization

In discussion of the phonological process of vowel nasalization and of the status of nasal vowels, evidence from Romance has figured prominently. Most influential has been the benchmark provided by the well-documented development of distinctive French nasal vowels – in the modern standard [ɑ̃], [ɛ̃], [ɔ̃] or [õ], and more marginally [œ̃], contrast with their oral counterparts (the nasal vowel being diacritically marked in the graphy by a silent nasal consonant):

(51)   *ange/âge* 'angel'/'age'; *feint/fait* 'pretends'/'does'; *bon/beau* 'good'/'hand-some'; *brun/preux* 'brown'/'valiant'.

The only other standard language with a salient series of nasal vowels (and diphthongs) is Portuguese, where their history is more confused, and their phonological status more ambiguous, even though the orthography sometimes picks them out even more distinctively by the use of a tilde or *til*:

(52)   *mão* /mau/ 'hand'/'bad'; *lã* /la/ 'wool'/'there'; *som/só* 'sound'/'alone'; *vendes/vedes*; 'you sell'/'you see'; *vim/vi* 'I came'/'I saw'; *pão/pano* 'bread'/'cloth'.

Among non-standard Romance varieties phonological vowel nasality is rather infrequent, but it is found in scattered dialects all over the Romance-speaking area:

(53)   Sard (Sàrrabus, South-East Campidanian) [maʔu]/[maʔu] 'hand'/'bad'; Span. ns. (Andalusia) [kãntã]/[kãnta] 'they sing'/'he sings'; North Ital. dial. (Milan) [sãː]/[san]'healthy' (m. sg.)/(f. pl.), (Imola) [kɛ̃ː]/[ɛːn] 'dog'/'year'; Francoprovençal [lãːna]/[aːno] 'wool'/'donkey'.

French and Portuguese creoles make use of the nasal–oral vowel distinction perhaps rather more frequently than their metropolitan equivalents:

(54)   Haiti [ʃãːm]/[ʃaːm] 'room'/'charm', *pãn/pan* 'hang'/'rag'; São Tomé [fũdu] / [fudu] 'deep'/'clean'.

In Romance phonetic nasality when the vowel is in contact with a nasal consonant, which may lose its segmental status, is fairly widespread and often acoustically salient, though sometimes frowned on by purists:

(55)   Rum. *dens* [dẽs] 'dense', *munti* [mtsj] 'mountains', *am* [ã] *fost* 'I have been'; Span. (Mexico) *corazón* [korasõ] 'heart'; French ns. (Acadia, Canada) *même* [mẽm] 'same'.

(i)   Phonologization

Phonologization of vowel nasality in French has been much discussed. The evidence of assonance and rhyme in medieval texts points to assimilatory nasalization under the influence of a following nasal consonant, and sixteenth-century descriptions of pronunciation leave us in no doubt that nasal vowels and diphthongs were phonetically salient at that time. However, it is usually assumed that phonologization of the distinction did not occur until preconsonantal and prepause nasal consonants (like other consonants) dropped out during the sixteenth century, leaving behind only the nasal quality of the vowel.

At about the same time, there began a process of denasalization of vowels followed by intervocalic nasal consonants. The truncation of atonic final vowels often left these in final position, so that there arose a contrast between nasal vowels (Ṽ) and *oral vowel + nasal consonant sequences* (VN), often in morphologically related forms:

(56)   *bon* 'good' (m.) [bõ] / *bonne* (f.) [bɔn], earlier [bõnə]; *vient* '(he) comes' [vjẽ] / *viennent* '(they) come' [vjɛn], earlier [vjẽnə].

Nasal vowels and diphthongs, now cut loose from their close link with the VN sequences, collapsed into a smaller inventory, tending to lower and/or simplify:

(57)   *fin* 'fine' (m.) [fẽ], earlier [fĩn] / *fine* (f.) [fin], earlier [fĩnə]; *brun* 'brown' (m.) [brœ̃], earlier [brỹn] / *brune* (f.) [bryn], earlier [brỹnə]; *vain* [vẽ], 'vain' (m.), earlier [vẽjn] / *vaine* (f.) [vɛn], earlier [vẽjnə].

Etymologizing orthography continued to use nasal consonant symbols to signal vowel nasalization; moreover in **liaison** contexts (see 7.2) the nasal vowel usually was resolved once more into a VN sequence:

(58)   *bon enfant* 'good child' (m.) [bɔnɑ̃fɑ̃]; *divin enfant* 'holy child' (m.) [divinɑ̃fɑ̃]; *vain effort* 'vain effort' (m.) [vɛnɛfɔʀ]; *un effort* 'an effort' [ynɛfɔʀ].

In more recent times (particularly in the last hundred years) such resolution is not mandatory, and *nasal vowel + nasal consonant* (ṼN) sequences have become normal in some liaison contexts:

(59)   *mon enfant* 'my child' (m. or f.) [mõnɑ̃fɑ̃]; *en été* 'in summer' [ɑ̃nete]; *un effort* [œ̃nɛfɔʀ] 'an effort'.

In spite of these anomalies, generative phonologists enamoured of 'abstract' analysis found in French nasal vowels an opportunity to elaborate a rule system by which the surface phonemic contrast was subordinated to a more 'underlying' uniformity. In the so-called 'classic' generative account, nasal vowels are synchronically derived from VN sequences, as they had been diachronically. In the synchronic account, however, the French nasalization rule could apply only in the presence of tautosyllabic nasal consonants, and must be followed by a rule truncating preconsonantal and prepause nasal consonants:

(60)   V –> [+nasal]   /_ N $\left\{ \begin{matrix} \# \\ C \end{matrix} \right\}$

             N –> ∅   / Ṽ _

The diachronic nasalization of preceding vowels by intervocalic consonants, and consequent denasalization, would not be reflected in the synchronic description.

> One snag in this type of account is that the orthographic vowels of atonic word-final syllables have to be postulated as present (even though they are not pronounced in the modern standard language) in the underlying forms, as they are required to account for the non-nasal character of the vowels in forms like:

(61)   *bonne* [bɔn], underlyingly /bonе/ 'good' (f.); *viennent* [vjɛn], underlyingly /venet/ '(they) come'.

> Once the final vowel (usually a schwa which serves as a morphological marker) has done its job it can be eliminated in a low-level phonetic rule.

Although the nasalization rules proposed were fairly unexceptionable, it was the status of schwa (**mute** *e*, *e muet* or *e instable*) in modern French that aroused controversy and provoked more 'concrete' generative accounts, which often distinguish non-alternating fully lexicalized nasal vowels from the morphologically determined alternations between Ṽ and VN.

> More recently multilinear phonology has neatly proposed descriptions of French nasalization by which a nasal consonant in the coda can 'float' extrametrically, losing its place and manner features, but transferring its nasality to the adjacent nuclear vowel: though the formalization is more satisfactory, the analysis has not changed much. The suggestion that so-called 'nasal vowels' are diphthongal in character receives some support from experimental data, especially for Portuguese and Canadian French.

The French example has prompted the widely held view that phonological nasalization normally develops from phonetic regressive assimilation as a result of the loss of the nasal consonant which provided the triggering context. In Portuguese, however, vowel nasalization can also be triggered by a preceding nasal consonant:

(62)   *mim* for *mi*, *mãe* < MATREM 'mother'; *muito* [mũĩⁿntu] < MULTU 'much'.

Discussion often revolves round the question of whether the triggering nasal consonant can still be articulated, allowing vowel nasality to be derived by low-level contextual phonetic rule. In Portuguese, for instance, where nasal vowels are frequently followed by some nasal occlusion in preconsonantal position, they are usually assumed to be synchronically derived from VN sequences, though some commentators prefer to regard them as lexicalized, and any nasal occlusion as **epenthetic**. Galician and Northern dialects of European Portuguese, which have no nasal vowels, can synchronically be viewed as closer to the synchronic underlying forms, even though it is likely that in these varieties nasalization was followed diachronically by denasalization, sometimes with nasal hardening:

(63)   [la]/[laŋ] 'wool' (Ptg. *lã*), *cais*, *cans* 'dogs' (Ptg. *cães*).

In standard Portuguese there is evidence for diachronic denasalization in certain contexts, with or without epenthesis of a nasal consonant:

(64)   *boa* < *bõa* < BONA 'good' (f.); *ter* < *tẽer* < TENERE 'hold, have'; *minha* < *mĩa*
         < MEA 'my' (f.); *cheio* < *chẽo* < PLENU 'full'.

         In Rumanian, the earliest (sixteenth-century) texts, written in Cyrillic script, frequently, but not consistently, use the nasalizing symbol ↑ with or without a graphical nasal consonant (or its rhotacizing substitute *r*), presumably to indicate nasalization of a vowel by a following nasal consonant:

(65)   *u↑bra*/*ubra* 'shadow'; *pri↑n* 'through' ; *mâ↑re* 'hand'; *lura* 'moon'.

In some cases an etymological nasal consonant has been definitively lost in all dialects; lexicalized nasalization and subsequent denasalization of the adjacent vowel is usually assumed for an early period:

(66)   *cât* 'how much?' < QUANTUM; *către* 'towards, against' < CONTRA.

The modern Daco-Rumanian nasal vowels are often ignored in synchronic descriptions, as they can readily be seen as surface realizations of VN sequences, with or without loss of nasal occlusion.

(ii)   Vowel height

The French case has also suggested that there is some sort of hierarchy of nasalization depending on vowel height, by which low vowels are more readily nasalized than high vowels. This widely held hypothesis is based not only on the well-attested lowering of nasal vowels in early modern period standard French, but also on the perception that Old French verse assonance patterns show separation of *an* and *en* sequences from their oral counterparts much earlier than is the case for *in* and *un* sequences. Statistical study of a wider range of texts has shown, however, that this perception is illusory and that apparent patterns of assonance are plausibly due to other factors, including the ready availability of certain endings, like present participle -*ant*, to satisfy verse conventions. Uncertainty about the constraints of assonancing conventions, and conflicting evidence from later rhyming verse, add to scepticism about the vowel height hierarchy hypothesis.

As it is likely that at the relevant time French vowel nasality was not yet phonologized, one of the factors to be considered is the possibly relatively inconspicuous acoustic salience of nasality with high vowels. In Portuguese high vowels are particularly prone to take on nasal resonance, even where no nasal consonant is in the environment:

(67)   *sim* 'yes', for *si* (traditionally thought to be influenced by *não* 'no' < NON,
            but *si* 'himself' is also frequently nasalized in non-standard varieties, here
            said to be influenced by *mim* 'me').

(iii)   Causes of nasalization

The classic works of Romance philology have sought the cause of French and Portuguese nasalizing tendencies in the Celtic substratum, whereas Rumanian was deemed to be influenced by Slavonic. One feature that these languages share and which has been linked to nasalization is their use of schwa-like vowels, that are readily elided, in atonic syllables. The strong accentuation that this feature implies might well have the effect of reducing the segmental status of nasal consonants. However, as we have seen, contextual phonetic vowel nasality is widespread in Romance (as indeed is reduction of atonic vowels). It can be maintained that only in French (and perhaps not even there) have nasal vowels become lexicalized, consequent on other radical changes in the phonological setup – in particular truncation processes in the early modern period. Phonologization (and morphologization) of vowel nasality can be viewed as due to reanalysis after denasalization processes had established a contrast between $\tilde{V}$(N) and VN sequences.

CONCLUSION

I have tried to give examples of how study of the Romance languages has contributed to knowledge about languages in general. Throughout the rest of this book I shall pinpoint discussions within Romance that are of interest to linguists in general, rather than attempt the sort of general account of Romance that is to be found in the classic manuals. This must mean that I neglect some aspects of Romance linguistics and that my choice of topic is somewhat subjective: I try, however, to retain some balance between treatment of phonology, morphology, syntax and lexicon, and to take into account social and historical factors. In being selective about the topics covered, I hope to look in rather more detail at some of them than would be possible in a general survey.

FURTHER READING

Posner (1966) is an elementary introduction to Romance linguistics. An account of the discipline,with full bibliographies, is to be found in Iordan, Orr & Posner (1970). More recent work is covered in Posner & Green eds. (1980–93). A useful select bibliography is Bal *et al.* (1997). A valuable collective survey of individual Romance languages, together with chapters on Latin and Romance, is Harris & Vincent eds. (1988, reprint 1996). See also Reinheimer & Tasmowski (1997). Encyclopedias, such as the *Encyclopedia Britannica*, Bright ed. (1991) and Asher & Simpson eds. (1994), have articles on Romance in general and on each principal language. Devoted solely to Romance is Sala ed. (1989). Still in process of publication is Holtus, Metzeltin & Schmitt eds. (1988–), which will give synchronic and historical accounts of each Romance area and overall surveys of the Romance family and its historiography. A similarly large-scale project on the history of the Romance languages (Ernst *et al.* (eds.) in preparation) is scheduled to begin publication in 2000. Each year the *Year's Work in Modern Languages* (published by the Modern Humanities Research Association) carries surveys of recent publications on the linguistics of Romance and of each individual Romance language. Current work is reported in the proceedings of the triennial international conference of the Société de Linguistique Romane and in the annual publications based on the American Symposium in Romance Linguistics, and the German Romanistentagen. Periodicals concerned with the Romance languages as a whole include the *Zeitschrift für romanische Philologie*, the *Revue de linguistique romane*, the *Revue des langues romanes*, *Romance Philology*, and (since 1989) *Probus*. For works mentioned explicitly in this chapter see the general bibliography, and for works on individual languages see chapter 5. See also, on the history of Romance linguistics, Bahner (1983), Niederehe & Schlieben-Lange (1987), Bossong (1990), and on unaccusativity Burzio (1986). On nasals, Tranel (1981), Hajek (1997).

PART I

The similarities

1

What is a Romance language? Part 1

1.1 WHAT IS A ROMANCE LANGUAGE?

If we knew nothing about the history and the geographical location of a Romance language, would we be able to recognize it as Romance from its linguistic features alone? Certainly, it seems that nothing in the phonetic or phonological makeup of those languages we are agreed on calling 'Romance' is particularly distinctive. The most obvious similarity is their shared **lexicon**: I shall leave that for discussion in the next chapter.

One difficulty that needs to be faced straightaway, though, is that some languages are not normally recognized as 'Romance' because of their morphosyntactic features. In particular, American, African and Asian creoles have quite decidedly 'Romance' vocabulary. Other languages – like Albanian, Basque, Maltese and even Berber – are sometimes regarded as even more borderline cases, because a substantial part of their vocabulary is identifiably 'Romance', but the basic vocabulary is rarely affected, and so we treat them as having extensively borrowed from Romance but not otherwise closely related.

(a) Morphosyntactic features

If we consider **creoles** – lexically related to French, Portuguese or Spanish – as not properly Romance, it is because their morphology and syntax are often markedly and consistently different from those of their metropolitan counterparts. Though they may differ phonologically from their respective lexifier languages, it is their shared morphosyntactic features that lead commentators to assign them to a separate category of languages, that includes other creoles, rather than to Romance. In chapter 2 I shall be paying particular attention to these in an attempt to define the bounds of Romanceness.

The standard Romance languages share many features that are lacking in creoles: for instance, **noun gender**, **agreement**, the **definite article** and, most important, morphological verb inflections. Usually the morphological features that are most clearly Latin remnants – surviving more intact in verbals than in nominals – are viewed as peculiarly Romance.

Typologically, however, there is comparatively little to distinguish the standard Romance languages from other modern Indo-European languages. If we compare them with English, for instance, we can note that they differ in the use of noun gender, in their richer verbal inflectional system, in the apparent absence of a distinct modal verb morphosyntactic category, in their distinctive system of clitic object pronouns and in their pronominal verbs. But they are similar in retaining morphologically marked number in nominals, and in having developed periphrastic perfect and passive forms.

It is usual to claim that Romance word order, in the core languages as well as the creoles, is dominantly SVO (subject–verb–object), unlike the SOV order of Latin. However, in many varieties 'atonic' object pronouns precede finite verb forms. Nearly everywhere surface word order is pragmatically determined, with a tendency to verb-first ordering. In some Swiss Rhaeto-Romance varieties (and in Old French) a Germanic-like verb-second order is dominant. In most varieties auxiliaries and modals precede the lexical verb in compound and periphrastic constructions, as in English: Sard and Rumanian are partial exceptions. Standard language noun–adjective order does differ from English: although, in unmarked sequences, adjectives usually follow the noun, there are many exceptions – especially in the literary languages, where stylistic effects can readily be achieved by variation of order (see 3.4).

> The comparison with English can, of course, only be by way of illustration: several of the features cited as distinguishing Romance from English are found in other Indo-European languages.

(b)   Romance 'archetype'

Typological identification of a language as 'Romance' is fraught with difficulties, for much will depend on what language is regarded as 'prototypically' Romance. Some Romance linguists – Rumanian-born Eugenio Coseriu in particular – seek to establish, within a 'holistic' or 'integral' typology, what the essential Romance characteristics are. Coseriu's contention is that the Romance guiding principle is that within the nominal system **syntagmatic** (or external) distinguishing features prevail, whereas in the verbal system, **paradigmatic** (internal or morphological) distinctions are more important. He goes further and attempts to motivate the difference functionally, by linking 'external functions' – those concerned with actualization within the sentence, like case relationships – with 'external' or syntagmatic expression features, while 'internal functions' – sometimes more directly related to reality, like noun number or verb tense and sometimes more specifically linguistic, like noun gender – are expressed paradigmatically.

Coseriu's 'Romance type' must, however, exclude modern French, which has changed since the Middle Ages into a more **analytic** language, relying, for instance, on subject pronouns to mark verb person, and losing the productive nominal diminutive formations that persist in other Romance languages. Coseriu places Rumanian too outside the Romance inner circle, at the other extreme from French. I prefer to identify Romanceness in terms of an archetype, not in the sense of the most 'neutral', but in that of the most 'central' of the languages – the model to which all the others may be most easily compared.

Occitan and Catalan are often seen, on morphological grounds, as the least distinctive Romance languages, the 'crossroads' of the Romance world. Catalan is spoken of as bridging the gulf between the closely knit Spanish and Portuguese grouping and the more central languages. However, this may be no more than a reflection of the conservative compromises arrived at in the standardization of Catalan and Occitan. Without official status for so long, their different regional varieties diverged quite widely. Standardizers attempted to take into account actual usage, while looking back to earlier literary conventions. In the case of Catalan, influence from Castilian in the modern period has been great, though the standard, as taught, attempts to minimize this effect.

On lexical and syntactic grounds, I regard standard Italian as the prime candidate for the status of Romance archetype, as a language which has most in common with each of the others. In some ways it is so close to Latin that it has even, as we have seen, been mistaken for a colloquial variety of the Latin literary language. It has been carefully nurtured throughout its history as an 'illustrious' language modelled on Classical Latin, so much so that some doubt that it can really be called a 'natural language'. The term standard Italian has even been described as a 'somewhat fictitious label. . . aiming to circumscribe a hopelessly vague concept', for the grammar book version is comparatively seldom heard, unsullied, in uneducated speech in Italy.

My choice of Italian (the modern geographical surrogate for a historical Popular Latin) as the archetype can be challenged as tending to confuse synchronic and diachronic criteria: my own view is that a comparison of Romance languages must take account of both criteria.

(c)   Degrees of Romanceness

Round the 'inner core' represented by standard Italian, the other languages cluster with greater or less cohesion. For instance, the Spanish-Argentinian scholar Amado Alonso, following Schuchardt, postulated a *Romania continua*, stretching from Portugal through Spain and southern France and into the Italian peninsula, leaving outside its bounds more maverick languages like French, Rumanian and Sardinian. This, and other attempts at sub-grouping, will be discussed in chapter 5: frequently, as we shall see, the intensity of 'Romanceness' is linked with postulated continuity of a Latin comparatively free from violent impact from barbarian tongues.

A rather different view is taken by the Brazilian scholar Theodoro Henrique Maurer, who stresses that many of the similarities of Western Romance standards are due to convergence stemming from conscious imitation of Latin models. Mutual influence has also led to convergence. Some sort of Sapirian 'drift' may also account for common features (see chapter 4).

(d)   Romance 'club' and Romance 'family'

A distinction has been drawn, within Romance, between 'organic' languages, untouched by conscious manipulation and remodelling, and 'inorganic' languages – interlects, or **koinai**, whether standard or non-standard. The definition of a 'language' as a 'dialect with an army and a navy' can presumably be applied only to 'inorganic languages'. Pure 'organic' languages, however, probably do not exist in complex societies, where we find what Coseriu calls 'historical languages' with characteristic intricate 'architecture', in which different linguistic systems and social norms interact.

Although local dialects and the like can still be counted as 'historical languages', we may find it useful to distinguish the exclusive Romance 'club' of national and literary languages, from the proliferating **family**, with its wide-spreading ramifications, ranging from the nuclear unit, still at home in southern Europe, to members of the extended family, fruits of emigration to outposts of former empires. One problem is to determine how far from the hub, or core, of Romanceness a language can stray without ceasing to be included in the extended family. This may be a sociocultural question rather than a linguistic one; we shall return to it in chapter 5.

These remarks of course apply to any large family of languages; but here we are trying to explore further any specifically linguistic traits that may be held to identify Romance languages. On the morphosyntactic level, I shall here examine verb inflections and noun gender, as these features are absent from creoles, which I believe fall decidedly outside the 'Romance type'. These Romance features reflect to a great degree a common Latin heritage: others that deviate from Latin will be discussed in chapter 6.

Although I view creoles as typologically un-Romance, I shall seek to demonstrate nevertheless that many of them remain within the Romance family, recognized by lexico-phonetic resemblances. Here as elsewhere I shall not confine my observations to the Romance club of literary languages, which owe much of their separate identity to deliberate differentiation in the course of standardization, but which have also retained, or restored, much of the Latin tradition and have also interacted culturally and linguistically with each other and with Latin at various stages of their history.

1.2   PERSON MARKERS

Verb morphology is, I repeat, one of the most diagnostic features for recognizing a Romance language. Let us take as an example morphological person markers in the verb system, which have similarities in all undisputed Romance languages. Nevertheless they present problems, synchronically and diachronically, that have not ceased to be discussed at length since the beginnings of Romance linguistics, especially in so far as they relate to use or non-use of subject pronouns.

I shall exemplify from the **present indicative** of regular verbs, at the risk of some considerable over-simplification. I cannot even then present systematically all the 'philological' detail, but I shall try to fill out the bare bones of the exposition by expanding some points, to give some impression of the complexities.

Table 1.1   Regular present indicative person endings in Latin, Spanish, Portuguese and Italian

	Latin	Spanish	Portuguese	Italian
1	-O	*-o*	*-o* [u]	*-o*
2	-S	*-s*	*-s* [ʃ]	*-i*
3	-T	Ø	Ø	Ø
4	-MUS	*-mos*	*-mos* [muʃ]	*-iamo*
5	-TIS	*-is*	*-is* [jʃ]	*-te*
6	-NT	*-n*	*-m* [˜]	*-no*

(a)   Spanish, Portuguese and Italian.

In the 'inner core' Romance standards, as in Latin, maximally six persons are morphologically marked by segmental bound inflectional endings, and subject pronouns are used only for some degree of emphasis. For ease of reference, I use the labels 'persons 1–6' (p.1–6), but it is sometimes more revealing to think of persons 4–6 as the plural of persons 1–3.

For the present indicative, which tends to have the richest system of person inflections, these mainly reflect regular derivation from Latin. The regular endings are as shown in table 1.1. Except in person 1, the Latin ending is preceded by the theme vowel: A, E or I. The accent falls on the root except in persons 4 and 5 (e.g. -AMUS, -ATIS), when a long theme vowel is accented (in Latin, accent regularly falls on the penultimate syllable unless its vowel is short and is in a free syllable: see 3.3). The three Romance languages cited continue, on the whole, the Latin forms, though they use a zero marker for person 3, having lost Latin -T, graphical reflexes of which are found in very early vernacular texts.

The picture is, however, much more complicated than this schematic account suggests. Some remarks are in order to give a more accurate picture of what is going on.

(i)   Spanish and Portuguese person 5

This was marked by *-des* < -TIS in the older language, as in some modern dialects. This phonetically regular ending gave way to the modern one in the standard language. It persisted until the seventeenth century, when stress fell on the antepenultimate syllable (as in the imperfect *cantávades*), but in the present indicative its decline began in the fourteenth century. In Portuguese *-des* is still used in the so-called **personal infinitive** and the **future subjunctive** (e.g. *falardes*). We shall see later that person 5 is replaced by other forms in some Latin-American varieties.

(ii)   Modern Italian person 4

The standard *-iamo* ending is used for all conjugations (compared with maximally differentiated *-amo*, *-emo*, *-imo* found still today in some dialects). The explanation usually given is that *-iamo* has spread analogically from a subjunctive, either of the *i*-conjugation, or via the 'be' form *siamo* (for SIMUS). Most dialects generalize *-amo* or *-emo*.

(iii)   Italian person 6

The *-no* ending in Italian is found in Tuscan texts from earliest times and is often said to be an analogical extension from *sono* (SUNT > *son*) 'they are', which in turn is crossed with *sono* (SUM > *so*) 'I am'. This latter allegedly acquired an *-o*, analysed as the characteristic ending of person 1. The frequent alternation of 'full' versus apocopated forms in person 1 lends support to this hypothesis. Other possible sources for the *-o* of person 6 may be analogy with the personal pronoun *loro* (< ILLŌRUM), though the use of this form as a subject pronoun probably postdates extension of *-o* to person 6, and there is no clear geographical correlation between the two developments. Analogy with the simple past *-ero* ending (e.g. *dièdero* < DĒDERUNT) is also possible. It is not irrelevant, perhaps, to note that Central and Southern Italian show a preference for vocalic word-finals. Southern dialects also use a vocalic final in person 6 (Sicilian *-anu*, *-inu*). This is not so in many North Italian dialects, where the person 6 ending is identical with person 3, though often obligatory clitic pronouns distinguish them. In old Northern texts, however, *-n* marks person 6, as today in Veneto:

(1)   *Cànten* 'They sing'

       In standard Italian *e*- and *i*- conjugations *o* replaces the theme vowel, perhaps also by analogy with *sono*:

(2)   *Tèmono* 'They fear' (*temere*), *Sèntono* 'They hear' (*sentire*).

In old Sienese -*ono* is also used in all conjugations, but in modern Florentine -*ano* sometimes occurs in the *e*- and *i*- conjugations. Other Tuscan dialects generalize -*eno* or -*ino*), tending to distinguish -*ano* (indicative) from -*ino* (subjunctive).

(iv)   Portuguese person 6

This is marked by nasalization of the thematic vowel: a regular development consequent on the loss of the nasal consonant. In Lisbon usage a nasal diphthong – [ẽw] *am*, [ẽj] *em* – is pronounced; in Brazil, however, nasal quality is often lost, so that person 6 is identical with person 3.

(b)   Catalan, Occitan and Sard

The Catalan and Occitan literary languages also morphologically distinguish six persons in the present indicative, as do Sardinian varieties. The endings in table 1.2 look very similar to those of Italian, Spanish and Portuguese, though how far they represent the reality of unfettered colloquial usage has been questioned.

Table 1.2   Regular present indicative person endings in Catalan, Occitan and Sard

	Catalan	Occitan	Sard Logudorian/Campidanian
1.	-*o*	-*i*/-*e*	-*o*/-*u*
2.	-*s*	-*s*	-*s*
3.	∅	∅	-*t*
4.	-*m*	-*m* [n]	-*mus*/-*us*
5.	-*u*	-*tz*	-*des*/-*is*
6.	-*n*	-*n*	-*n*/-*nt*

Consonant-final Sard forms very frequently – some say regularly – have an added **paragogic** vowel that is identical to a theme vowel:

(3)   Campidanian *Cantauzu* 'We sing', *Cantaizi* 'You sing', *Cantanta* 'They sing'.

In some Catalan and Occitan varieties persons 1 and 3 are not clearly distinguished. The standard Catalan -*o* for person 1 is a comparatively recent acquisition found in Central and Western dialects. Elsewhere person 1 is sometimes identical with person 3. In Occitan, too, the person 1 ending *-i/-e* (or, sometimes in Provençal, *-o*) is not consistently used, except when the form would otherwise end in a consonant cluster (as in *cobre, cobri* 'I cover'). In the old literary language persons 1 and 3 were identical except in the *a*-conjugation.

Many modern Occitan varieties – since the seventeenth century perhaps through French influence – have tended to generalize use of the subject pronoun especially with person 3 forms:

(4)   *L'ome el plora* 'The man weeps', *El plóu* 'It is raining'.

The bare verb form, however, can be used, apparently with affective import, especially when the lexical subject is in focus:

(5)   *plóu de peiras* 'it's raining stones', *canta l'ausèl* (French *ça chante, l'oiseau*) 'it's singing, the bird is'.

(c)   Rumanian

The standard Rumanian language does not normally distinguish more than five personal endings in the present indicative, but does not obligatorily make use of subject pronouns. In the *a*-conjugation, person 3 is identical with person 6:

(6)   *Cîntă* 'He sings, they sing' / *Cînt* 'I sing':

whereas in the other conjugations person 1 is the same as person 6:

(7)   *Ţin* 'I, they hold', *Dorm* 'I, they sleep'.

In some Istro-Rumanian varieties numerous verbs do distinguish six persons in the present indicative. The other standard Rumanian person endings are as follows:

Regular present indicative person endings in Rumanian

2 *-i*,   4 *-m*,   5 *-ţi* [tsʲ]

The Rumanian p. 2 *-i* ending (a graphy used for [j] after vowels or marking palatalization of a preceding consonant) is reminiscent of Italian: for both these languages some see the palatal vowel or glide as a phonetic development of final Latin *-s*, or even of *-ᴀs* (see 6.2).

(d)   **Rhaeto-Romance**

The Rhaeto-Romance varieties sometimes distinguish six personal endings: in the Engadine, for instance, persons 1 and 3 differ in that the latter
retains the thematic vowel:

(8)   *lef* 'I lift' / *leva* 'he lifts'.

The *-s* (or [ʃ]) person 2 ending is most often reinforced by a *-t* that presumably derives from an enclitic pronoun (TU) and which is sometimes
extended to person 5.

> Thus at Santa Maria, in the Lower Engadine, person 2 in the *a*-conjugation
> has an atonic ending [aʃt] compared with the person 5 tonic -['at]:

(9)   *lávast* (sg.) / *lavát* (pl.) 'you wash':

> whereas at nearby Remüs the comparable endings are p. 2 [aʃt] and p. 5 ['aj-
> vat], where TU and VOS elements seem to be incorporated (compared with, for
> instance, Zernez where we find -[aʃ]/-['ajs] and Zuoz, Upper Engadine, where
> the endings are -[aʃt]/-['ajs]). In some Surmeiran varieties the retention of
> etymological [s] rather than the [ʃ] characteristic of /st/ clusters suggests a
> morpheme juncture between the two elements.

In some Upper-Rhine Surselvan varieties – as at Tavetsch – persons 1 and 3
are identical. Many others (especially in the north-east of the region) have
added an *-l* to person 1 in the present and imperfect indicative, and this
ending is adopted by the standard. In all Surselvan dialects the use of the
disjunctive pronoun is required, even when the persons are distinguished
by inflectional endings:

(10)   Brigels *Jéu lával* '(I) wash' / *El láva* '(he) washes'.

> Sporadic evidence for the suffixed *-l* (not found in the earliest texts) dates from
> the beginning of the eighteenth century. It has been suggested that it repre-
> sents an enclitic pronoun object (< ILLUM) or that it is introduced by analogy
> with verbs with an *l* in the stem (e.g. *affel* < AFFLO). Although the former sug-
> gestion may appear unmotivated, we may compare the 'pleonastic' use of a
> feminine (originally neuter?) pronoun *la* in, for instance, Florentine:

(11)   *O che la fai?* 'what are you doing?' *Io la prendo il treno* 'I am taking the train'.

> It is possible that in Surselvan, which no longer uses atonic pronouns, the *-l* is a
> relic of a similar former 'pleonastic' enclitic pronoun. Another suggestion is
> that the *-el* element represents a hypercorrect reformation of borrowed Italian
> *-o*, parallel with e.g. *staunchel* = Ital. *stanco* 'tired'. However, an *-el* adjectival

and nominal suffix (often originally from -ĪLIS) is very common in this variety
and there is no good reason to associate it with Italian *-o*. More plausible morphologically would be the agglutination to the verb of an obsolete enclitic person 1 pronoun, parallel to disjunctive *jéu*. There is, however, no phonological
evidence to support the postulated change [ew] > [əl], even though hardening of
glides (to velars) is regular in some localities, and the change of [aw] to [al] in
some contexts is found in a number of North Italian dialects.

Some marginal Ladin dialects also require use of the disjunctive pronoun
apparently to distinguish homophonous persons 3 and 6:

(12)   Pàdola (Comelico) *Luj s lava* 'He gets washed'/ *Lueri s lava* 'They get washed'.

         Dolomite varieties, however, regularly use a subject clitic for persons 2, 3 and
         6, whereas p.1 does not require a clitic:

(13)   Ampezzo *lave* / *te laves* (compare Pàdola *lavi* /*lavî*)/ *l lava* / *i lava* 'I / you wash /
         he washes / they wash'.

In the literary variety of Friuli, where subject clitics are regularly used,
persons 1 and 3 are identical except in the *a*-conjugation:

(14)   *i/a ciol* 'I take, he takes', but *I cianti* 'I sing' / *A ciante* 'He sings'.

         The *-i* person 1 ending often found in North Italian varieties is thought by some
         to derive from an enclitic subject pronoun (cf. Ital. *io*).

(e)   French

Modern spoken French seems to be furthest from the Romance archetype, in
that inflectional person endings are even less consistently used than elsewhere.
In the present indicative of most verbs persons 1, 2, 3 and 6 have zero markers. Persons 4 and 5 are, however, differentiated by [ʃ] and [e] endings, and
sometimes by difference of stem. The graphical form reflects to some extent
an earlier stage of the language which did apparently differentiate six persons:

(15)   *chante* (Old French *chant*), *-es*, *-e*, *-ons*, *-ez*, *-ent*.

Loss of unstressed final vowels and of consonants, completed by the
beginning of the modern French period (early seventeenth century), led, in
the standard language, to homonymy of all the stem-stressed forms, and
by the same period subject pronouns came to be obligatorily used, except
when there is a noun subject. Dialects sometimes distinguish singular from
plural verb forms inflectionally, rather than by different pronouns:

(16)   *Je chante / Je chantons* 'I / We sing'.

Some generative phonologists have maintained that (highly abstract) underlying forms still distinguish the different persons in standard French. Most scholars agree, however, that the burden of distinguishing the persons has shifted from the verb endings to the proclitic subject pronouns. Even when there is a noun subject, popular varieties of French use fairly consistently the 'pleonastic' subject pronoun:

(17)   *Mon père il chante* 'My father [he] sings'.

This is similar to what happens in many dialects of north Italy and neighbouring areas, where the pronoun can be virtually obligatory:

(18)   Tessin *ul me pa al canta* '[the] my father [he] sings'.

> The preverbal *i* in some Indian Ocean creoles can be seen as an extension of such constructions, though other origins have been suggested.

Some would maintain that examples like (17) and (18) involve **left dislocation**, by which the noun subject is placed in an extraposed topic position, to be echoed by the pronoun within the clause proper. Others claim that the pronoun is part of the verb inflection. Much depends on judgements about intonation patterns, and on the possibility of use of the pronoun to echo indefinite noun subjects (like 'someone' etc.). In standard French, for instance, this does not happen, whereas in many dialectal varieties it does:

(19)   French *Quelqu'un* (*il*) *a demandé*, Francoprovençal (Val d'Aosta) *Quatsun l'at demandà* 'Someone has asked' (where, admittedly, the *l* could be a subject or an object clitic); French dial. (Picard, Démuin) *Chacan i a ker l'indrot adù qu'i est vnu au monne* / standard *Chacun* (*il*) *a le cœur là où il est venu au monde* 'Everyone has his heart in the place where he came into the world'.

Note, however, that a clitic subject apparently echoes *personne* 'no-one' in questions in standard French:

(20)   *Personne ne vient-il?* 'Is nobody coming?'

In non-standard French, too, clitic copying with indefinites is also not unknown (see the film title *Tout le monde il est beau, tout le monde il est gentil* 'Everybody [he]'s good-looking, everybody [he]'s nice').

In both French and North Italian varieties, unlike standard Italian, a 'dummy' (**expletive**) pronoun is used in **impersonals**, where no logical subject is involved:

(21)   French *Il pleut, il faut* / Ital. *Piove, bisogna* 'It is raining' / 'it is necessary that. . .'.

In French, even with the clitic subject, person 3 is identical with person 6, except when the pronoun is followed by a vocalic initial:

(22)   [i'ʃɑ̃t] *Il(s) chante(nt)* 'He sings, they sing', but [i'lɛm] *il aime* 'he loves' / [i'zɛm]
              ils aiment 'they love'.

(f)   Anaphoric and deictic pronouns

Persons 3 and 6 are, as we have seen, homophonous in some other Romance languages, and, normally, these persons would, in the absence of a lexical subject, call for a 'substitute' **anaphoric** subject pronoun. However, in those Romance languages in which use of the subject pronoun is not obligatory it is the discourse or **deictic** pronouns – first and second persons – that are most frequently used, and not the third-person pronouns. This usage is presumably pragmatically motivated, in that the discourse pronouns closely implicate the interlocutors.

(g)   First and second persons plural

Yet, morphologically, it is persons 4 and 5 that appear to be most often clearly differentiated, not only by distinctive endings, but also often by stem changes that historically owe their origin to the Latin accentuation pattern (see 7.3):

(23)   French *il vient* / *nous venons* / *vous venez*, Ital. *viene* / *veniamo* / *venite*, Span.
              viene / *venimos* / *venís* 'he comes / we come / you come'.

Persons 4 and 5 behave in unexpected ways in several languages. We have already mentioned that Italian has generalized the ending -*iamo* in all conjugations. French, too, has adopted a uniform ending for each of these persons: -*ons* is sometimes said to come from SŬMUS (French *sommes* '(we) are') or, perhaps, from a deviant development of -AMUS (Old French -*ens*), while -*ez* is a regular outcome of -ATIS.

In the Spanish and Portuguese standard languages persons 4 and 5 of the present indicative are the only finite forms that distinguish three conjugations rather than two:

(24)   p.4: -*amos, -emos, -imos*; p.5: Span. -*áis, -éis, -ís* / Ptg. -*ais, -eis, -is*.

One may well wonder what it is about these two persons that calls for special characterization. Perhaps it is something to do with their semantic complexity – 'we' can indicate the inclusive 'I and you' or the exclusive 'I + he or they' (a distinction not grammaticalized in Romance), while 'you', originally plural, can often be used as a polite form of address to a single person.

> In several languages, though, there seems to be a tendency to avoid use of the morphologically marked persons 4 and 5 forms (see below).

(i)   Honorifics

Some languages prefer a person 3 honorific form, with third person verb agreement, to the polite use of the person 5 form in addressing a single individual:

(25)   Span. *usted* (originally *vuestra merced* 'your grace') and also *él, ella* in the older language and in dialectal use; Ital. dial. (Genoa) *vosá* (from *vostra signoría* 'your lordship'); Ptg. *o senhor* 'the lord', *você* (from *vosse mercê* 'your grace').

Rumanian *Dumneată* (*Matà* for short) or less familiar *Dumneavoastră* are used with person 2 and 5 verb forms respectively.

Italian *voi* (person 5 pronoun) and *Lei* (feminine person 3 pronoun) are today often regarded as regional (South and North) variants of the honorific pronoun, but they have apparently always alternated, without clear pragmatic differentiation.

> Interestingly enough, some Louisiana (*cajun*) French varieties differentiate the polite *vous* person from the familiar plural *vous autres* 'you others' (see 2.2):

(26)   *Vous chante / Vous-autres chantez* or *vous-autres ça chante* 'You sing' (sg./pl.).

> Another isolated related, and now virtually obsolete, American French dialect, that of Old Mines, Missouri, does not retain even traces of the *-ez* person 5 ending, except in a few fossilized forms. A distinction in person 5 pronouns similar to that of *cajun* is found in Friulian, the polite *vo* form being used in addressing a friend or relative, and *voaltris* as a plural. However, third person forms are used to address strangers or superiors.

(ii)   Voseo

Some American Spanish varieties apparently make no use at all of the person 5 forms, employing the subject pronoun *vos* apparently with person 2 verb forms (a phenomenon known as *voseo*) to address single individuals. However, the stress pattern of some of these verb forms, as in the Plata region of Argentina, suggests that there may be person 5 rather than person 2 agreement:

(27)   *Vos cantás* (< *cantáis?* rather than *cántas*) 'You sing'.

In Argentina *vos* is apparently used with person 2 agreement in most tenses:

(28)   *vos cantarás, vos has cantado, vos cantabas*

but in the preterite popular usage adds a *-s* marker to the *-áste* person 2 verb form (in place of the standard person 5 *-astéis* form):

(29)   *Vos cantastes* (popular) / *cantaste* 'You sang'.

Elsewhere (for instance, in Chile) person 5 verb forms are certainly used in *voseo*.

> Perhaps significantly, in many of the *voseo* dialects syllable-final *s* is phonetically realised as a spirant, or has disappeared altogether (see 6.2). For the plural, *ustedes* (with p. 6 agreement) is used in *voseo* dialects. In West Andalusia the same form, a honorific, is used with a person 5 agreement:

(30)   *Ustedes cantáis* 'You (pl.) sing'.

(iii)   Person 4

The first person plural inflected form is apparently avoided in popular varieties of several languages. In colloquial French, for instance:

(31)   *On chante* 'One sings' is frequently substituted for *nous chantons*; *nous on va* 'we are going'.

The *on* form (see 6.5) seems to be the only colloquial person 4 form in most American varieties.

In colloquial Tuscan varieties of Italian the use of a person 3 pronominal (reflexive) form has virtually replaced the person 4 form:

(32)   *Noi si canta* for *Cantiamo* 'We sing'.

Similar forms are found elsewhere in Italy (especially in the north), even where the inflectional ending is well preserved.

In some popular Brazilian Portuguese varieties the person 4 *-mos* ending is virtually unknown, the person being marked by an obligatory, preposed pronoun:

(33)   *Nos deve* for *devemos* 'We ought'.

Even where the characteristic -MUS person 4 ending appears to be intact, there is sometimes confusion with the NOS 'we' pronoun. In some languages such confusion is undetectable as it is overlaid by other phonological changes, but in parts of south-west France, north Spain and central Italy it looks as if the inflectional and pronominal morphemes have tended to fuse. In the pronoun not infrequently the initial phoneme appears as /m/ (a phenomenon found also in south-east France).

Even more often the inflectional ending could conceivably be a reflex of the NOS pronoun, rather than of the -MUS ending. This is particularly so in Spain (examples from Leon, Aragon and Asturias have been cited, most frequently in the imperfect indicative and the present subjunctive) and in American Spanish. The *-nos* forms (as distinct from the *-mos* forms) may be stressed on the stem, not on the thematic vowel:

(34)   North American (*chicano*) Span. *Trabájenos* / standard *Trabajémos* 'Let's work'.

This stress patterning suggests that the ending may have been reanalysed as *trabáje* (person 1 or person 3) + *nos*.

Old Tuscan *-no* person 4 endings were frequent from the thirteenth century: analogy with person 6 is the favoured explanation. For instance, in the attested medieval form:

(35)   *Penseno* 'We think'

where there is no stress marking in the graphy, it is possible stress was on the stem as in person 6 (*pénseno*). But similar forms survive in varieties of modern Tuscany, with the stress on the ending. It is possible that here we have enclisis of the *no* 'we' pronoun to an apocopated person 4 form. Thus:

(36)   *faciém*(*o*) + *no* > *faciéno* = Ital. *facciamo* 'we do' (compare R-R (Friuli) *mangín* = Ital. *mangiamo* 'we eat').

We note, however, that in Liguria persons 4 and 6 of the imperfect indicative can be identical:

(37)   *Mingáven* = standard *Mangiavámo*/*Mangiávano* 'We/they were eating'.

Shift of stress in the inflected person 4 form may also occur in the North Italian Cremona dialect:

(38)   *Kantúm/Kántum* 'We sing'.

The stem-stressed form seems to be associated with:

(39)   *Um kánta* 'One sings, we sing'.

In French there may once have been similar associations: see example (31) above. The interaction of person endings and person pronouns, as shown by analogical reformation of one or the other, by reanalysis of the endings as pronouns, or the fusion of pronouns to the verb as inflections, occurs sporadically throughout the Romance area, more often in non-standard varieties than in the standard languages.

(h)   Person markers and subject pronouns

In none of the creoles are there person inflections, but an invariable lexical verb form is obligatorily preceded by a disjunctive non-case-marked personal pronoun, except when a lexical subject is present. Compared with our 'archetypical' Romance language, the typological difference appears radical.

We have seen, however, that within the Romance languages there is a shading which, at the outer limit, no longer presents sharp contrast with the creoles. Some would place the dividing line between those languages that still rely primarily on inflectional endings to mark the person of the verb (identified broadly with the **null subject** or **pro-drop** languages of current generative studies), and those that make use of preposed subject pronouns: French, Northern Italian, the Spanish of San Domingo and the Portuguese of Brazil would then fall on the side of the creoles.

The hypothesis of a difference in parametrical setting that divides the Romance languages into two groups on this basis has encountered many empirical problems, and has led to refinements of the hypothesis that sometimes appear to lack close direct links with the data. For instance, a distinction is made between 'phonological clitics' in North Italian varieties, where the pronominal form is treated as part of the inflection, and 'syntactic clitics' in French, where the pronoun is assumed to occupy a syntactic slot of its own. If we take into account non-standard usage, this distinction is not so clear-cut.

Here we should return to the earlier remark that the modern Romance languages may be moving to verb-first (V1) ordering. If the subject clitic does

indeed become a verb inflection then in many cases a change from SV to V1
ordering has been effected.

Undoubtedly phonetic attrition of personal inflections favours increase in
use of pronouns. But the direction of causation is not uncontroversial;
indeed historical evidence seems to indicate no direct chronological correlation between loss of inflections and obligatory use of overt pronouns. After
all, as we have seen, some languages have buttressed their doomed inherited
inflections with postposed vestigial pronouns, and some use clitic or non-
clitic pronouns obligatorily, even though most inflectional endings are kept
distinct. As an example of belt-and-braces differentiation of persons, we can
cite a Lombardy paradigm, which distinguishes person endings, in which at
least one pronoun is obligatory, either the disjunctive (*mi canti*), or the clitic
(*a canti*), but often both are used (*mi a canti*). The proclitic pronoun, in some
varieties, differentiates persons 2, 3 and 6, and occasionally person 1.

Lombard person markers

mi a (*/mi*) *kánti*; 'me he (/I) I-sing';
ti ty (*/a*) *kántat*; 'you you (/he) you-sing';
ly al (*/a*) *kánta*; 'him he sings';
le la kánta; 'her she sings';
ny (*m*) *a kantom* 'we he we-sing'/ *ny* (*m*) *am kántawe* = 'we one sings';
vy / *vialtri a kantá(f)* 'you/you-all he you-sing';
lor i (*/a*) *kánta* 'them they (/he) sings'.

Indeed, here, the hypercharacterization can be so marked that one colleague has called it 'belt, braces *and* hands'.

Other North Italian varieties also make similar use of pronouns though not
always so consistently. In most Veneto varieties a clitic pronoun is obligatory
with only persons 3 and 6, which have identical verb endings:

(40)   *el/i crede* 'he believes / they believe'.

In Venice clitic *ti* is obligatory also with person 2; however, the person 3 clitic is
not used with 'impersonals', or 'indefinites', nor, curiously, when the lexical
subject is postposed to the verb (though note that in this example there is an
unaccusative verb):

(41)   *Toni el ze rivà* / *Ze rivà Toni* 'Tony has arrived'.

It has been argued that in this variety the person 3 clitic is an argumental element which cannot be associated with the expletive null element that is
assumed to occupy subject position (e.g. in unaccusatives). In varieties of

Central Veneto an invariable particle *a* accompanies persons 2 and 3 clitics, apparently always verb-phrase initially:

(42)   *A te ve via* 'You are going away', *A veto via*? 'Are you going away?', *A no te parli mai* 'You never speak'.

It is also used with 'impersonals', like weather verbs; whether it is better viewed as a pronoun or as a verb-phrase marker is debatable:

(43)   *A névega* 'It is snowing'.

In the dialect of Genoa, like that of Venice, a clitic pronoun is obligatory with persons 2, 3 and 6, but also with the polite form – see example (25) above – used with persons 3 and 6 agreement:

(44)   [(vuˈʃa) ʃa sa] = Ital. *Lei sa* 'you know'.

Pro-drop in French

The problems posed by the history of French person markers has in recent times sparked off copious research activity, as the transition from pro-drop to non-pro-drop was apparently made in fairly recent times (completed by the seventeenth century). For French, unlike most North Italian varieties, there is ample documentation of all kinds and for most periods. The main facts of the case have long been known: in Old French texts subject pronouns are not used in contexts in which they would be obligatory in modern French. Old French texts also tolerate more variation in word order and show a richer verbal morphology than modern French, and so it has frequently been assumed that Old French was more 'prototypically' Romance than the modern language.

The Old French of the early texts has, however, apparently non-Romance syntactic features that some have linked to putative Germanic influence (presumably owing to the prestige of the Franks, who constituted the ruling class in north Gaul after the disintegration of the Western Romance Empire). These features include the apparent predominance of the so-called verb-second (V2) word order that is usually assumed to be a defining characteristic of Germanic languages. The link between V2 and non-use of pronoun subjects in Old French texts has long been recognized. Where we would expect a subject pronoun to follow the verb, displaced by another element preceding the verb in the clause, most frequently no overt pronoun is used (or 'the pronoun is omitted').

In modern French V2 ordering is no longer extant (except in some fossils –
like *ainsi soit-il* 'so be it'). Attempts to trace in texts a direct link between loss
of V2 and obligatory use of pronouns have not been completely successful.
That there is no simple causal connection is suggested by comparison with
those Surselvan Rhaeto-Romance varieties that have V2 and a rich verb morphology, but also obligatorily use disjunctive case-marked pronouns:

(45)   *Jeu cumprel, ti cumpras, el cumpra* 'I, you buy, he buys'.

Sociolinguistic factors

One thing that has to be borne in mind is that modern French is highly standardized. Seventeenth-century linguistic arbiters decreed that variants that
permitted non-use of subject pronouns were unacceptable and archaic, on
the grounds that they were potentially ambiguous. Texts before this time
show more variation, but documentation of truly colloquial usage is hard to
come by. So we can only extrapolate from incomplete evidence, testing
hypotheses that can be formulated within the framework of current theories.

Standardization in this instance, as in others, had the effect of distancing French from the inner circle of the Romance 'club'. Seventeenth-century fashionable society in France swept aside tradition and fostered radical
modernity. The ideal of clarity and elegance in language use eschewed
ellipsis and favoured overt marking of sentence constituents.

French subject pronouns by the seventeenth-century were always proclitic to the verb and could not receive stress. Stressed **disjunctive** forms
that were originally non-nominative (like *moi, toi* < ME, TE) were used for
emphasis, alongside the clitics:

(46)   *Moi, je chante, Toi, tu chante* '*I* sing, *you* sing'.

In the modern standard, exceptionally, it is still possible to use the third
person disjunctive pronoun without a clitic, usually with adversative
import:

(47)   *Lui vient et non elle* '*He*'s coming, and not *her*'.

It is the disjunctive forms, not the clitics, that yielded the only personal
pronouns of French creoles. There is a closer resemblance in this respect
between French and North Italian varieties, where the subject clitic can be
viewed as an inflectional element, than between French and the creoles.

Thus we can maintain that in the use of person markers most creoles stand apart from the Romance languages proper, though Surselvan Rhaeto-Romance and non-standard Brazilian Portuguese have creole-like properties.

1.3 NOUN GENDER

In the Romance languages proper, as distinct from the creoles, nouns fall into two gender classes, known as **masculine** (m.) and **feminine** (f.) because there is a reasonably good, though far from perfect, correlation with sex differences where referents are animate beings. Unlike Latin, there is no third **neuter** (n.) gender, even though, as we shall see, there are forms that can be regarded as resembling a neuter. Within the Indo-European family the historical collapse of a three-gender system into one distinguishing animate from neuter is frequent, but the maintenance of a masculine/feminine distinction, with the concomitant loss of the neuter, seems to be unique to Romance (though it is found outside Indo-European).

Romance gender differences are marked most consistently by agreement of determiners and adjectives, though, as we shall see, the phonological shape of the noun can serve as a good, though not infallible, signal to its gender. Gender of non-animates appears to be fairly random though some semantic patterns can be discerned, usually reproducing those of Latin: for instance, 'abstract nouns of quality' – noun derivatives of qualitative adjectives – are normally feminine.

The Latin A-class (first declension) and Ŭ-class (second declension) nouns were overwhelmingly feminine and masculine respectively, and remain so in Romance. Where the final vowels have survived (as in Spanish and Italian) -*a* is still seen as the feminine marker, -*o* as the masculine, mainly because those adjectives that distinguish gender make use of these inherited marks. Even in French, where all unstressed final vowels eventually were lost, the -*e* that continued Latin -A is seen as a feminine marker; nowadays, in the standard language it is a graphical marker usually indicating that the preceding graphical consonant is pronounced. In some varieties, on the other hand, it is heard as a schwa [ə], and in some dialects (e.g. in Normandy) it changed the *timbre* or length of a preceding vowel before being lost.

The first- and second-declension word markers in Latin are not, however, totally reliable indicators of gender: in particular some -A forms are masculine and designate male human beings:

(48)   AGRICOLA 'farmer', POETA 'poet'.

Romance conserves some apparently anomalous cases: Italian *poeta* has the regular masculine plural form *poeti*, whereas Spanish *poetas* looks morphologically like a feminine plural.

(a)   Latin neuters

The Latin third gender – the neuter – has no direct reflex in nouns in the Romance languages (but see below). Neuters in the ŭ-class normally become masculine:

(49)   PRATUM 'meadow': French *pré*, Ital. *prato*, Span., Ptg. *prado*, Occ., Cat. *prat*;
        OVUM 'egg': French *œuf*, Span. *huevo*, Ptg. *ovo*, Occ. *uou*, Cat. *ou* (for Rum./Ital.
        m. *ou/uovo*, f. plural *oua/uova* – see below).

Some third-declension neuter nouns with a U in the final syllable are also incorporated into the same class:

(50)   CAPUT 'head' : French *chef*, Ital. *capo*, Span., Ptg. *cabo*; Occ., Cat. *cap* m.,
        capete f. pl.; PECTUS 'chest': Old French *piz*, Ital. *petto*, Span. *pecho*, Ptg. *peito*,
        Occ. *peitz*, Cat. *pit* (Rum. *piept* 'breast of coat' is masculine, but see below for
        piept 'chest').

In some cases (but see below) the plural second-declension neuter form in -A is reanalysed as a feminine singular (with originally collective import):

(51)   OVA 'eggs' (/OVUM): Span. *hueva* 'roe' (/*huevo*); FATA 'fates': French *fée*, Ital.
        fata, Span. *hada*, Ptg., Occ., Cat., *fada* 'fairy' (see Span. *hado* 'fate', Ptg. *fado* 'a
        kind of song, dirge' < FATUM); FOLIA 'leaves': French *feuille* (Old French also
        fueil m.), Ital. *foglia* (/*foglio* 'sheet of paper'), Span. *hoja*, Ptg. *folha*, Occ. *folha*
        (/*folh*), Cat. *fulla* (/*full*), Rum. *foaie*; GAUDIA 'joys': French *joie* (Old French
        also *joi* m.), Ital. *gioia* 'joy, gem', Span. *joya* 'gem', etc. seem to be borrowed
        from French (compare Span. *gozo* 'delight').

(b)   Fluctuating gender

Most descendants of Latin third declension nouns lack an overt mark of gender. Not surprisingly, Romance languages frequently hesitate about allotting them to one class or another, even when they were not originally neuter nouns:

(52)   MAR, MARIS n. 'sea': French *mer* f., Ital *mare* m., Span., Ptg. *mar* m.
        (f. in Old Spanish and in modern dialects as well as in some idioms e.g. *en alta mar*

'on the high seas'), Occ. *mar* m. or f., Cat. *mar* m. 'body of water', f. in other uses, Rum. *mare* f.; LAC, LACTIS n. 'milk': French *lait* m., Ital. *latte* m., Sard *latte* f., Sp. *leche* f., Ptg. *leite* m., Occ. *lach* m., Cat. *llet* f. (for Rum. *lăpte*, see below). SANGUEN, SANGUINIS n. / SANGUIS, SANGUINIS m. 'blood': m. nearly everywhere except Occ. *sang* m. or f., Cat. *sang* f. and Span. *sangre* f. (for Rum. *sînge*, see below). MEL, MELLIS n. 'honey': f. in Rum. (*miere*), many Ital. and R-R dialects, Cat. (*mel*) and Span. (*miel*), m., but elsewhere; PONS, PONTIS m. 'bridge': French *pont*, Ital. *ponte*, Span. *puente* m., but Ptg. *ponte*, OSpan. *puente* f.; VALLES, VALLIS f. 'valley': Ital. *valle*, Rum. *vale* f., French *val*, Span. *valle* m.

It is not unknown for both masculine and feminine reflexes of Latin third-declension nouns to be found in the same language:

(53)   Span. *la frente*, Ital. *la fronte* 'forehead' / Span. *el frente*, Ital. *il fronte* 'front (military, weather)' (FRONS, FRONTIS f.); Ital. *la fine* 'end' / *il fine* 'purpose' (FINIS m. sometimes f.); French *de vieilles gens* (f.) 'old people' / *des gens ennuyeux* (m.) 'boring people' (GENS, GENTIS f.).

Latin fourth-declension nouns in -U- are usually treated as masculine, whatever their original gender:

(54)   DOMUS f. 'home': Ital. *duomo* 'cathedral'; PORTICUS f. 'porch': French *porche*, Ital. *portico*; CORNŪ n. 'horn': French *cor*, Ital. *corno*, Span. *cuerno*, Ptg. *corno* (but NURUS 'daughter-in-law' was early attested in the form NORA).

In the (Southern Italian) dialects of Campania distinctive traces of the fourth declension survive: the same form is used for the feminine singular and plural in these words:

(55)   ACUS, ACŪS, f. 'needle' > *ago* (Ital. m. *ago/aghi*); FICUS, FICŪS. f. 'fig-tree' *fico* (Ital. m. *fico/fichi*).

MANUS 'hand' (a word learned in early infancy) has, exceptionally, retained its feminine gender nearly everywhere, even where it has a masculine-type final vowel:

(56)   Ital. *mano*, Sard *manu*, Span. *mano*, Ptg. *mão*.

In the Rhaeto-Romance of the Engadine, however, *maun, màn* is masculine – a gender also attested in Old French and Old Occitan. In Rumanian and some Italian dialects the form of the word has changed to match its gender:

(57)   *mînă, mana.*

It appears that the plural forms of this word succumb more readily to such analogical change in dialectal usage. Nearly everywhere diminutive and other derivatives of MANUS have overtly feminine endings (though in the Engadine *maunin* is feminine and *manut* masculine):

(58)   Ital. *manina, manuccia,* Span. *manita,* Ptg. *mãozinha,* Rum. *mînuţă*

Not infrequently, any gender fluctuations that affected nouns in the Middle Ages were eventually resolved in favour of the Latin tradition, at the period of codification of the languages by normative grammarians, who were keen that the prestige of Latin should rub off on to the newly elevated 'vulgar' varieties. This is particularly true of French, where erosion of final vowels has left nouns with no overt gender marker:

(59)   *amour* f. → m. 'love' (AMOR, AMORIS m.), *honneur* f. → m. (HONOS, HONORIS m.), *espace* f. → m. 'space' (SPATIUM n.), *image* m. (originally non-nominative) → f. 'image' (IMAGO, IMAGINE f.).

(c)   'Neuter' gender in Romance?

For some languages a third gender is sometimes postulated and linked with the Latin neuter. I shall examine these so-called 'neuters' and seek to show that they do not in Romance constitute a separate gender class.

(i)   Spanish

In standard Spanish nominalized masculine adjectival forms are differentiated into animates and abstracts apparently by the choice of the form of the definite article (*el* m., *lo* n.):

(60)   *el bueno* 'the good one (m.)' / *lo bueno* 'the good'.

Furthermore the *lo*-neuter can be used, though very rarely, with nouns to express the inherent quality of the objects referred to:

(61)   *lo mujer* 'femininity' / *la mujer* 'the woman'; *lo rey* 'kingliness' / *el rey* 'the king'.

Lo can more readily be used with plural or feminine 'gradable' adjectives:

(62)   a. *En lo*   *valientes*   *y*   *sufridos*   *ningún*
           in the (n.) valiant   and enduring (m. pl.) no

           soldado aventaja   *a los* *españoles.*
           soldier   surpasses to the Spanish

           'There are no better soldiers than Spaniards in respect of valour and suffering hardships.'

b. *Había olvidado   lo   guapa   que eres*
I-had forgotten   the (n.) handsome(f.) that you-are
'I had forgotten how pretty you are.'

A similar usage is occasionally found in Portuguese, where there is no formal distinction between 'masculine' and 'neuter'; a translation of (62b) is:

(63)   *Tinha esquecido o   bonita   que es*
I-had forgotten the (m.) pretty (f.) that you-are

This may, however, be regarded as more an imitation of Spanish than as authentic Portuguese.

Lo in these uses may be more readily understood as a pronoun than as an article: we can compare, for instance, *¡Lo que eres es guapa!* 'How handsome you are!' (literally 'That which you are is handsome'). For the close relationship of determiners and pronouns in Romance see 3.3. and 7.5. The distinction between determiner and pronoun accompanying an adjective is more obvious in Spanish with the indefinite form. In this case the pronominal (*uno*) can be understood as a numeral:

(64)   *En la playa vi a cuatro chicos morenos y un/uno rubio* 'On the beach I saw four dark boys and a/one fair [one]'.

A 'definite' pronoun in such a context would be understood as closer to a demonstrative ('that') (though without the localization implied by the demonstrative).

For the use of the definite pronoun/article with possessives see 6.5.

The *lo* pronoun/determiner can also be used to nominalize other syntagmata; in these cases it looks even more akin to a pronoun than a determiner:

(65)   *lo de ayer* (literally, 'the [thing] of yesterday') 'what happened yesterday'; *No me di cuenta de lo rápidamente que trascurrían las horas* 'I didn't realize how (the n.) quickly the hours passed'.

The Spanish 'neuter' is clearly not functionally derived from the Latin neuter, even though morphologically *lo* may well continue the neuter demonstrative form ILLUD. It can be seen today as a pronoun with [–specific] semantic import. It is difficult to discern how far the Spanish 'neuter' function was an ancient popular development, as, in Old Spanish, the masculine definite article *el*, rather than *lo*, could be used with substantivized adjectives – though it is true that *lo* was used with possessives (*lo mío* etc.).

In modern times (since the eighteenth century), some writers have used the *el* form with adjectives, though this use may be regarded as rather affected:

(66)   *Infelices cuya existencia se reduce al mero necesario* 'Unhappy [people] whose existence is reduced to the (m.) mere necessary'.

For the morphological relationship between *el* and *lo* see 7.5.

(ii)   Asturias

In Central Asturian dialects of Spain, alongside the 'abstract neuter' is found another phenomenon, which is often described as a *neutro de materia* or a 'collective neuter'. In Asturian there is no special definite article form, but in some varieties nouns with non-count meaning can have a final *-o* distinct from the normal masculine *-u*, sometimes triggering metaphony (4.2).

(67)   *Ten   el pelo* (n.)   *rojo   Kayu   i   un pilu* (m.).
         he-has   the hair   red   It-falls-to-him   a hair

         'He has red hair.' 'One of his hairs fell out.'

         Ye   de fierro (n.)   *da   me isi   fiirru* (m.)
         'It is   [made] of iron.'   'Give me that iron.'

Usually, however, mass-noun status is indicated only by the neuter form of the (dis)agreeing adjective:

(68)   *Apúrreme la cebolla blanca* (f.) 'Peel me the white onion' / *Semó la cebolla blanco* (n.) 'He sowed the white [species of] onion'; *el pie fríu* (m.) 'the cold foot' / *el arroz frío* (n.) '(the) cold rice'; *la casa fría* (f.) 'the cold house' / *el agua frío* (m.) '(the) cold water'; *el ome buenu* (m.) 'the good man' / *la mujer buena* (f.) 'the good woman' / *la gente bueno* (n.) '(the) good folk'.

It has been suggested that the *-u* form derives from Latin -US (m. nom. sg.), while the *-o* 'collective' comes from neuter -UM. More plausible, phonologically and semantically, is the suggestion that the *-o* derives originally from an ablative, or a genitive–dative, inflectional ending used with partitive sense, and that the 'disagreement' has a function similar to that of the partitive article in French. The distinction would therefore be one of case, marked only on the adjective in some varieties, rather than of gender.

(iii)   Southern Italy

A similar phenomenon is also found in parts of Abruzzo, in and near Bari and in Lucania (Basilicata). It takes various phonological guises, including a word-final vowel (*-o/-u*) distinction and/or umlauted vocalism (in the *-u* forms):

(69)   *lo ferro* (n.) '(the) iron', *lo pescio* (n.) '(the) fish' / *lu pjettu* (m.) 'the chest', *lu pesciu* (m.) 'the fish'.

Here the distinction, as in Asturias, seems to be one of case, rather than of gender.

In some dialects only the form of the 'definite article' marks the non-count status of the noun. The form of these articles varies from dialect to dialect but contrasts are regularly made:

(70)   *o latte* (n.) '(the) milk' / *u pratu* (m.) 'the meadow'; *lu pan* (n.) '(the) bread' / *ju kane* (m.) 'the dog'; *le sangue* (n.) '(the) blood' / *i pete* (m.) 'the foot'; *le pesce* (n.) '(the) fish' / *la pesce* (f.) 'the fish'.

Sometimes the 'neuter' article shows that the noun has an abstract meaning, while the masculine indicates a more concrete sense:

(71)   Abruzzo *le fúoke* (n.) '(the) heat' / *lu fúoke* (m.) 'the fire'; *le kore* (n.) 'the heart' (figurative, as in *le kore de la notte* 'the dead of the night') / *lu kore* (m.) 'the heart' (in other senses).

The Abruzzo neuter article is not only used with mass nouns, but also, as in Spanish, with substantivized adjectives, infinitives and past participles:

(72)   *le bielle* 'the beautiful', [lə maˈɲɲa] = Ital. *il mangiare* 'eating, food', [lə ˈskrettə] = Ital. *lo scritto* 'what has been written'.

The 'neuter' article is also used in Western Abruzzo with forms deriving from Latin neuter plurals:

(73)   *le prate* < PRATA 'meadows', *le corpore* < CORPORA 'bodies'

and with newer formations of the same type:

(74)   *le capere* < CAP(UT) + -ORA 'heads'.

In Western Abruzzo, too, an 'indefinite neuter' article ([nə]/[nu] m., [na] f.) is also found: it is used with a singular mass noun, or with a masculine plural to indicate excellence ('quite something'):

(75)   [nəˈvinə] 'high-quality wine' / [nuˈvinə] 'a wine'; [nəkaˈvɛllə] 'thoroughbred horses' / [ikaˈvɛllə] 'the horses'.

In several Southern Italian varieties the initial consonant of mass nouns shows a 'syntactic doubling' (see 6.3), not found in comparable masculine nouns, suggesting that the preceding definite article, although phonetically identical with the masculine form, is phonologically distinct:

(76)   *lu ppane* (n.) '(the) bread' / *lu liettu* (m.) 'the bed'; *u ssale* (n.) '(the) salt' / *u nase* (m.) 'the nose'.

The distinctive marking of the mass noun is often marginal and fragile. In some parts of Lucania, for example, a few nouns are marked by 'neuter' article *ru*:

(77)   *ru ssale* 'salt', *ru ppane* 'bread'

but neighbouring varieties incorporate them into the masculine gender class:

(78)   *u ppane* 'bread'.

Are the Asturian and Abruzzan 'neuters' related?

It has been suggested that the South Italian and the Asturian 'neuters' are directly related historically (perhaps through colonization of parts of Hispania by Oscans, during the Imperial period) and that they are relics of a once more widespread phenomenon. In Italy, however, agreement phenomena may not be involved, in the way they are in Asturias. Admittedly, reduction of final vowels, in many of the Italian varieties, means that adjectival agreement is not shown overtly. However, one might expect evidence of metaphonic ('umlauted', see 3.2) stem-vowel differences in some varieties (where, for instance, a distinction is made between *nire* (m.) and *nere* (f.) 'black'). The syntactic evidence available about these dialects is so patchy, though, that we do not at present know for certain what happens.

One bit of negative evidence can be found in the nominalized adjectival forms at Sulmona (Abruzzo):

(79)   *le nire* (n.) '(the) blackness' / *lu nire* (m.) 'the black man'

where, unexpectedly, the 'neuter' form is umlauted; however, it may be a lexicalized fossil. Another apparently contradictory bit of evidence comes from Servigliana (Ascoli Piceno), in the Marche region, where the 'neuter' has an *-o* ending (*lo vi* 'wine'), compared with the masculine *-u* (*lu patru* 'the father'). Here there is, in the compound perfect, agreement of the past participle with the masculine subject of the 'unaccusative' (see page 19):

(80)   *Issu è vinutu* 'He has [is] come'.

Conversely the non-agreeing past participle in transitive verbs:

(81)   *Issu ha magnato* 'He has eaten'

seems to have a 'neuter' (or default?) gender mark.

The similarities and differences between the Asturian and Southern Italian cases suggest a marginal and independent survival of an inherited case distinction, functioning as a mass/count noun distinction, rather than an innovation within the gender system.

For a possible parallel in Alpine Romance, see 3.3.

(iv)   Italian

Yet another type of phenomenon that is often associated with the Latin neuter is that of ambigenous nouns in standard Italian and Rumanian: these have masculine gender in the singular and feminine in the plural. In other standard languages a few marginal cases of ambigeneity are found:

(82)   Span. *el arte gótico* (m.) 'Gothic art' (but *el arte poética* (f.) 'Ars Poetica') / *las bellas artes* (f.) 'fine arts' (ARS, ARTIS f.); French *un délice* (m.) / *les délices* (f.) (DELICIAE f. pl. 'delights').

In Italian more, but still comparatively few, nouns – mainly designating parts of the body – are at issue. The feminine plural forms in -*a* (apparently originating as the Latin second-declension neuter nominative–accusative plural ending -A) often have collective or dual purport:

(83)   *il braccio* 'the arm' / *le braccia* 'the arms' (BRACCHIUM n.); *il labbro* 'the lip' / *le labbra* 'the lips (of human)' / *i labbri* 'the lips (figurative), brims, rims', also in the anatomical sense for 'closed lips' (LABRUM n.); *il frutto* 'the fruit' / *le frutta, i frutti* (more frequent) 'fruits', also *la frutta* 'fruit' (collectively) with the plural *le frutte* or (more archaic) *le frutta* (see Span. *el fruto* 'fruit' [growing] / *la fruta* 'fruit' [gathered]) (FRUCTUS m. 4th declension); *l'uovo* 'the egg' / *le uova* '[the] eggs' (OVUM n.).

In Swiss Rhaeto-Romance there are traces of a similar distinction:

(84)   Surmeiran *igl meil* 'the apple' / *la meila* '[the] apples'; Engadine *il daint* 'the finger' / *la dainta* '[the] fingers'; *il bosca* 'tree' / *la bosca* 'the wood'.

One indication of the marginal character of ambigenous nouns in modern

Italian is the degree of hesitation about gender agreement in co-referent pronouns, as in the following literary examples:

(85)   a. *dodici uova*   *avvoltate*   *ciascuna*   *in un foglio*
             twelve eggs (f.pl.)   wrapped (f. pl.)   each (f. sg.) in a sheet (of paper)

         b. *come   insomma   se   le dita*   *dei piedi*   *non li*
             as   in-short   if   the fingers (f. pl.)   of the feet(m.pl.)   not them
                                                                                                (m. pl.)

         avessi.
         I-had.

         'as if I hadn't any toes (? feet)'.

         Some dialects appear to treat the dual form as a masculine singular (as in Tuscan) or as a masculine plural (as in Sicilian), while elsewhere (as in some South Central dialects and in Old Surselvan Rhaeto-Romance) adjectival agreement suggests feminine singular status.

In older Italian more ambigenous words were current:

(86)   *letta* 'beds' / modern *letti* (LECTUS m.).

There was also a greater number of words with reflexes of the Latin (unaccented) third-declension neuter plural ending - ŎRA:

(87)   *corpora* 'bodies' / modern *corpi* (CORPUS, CORPORA n.).

Some Central and Southern dialects still make greater use of such forms, which are treated as feminine plurals. Although -*e* remains the most frequent feminine plural marker, it is rivalled in some areas (e.g. near Salento) by -*uri* etc.:

(88)   Abbruzzo *tempere* 'times' (TEMPUS, TEMPORA n.), *tettere* 'roofs' (TECTUM n.); Sicily *corpure* 'bodies'; Salento *manure* 'hands' (MANUS f.), *akure* 'needles' (ACUS f.).

         In some Western Abbruzzo dialects a collective sense is indicated by a suffixless form, while the normal plural is marked by the -ORA suffix, both plural forms being used with the 'neuter' article – see also examples (73) and (74) above:

(89)   *lu dite* 'the finger' / *le dete* '(set of) fingers' / *le detere* 'fingers (individually)' (DIGITUS m.); *lu vracce* 'the arm', *le vracce* 'pair of arms', *le vraccere* 'arms (individually)' (BRACCHIUM n.).

(v)   Rumanian

In Rumanian ambigenous nouns (masculine in the singular and feminine in the plural) are much more frequent than in Italian; indeed, some 25–30 per cent of nouns fall into this class, for which the term 'neuter' is often used. Slavonic influence is sometimes argued. About a third of the relevant nouns have -ŏRA (modern -*uri*, earlier -*ure*) plural forms:

(90)   *fir* (m. sg.) / *fire* (f. pl.). 'wire(s)' (FILUM n.); *piept* (m. sg.) / *piepturi* (f. pl.)
         'chest(s)' (PECTUS, PECTORA n.); *timp* (m. sg.) / *timpuri* (f. pl.) 'time(s), tense(s)' /
         timpi (m. pl.) 'tempos, epochs' (TEMPUS, TEMPORA n.); *frig* (m. sg.) 'cold', *frig-*
         uri (f. pl.) 'shivers' (FRIGUS, FRIGORA n.); *sînge* (m. sg.) 'blood', *sîngiuri* (rare f.
         pl.) 'murders' (SANGUEN, SANGUINIS n. / SANGUIS, SANGUINIS m.); *lapte* (m. sg.)
         'milk', *lăpturi* (rare f. pl.) 'sorts of milk' (LAC, LACTA n.); *corp* (m. sg.) 'body',
         corpuri (f. pl.) 'bodies' / *corpi* (m. pl.) 'bodies (in scientific terminology)' (COR-
         PUS, CORPORA n.); *ochi* (m. sg. and pl.) 'eye(s)' / *ochiuri* (f. pl.) 'fried or poached
         eggs, orifices' (OCULUS, OCULI m.).

The -*uri* feminine plural appears to be productive, unlike its equivalent in standard Italian, having spread to words of non-Romance origin, especially monosyllabic words:

(91)   *drum* (-*uri*) (from Byzantine Greek via Slavonic) 'road(s)', *pod* (-*uri*) 'bridge(s)',
         ceas (-*uri*) 'hour(s)' (from Slavonic).

         In the modern language there is sometimes oscillation between the -*uri* and the
         -*e* feminine plural form, with preference for the latter, which is viewed as 'more
         Romance'.

(92)   *nucleuri/nuclee* 'nuclei'; *aerodromuri/aerodroame* 'aerodromes'.

         In some cases the two plural forms are differentiated semantically:

(93)   *raporturi* 'relationships' / *rapoarte* 'reports'; *resorturi* 'mechanisms' / *resoarte*
         'departments'.

It seems that Rumanian ambigenous nouns are usually inanimate (or at any rate 'sexless'), whereas the masculine nouns are predominantly animate. The feminine class is by far the largest one and contains mostly inanimate nouns; it can be considered as the unmarked gender class. Latin neuter nouns normally have become feminine in Rumanian, except when they end in a consonant, in which case they most usually are ambigenous. The motivation for the ambigenous treatment may be morphophonological, as straightforwardly 'feminine' nouns nearly always end in a vowel in the singular.

Rumanian gender is not directly related to sex reference: indeed, compared with Spanish or Italian, Rumanian makes little use of noun-form class to differentiate the sex of animates. The so-called 'neuter' can be viewed as a sub-class of the 'feminine', or 'genderless', class, in which 'masculine' agreement is used with the consonant-final singular forms: 'masculine' adjectival forms, when they differ from 'feminine' forms, usually end in *-u* or a consonant, whereas the characteristic feminine ending is *-ă*. Exploitation of the possibility of use of feminine plural forms to match the singular of some masculine vowel-final non-count nouns – like *sînge*, *lapte*, see example (90) above – is attested, but not widespread, and considered by some educated speakers to be deviant.

It is noteworthy that adjectival forms used as abstract nouns occur, with a definite article, in the masculine singular or the feminine plural:

(94)   *răul* (m. sg.) or *relele* (f. pl.) 'the evil' (from the adjective *rău* (m. sg.), *reă* (f. sg.), *răi* (m. pl.), *rele* (f. pl.) 'bad').

This suggests that the ambigenous type is treated as gender-neutral.

(d)   Function of gender

The functional role of gender class in Romance nouns is difficult to discern, though some languages – especially Spanish – make extensive use of it to differentiate otherwise homophonous nouns. Among animates, gender can be used as an indicator of sex, most often when there is an overt *-o/-a* gender marker:

(95)   Span. *hermano/hermana*, 'brother/sister', Ital. *ragazzo/ragazza* 'boy/girl'.

Both in Spanish and in Italian, non-standard varieties make greater use of sex–gender marking than the standard.

Gender differentiation can also hint at other types of relationship:

(96)   Span. *la ayuda* 'help' / *el ayuda* 'valet', *la trompeta* 'trumpet' / *el trompeta* 'trumpet player'; Ital. *il brodo* 'broth' / *la broda* 'dish-water'.

In some cases the feminine is more affective: Italian in particular appears to use the feminine form of doublets in a wider range of metaphorical and non-concrete senses. For example:

(97)   *tavolo/tavola* 'table'

where the rarer masculine (sometimes characterized as non-Tuscan) is exclusively used for an item of furniture, whereas the feminine can designate a wider range of things, like 'list, index, statistical table' as well as 'board, plank' and so on.

Even in French, where overt gender markers in the noun itself have mostly disappeared, gender can be used to distinguish homonyms (with postulated elision of other nouns):

(98)   *le* [*vin de*] *Champagne* 'champagne (the wine)' / *la Champagne* 'Champagne (the region)'; *le* [*bateau à*] *vapeur* 'steam boat' / *la vapeur* 'steam', *le* [*paquebot*] France 'the [ocean liner] *France*' / *la France* 'France (the country)'.

Italian also makes use of this device:

(99)   *la* Roma 'the battleship (*nave* f.) *Rome*' / *il* Roma 'the cruiser (*incrociatore* m.) *Rome*'.

Size differences

One rather curious feature of lexical gender-differentiated pairs in Romance is that gender sometimes signals a difference in size. More often, but not always, the feminine denotes the bigger one of the pair. This phenomenon appears to be absent from Rumanian and rare in French, but it is otherwise quite widespread:

(100)   Span. *cuchillo* 'knife' / *cuchilla* 'cleaver' (though in Italian *coltello* and *coltella* appear to be interchangeable and in some Spanish varieties the feminine is actually smaller – in Puerto Rico, Costa Rica and Peru *cuchilla* 'penknife'); Span. *gorro* 'cap without a visor' / *gorra* 'cap with a visor' (but *talego* 'sack' / *talega* 'small sack'); Ptg. *caldeiro* 'small kettle' / *caldeira* 'cauldron'; Ital. *cavicchio* 'wooden pin' / *cavicchia* 'large bolt, peg', *buco* 'hole' / *buca* 'cavity, large hole' (but the more archaic *tina* 'vat' denotes a smaller vessel than *tino*); Cat. *anell* 'ring' / *anella* 'large ring'.

The semantic motivation of such differentiation has been seen as connected with the larger size of the female in some insect species, or with the effect of pregnancy on female mammals. Perhaps more plausibly, it is a remnant of a spill-over from the frequent phonetic identity of Latin feminine singular nominatives (in -A) with neuter plural nominatives. It has been suggested that the equation 'feminine = larger' was found in older stages of the languages, overlaid later by an association of feminine with diminutives and endearment.

On the whole, however, noun gender's main effect is to trigger off agreement in determiners and adjectives modifying the noun.

(e)   Robustness of gender distinctions

Although the gender agreement system is by no means watertight in most
Romance languages (and especially in French), there can be little doubt
that their speakers are conscious of gender differences, and acquire knowledge of the gender of common words simultaneously with their form and
meaning. In the creoles there is no gender agreement, nor, it appears, consciousness of grammatical gender differences – though in Guadeloupe
some remnants of adjectival agreement (as in *mové/movez* = French *mau-
vais(e)*) are found with animate nouns, and São Tomé uses lexicalized distinctions like *mano/mana* 'brother/sister'. However, it is to be noted that in
some lexical items especially in French creoles (more frequently in Indian
Ocean than in New World creoles) the original gender-marked definite
article has been incorporated into the noun:

(101)   French creole *latab* 'table', *lisu* (*chou*) 'cabbage' (cf. also Principe *upã* (*o pão*)
          'bread', *ufogu* (*o fogo*) 'fire').

This suggests that the gender-marked inherited forms had been understood as genderless, unanalysable entities.

Uncertainty about gender

Within 'core' Romance, speakers sometimes have doubts about the gender
of nouns: I have already mentioned fluctuations in reflexes of the Latin
third-declension nouns which had no overt gender marker. In French few
nouns are overtly marked for gender, though it is possible to make a reasonably good guess at the gender of a noun on the basis of its phonetic
shape and, in particular, its final phoneme. Moreover nouns hardly ever
occur in speech without a determiner which is usually, in the singular,
clearly marked for gender (but see, for Picard, 7.5).

Where, however, a French word begins with a vowel, clues to its gender
will be relatively rare in discourse: for the singular, the immediately preceding definite article has the single form *l'*, the demonstrative the single form
[sɛt] (*cet(te)*), the possessive the single form *mon* and so on. Admittedly the
indefinite article today differentiates *un* [œ̃] masculine from [yn] feminine
before vowels in the standard, but this is a relatively recent development
and some non-standard dialects still use the prevocalic [yn] form for both
genders (e.g. *un élève* 'a pupil' [œ̃nelɛv], earlier [ynelɛv], identical with *une*

élève). It is not surprising then that less-educated native speakers mistake the gender of such forms as:

(102)   *l'éclair* (m.) '[the] lightning', *l'horloge* (f.) 'the clock', *l'ouvrage* (m.) 'the piece of work'.

In non-standard varieties of French, uncommon words beginning with a vowel and ending in a consonant are almost regularly assigned feminine gender, as indeed were some such words in Old French. Whereas in older stages of the Romance languages, feminine nouns were probably more numerous (as they certainly were in French), in most of the modern languages there are about equal numbers of masculine and feminine nouns. This may be due to the, already mentioned, pressure by grammarians to retain or restore Latin gender in Romance reflexes, or to a tendency to assign more recent non-Romance loanwords to the masculine gender. It is likely that changes in balance between forms with different derivational suffixes and borrowings from other languages have had some effect on the relative frequency of gender assignment.

Elsewhere the grammatical tradition, and the partial correlation of gender with sex-reference, has helped to retain and reinforce what threatened to become a redundant system. Lack of grammatical gender can be counted a defining characteristic of a Romance creole, as distinct from those varieties that have retained even the most tenuous link with the Romance tradition. In Rumanian, unlike the other Romance languages, there appears to have been, over time, a reduction in the number of purely masculine nouns and a corresponding increase in 'genderless' (feminine and ambigenous) nouns. Here, as we have seen, there appears to be some tendency to distinguish between animates and inanimates on this basis.

1.4   IN PLACE OF A PARTIAL CONCLUSION

In this chapter we have seen that the Romance languages have in common some morphosyntactic features that are not directly inherited from Latin. There are even more such features that can be seen as descending from Latin: the relationship between Latin and Romance will be explored further in chapter 3.

The systems by which person is marked in the verb paradigm reflect the Latin system, but deviate from it in detail. Even in French, however, where the Latin system has been most eroded, there is sufficient similarity to other more mainstream languages for it to be set in the Romance rather than in the creole camp. In the two-gender system, absent from the creoles, we find a clearer Romance identity. The so-called 'neuter' gender form of some languages I claim does not constitute a separate class and does not continue the Latin system.

The most diagnostic criterion for Romanceness, however, has traditionally been shared lexicon, part of which can be traced back to Indo-European origins. In the next chapter we shall look at the common Romance lexicon and try to draw some conclusions about the light it sheds on our question: What is a Romance language? I shall begin by looking at the way creoles use Romance lexical material for grammatical functions that look very un-Romance, and consider further the question of whether we can distinguish a 'Romance type' from the more traditional 'Romance family'.

FURTHER READING

On typology, Croft (1990), on grammaticalization, Hopper & Traugott (1993). For Romance typology, Coseriu (1988), Manoliu-Manea (1985), Raible ed. (1989), Guillet & la Fauci eds. (1984). On morphology, Matthews (1991), Plank ed.(1991), Zimmer (1992), Drijkoningen (1989), Fisiak (1980). On Romance verb morphology, Bybee (1985), Hall (1983) and especially Iliescu & Mourin (1991) – a second volume on diachronic factors is forthcoming. On parameter setting, Lightfoot (1991), Ouhalla (1991), Bellettti & Rizzi (1994). On the pro-drop question and the status of subject clitics, Jaeggli & Safir eds. (1989), and on French, Adams (1988), Vance (1988), Battye & Roberts eds. (1995). On gender, Corbett (1991).

2

What is a Romance language?
Part 2

2.1   ROMANCE 'FAMILY' AND ROMANCE 'TYPE'

I distinguished earlier between the Romance type and the more traditional Romance family. The most convincing and obvious mark of similarity between the Romance languages – here not excluding the creoles – is the degree to which they share lexicon. Phonological differences sometimes obscure the similarities from the casual observer, but even the most naïve speaker can, with a little effort, discern regular relationships. A high proportion of lexico-phonetic correspondences is the criterion used by traditional comparative philology to define the language family – members of which, it is assumed, have developed from one and the same language spoken by a single language community at some time in the past. The most telling evidence is to be found in everyday, 'basic' vocabulary and in grammatical items, as these are more likely to have been handed on from generation to generation, and less likely to have been borrowed from foreign tongues. However, the Romance creoles, though sharing most of their vocabulary with the rest of the Romance languages, seem to be typologically diverse. I shall later in this chapter discuss how 'Romance' they can be considered to be. But first I shall examine the sort of vocabulary that is shared by all Romance languages, and discuss the implications for classification.

2.2   ROMANCE FUNCTIONAL MORPHEMES

In the Romance context, it is not surprising that the shared 'basic' lexicon is, very often, similar to that of Latin, or at least of a popular version of Latin. We have already seen that Romance verb person markers can be linked to Latin forms. Other morphological features will be examined in the next chapter, where Romance is systematically compared with Latin.

Here we shall concentrate on some 'function words'. To begin with we shall look at forms that have been adopted by the creoles and put to uses that are unfamiliar in 'core' Romance – the so-called **TAM** (tense/ aspect/mood) markers that distinguish most sharply the creoles from other Romance languages.

(a)   Creole tense/aspect/modal markers

Even more than the absence of verb person endings the morphosyntactic feature that most clearly excludes the Romance creoles from the 'Romance type' is the fact that they have no synthetic verb **tenses** or **moods**, but, instead, prefix tense, aspect or modality markers, in various combinations, to invariable lexical verb forms. What is striking in this respect is that the TAM forms used in the creoles are nearly always of Romance origin. The use to which they are put looks totally unlike Romance, but they may sometimes reflect Romance periphrastic constructions (see 3.3, 4.5). The purport of the verb prefixes varies from one creole to another, but the overall pattern is so similar, whatever the lexifier language, that many theorists believe that it must be taken over from another language type – Western African languages, for instance.

In Indian Ocean (Seychelles and Mauritius) French creoles, for instance, the preverbal markers have the following forms (approximate functions are indicated in capitals):

TAM markers in Indian Ocean creoles, with French equivalents

PAST: *ti/te* (< *était*) 'was';

PROGRESSIVE: (*a*)*pe* (< *après*; cf. the seventeenth-century and Canadian French periphrastic progressive *je suis après faire* 'I am (after) doing');

PERFECTIVE: *fi* (*n*) (< *finir* 'finish');

RECENT PAST: *fek* (< *ne fait que* = '(he) has only just done') or *soti* (< *sortir* 'go out'; cf. *il vient de . . .* 'he comes from . . .,' i.e. 'he has just. . .');

NEGATIVE: *pa* (< *pas*);

FUTURE: *a* (< *va*; cf. *il va faire* 'he is going to do', *pu* (< *pour* or *pouvoir*? Cf. archaic *il est pour faire* 'he is about to do' and *il peut faire* 'he can do').

> The two FUTURE markers seem to have slightly different modal meanings: *a* is variously described as 'indefinite', or 'expressing certitude', while *pu* is 'definite', 'immediate' or 'uncertain'. *Ule/vle* (< *vouloir*) is also used apparently as a FUTURE marker: in nonstandard French *il veut faire* 'he can do' can be used in the same way as *il va faire* 'he's going to do'.

French creoles in America and the Caribbean use similar markers: besides *ape* (*ap, apr, pe*), *te*, (*fi*)*n* and (*v*)*a* we find *s*(*r*)*e* (< *serait*) as a CONDITIONAL marker. Forms for which no obvious French etymon can be found include *ka* or *ko* as a HABITUAL marker (of African origin, or < *capable*?) and also, in some parts, a FUTURE marker *ke*, which is usually seen as a West African particle. In the Caribbean islands St Barth and St Thomas, the *patois*, like some Louisiana *cajun* varieties, use a construction with *ki* (*qui*) which may, however, be at the root of *ke*:

(1)   *Je suis qui va /   Ma   qui va   le faire*
        I- am   who goes /   me-go who goes it to-do

        'I am going' / 'I shall do it'

Portuguese creoles also use markers in similar ways but with variable forms. In the *crioulo* of Guinea-Bissau and Cape Verde, for instance, *na* (Ptg. 'in the f.') is a PROGRESSIVE verb marker, as well as indicating location when used with an inherited noun:

(2)   *I na kuúri* 'He is running' / *I sta na kasa* 'He is in the house'.

Here, as in some other creoles, there is no clear distinction between noun and verb, and *na* seems to be used to denote some sort of continuity in space or time, as in some African languages. Cape Verde varieties also use a more Portuguese-looking continuous verb form:

(3)   *Sta entrano* = Ptg. *Està entrando* 'They are coming in':

as well as an apparently periphrastic FUTURE:

(4)   *N sta faze* 'I am to do'

and a *jà* ('already') COMPLETIVE in which the TAM marker uncharacteristically precedes the subject pronoun and sometimes is repeated after the verb:

(5)   *Dja n daba nha palabra* 'I have given my word' / *Dja'l comê dja* 'He has eaten already'.

In other African Portuguese creoles the *jà* particle occurs clause-finally:

(6)   Guinea-Bissau *I baj dja* 'He has gone'; São Tomé *N fla za* 'I have spoken'.

        In Kristang (< Ptg. *cristão* 'christian') spoken by some 1,500 people in Malacca, Western Malaysia, *já* acts, on the other hand, like other preverbal markers:

(7)   *Yo ja chegá* 'I arrived'.

The *FUTURE* marker in *crioulo* is *ba* (< *vai* 'go') or *al*. The marker *ta* (< *està*) is probably basically a non-past, non-continuous marker, used as a *HABITUAL* or *ITERATIVE*. In the Portuguese-based Gulf of Guinea creoles, on the other hand, an apparently non-Portuguese *ka* is the *HABITUAL* marker (as in the Asian Portuguese). *Na* (< *não*) is here used for the *NEGA-TIVE* marker, which in some other Portuguese-based creoles has the form *ka* (< *nunca*). In São Tomé, however, we find for the *NEGATIVE*, besides *na*, a clause-final *fa*, perhaps of African origin. A more familiar looking *ska* (< *sa* 'be' + *ka*) here marks the *PROGRESSIVE*, *te* (< *ter* 'have') the *DISTANT FUTURE*, *ta* (< *està*) the *PAST*, and *bi* (< *vir* 'come') some degree of compulsion. In Sri Lanka the *PROGRESSIVE* form is *te*.

In Curaçao *papiamento IMPERFECTIVE ta* and *HABITUAL sa* (? < *saber* 'know') markers are found; *ke* (? < *querer* 'want') seems to be a modal, while *IRREALIS lo* (< *logo* 'then') can be used as a *FUTURE* marker (as it is in Asian creoles, but there it usually precedes the subject pronoun, acting like a sentence adverbial). The *PAST tabata* (older *taba*, colloquial *ta'a*) seems to be derived from the Hispanic imperfect *estaba* with agglutination of *ta* 'to be' (cf. *tabatin* 'had' with agglutination of *tin* 'have, hold').

Philippine Spanish varieties also make use of particles of apparently Romance origin, prefixed to invariable verb forms: *ta NON-PUNCTUAL* (*HABITUAL* and *PROGRESSIVE*), *ya* 'now, already' *PERFECTIVE* (also post-posed to the verb) and *de* or *aj* (? < *de* 'of', *hay* 'there is') *FUTURE*.

One notable feature of many Portuguese creoles, and of Colombian Spanish-based *palenquero*, is their use of a *ba* (or *va*) particle to indicate *PAST* tense. This does not seem to be related to the Catalan *va* preterite (see 4.6) but may be derived from the **imperfect** *-aba* inflection of Portuguese (see 3.3). It is sometimes used in a different way from verb prefixes:

(8)   Guinea-Bissau *I bin ba* 'He came'; *I profesor ba* 'He was a professor'; *I kõse-bu bã* 'He knew you'; Cape Verde *El ta ba chigá* / *El ta chigá ba* 'He used to arrive'; São Tomé *E ta va nda* 'He went', *E ta va ka nda* 'He was going'.

Some think the *ba* particle is of African origin, but it is possible that here we have an agglutination of the Portuguese verb inflection rather than the development of a suffixed particle.

Interestingly enough, in other rather conservative creoles – in Louisiana and the Indian Ocean island of Réunion – remnants of an imperfect inflection have survived:

(9)   Louisiana (St Martin) *mo kup* 'I cut' (present) / *mo kupe* 'I cut' (past) = *moi coupe / moi coupais*; Réunion *mi i mãz / mi i mãzé* 'I eat / ate'.

Some linguists see in such forms the effects of a **decreolization** process that has re-introduced flectional endings into languages that normally use agglutinated prefixes. Whether the imperfect flections are survivals or re-introductions, their existence helps to blur the distinction between Romance 'dialects' and creoles (see 5.7). That the imperfect flection is the only one to be found among creoles may be of particular significance, for, as we shall see, the only two Latin tense-aspect forms that survive intact in every Romance 'dialect' are the (unmarked) 'present' and the (past) 'imperfect'.

It can be maintained that creole verb prefixes are so alien to Romance (and to other Indo-European languages) that their origin must be sought elsewhere – especially as similar features are found in non-Romance creoles. Yet it is true that all Romance dialects have developed compound and periphrastic verb forms in which an auxiliary precedes a non-finite form of the lexical verb. Some Romance languages make greater use of such forms than others.

One notable feature is that, usually, the non-finite lexical verb form contributes to the aspectual or modal meaning conveyed: a **gerund(ive)** for progressive aspect, a **past participle** for perfective or resultative, and an **infinitive** for modalities. In creoles the verb form is nearly always clearly derived from an original infinitive. Portuguese and Spanish creoles, however, often retain Romance-like forms (as we have seen for Cape Verde). *Papiamento*, for instance, distinguishes *máta* 'kill' from *matá* (< *matado*) 'killed', as well as, like *palenquero*, retaining remnants of the PROGRESSIVE type *estar* + present participle:

(10)   Papiamento *E tabata papyando* 'He was talking'; Palenquero *I ta kanta(ndo)* 'I am singing'.

It is noteworthy that in French, periphrastic formations with the gerund(ive), or present participle, have fallen out of use, while those which use the infinitive have been extended (see 4.5). Moreover, the past participle is often indistinguishable from the infinitive, so that, for instance, a form like *Il a chanté* [ilaʃãte] 'He sang, he has sung', could readily be reanalysed as a structure similar to *Il va chanter* [ivaʃãte] 'He is-going to-sing'.

> French, especially in its 'popular' varieties, is often regarded as the most 'advanced' of the Romance languages, in the sense that it is nearer to creoles than the other languages. We shall later (5.7) compare and contrast extreme

versions of French *patois* that exist alongside French creoles (in Louisiana and the Caribbean), in the light of the hypothesis that creoles are new creations fashioned by a language bioprogramme.

There is little to suggest that in the Romance creoles the TAM markers are, or were at one time, limited to Bickerton's bioprogrammatic functions of *ANTERIOR* (? = my *PAST*), *IRREAL* and *NON-PUNCTUAL*. Most Romance creoles distinguish *FUTURE*, *HABITUAL* and *PROGRESSIVE*, but in these latter two cases some creoles use a bare verb form for one or the other. In nearly all cases the TAM markers can be linked etymologically, and to some degree functionally, to Romance periphrastic formations with similar functions. One difference, however, which does seem to hive off the creoles from other Romance languages is the way in which negation often appears to be treated as a modal and so part of their TAM system (for discussion of Romance negation see 7.4).

Certainly the creole TAM systems are very different from those of Romance, which still relies on morphological inflections rather than independent morphemic markers to signal tense, aspect and mood. Where compound or periphrastic verb forms have been developed in Romance, they have tended to be grammaticalized to become virtually new inflections. On the other hand, some of the so-called creoles do have verb features that resemble those of 'core' Romance. For the question of 'decreolization', alleged dilution of creole features due to close contact with non-creole Romance languages, see 5.8.

(b)   Personal and possessive pronouns

The 'discourse' pronouns (persons 1, 2, 4, 5) in the Romance languages are strikingly similar to those of Latin (for persons 3 and 6 pronouns see 7.5). It is noteworthy that the Latin pattern holds for most Indo-European languages, so we may talk here of long-term retention of Indo-European forms, rather than specifically Latin-to-Romance conservatism.

It is hardly necessary here to reproduce the tables of pronominal forms that are to be found in all the manuals. Some comments are, however, called for.

No Romance language perpetuates the Latin genitive forms MEI, TUI, NOSTRI, VESTRI, but most use adjectival possessives of the MEUS, TUUS, NOSTER, VESTER type. Many of the modern forms, however, show irregular phonological development, often due presumably to paradigmatic levelling.

Thus a proto-Romance *VOSTRU is postulated as the predecessor of most person 5 forms, and some person 2 forms have been remodelled on person 1:

(11) *TEUM: French *tien*, Ptg. *teu* (but feminine *tua*), Cat. *teu*, Rum. *tău* / TUUM: Ital. *tuo*, French, Cat. *ton*, Span. *tu*, *tuyo* (influenced by *cuyo* < CUIUS ?).

In Surselvan and Engadine Rhaeto-Romance and in Portuguese persons 4 and 5 pronouns appear to derive from unattested (archaic or dialectal?) forms *NOSSU, *VOSSU.

In those parts of Southern Italy where final vowels are reduced to schwa, the possessive often has a form identical with that of the object pronoun and is enclitic to the noun:

(12) Abruzzo [lu'libbrəmə] '[the] my book'.
(For the use of the definite article with possessives see 6.5.)

Enclitic possessive forms were also used, without a definite article, in literary Tuscan until the fourteenth century, when they were condemned as 'low', but they were always distinct from object pronouns:

(13) *mógliata* 'your wife', *signorso* 'his lord'.

Creoles often use invariable postposed pronouns as possessives, with or without a preposition:

(14) Guadeloupe *timu-a-u* 'little-person-to-you' i.e. 'your child'; Haiti (Port-au-Prince) *pitit mwẽ*, (Northern) *pita-m* 'my child'; São Tomé *manu-m* 'my brother', *ke nõ* 'our house'.

Some creole varieties, however, use reflexes of the possessive (sometimes, in Portuguese creoles, generalizing the feminine form):

(15) Mauritius *mo madam* 'my wife', *nu lakas* 'our house'; Cape Verde *mye irmõ* 'my brother', Asian Portuguese *minha pai* 'my father'.
Some 'core' Romance varieties also prefer a combination of preposition A(D) or DE with a pronoun to specifically possessive forms.

The distinction between nominative EGO, TU and accusative ME, TE is maintained by the 'core' languages (though phonetic erosion has often rendered TU and TE indistinguishable). However, some dialects, in particular in France and north Italy, use, as disjunctive pronouns in all sentences roles, stressed reflexes of the old accusative forms:

(16) French *Moi, je te donne ça, à toi* 'Me, I give that to you'.

In most French creoles an originally stressed-type pronoun, *mwĕ/mo* etc., is found in every sentence role and there is no cliticized nominative. African Portuguese creole *n/[ɲ]* unstressed person 1 pronoun may be a phonetic development of *mi*, or it may be of Bantu origin. Other Portuguese creoles prefer reflexes of *eu*.

For persons 4 and 5, whereas Latin did not distinguish nominative from accusative, some Romance languages tend to add an element ALTERI /-OS 'others' to the nominative, or at least to the disjunctive, form. In post-medieval Spanish and Catalan, the element is obligatory:

(17)   disjunctive *nosotros/-as*, *nosaltres* and *vosotros/-as*, *vosaltres*, alongside clitic accusative–dative *nos*, *os* and *vos*, *us*.

In standard Italian *noialtri* and standard French *nous autres* are optionally used for *noi* and *nous*. In some French creoles *zot* (from *vous-autres*) is the only form for person 5 (and, sometimes, for person 6). In Friulian *no(altris)*, *vo(altris)*, the *altris* appears to be obligatory for the postprepositional pronoun.

In Italian the accusative–dative clitics of **adverbial** origin, *ci* and *vi*, alongside disjunctive *noi*, *voi*, began to replace *no* and *vo*, from the thirteenth century.

Generalization of VOS, originally used as a polite substitute for TU (see 1.2), is found in several areas, including Haitian and most African Portuguese creoles (except in Principe). In American Spanish, *vos* is often used as the familiar nominative form (*voseo* – see 1.2), though *te* may be retained as the object clitic pronoun. Some Portuguese creoles, however, have generalized other originally honorific forms:

(18)   Cape Verde (Sotavento) (*ños/ñozi*) (from *os señores*), (Barlavento) *bosés* (from *você + s*), São Tomé (*i*)*nanse*, Anobom *namesezi* (perhaps from *nã*, a pluralizer of African origin + *mercês* 'grace').

In Colombian *palenquero, uté* (Spanish *usted*) has similarly been generalized. In Argentinian popular speech the definite-article form *los* is used for the clitic reflexive *nos*:

(19)   *Los vamos* 'Lĕt's go' (more vulgarly *Se vamos*, with person 3 reflexive generalized to all persons).

Most languages have no reflex of the Latin accusative/dative distinction (ME/MIHI, TE/TIBI, NOS/NOBIS, VOS/VOBIS). One apparent puzzle is the relationship of Italian (tonic) *me, te* / (atonic) *mi, ti*, to Spanish (tonic) *mi, ti* / (atonic) *me, te*. Are these a result of different phonological rules, or are they haphazardly derived from ME, TE / MIHI, TIBI? Even more puzzling are such Spanish forms as *migo* (? < MIHI + CUM) used after *con* (< CUM).

> Sard, Southern Italian dialects, Rumanian and Galician retain some reflexes of both accusative and dative forms, but do not use them in their Latin functions (see 3.3).

Whereas in Latin personal pronouns were full nominals, in the Romance languages clitic (conjunctive) forms have evolved, derived from unaccented forms, alongside originally accented disjunctive (autonomous or post-prepositional) forms. In the creoles, as we have seen, there is no such systematic distinction, nor is there in modern Surselvan Rhaeto-Romance, where use of disjunctive forms, instead of earlier clitics, is thought to be a recent innovation, due to influence from German. In all other languages, object pronouns are cliticized (see 4.4); in French and North Italian varieties, clitic subject pronouns have become, as we have seen (1.2), virtually bound person markers.

(c)   Prepositions

More than a third of the prepositions in common use in Romance are recognizably related to Latin ones, though often they do not mean exactly the same. The following are some of the virtually pan-Romance items, preceded by approximate English translations:

Some pan-Romance prepositions

'above, on': SUPER, SUPRA,: French *sur*, Ital. *sopra*, Span. *sobre*. The Latin adverb SURSUM
    'up(wards), over' also has reflexes in most languages: French (*au des*) *sus* (*de*),
    Rum. *sus* 'above' / *spre* < SUPER 'towards' / *pe* < PER 'on', Old Span. *suso*, Ital.
    su. In some French creoles *lao* (*là-haut* '(high) up there') replaces *sur*.

'against': CONTRA: French *contre*, Old Ital., Sard, Span., Ptg., Occ., Cat. *contra*, modern Ital.
    contro, Rum. *cătră*, Engadine *kunter*, Friulian *kuintri*.

'at, to': AD: *a* everywhere – in Rumanian it is used only in adverbial phrases, *la* (< ILLAC-AD)
    'there' replacing AD in its original sense: a similar form is used in Abruzzo and
    Friuli. Some French creoles use [kot] (< (*à*) *côté* (*de*) 'by the side of', for
    French *à*.

'before, in front of': ANTE, including various combinations with other prepositions
    (AB/DE/IN/DE, AB/DE, IN/AD, AD/DE). Usually temporal use is distinguished
    from spatial: French *avant*, *devant*, Ital. *avanti*, *davanti*, *innanzi*, *dinanzi*, Span.
    antes, *delante* (older *denante*), Ptg. *antes*, *adiante*, Rum. *înaintea* / *dinainte*.

'between': INTER: spelt *entre* nearly everywhere; Sard *inter*, Rum. *între*.

'from, of': DE: *de* nearly everywhere, Ital. *di*; composite forms include Ital., R-R (Engadine) *da* < DE + AB, Rum. *din* < DE + IN and Span. *desde* < DE + EX + DE.

It has been claimed that 'true' creoles lack a range of prepositions, using instead serial-verb constructions:

(20)   Guyana *Li pote sa bay mo* (< French *Lui porter ça baille* ('give') *moi*) 'He brought it for me'; Haiti *Mwẽ kouri ale lakay li* (< French *Moi courir aller la case lui*) 'I run to his house'.

Serial verbs are found in a number of Romance creoles, though not in Indian Ocean French creoles. However even those varieties that use verb serialization still have a range of prepositions that match those of their lexifier language: thus Haiti *ak* 'with', *pu* 'for' from French *avec, pour*, compared with Principe *ki, pa* from Portuguese *con, para*.

2.3   WORD FORMATION

In the modern Romance literary languages between 60 per cent and 80 per cent of any text will consist of words apparently used uninterruptedly from Roman times and clearly related to Latin. Among loanwords, a large proportion are borrowed directly from Latin or the other Romance languages, so that the 'Romance' character of the vocabulary is overwhelmingly obvious. Moreover, about 10 per cent of the words in any text will be created from native sources: it is not always certain whether such words were already in use during the Imperial period or whether they were later creations.

The resources for creating new words are similar in all the Romance languages. Change of function class – from noun to adjective and vice versa and from verb infinitive to noun, or from participle to adjective etc. – is particularly frequent.

Reduplication of adjectives or of verbs for intensification is also widespread in the colloquial varieties:

(21)   Ital. *pian piano* 'very quiet'; Span. *Entender, entiendo* 'I certainly understand'.

Creoles make even wider use of this device, some believe under African influence:

(22)   Mauritius *Li ti marse marse* 'He trudged on and on'; São Tomé *O pega pega pishi* 'He catches fish often'.

However, it is to be noted that Sard varieties also make extensive use of similar reduplication:

(23)   Nuoro *Mori mori* 'He dies, he dies', i.e. 'He is about to die', *Time time* 'He

fears, he fears', i.e. 'He is terrified'.

(a)   Compound words

Compounding seems to be less common in Romance than in Germanic languages, though it appears to be on the increase, and has always been a possibility:

(24)   French *gratte-ciel* 'scratch-sky', i.e. 'sky-scraper', *rouge-gorge* 'red-throat', i.e.
            'robin'; Ital. *dopopranzo* 'after-lunch', i.e. 'afternoon', *nettadenti* 'clean-teeth',
            i.e. 'toothpick'; Rum. *floarea-soarelui* 'flower of the sun', i.e. 'sunflower', *papă-lapte* 'pope-milk', i.e. 'milksop'; Span. *lavamanos* 'wash-hands', i.e. 'wash-basin', *aguardiente* 'water-burning', i.e. 'brandy'.

Adverbs in *-mente*

The most widespread (though not pan-Romance) procedure for formation of adverbs also originated as compounding, though in most of the languages it is now suffixal. Already in Classical Latin, instead of an adverbial form of -ITER, the ablative of the word for 'mind' (MENS, f., ablative MENTE), most often following an agreeing adjective, could be used to indicate the manner in which an action is performed: as in PLACIDA MENTE 'with peaceful mind'. MENTE was to become virtually an adverbializer, which could be suffixed to nearly all qualifying adjectives:

(25)   French *doucement* 'softly', Ital. *raramente* 'rarely', Ital. dial. (Bologna) *breve-meint* 'briefly', Occ., Cat., *bellamen(t)* 'beautifully', Span. *distintamente* 'distinctly', Ptg. *cruamente* 'cruelly', R-R (Engadine) *puramaing* 'purely', (Surselvan) *finalmein* 'finally', Dalmatian (Veglia) *fuartemiant* 'strongly', Sard *finalmenti(s)* 'finally'.

Constraints on use of the MENTE suffix have led some linguists to postulate that it still retains some autonomy. For instance, rather like the English suffix *-ly*, it is less readily used with adjectives referring to strictly physical properties, suggesting that it still has a 'mental' tinge:

(26)   Ital. **giallamente* '?yellowly', **bruttamente* '*uglily', **lungamente* (with reference to space) '*longly'.

In early Romance the two parts of the syntagma probably retained greater autonomy, as other words could be interposed, and, as in sequences of two adverbial phrases, the MENTE could be omitted in one –

most frequently the first (as in modern standard Spanish and Portuguese) but also the second (as in Old Occitan and Catalan):

(27)   Ptg. *clara e distintamente* 'clearly and distinctly', Span. *lenta y cuidadosamente* 'slowly and carefully', Cat. *bellament i dolça* 'nicely and gently'.

In modern Spanish and Portuguese, adverbial forms in *-mente* also, unusually, have two stresses, suggesting that they are treated as two words.

In Old French there seem to be no unambiguous examples of omission of *-ment* in sequences, and it is probable that it was already an adverbial suffix, homophonous with the -MENTUM suffix (see below). French appears to have retained no other inherited trace of the Latin word MENS, except in the now extinct word for 'remember', *mentevoir*. In modern French, too, the adjectival element is not always distinctively marked as feminine (see *évidemment* [evidamã] with *évidente* f. [evidãt]).

Apart from modern Occitan and Dalmatian, the other Romance languages do have reflexes of the word MENTE, though some of them may be Latinisms:

(28)   Ital., Sard (Logudorian), Span., Ptg. *mente*, Rum. *minte*, Dolomite R-R (Gardena) *ment*. Old Span. *miente* survived till the Golden Age and till this day in expressions like *traer a las mientes* 'to bring to mind'. Old Occ. *men* (f.) is not now current; Cat. *ment* (m.) is not common and is possibly modern.

In some languages the adverbial suffix was differentiated from the noun by the addition of a so-called 'adverbial *-s*', allegedly on the analogy of adverbials like MINUS:

(29)   Old Occ. *fortamens* 'strongly', Old Ptg. *claramentes* 'clearly'.

Elsewhere an *-r-* was incorporated into the MENTE element:

(30)   Old Span. *solamientre/solamiente*, Ital. dial. (Veneto) *solamentre* 'only'; Old Lombard *malamentre* 'badly'; R-R (Friuli) *stupidamentri* 'stupidly', (Dolomites) *fermamenter* 'firmly'; Rum. *altminteri/aimintre* 'otherwise'.

The most likely source of the *-r-* is the Latin adverbial marker -ITER, which may have become attached to MENTE (*MENTER?). Spanish *mientre*, ousted in the fourteenth century by 'learned' *mente*, is thought by some to show contamination with (*do*)*mientre* < (DUM)-INTERIM 'while'.

Whatever their origin, it does seem that the additions differentiated the adverbial ending from the MENTE noun forms: it is possible that learned influence led to the restoration of more transparent forms in Spanish and Portuguese at the beginning of the modern era. It has also been maintained that Italian *-mente* (unattested before the mid-eleventh century) was a borrowing from either French or Latin rather than a native development, and so evidence about its status as a bound suffix or free form is unclear.

In the extreme south of Italy and in Rumania the MENTE construction does not appear to have caught on, though some examples, presumably loanwords, are found (e.g. Rum. *literalmente*). The most usual device continues the use of the neuter adjectival form as an adverb, which was frequent in later Latin:

(31)   Rum. *cîntà frumos* 'to sing beautiful(ly)', Calabria *mi dúnanu sulu* 'They only [alone m.] give me' = Ital. *mi offrono solamente*.

In Latin America, especially, similar usage is frequent in popular speech; indeed, with intransitive verbs it is common in all Spanish colloquial speech.

In some Southern Italian dialects the adjectival form used in this way can agree in gender with the subject of the verb:

(32)   Conidoni (Calabria) *Kusísti bonu/bona*, San Chirico Raparo (Lucania) *Ai kusú-tu bwenu/bwena* 'You have cooked well [good m./f.]' = Ital. *Hai cucito bene*

A not dissimilar usage is normal in Spanish with some verbs:

(33)   *Hablas ligero/a* 'You talk quickly (quick m. /f.)'.

It has been maintained that the MENTE construction was unknown in 'Eastern' Latin – though examples from Dalmatian (25 above) and Rumanian (30 above) suggest that this cannot be wholly true. The absence of the MENTE construction in Campania, Abruzzo, Apulia, Lucania and Calabria has been ascribed to the influence of Greek as used in Magna Graecia (the part of southern Italy that was within the Eastern Empire), in which adverbs were frequently phonetically identical to adjectives.

Even in the languages where -MENTE is the normal adverbial suffix, short and much-used adjectives double as adverbs, in their masculine singular form:

(34)   French *faux, fort*; Ital. *alto, piano*; Span. *claro, temprano*.

We should note that in Rumanian the numerous adjectives in *-esc* (< ISCU, or of Slavonic origin?) have a special adverbial form in *-eşte*:

(35)   *proteşte* 'foolishly' / *protesc* 'foolish'.

(b)   Derivation

Apart from this Rumanian case, derivational procedures are strikingly similar in all the Romance languages: a number of **suffixes** and **prefixes** are pan-Romance and, though not always fully productive in modern times, they are usually easily recognizable as bound morphemes. Some of them, admittedly, are virtually pan-European – borrowed from Latin or Greek – but Romance languages probably make greater use of them than do other languages. Standard French has, since the seventeenth century, tended to restrict derivation, except with 'learned' affixes, though Canadian French continues the earlier habit of proliferating near-synonymous derivatives.

All the Romance languages, except modern French, make great productive use of expressive suffixes, especially diminutives, augmentatives and depreciatives:

(36)   Span. *hermanito* 'little brother', Ital. *omaccione* 'nasty big man', Ptg. *livrinho*, Rum. *carticcică* 'little book', Cat. *cadirota* 'ugly old chair', Occ. *galinassa* 'great big hen', R-R (Surselvan) *viatscha* 'bad road', Sard (Nuoro) *minoreddeddéddu* 'very, very little' (with three repetitions of the diminutive suffix).

In the creoles, on the other hand, bound derivational affixes play little or no role in lexical creation, though *crioulo* (Guinea-Bissau and Senegal) has a productive causative *-nt-* affix (perhaps of Madinka origin, or generalized from verbs like *levantar* 'to raise', *adiantar* 'to put forward'):

(37)   *tjoránta* 'to make weep' / *tjora* 'to weep' = Ptg. *chorar*.

(i)   Prefixes

Some Romance prefixes were originally detachable prepositions (DE, AB, AD, CONTRA, CUM, EX, IN, SUB) that have become agglutinated to free forms, especially to verbs. It is thought that spoken Latin must have had a predilection for extended forms – with intensive or expressive affixes – which have often survived into Romance at the expense of the simple forms and are no longer recognized as derivatives:

(38)   French *acheter* 'buy' < AD-CAPTARE; Ital. *cominciare*, French *commencer*, Cat. *comensar*, Span. *comenzar*, Ptg. *começar* < CUM-INITIARE; French *souffler*, Ital. *soffiare*, Ptg. *soprar*, Rum. *suflá* 'blow' < SUB-FLARE.

A prefix that is still analysable as such, if not productive in all languages, is the iterative or intensive bound form RE-:

(39)   Ital. *riandare*, 'go again, go back', Span. *realzar*, Ptg. *realçar* 'elevate, enhance, raise up' (intensive), French *ravoir* 'regain, have again', Rum. *revedea*, 'see again'.

This prefix is also productive in the creole of Mauritius:

(40)   *Li n re-vini* 'He came again', *Mo ti re-ekrir zot* 'I wrote to them again'.

The French creole of St Lucia seems to use a *de-* prefix in a similar way as an intensive or iterative:

(41)   *depale* 'rant' / *pale* 'speak' = French *parler*

DIS- is widespread with negative force, like English *un-* or *dis-*:

(42)   Ital. *discaricare*, Span. *descargar* 'unload', French *défaire*, Rum. *desface* 'undo'.

(ii)   Suffixes

Suffixation is the most common means of derivation in Romance, and most of the pan-Romance suffixes are reflexes of Latin ones. Not infrequently a Latinate borrowing has ousted a cognate native suffix, as in French, where *-aison* (e.g. *pendaison* 'hanging') from -ATIONE(M) is no longer productive, while more modern *-ation* (e.g. *cultivation*) remains so. Less clearly one of borrowing as against popular development is the contrast between [a'tsjone] and [a'dʒone] in Italian and between [a'θjon] and [a'θon] in Spanish:

(43)   Ital. *salvazione* 'salvation' / *venagione* 'game, venison'; Span. *ligación,* 'tying, binding' / *ligazón* 'tie, bond'.

The -TIONE(M) suffix is very productive :

(44)   Rum. *putreziciune* 'dissolution'; Span. *embarcación* 'embarkation, ship'; Ptg. *liquidação* 'liquidation'; Sard (Logudorian) [kan'ðone] 'singing, song'.

Other still more or less recognizable pan-Romance abstract noun suffixes include:

Pan-Romance abstract noun suffixes

-MENTU: French *logement* 'lodging', Ital. *stiramento* 'pulling', Span. *acercamiento* 'approach', Rum. *vesmînt* 'clothing', Sard (Campidanian) *iuvamento* 'help', Curaçao (*papi-amento*) *perdementu* 'loss';

-TATE: French *cherté* 'dearness', *actualité* 'current happening', Ital. *sanità* 'health', Span. *leal-tad* 'loyalty', *realidad* 'reality', Cat. *falsedat* 'falseness', Rum. *puţinate*, Sard (Nuoran) *minoridade* 'smallness';

-ITIA: French *franchise* 'frankness', *finesse* 'fineness', Span. *limpieza* 'cleanness', Ital. *bellezza*,
  Rum. *dulceaţa*, 'sweetness', Cat. *aridesa* 'dryness', Ptg. *magreza* 'thinness',
  Sard (Logudorian) *bonissja* 'goodness';
-IA: French *courtoisie* 'courtliness', Ital. *pazzia* 'madness', Span. *alegría* 'happiness', Rum.
  avuţie 'wealth', Sard (Logudorian) *nobilia* 'nobility'.

Agentive or instrumental nouns in -ORE(M) and -ARIU(M) are still sometimes productive:

(45)   French *chercheur* 'researcher', *fermier* 'farmer'; Span. *hablador* 'talker', *cartero*
        'postman'; Ital. *cacciatore* 'hunter', *calzolaio* 'cobbler'; Cat. *bevedor* 'drinker',
        mariner 'seaman'; Rum. *cîntător* 'singer' (not directly from Latin CANTATOR,
        but from *cînt* + suffix *-ator*), *plugar* 'ploughman'; R-R (Surselvan) *mulgíder*
        'dairy-man, milker'; Sard (Logudorian) *piskadore* 'fisherman', *krabardzu* 'goat-
        herd'.

The originally diminutive suffix -ELLU has reflexes everywhere (though
sometimes it is no longer a separable morpheme in modern languages, as
in French *couteau*, Ital. *coltello*, Span. *cuchillo* 'knife'< CULTELLUS 'little
knife' from CULTER 'knife'). Romance derivatives include:

(46)   French *ruelle* 'little street, alley', Ital. *paesello* 'small village', Span. *bolsillo*
        'small bag, purse'; Rum. *bărbătel* 'little man', Sard *kateddu* 'little dog, puppy'.

Other adjectival suffixes that have, on the whole, remained productive, or
at least separable, include:

Adjectival suffixes

-ALE(M): French *hivernal* 'wintry', *mortel* 'fatal, mortal' (with a distinction between learned
        and popular development), Ital. *invernale, mortale*, Sard (Logudorian) *istadi-
        ale* 'summery', Span. *gubernamental* 'governmental', Rum. *pastoral* 'rustic'
        (possibly a French borrowing);
-BILE(M): French *blâmable* 'reprehensible', Ital. *agevole* 'easy, manageable', Span. *razonable*
        'reasonable', R-R (Surselvan) *kusteival* 'costly', Sard (Logudorian) *addegibile*
        'decent'. Words like Rum. *remarcabil* are borrowings (cf. *vandabil* 'saleable'
        from French *vendable*) and it seems that this suffix has never been productive in
        Rumanian.
-IVU(M): French *pensif* 'thoughtful', Ital. *tardivo*, Span. *tardío* 'tardy, backward, dilatory',
        Rum. *dulciu* 'sweetish', R-R (Engadine) *sulaglif* 'sunny', Sard *bagantiu* 'fallow
        [vacant] (of field)';
-OSU(M): French *ennuyeux* 'boring', Ital. *pauroso* 'fearful', Span. *arenoso* 'sandy', Cat.
        coratjós' 'courageous', Rum. *barbos* 'bearded', Sard (Logudorian) *fodzosu*
        'leafy'.

-ENSE(M) is also fairly productive, especially to form adjectives from place-names:

(47)   French *bolognais, namurois*; Ital. *milanese*; Span. *aragonés*, Rum. *englez*, Sard *kagliaresu*.

2.4   SHARED LEXICON

Anyone familiar with one Romance language will have little difficulty in recognizing in the vocabulary of another at least half of the common words: Rumanian will present more vocabulary difficulties than any other. In the case of some pairs of languages – Spanish and Portuguese, for instance, or French and Occitan – some 90 per cent of the 'basic' vocabulary will look familiar. Italian is again the 'archetype' – the most 'central' of the languages, which has some 80 per cent of its 'basic' vocabulary in common with most languages.

It is not surprising, then, that among Romance speakers there is some degree of mutual intelligibility or that, at any rate, they have comparatively little difficulty in learning each other's language. Barriers are raised more by differences in phonetic shape than by lexical differences. In the next two sections I shall exemplify first from the numerals in Romance and then from other 'basic vocabulary'.

(a)   Numerals

The Indo-European names of numbers have on the whole persisted into Romance, but there are some noteworthy differences.

(i)   Numerals 1–10

In all the Romance languages the cardinal numbers 1–10 are clearly related to their Latin counterparts. The **indefinite article** is often identical with the numeral 1, and agrees with the noun to which it refers. In Dolomite Rhaeto-Romance varieties, however, the reduced article form can be used in conjunction with the numeral 1:

(48)   Gardena *una na rama* 'one branch'.

The number 2 (DŬO, DŬAE) inflected for gender in most languages at an earlier stage and still does in some languages:

(49)   (m./f.) Rum. *doi/douǎ*, Sard *duos/duas*, Ptg. *dois/duas*, R-R (Müstair) *doi/ dos*,
          Ital. dial. (Venice) *du/do*.

In Italian the former feminine *due* has ousted the old masculine and
'neuter' forms *dui* and *dua* (the latter survives in Sard).

> In Swiss Rhaeto-Romance varieties 'neuter' or 'collective' forms for both 2 and
> 3 (TRES, TRIA) are attested:

(50)   Engadine *dua* (*traia*) *bratscha*, Surselvan *dua* (*trei*) *bratscha* 'two (three) arms'.

In some languages numbers between 3 and 10 are less uniformly derived.

> In the Rumanian dialects of the Istrian peninsula, Croatian forms are found
> alongside the Latinate ones, for the numbers 5–10 (for 9 the Latin form has
> apparently not survived anywhere and for 8 and 10 the Croatian form has oust-
> ed the Latin one in some varieties):

> *Istro-Rumanian numbers 5–8*

5 [cinc]/ [pet]	Daco-Rumanian *cinci*	< QUINQUE
6 [ʃase]/ [ʃest]		*şaşe*	< SEX
7 [ʃapte]/[sedṛm]		*şapte*	< SEPTEM
8 [opt]/[osṛm]		*opt*	< OCTO

> For higher numbers Slavonic numerals are preferred in both varieties; but for
> 5–10, Southern varieties (which had until recently more contact with North
> Italian dialects) seem to use the Latinate numerals (and other basic vocabulary
> items) more than the Northern do.

(51)   South *cinc zile* / North *pet dṃ*'five days'.
          Both varieties use Latinate numerals for counting domestic animals, but
          Croatian numerals for telling the time:

(52)   [ʃapte kali] 'seven horses' / [sedṛm miˈnutii] 'seven minutes'.

> Angolar creole, spoken on São Tomé by some 9,000 descendants of runaway,
> or shipwrecked, slaves, uses Portuguese forms for 1–3, but for higher numbers
> Bantu (Kimbundu) forms are current.

(ii)   Teens

In Daco-Rumanian, numerals 11–19 are in origin periphrastic ('one, two,
etc. – on – ten'):

(53)   *unsprezece*, *doisprezece*, etc. (reduced in colloquial usage to [unʃpe] etc.).

It is suggested that although lexically derived from Latin (UNU – SUPER – DECEM etc.) these forms are modelled on Slavonic. In Arumanian dialects south of the Danube, however, 21-9 are constructed, unlike Slavonic, on a similar pattern (*umspräyginti* 'twenty-one' etc.).

The late teens in most Romance languages are also periphrastic:

(54)   17: 10-7: French *dix-sept*, Cat. *dissèt*, Sard *deghesette*; 10 AC 7: Ital. *diciassette*, Ptg. *dezassette*; 10 ET 7: Span. *diecisiete*, Old Occ. *detze e set*.

For 11–15, though, the Latin type UNDECIM etc. survives. For the number 16 different solutions are chosen:

(55)   French *seize*, Ital. *sedici*, Cat. *setze*, Engadine *saidesch* < SEDECIM / Span *diez y seis, dieciséis*, Ptg. *dezasseis*.

(iii)   Tens

The Rumanian names for 'tens' are periphrastic (*douăzéci, treizéci* '2/3 tens' etc.), compared with reflexes of VIGINTI and TRIGINTA etc. in other languages (Ital. *venti, trenta*; French *vingt, trente*, Span. *véinte, tréinta*).

Sometimes held to be Celtic in character are such forms as:

(56)   standard French *soixante-dix* '60-10' (70); *quatre-vingt(s)* '4 x 20(s)' (80).

Belgian and Swiss French *septante* and *octante* fit better into the general Romance pattern.

(iv)   Hundreds

Rumanian uses a Slavonic *sută* 'hundred' (Istro-Rumanian *sto*), instead of the CENTUM that survives elsewhere: the Rumanian slang form *centă* '100 lei note' may be a French borrowing.

For the hundreds most languages prefer an analytic construction:

(57)   Rum. *două sute*, Ital. *duecento*, Cat. *doscents*, R-R (Engadine) *diatschient*, French *deux cents*, Span. *doscientos* '200' (i.e. '2 – 100(s)' compared with the Latin lexicalized DUCENTI).

Nevertheless some less transparent etymological forms survive:

(58)   Sard *dughentos, treghentos*, Ptg. *duzentos, trezentos* '200, 300' (DUCENTI, TRECEN-TI); Span. *quinientos*, Ptg. *quinhentos* '500' (QUINGENTI).

(b)   Basic vocabulary

If we consider the 'most representative' Romance vocabulary of some 3,000 words (measured by frequency, morphological productivity and semantic range), about a fifth of the inherited Latin forms are pan-Romance, and many more are shared by several languages. The factors that make for similarity and differentiation are discussed in chapters 3, 4, 6 and 7. Here let us illustrate the similarities in 'basic' vocabulary by examining Romance translations of a version of the 'Swadesh' word lists, devised to provide a practicable means of comparing common vocabulary items across languages. One count using a limited range of languages concluded that pairwise scores of 'look-alikes' range from 70 per cent (Italian–Rumanian) to 89 per cent (French–Italian and Spanish–Portuguese). Similar counts on Romance creoles reckon that their basic vocabulary is often well-nigh identical with that of their lexifier languages.

Some creoles, however, have incorporated so much vocabulary from other sources that they can no longer be called Romance. This is particularly so for Saramaccan, spoken by some 20,000 descendants of runaway slaves (maroons) in Surinam. Though some maintain that it was once a Portuguese-based creole, it now is reckoned to have only some 37 per cent of basic Portuguese lexical items, compared with 54 per cent English, 4 per cent Dutch and 4 per cent African. The Romance linguist Schuchardt, one of the first to take a serious interest in creoles, in 1914 wrote an article on this 'Bush Negro' variety, known by its speakers as *Djoe-tongo* 'Jew language', presumably because it was allegedly used on plantations owned by Jews from Brazil. His information was based largely on reports from *Herrnhuters* (Moravian Brethren missionaries), and he estimated, at that time, that the English lexical stock was almost equal to the Portuguese – the personal pronouns (except perhaps *mim*) and the TAM markers (see 2.2) were already of English origin, but prepositions (*com, na*) and adverbs like *aqui* were still Portuguese, as were common adjectives like *bom, grande* and *pequen(in)o*.

Another 'maroon' creole, Angolar in São Tomé, still has, on the other hand, nearly 70 per cent of its basic lexical items cognate with Portuguese. Curaçao *papiamento* is also still recognizably Romance even though some 28–30 per cent of its vocabulary is clearly of Dutch origin, located mainly in less 'basic' areas of the lexicon, but including, for instance:

(59)   *lep* 'lip', *smal* 'narrow', *stul* 'chair', *hel* 'yellow'.

Of the 100 words in one version of the Swadesh list the following forty-three seem to be pan-Romance – the English gloss appears in alphabetic order and apparent Latin etymons are given in the form which seems to have survived (nouns are usually from the Latin accusative):

Pan-Romance basic vocabulary

all TOTU; **and** ET (but modern Daco-Rumanian *şi* < SIC 'thus'); **animal** ANIMALE (also BESTIA); **blood** SANGUE; **bone** OSSE; **come** VENIRE; **die** MORI[RE]; **drink** BIBERE; **ear** AURICULA (though in Spanish *oído* is more polite than *oreja* when referring to humans); **egg** OVU; **eye** OCULU; **fire** FOCU (for IGNE) (though words for 'light' are also used: Span. *la lumbre*, Sicilian *lu luci* = 'fire' / *la luci* = 'light'); **fish** PISCE; **full** PLENU; **good** BONU ; **green** VIR(I)DE; **horn** CORNU; **I** EGO (cf. 2.2); **know** COGNOSC[ERE] (most languages distinguish 'know for a fact' *SAPERE (SAPERE)/SCIRE from 'be acquainted with' COGNOSCERE, though Louisiana creole has generalized the *connaître* form, and Rumanian popular usage substitutes *cunoaşte* for *şti*); **leaf** FOLIU (though FRONDE is also widespread); **louse** PEDUCULU; **moon** LUNA (in standard Rumanian the same word is used also for 'month' as in Slavonic); **name** NOMINE (in Haiti this word is used only for the forename, while the surname is *signati* = French *signature*); **new** NOVU; **night** NOCTE; **not** NON (rivalled in French and modern Occitan by *pas*, used in French creoles as the main negative particle); **one** UNU; **person** PERSONA (in most French creoles (*di*)*mun* < French (*du*) *monde* 'world, people', is the usual word); **rain** PLUVIA (the word for 'water' AQUA is used more often in Sardinia and southern Italy); **round** ROTUNDU; **see** VIDERE; **skin** PELLE; **sleep** DORMIRE; **smoke** FUMU; **star** STELLA; **stone** PETRA (in Haitian creole [*pie*] < *pierre* is specialized in the sense of 'fetish' and *roche* 'rock' is used more generally); **thou** TU (see 2.2); **tongue** LINGUA; **tooth** DENTE; **two** DUO; **water** AQUA; **we** NOS (see 2.2); **what** QUID.

In seven cases different derivatives or related forms are used but it is not difficult to discern a relationship:

Related basic lexical items in Romance

ashes CINERE, Ital. *cenere*, French *cendre*, R-R (Engadine) *cendra* / CINISIA Dalmatian (Veglia) *kanaisa*, Sard *kijina*, Span. *ceniza*, Ptg. *cinza*, Rum. *cenuşă* (*scrum* 'cold ashes' is similar to words in Bulgarian and Albanian); **fly** VOLARE French *voler* / EXVOLARE Rum. *zburá* ; **sit** SEDERE French (*as*)*seoir* / SEDENTARE Span. *sentar* (Haiti [*ʃita*] seems to come from the French imperative *assied-toi*, Mauritius [asize] is clearly formed from the French past participle *assis* – cf. [debute] 'to stand up' < *debout* 'standing'); **sun** SOLE Ital. *sole* / SOLICULU French *soleil*; **this** ISTU/ECCE-ISTU and **that** ILLU/ECCE-ILLU; **who** QUI French *qui*, Ital. *chi* / QUEM Span. *quien*, Ptg. *quem*, Rum. *cine*.

Sometimes Rumanian is the odd-man-out:

Basic lexical differences in Rumanian

cold FRIGIDU: Rum. *rece* RECENS 'fresh' (cf. Old French *roisent*; the Rumanian noun *frig* 'coldness' is from FRIGUS, FRIGORIS); **dry** SICCU: Rum *uscat* EXSUCATU (cf. Ital. *asciugare* 'to dry' etc.; Rum. *sec* is less popular); **earth** TERRA: although *ţara* = 'land' in Daco-Rumanian (also = 'earth' in Arumanian), **earth** is rendered in the standard language by *pamînt* PAVIMENTU (cf. Sard *pamentu* 'floor, ground'); **foot** PEDE: but Rum. *picior* < PECIOLU 'stalk' – cf. Ital *picciuolo* 'petiole'); **heart** COR: Rum. *inimă* ANIMA 'spirit, soul' (cf. French *âme*); **man** HOMINE: Rum *bărbat* BARBATU 'bearded one' / *om* 'human being' (in French creoles the equivalents of the French word *nègre* or *bougre* are often used to designate a male human); **mouth** BUCCA (for OS, ORIS): Rum *bucă* keeps the Latin meaning 'cheek' while 'mouth' is rendered by *gură* (GULA 'throat', but cf. French *gueule* 'jaw', used slangily and in creoles for 'mouth'); **tree** ARBORE: although in Old Daco-Rumanian and in Arumanian *arbure* = 'tree' (also Megleno-Rumanian *arbur* = 'oak'), an Albanian (or Thraco-Dacian) word *copac* is the usual Daco-Rumanian general word, while *pom* (POMU) means 'fruit-tree' (in many parts of Italy PLANTA 'plant, sole of the foot' is used for 'tree' while Haitian Creole uses [pje] < French *pied* 'foot' and in the Engadine *bösch*, of Germanic origin (cf. French *bois* 'wood') is preferred to *alber*).

It will be seen that the deviations in Rumanian seem to stem mainly from a differentiation in Latin vocabulary rather than borrowing from other languages. As far as 'basic' vocabulary is concerned this is true for many of the lexical differences between the modern Romance languages, as we shall see later. Not infrequently similar differences are found between neighbouring and mutually intelligible dialects; indeed it can be claimed that speakers in one small community may even, for normal use, select, from the possible synonyms, those items that are *not* used in a near-by village. In this way, the community can emphasize its separate identity, without impairing bread-and-butter communication (see 5.4).

Differences in basic vocabulary between creoles and 'core' languages seem often to be the consequence of semantic shifts that may be connected with environmental and sociocultural conditions. French creoles, for instance, often use more archaic or popular words than the standard:

(60)   *ba(j)* < *bailler* for *donner* 'give', *guetter* 'to watch out for' for *regarder* 'to look at', *rete* < *rester* 'stay' for *habiter* 'inhabit'.

Originally nautical words are also generalized – like *amarrer* 'to moor a ship', *chavirer* 'capsize' and so on. This sort of generalization is found in other Romance languages:

(61)   *ADRIPARE 'to come to shore' > Ital. *arrivare*, Sard *arribare*, French *arriver*,
         Cat., Occ. *arribar* 'to arrive', PLICARE 'to fold' (of sails) > Span. *llegar*, Ptg.
         chegar 'to arrive', Rum. *a pleca* 'to leave'.

2.5   LOANWORDS

Borrowing from other languages is mainly a factor in the differentiation of Romance lexicon, which will be discussed in chapters 6 and 8. The standard languages have had in common, from late medieval times, the tendency to borrow more extensively from Latin (see 3.4) and from other Romance languages than from non-Romance tongues, while dialects tend to borrow from their national language (see 4.8).

> Isolated Romance-speaking communities are clearly under pressure to use non-Romance forms: an extreme example are the tiny Istro-Rumanian groups that have at their disposal a number of synonymous pairs of Rumanian and Croatian words, especially in verb aspectual pairs in which a Romance form is used for the imperfective, and the Slavonic for the perfective:

(62)   *be* (BIBERE) / *popii* 'to drink'; *munká* (*MANDUCARE) / *poidii* 'to eat'.

> Similarly *papiamento* in Curaçao often alternates between equivalent items of Romance (Spanish/Portuguese) and Dutch origin in its vocabulary – see example (59) above. Creoles have to a differing extent borrowed from African or Asian languages. We may compare, in this respect, Cape Verde with São Tomé Portuguese creoles, with the latter admitting many more African words:

(63)   'body' São Tomé *ubwé* / Cape Verde *korpe* (Ptg. *corpo*); 'empty' São Tomé *duji* /
         Cape Verde *baziu* (Ptg. *vazio*).

Massive borrowing from neighbouring languages can be a sign of imminent 'language death', as speakers shift their loyalty from one language to another: this is presumably what is happening to Istro-Rumanian, and to many Asian Portuguese, and Philippine Spanish varieties. The Saramaccan and *papiamento* examples are of different character, involving the complex, and not yet fully understood, process of creolization, which I shall return to in chapter 5.

2.6   HOW CLOSE ARE ROMANCE LEXICONS?

Although many of the common lexical items in the Romance languages are cognate, they may have very different phonetic shapes in different languages. Most of the studies on divergence between languages are concerned principally with the phonetic changes that have cleft the languages apart. But in many cases it is fairly easy to formulate translation rules which allow speakers to recognize their own indigenous items in the unfamiliar shapes of other languages. For instance, the voicing and opening of intervocalic voiceless stops in Spanish, compared with their preservation in Italian, causes little hindrance to recognition when the regular correspondence is discerned:

(64)   [biða] / [vita] 'life'; [amiɣo] / [amiko] 'friend'.

More difficulty is caused by the complete disappearance of these stops in modern French, so that there is no way of discovering *which* stop is missing:

(65)   [vi], [ami].

However, the difficulty is reduced by the existence of 'learned borrowings' which are semantically and phonetically related to the 'popular' words, but which still preserve the original stops:

(66)   [vital] 'vital', [amikal] 'friendly'.

In so far as speakers link [vi] with [vital], for instance, it is possible that they are conscious, synchronically, of the type of close resemblance between the lexical items of different Romance languages that would otherwise have been rent asunder by diverse phonological developments.

Thus one may make bold to suggest that, from the late medieval period, the predilection for Latinisms has closed some of the gaps that were opened in the Dark Ages (see 3.4). Latinisms are particularly frequent in the fundamental vocabulary of Italian, Spanish, French and Portuguese (in that order), and least frequent in Sard and Rumanian. If we take into account both inherited and borrowed Latin vocabulary, the most 'Romance' of the languages is Italian, and the least, Rumanian.

2.7   ROMANCENESS AS A CONTINUUM?

Latinizing tendencies, especially in lexicon, but also in grammar are a mark of literary languages that form part of the Romance 'club' – of which

Rumanian is a fairly recently joined member – and trickle down to a greater or lesser extent to the varieties that shelter under the 'roof' of these languages. We shall see in the next chapter that this 'club' of languages also shares certain features that are absent from Latin. One answer to the question we asked originally – 'What is a Romance language?' – could be answered by reference to the 'club-land' metaphor, which I shall develop further in chapter 4. A Romance language is one whose speakers have a representation of their language that associates it with prestigious 'Neo-Latin' club members, and especially with Latin itself. As speakers of such varieties that lack the status associated with the nation–state – like Catalan, Occitan, Galician, Romansh, Sard – seek to nurture self-esteem, they will usually assert their independent affiliation to Latin, as full members of the club and not merely satellites of the 'big' languages. Other varieties – like some of the creoles – seek their cultural identity elsewhere. Others are doomed to decline and death as speakers disappear or shift their allegiance to other languages. This is happening now to Asian Portuguese, to Louisiana French, to Judeo-Spanish, to Istro-Rumanian varieties, as it has in the past to the Romance varieties that were certainly spoken in Dalmatia and in some areas that are now German-speaking, and to those probably spoken in North Africa and Britain.

But, of course, not just any language can join the club. It would have first to be related to the Romance family. This is a classic metaphor in comparative philology, which refers to a group of languages that are related, in the sense that they are modern variants of what was in the past a single language. The (inexact) analogy, with a parent and her children, reflects the view of languages as organisms that are born, grow old and die.

Here I have used lexico-phonetic correspondences among basic lexical items and grammatical morphemes as the bench-mark for family membership. Where to draw the line is of course an arbitrary decision: perhaps a language with more than 50 per cent of core items that are recognizably Romance can be included. This would exclude English (even though in the wider vocabulary numerous French and Latin words are used) and Saramaccan. It would include most other 'Romance creoles', even Angolar, and, still (but for how long?) Istro-Rumanian.

Within the family there would still be more or less distant relatives: I have suggested that Italian seems to be at the centre of the family group, with Rumanian and French (including French creoles) more on the periphery. Rumanian, unattested before the sixteenth century, seems to have been drawn further into the family since the eighteenth century, when its more prestigious speakers began to solicit for membership of the 'club', by favouring Romance lexical variants at the expense of Slavonic, Turkish, Albanian or Greek.

I have broached, without resolving it, however, the question of a Romance 'type', which would be defined by synchronic morphosyntactic, rather than by sociocultural or historical, criteria. I shall pay more attention to sociocultural factors in chapter 8, while in chapter 5 I discuss creolization as a historical process.

One thing I think I have demonstrated is that, at the extreme, creoles can have a different sort of verbal system from other Romance languages, even though the 'Romance verb' and the 'creole verb' themselves show a great deal of variation and sometimes overlap. I have also maintained that a nominal two-gender system, as distinct from the Latin three-gender system, is a Romance characteristic, not found in any of the creoles.

Most, but not all, of the common features of Romance are inherited from Latin. In the next chapter I shall look more closely at the relationship between Latin and Romance, emphasizing the differences as well as the similarities. In chapter 4, I shall consider especially features that are shared by most Romance languages but absent from Latin.

FURTHER READING

On 'family' relationships and reconstruction, Polomé & Winter eds. (1992). On creoles, Holm (1988–9). Volume I of Posner & Green eds. (1980–93) gives an account of lexicological studies in Romance, with a complete bibliography up to that time. More recent important comparative works include Sala ed. (1988), a detailed study of the 'representative' vocabulary of nine Romance languages and of Latin, and comparison between them. Vernay (1991–), of which four volumes have appeared to date (1996), is less a dictionary than an account of Romance words for selected concepts grouped according to their semantic field ('moral concepts', 'parts of the body', etc.). On word formation, see Kursschildgen (1983), Klingebiel (1989), Malkiel (1989). On etymology, see especially Malkiel (1992, 1993). Most comparative works concentrate on differentiation of vocabulary: for instance Rohlfs (1986). On -*mente*, Karlsson (1981).

3

Latin and Romance

3.1   DERIVATION

I asked in the last chapter 'What is a Romance language?' For most Romanists, the answer is obvious: 'It is a language derived from Latin.' But what is meant by derivation is not obvious. As a metaphor, based on the Latinate form DE-RIVUS 'from a stream' (implying originally 'diversion of a water channel'), we can conjure up a picture of a river flowing from its source, expanding as it is fed from various other sources and splitting up into an estuary as it nears the sea. An even more vivid metaphor is that of a tree, from the trunk of which various branches sprout. But in both these cases the parent remains, with the off-shoots still part of it. The comforting metaphor of a family, which I used before, is misleading too, because that implies discontinuity and the birth and death of discrete individuals.

What we are looking for is a metaphor that implies continuity and diversification, but also the slow withering away of the parent stock: my far from glamorous suggestion is that of vegetative reproduction, as with a rhizome. The Romance languages, the newer sprouts, are living versions of Latin, a root-stock that is now dead – in the sense that it is now represented only by a closed corpus of texts and that it is no longer the mother-tongue of any speaker. How and when the death of Latin came about we shall discuss later.

I have already emphasized that traditional comparative philology assumes that distinct languages which share a large number of basic lexical elements, the phonological shapes of which are related in a regular way, must at an earlier period have been one and the same language. The methods developed for reconstruction of the original proto-language are, as we have seen, vindicated by the results of Romance reconstructions, which often closely match the actually attested Latin forms. But it is also true that some shared features of the Romance languages are not attested in Latin; hence the disputes about how reconstructed Proto-Romance, or Vulgar Latin, relates to the language of our Classical texts.

3.2   PROTO-ROMANCE OR VULGAR LATIN

The much-used term **Vulgar Latin** fills some Romanists with consternation, because it is used in many vague, and sometimes contradictory, ways: one commentator counts thirteen distinct meanings for the term. It implies for most users the Latin of 'the people', unsullied by excessive grammatical learning, lively, and expressive, but, perhaps, slovenly, unsubtle and imprecise. Recall (page 3) that some sixteenth-century thinkers claimed that even in Republican times the Roman populace may have spoken Italian. They did not envisage that languages change over time, merely that one social variant replaces another, when there is decay of social constraints. The idea that change implies decay from God-given complexity and uniqueness towards animal-like communicative simplicity survived well into the era of scientific linguistics. Classical Latin would, in the view adopted by most respected nineteenth-century linguists, be maintained only by discipline and educational rigour, while a relaxing of standards gave rise to a less intellectually subtle, but perhaps more crudely expressive, vulgar version of the language. Thus the sources of Romance were to be sought in scantily attested colloquial Latin. It was well known that social differences in Republican Rome were stark and it has even been suggested that the non-senatorial class had virtually no access to the prestige language that was committed to writing.

The notion that the proto-language of Romance could be reconstructed in a way similar to that used for unattested Proto-Germanic or Indo-European did not catch on until quite late in the nineteenth century. Only more recently has much attention been paid to the discrepancies between the sparse textual evidence for colloquial Latin and the reconstructed Proto-Romance.

(a)   Popular Latin

It could not fail to strike observers that early Latin and Italic dialects displayed some of the features that resurfaced in the late texts that foreshadowed Romance. Let us take as an example **syncope**, a term used for amply attested Late Latin truncation of a penultimate syllable containing a short vowel (ῐ or ῠ), in classical forms in which the accent falls, exceptionally, on the antepenultimate syllable:

(1)   VῙRDE for VῙRῘDE(M) 'green' (cf. Ital. *verde* etc.); AURICLU for
          AURῙCῠLU(S) 'ear' (cf. Ital. *orecchio* etc.).

Such truncation is usually associated with the postulated change from tonal to stress accentuation in later Latin: unaccented vowels tend to reduce and disappear between two stressed syllables, whereas the contrast between high-tone and low-tone vowels would not be expected to produce the same effect. There is no universal tendency to reduce and drop vowels in atonic syllables, so perhaps in Latin the vowels written ῐ and ῠ were schwa-type vowels that were in some sense evanescent.

Evidence suggests that early Latin may also have had stress accentuation: certainly there are examples of apparently syncopated forms from this period:

(2)   CALDUS, for CALῙDUS 'hot' (cf. Ital. *caldo*).

          The Emperor Augustus is said to have regarded the unsyncopated form of this
          word as affected.

Some scholars believe that the tonal accent, described by Latin grammarians, may in fact have been an artefact of the literary language, imitated from prestigious Greek. Some of the short vowels found in classical penultimate syllables may then be a consequence of insertion (**anaptyxis**) between certain consonant sequences, perhaps favoured by fashionable 'tonal' pronunciation. In this case it is likely that it was never totally adopted in the colloquial language. A parallel can be drawn with later developments in Romance. In standard Italian, for instance, unsyncopated forms apparently survive (see 7.2):

(3)   Compare Ital. *tavola* with French *table* < TABῠLA; TABLA in the *Appendix Probi*
          (note that BL was a very infrequent cluster in Latin).

Here we seem to be faced with 'semi-learned' forms; 'regular' counterparts would derive from a form like TABLA, *TAVLA, *TAULA, which ends up as:

(4)   Ital. dial. *tola*, *tabia* in various specialized uses like 'shoemaker's bench, chess-
          board, etc.', French *tôle* 'sheet metal'.

Compare also:

(5)   modern Ital. *anima* 'spirit, soul', Rum. *înima* 'heart' / Old Ital. *alma, arma*,
            French *âme* (old *arme*), Span., Ptg. *alma* < ANĬMA.

So-called *sdrucciole*, with antepenultimate stress, are fairly common in Italian, not only in learned words. There is often hesitation about the correct pronunciation, with, on the whole, avoidance of accentuation of suffix-like sequences like *-ola, -ula*. Evidence that there has been restoration, rather than retention, of the atonic penultimate is provided by the not infrequent lack of correspondence between the vowel and that of the Latin etymon:

(6)   *attimo* 'moment'< ATOMU; *debole* 'weak'< DEBILE; *sedano* 'celery'< SELINON.

The suggestion that lower class Latin continued to use syncopated forms throughout the classical period is supported by evidence from graffiti from Pompeii (which was destroyed by an eruption of Vesuvius in AD 79):

(7)   DOMNUS for DOMĬNUS 'master'; COLICLO for CAULĬCULUS 'little cabbage' (also
            with 'popular' reduction of diphthong AU to O); MANUPLUS for MĂNĬPŬLUS
            'bundle'.

There was also abundant attestation in later texts.

            In some sequences the short vowel in the penultimate syllable seems to have
            distinctive value:

(8)   MANCUS 'maimed' > Ital., Span., Ptg., Cat. *manco*, Old French, Occ. *manc* /
            MANĬCUS 'grip' > Ital. *manico*, Span., Ptg. *mango*, French *manche*, Occ. *margue*.

One type of social variation is obvious to all: different choice of vocabulary. In many cases the Latin word that survives into Romance is more popular in its flavour than the word preferred in high literary style. Among common words we can cite:

Pan-Romance popular Latin words

BELLUS 'fine, beautiful' which survives in all Romance languages, although in Spanish,
            Portugese and Sard it is probably a loanword from Italian. PULCHER is quite
            lost, while FORMŌSUS 'beautifully formed' persists in Spanish, Portuguese and
            Rumanian.
CABALLUS 'horse', originally a Celtic word, replaces EQUUS everywhere.
ŌS 'mouth' is replaced by BŬCCA 'puffed-up cheek', or GŬLA 'gullet'.
FLĒRE 'to weep' gives way to PLORARE 'to lament, to wail', or PLANGERE 'to bewail'.
LŪDĔRE 'to play' is replaced by IOCĂRE 'to joke'.

PORTĀRE 'to carry' – a word already used by the early comedian Plautus – replaces FERRE 'to bear'.

ĒDERE 'to eat' survives in derived forms like Span. *comer*; some other languages use a verb formed on the name of a gluttonous character of comedy – MANDŪCĀRE.

The popular idiom, and Romance, often preferred longer, derived forms to a shorter word. Diminutives were particularly favoured:

(9)   AURĪCULA, AVĪCELLA, GENŬCULUM 'little ear, bird, knee'.

So were frequentatives:

(10)   CANTĀRE 'to keep on singing' for CANĔRE 'to sing'.

(b)   Italic dialect

It can be argued that the differences between reconstructed Proto-Romance and Classical Latin are great enough for us to postulate another, related language as the 'mother' of the Romance family. Some, for instance, postulate a variety that deviated from Latin at an early stage, perhaps before the third century BC, when the earliest literary texts were written. Others, more radically, suggest that a regional dialect (probably from southern Italy) was at the origin of the spoken language that spread through the Empire. For instance, reconstruction of the medial cluster in:

(11)   French *nuit*, Ital. *notte*, Span. *noche*, Rum. *noapte* 'night'

which are usually derived from NOCTE, causes difficulty, because of the deviant Rumanian reflex. A plausible proto-form would have /k^{w}t/; the QU /k^w/ of Latin, as in AQUA 'water', comes out in Rumanian like the second labial element:

(12)   Rum. *apă* / Ital. *acqua*.

Note that /k^{w}t/ and /kt/ could be related in a similar way as literary -CŬL- and syncopated -CL-. It may also be that Latin QU represented a cluster /kw/ rather than a unitary phoneme.

Even more controversial is the suggestion that the Romance mother may have been an **umlauting (metaphonic)** language, in which a final ī or ŭ raised the vowel of the preceding tonic syllable. Such umlauting is found in various Romance dialects, particularly in central and southern Italy. The 'mass neuter' forms of Asturias and Abruzzo (see 1.4) can be connected with the same phenomenon. There are traces too of umlauting in French:

(13)   *fis* < FĒCĪ 'I did'; *il* < *ILLĪ 'he'.

More widespread is the **diphthongization** that some see as a consequence originally of umlaut (see 4.2).

It has been claimed that Proto-Romance can best be reconstructed as an umlauting language, like Germanic languages. As Latin, even in its popular varieties, shows no signs of umlaut it could not therefore be equated with the Romance mother-language.

(c)   Late Latin

It is generally assumed that after the Latin Golden Age (*c.* 90 BC to AD 14), as social structures became less rigid and linguistic habits became more variable with the spread of the Empire, there was relaxation of the tight control over the written language that had characterized the classical period. Even those who do not subscribe to the view that popular Latin always differed considerably from the prestigious variety recognize that the later Latin texts display certain features that foreshadow Romance.

Petronius, who died in AD 66, is often cited as one of the heralds of the Romance languages. His depiction of vulgar feasting in *Cena Trimalchionis* includes well-known 'Vulgar Latin' features, such as syncope:

(14)   COLPUS, OCLUS, CALDUS, ORICLA, etc.

and 'popular' vocabulary:

(15)   BELLUS, PLORARE, BUCCA, CABALLUS, MANDUCARE, etc.

The letters of Claudius Terentianus from the first quarter of the second century AD – personal letters, written in Egypt by professional scribes (both in Greek and in Latin) – are recently studied texts among the many papyrus documents now available. They show even more evidence of 'Vulgar' features.

The best-known early 'Vulgar text' is the *Appendix Probi*, a curious list of correct and incorrect spellings forming part of a seventh- or eighth-century manuscript. Its date and place of composition is disputed. If indeed it is from the third century, it provides ample mainly phonological evidence, especially of syncope:

(16)   VIRDIS, TABLA, OCLUS etc.

of jodization:

(17)   ALIUM NON ALEUM, COCHLEA NON COCHLIA, etc.

and of loss of final -M:

(18)   OLIM NON OLI, PASSIM NON PASSI.

It is disappointingly inconclusive on some other changes that we think should have happened by then. One problem about the text is that we do not know what its purpose could have been: a school exercise? A consultative manual for scribes? Certainly the choice of words in the list is eccentric and does not always reflect Romance outcomes.

Another text that is given favoured status in the study of Vulgar Latin is the so-called *Peregrinatio Aetheriae* (or *Egeriae*), which we have in an incomplete eleventh-century manuscript. It is a nun's first-hand account of a pilgrimage to the Holy Land, dated, on external evidence, to between AD 363 and 431. The value of this text is that it provides evidence of syntactic changes, and in particular of the comparative infrequency of the verb-last ordering that characterized Classical Latin. The Terentianus letters had also shown a similar trend: in all the Romance languages a SVO (subject–verb–object) ordering is seen as basic (but for preposing of object clitics, see 4.4).

In the Late Latin period there were numerous grammatical treatises, presumably aimed at speakers who were conscious of their imperfect command of Latin. Much of the evidence is ambiguous, but some does bear out the predictions suggested by our reconstruction of Proto-Romance.

Texts and inscriptions in Latin continued to be produced throughout the Dark Ages. The 'mistakes' in these texts can be interpreted to match the changes that were to produce Romance, and as time goes on they tend to become more numerous. But clearly the writers were versed enough in the Latin tradition to make a shot at correctness, and they continued to use forms – like the Latin passive (see 4.7) and future (see 4.6) – which disappeared completely from Romance.

How far can we guess what sort of language they were speaking? What we cannot say for certain is that the Latin of these texts represents the 'same language' as reconstructed Proto-Romance.

3.3   DIFFERENCES BETWEEN LATIN AND ROMANCE

(a)   Language names

The use of the collective term **Romance** has always been seen as indicative of the separate status of these languages. **Latin** is the name traditionally used for the literary language known from classical texts, as well as for **Medieval Latin**, and for **Neo-Latin**, as the Renaissance use of the language is designated, and for Church Latin. The name derives from the ancient peoples of Latium, but the standard and preferred form was always the usage of Rome. In ancient texts LINGUA ROMANA seems to have been used synonymously with LINGUA LATINA, though often with the suggestion that the urban use was more sophisticated than the regional.

For Classical Latin, the Romance languages now use, like English, Latinized forms of the name. These are learned borrowings that date, in French, from the twelfth century, and in Spanish probably from the fifteenth or sixteenth centuries. Standard Italian *latino* could be a popular form, but Latin was known as LITTERAE in the twelfth century, and GRAMMATICA in the thirteenth (both implying a written language). In Rumanian there is no popular reflex of LATINUS.

Popular reflexes, typically *ladin(o)*, are today used for some Romance languages, all in contact with non-Romance tongues: the now-extinct Dalmatian language, the written language used for literal translation from Hebrew and Aramaic texts by Sephardic Jews (whose vernacular is a Spanish variety), and Engadine and Dolomite Rhaeto-Romance. This originally bookish usage probably dates from the nineteenth century, but earlier similar names were used for many North Italian varieties. Till about the seventeenth century, the word was used, as it is today in the United States, for Spanish-speaking foreigners.

> Everyday words deriving from LATINUS in the Romance languages are frequent in the general sense 'language' (including for instance 'birdsong', also for 'gibberish') and, as an adjective, with meanings like 'clever', 'smooth', 'slippery', 'nimble', 'easy'. Non-Romance speakers often use the name for Roman Catholics: in some Germanic dialects it means 'bondsman'. Spanish Arabic used the name for Christians.

One commonly held belief is that in the later part of the first century AD the names LINGUA LATINA and LINGUA ROMANA were differentiated, with the former indicating the written, learned language, and the latter one or several spoken Romance tongues that are not recorded in writing. It has been shown, however, that this distinction is not made in texts before the ninth century. Even then it is not wholly consistently made, though the addition of an adjective like RUSTICA sometimes makes clear that LINGUA ROMANA is meant to designate vernacular use.

Romance speakers throughout the Middle Ages tended to differentiate themselves from Germans or Slavs by calling themselves **Romans**; the Germans called them by varieties of the name **Welsh** (see, for instance, **Walloon** in Belgium, old *Churwälsch* for Romansh or Surselvan, and **Vlach** for Rumanian). Today the Roman name survives only in regions where the language is in contact with other tongues – in Suisse Romande, in Rumania, in Romansh territories, and in *sefardí* Jewish communities.

> Names for the individual languages usually arose in the Middle Ages, frequently with a geographical or historical origin. FRANCISCA seems originally to have been used for Germanic Frankish; for French *romanz* was still in use at the beginning of the twelfth century, to be replaced only later by *franceis*. In Occitan *romans* was usual, with *lemosí* and *provenzal* fairly rarely used before the thirteenth century. *Langue d'oc* seems to be a northern name, used from the late thirteenth century, and *Occitan* a modern usage. In Spain *romance* was the usual name before the second half of the thirteenth century, when *castellano* (belonging to the 'castle area') began to be used. *Español* (formed on HISPANIA) dates from the end of the fifteenth century. In the west *romanço* was current from the fourteenth century, *portugues*, from the sixteenth century. *Catalá* dates from the fourteenth century; *romanç* was usual in the thirteenth century. In Italy, the vernacular was called *volgare*, though the name *italiano* was introduced first in the thirteenth century. For Rumanian we have little evidence before the sixteenth century. It is claimed that the name *Vlach* was not used by speakers themselves, who always called themselves Romans.

(b)   Phonology

The differences between the Romance languages are discernible most at the phonological level, and it is on this aspect that traditional Romance linguistics has concentrated. Where Romance languages share phonological characteristics that are absent from Latin, it is usual to look to the proto-language for their source. We shall here examine some phonological developments that may date from a common Romance period.

(i)   Vowel length

The Latin phonemic vowel system comprised two inventories, one long (two **moras**) and one short (one mora). The long-vowel inventory had, besides the five vowels matched in the short system (I, U, E, O, A), three diphthongs. In Romance the diphthongs OE and AE were merged into the long and short E respectively. The diphthong AU, which in popular Latin usage seems to have merged with ō:

(19)   CAUDA > CŌDA > French *queue*, Occ. *coza*

is retained in some Romance languages, but merges eventually with ŏ in most:

(20)   CAUSA > French *chose*, Occ. *cauza*.

One salient difference between Latin and Romance is that the latter inherits no phonological length distinctions from Latin (where lexically determined long vowels were fixed by poetic authority, and metrical long vowels 'by position'). Even though it was never consistently marked in graphy, vowel length was indubitably distinctive in Latin, with minimal pairs like:

Long and short vowels in Latin

/iː/	PĪLUM	'javelin'	/i/	PĬLUM	'hair' (acc. sg.);
/eː/	LĒVIS	'smooth'	/e/	LĔVIS	'light';
/aː/	MĀLUM	'apple'	/a/	MĂLUM	'evil' (acc. sg.);
/oː/	ŌS	'mouth'	/o/	ŎS	'bone';
/uː/	FŪRIS	'of a thief'	/u/	FŬRIS	'you rage'.

Admittedly there seems to have been some morphological relationship between short and long vowels:

(21)   FĬDES 'faith' / FĪDES 'you will trust'; SŬO 'I sew' / SŪTOR 'cobbler'; ATTRĂCTUS 'attracted' / ATTRĀXI 'I attracted'.

There was also some interchange between long vowels and long consonants (**geminates**):

(22)   MŪCUS/MŬCCUS 'mucus', TŌTUS/TŎTTUS 'all', BĀCA/BĂCCA 'berry'.

> Combinations of long vowel and long consonant are extremely rare in Latin: apart from derived forms, only STĒLLA 'star' and VĪLLA are usually cited. In the former case, the geminate is supported by other Indo-European evidence, which suggests assimilation from an earlier cluster. In Latin such clusters are usually simplified after a long vowel:

(23)   MĒD-CUM > MĒCUM 'with me'.

> Although Span. *estrella* and Ital. *stella* imply a Latin geminate, the diphthong
> of French *étoile* indicates a form with single *l*.

How far the quantity differences were consistently functional in Latin has been debated. In atonic syllables, for instance, short vowels predominate. I have already suggested a tendency to schwa-like reduction. In tonic syllables, too, Ĕ, Ĭ and Ŭ are frequent.

That the long and short vowels were acoustically similar is evidenced by loanwords – for instance, in Basque – which do not distinguish them. Moreover in Sard dialects long and short vowels fall together; this is also true of some of the vowels in Southern Italian dialects and Rumanian. Most languages, however, distinguish inherited Latin vowels by **quality** and not by **quantity**. Thus, inherited short vowels tend to have lower pronunciation than long vowels: Ē, for instance, would be [e], whereas Ĕ is [ɛ]. It is often assumed that colloquial Latin at some period must have had similar qualitative differences, which came to displace the redundant quantitative differences.

It is from Romance data impossible to reconstruct the fact that Latin had distinctive vowel length. Vowel length differences may have been neglected in rapid speech, especially in varieties with a stress accent, and were therefore frequently accompanied or supplanted by qualitative differences.

> It has been suggested that differences in accent placement can be used to reconstruct Latin vowel quantity. However, this would depend on reconstruction of short vowels in penultimate syllables – which, we have seen, were probably regularly syncopated (though sometimes apparently restored). In any case accent placement in Latin depended not on vowel length but on syllable weight.

Vowel reconstruction seems clearly to distinguish **West Romance** from **East Romance** (see 5.2). In the former Ē falls together with Ĭ, and Ō with Ŭ:

(24)   CRĒDIT 'he believes' > /krede/, PĬRA 'pear' > /pera/; FLŌREM 'flower' > /flore/,
             MŬSCA 'fly' > /mosca/ .

The differences in treatment of vowels are linked by many Romanists to historically attested political separation of some areas from the Roman orbit: thus Sardinia was isolated from the second century, Rumania from the third. It is therefore assumed that the specifically Western developments – attested in France, the Iberian peninsula and northern and central Italy (and, incidentally, in Britain) – must have occurred at a later stage.

> Diphthongization in tonic syllables in early Romance is connected with sylla-
> ble structure and is thought by some to result from lengthening of vowels in
> open syllables (see 4.2). This process seems to have no connection with Latin
> vowel length.

Compensatory lengthening, by which merger of two phonological seg-
ments results in one long one, was at the origin of many of the Latin long
vowels. Similar processes took place later in separate Romance languages,
so that some developed vowel length differences at some stage during their
history. For instance, in the course of Old French the loss of medial syllable-final consonants led to the creation of distinctions like these (where
the circumflex accent marks a long vowel):

(25)   *pâte* < PASTA 'paste' / *patte* 'paw' (probably of onomatopoeic origin); *bête* <
         BEST(I)A 'beast' / *bette* < BETA 'beetroot'.

In most varieties of French these length distinctions have now been lost.

(ii)   Accent

There is some dispute, as we have seen, about the nature of the Latin
accent. Certainly in all the Romance languages the accent is one of stress
(although some creoles seem to have tonal characteristics, like neighbouring African languages).

The position of the accent in Latin was determined by morpheme and
syllable structure, and was not distinctive. Within the word (not including
any clitics, but embracing also affixes) the accent fell on the penultimate
syllable, except when that syllable was **light** – that is, contained a short
vowel not followed by a tautosyllabic consonant.

> In Jakobson's formulation, the accent falls upon that syllable which contains
> the second mora counted from the final syllable (where a short vowel has one
> mora, and a long vowel, two).

The regularity of accent placement relative to syllabic structure is
demonstrated by the way Latin displaces the accent of Greek loanwords
to conform to its own pattern:

(26)   *kámelos* > CAMĒLUS ; *kamára* > CAMĔRA

In nearly every case the stress falls on the same syllable in Romance as it
did in the Latin etymon. Occasionally, especially where the word was
proparoxytonic, Romance has changed the stress pattern. This sometimes

happens as a result of lengthening the short vowel, so that the penultimate syllable becomes heavy:

(27)   *SAPĒRE for SAPĔRE 'to taste, to know': Ital. *sapere*, Span., Ptg. *saber*, French *savoir*, Catalan *saber* (but also *sebre*).

One group of words fairly consistently shows displacement of accent: these are proparoxytones with a penultimate short vowel followed by an *obstruent* + *r* cluster. In Latin such clusters did not 'make position' – so that the preceding syllable was not heavy. In popular Romance reflexes, however, the accent falls on the penultimate syllable, and not, as in Latin, on the antepenultimate:

(28)   ĀLĂCREM 'lively': Ital. *allegro*, Old French *halaigre* (< *ALECREM); COLŬBRA 'female snake': French *couleuvre*, Span. *culebra* (but Ptg. *cobra* perhaps from the proparoxytonic form); INTĔGRUM 'whole': Rum. *întreg*, French *entier* (but also Old French *entre*), Ital. *intero*, Old Span. *intrego* (modern *entero*); CATHĔDRA 'chair': Old French *chaiere* (modern *chaire*, *chaise*), Span. *cadera* 'hip' (Span. *cátedra*, Ital. *cattedra* are Latinisms).

As a result of syncope, with loss of the short vowel in the penultimate syllable, many Latin proparoxytones became Romance paroxytones. Similarly, apocope of the final syllable results in a Romance oxytone:

(29)   SANITĀTEM 'health': Ital. *sanità*, French *santé*.

              In Italian, in particular, the short vowel that should have been lost by syncope seems still to be retained in the modern standard, so that proparoxytones, as we have seen, are quite frequent:

(30)   HĔDĔRA 'ivy': Ital *èdera* / French *lierre* (Old *iere*), Span. *hiedra*; LITTĔRA 'letter': Ital. *lettera* / French *lettre*, Span. *letra*.

              Whether this is an effect of influence from Latin, or of anaptyxis of vowels to avoid awkward clusters, is not certain (see 7.2).

The stress pattern in most of the languages is not now predictable from the syllable structure of the word and in the orthography the position of stress may be marked (consistently in Spanish, less so in Italian). Position of the stress may differentiate inflectional forms, as in:

(31)   Span. *hablo/habló*, Ital. *parlo/parlò*   'I speak/he spoke'.

              In French, where unstressed syllables were reduced and lost by the modern period, the stress falls regularly on the final syllable of the isolated word.

Occasionally a shift of stress can be used for emphasis (*accent d'insistance*), and some public speakers affect a diction which favours stress on the first sylla- ble of the word. However, modern French does not normally use word stress but rhythmic group stress, with only the last syllable of the group receiving stress. The modern habit seems to have become established in the early modern period. Evidence from the sound changes suggests that Old French had a heavy word stress but that by the sixteenth century words were no longer distin- guished within the rhythmic group (see 7.2).

(iii)   Palatals

As an example of the way the phonology of Romance languages differs collectively from Latin, let us consider the phenomenon of **palatalization**. What seems to have happened to differing degrees in each of the Romance languages is the movement of back and front consonants towards the cen- tral palatal position, thus creating new phonological distinctions and a series of palatal consonants. The processes involved are usually the well- known ones of **assimilation**, by which features of one segment are trans- mitted to a juxtaposed one. Similar changes are widely attested in other languages.

In Romance, the picture that is usually drawn is of a rich array of palatal and palatalized consonants at some unspecified medieval period, with some of these merging or moving forward to dental position in more modern periods. It is difficult to decide for sure how far these postulated palatal consonants were, at any particular stage in the past, distinct phonological units, rather than merely phonetic variants of other units.

Other interlocking sound changes have to be taken into account, so that, for instance, palatalization of Latin c /k/ has to be related to the simplification of QU (/k^w/ or /kw/):

(32)   *CINQUE [k-] (dissimilated from QUINQUE) 'five'. > French *cinq* [s], Italian *cinque* [ʧ], Span. *cinco* [θ] / QUINDECIM [k^w] 'fifteen' > French *quinze*, Span. *quince* [k], but Ital. *quindici* [kw] / QUI/QUEM [k^w] 'who/whom' > French *qui* [k], Ital. *chi* [k], Span. *quien* [k] / Rum. *cine* [ʧ].

Shifts in the lexical stock of the languages probably had an effect on the phonological status of the consonants, and perhaps led to some simplifi- cation of the variation range. This happened especially when frankly Latinized forms were borrowed, particularly in the late Middle Ages and the Renaissance period.

Latin consonantal ɪ

In Classical Latin there were no phonological palatal consonants. The vowel ĭ, however, had as a phonetic variant, palatal glide [j]. There were no minimal pairs that distinguished the vocalic and the consonantal variants, but, because prevocalic ɪ in word-initial position is often cognate with an initial jod in other Indo-European languages, it is assumed that in Latin too it was consonantal. However, in the literary language, word-initial prevocalic ĭ sometimes counted as a syllable, while postconsonantally it often 'hardened' to a non-syllabic (**jodization**).

In Romance, Latin word-initial Ī gives in nearly all languages the same outcome as word-initial G+^{E,I} and as [dj], which suggests hardening:

(33)   ɪAM 'already' > Ital. *già* [ʤ], French *ja* [ʒ] (as in *déjà*), Span. *ya* [j]; GELU
        'frost'> Ital. *gelo*, French *gel*, Span. *hielo*; DIURNU 'day' > Ital. *giorno*, French
        jour / HODIE 'today' > Ital. *oggi*, Span. *hoy*.

Those who maintain that colloquial Latin had a stress accent also assume that prevocalic ĭ was always pronounced as jod. In intervocalic position the testimony of grammarians confirms that ɪ was a geminate [jj]. Furthermore it 'made position' so that the preceding vowel was counted as long for metrical purposes.

Late Latin texts provide ample evidence that clusters of *consonant + jod* were tending to assimilate to produce an intermediate palatal consonant (for instance, [dj] was written as z, and [kj] and [tj] were frequently confused). The almost regular confusion of prevocalic Ě and Ĭ suggests that both had merged as jod. The *Appendix Probi*, for instance, cites forms like:

(34)   VINEA NON VINIA, ALLIUM NON ALLEUM

heralding the palatalization in all the Romance languages:

(35)   Rum. *vie* (dialectal *viñe*), Ital. *vigna*, French *vigne*, Span. *viña*, Ptg. *vinha*, Sard
        bindza 'vine'; Rum. *aiu*, Ital. *aglio*, French *ail*, Span. *ajo*, Ptg. *alho* 'garlic'.

Latin consonantal clusters

Other Late Latin combinations which were ripe for palatalization were those composed of a velar consonant and a front consonant – like L (including clusters resulting from syncope of the intertonic short vowel, as in the diminutive suffix -CLU) or T, as in, for instance, FACTUM. In the former case, as we have seen, the cluster palatalizes everywhere, whereas in the latter there has been resistance to palatalization in some languages (see example (11) above).

> Latin GN poses a particular problem, as it is not clear whether this indeed represented a cluster, a geminate or a single segment. In Western Romance languages it palatalized to [ɲ]:

(36)   AGNELLU 'lamb' > Ital. *agnello*, French *agneau*, Cat. *anyell*; LIGNU 'wood' > Ital. *legno*, Old French *lein*, Span. *leño*, Ptg. *lenho* (but Rum. *miel* (dialectal / *ñel*), Southern Ital. dial. *líunu*, Sard *linnu*).

Most Romance languages retain a palatal *n* [ɲ], and a palatal *l* [ʎ] (in French it simplified to jod in the eighteenth century, and in modern Spanish varieties it has been transmogrified to [j] or [ʒ]).

> In Spanish and Catalan a geminate N or L also resulted in palatal [ɲ] and [ʎ]:

(37)   ANNU 'year'> *año, any*, CASTELLU 'castle' > *castillo, castell*.

> Catalan also palatalizes L in initial position to [ʎ]:

(38)   *llengua* / Span. *lengua* < LINGUA.

> In Spanish, word-initial clusters composed of a *consonant* + *l* palatalize to [ʎ]:

(39)   CLAMARE 'to call'> *llamar*, PLORARE 'to deplore' > *llorar*, 'to weep' / Cat. *clamar, plorar*, Ptg. *chamar, chorar*, Ital. *chiamare*, Old *piorare* (modern *piangere* < PLANGERE).

> In Italian, on the other hand, the geminates are retained and [ʎ] derives only from medial GL or [lj] clusters:

(40)   VIG(I)LARE > *vegliare* 'to watch at night' (but cf. Old *vegghiare*), MELIUS 'better' > *meglio*.

Latin velar consonants

A striking feature of Romance is the almost universal palatalization of Latin velar consonants when followed by front vowels – a fact that causes confusion in school pronunciation of Latin, with CAESAR pronounced e.g. [sezar] or [ʧesar], rather than the [kajsar], which is vouchsafed by the German loanword, *Kaiser*. It is usually assumed that in Proto-Romance assimilation of back consonants to a following front vowel must have already begun, but whether this merely resulted in phonetic variants or in phonological splits is disputed.

The Late Latin texts provide very little help in dating the changes. Certainly in Sard the palatalization did not take place: this is usually linked to the early dissociation of the island from the rest of the Latin-speaking world. There is evidence of a similar, but inconsistent, resistance to this type of palatalization in Dalmatian:

(41)   Veglia *kaina* < CĒNA 'dinner'.

To take as an example the treatment of word-initial /k/ + $^{E, I}$, nearly everywhere in Romance it acts like medial /kj/:

(42)   CIVITATE 'city' > [ʧ] Ital. *città*; [s] French *cité*, Ptg. *cidade*, Cat. *ciutat*; [θ] Span. *ciudad* / FACIA/FACIES 'face' > Ital. *faccia*, French *face*, Ptg. *face*, Cat. *fas*, Span. *haz* (but Rum. *cetate* [ʧ] / *faṭā* [ts]).

This suggests a palatal glide transition between consonant and vowel, or at any rate transfer of palatal feature from the vowel to the consonant.

Despite such similarities, Romance languages (leaving aside Sard) seem to split into two groups. The palatalized [k] can end up as a dental affricate (and then usually a sibilant), eventually losing palatal features:

(43)   CENTU 'hundred'> French *cent* [s], Spanish *ciento* [θ] or [s]

where earlier evidence reveals that the initial consonant was an affricate [ts]. Or it can turn into a palatal plosive or palatal-alveolar affricate (sometimes simplifying to a fricative):

(44)   Ital. *cento*, Dalmatian (Veglia) *čant*, R-R (Engadine) *čaint* [ʧ] (cf. Sard *kentu*).

We assume that the former had an apical and the latter a laminal articulation. Whether one of these outcomes can be traced as having passed through the other is hotly disputed. The dental (apical) outcome is less widespread in Romance than the palatal-alveolar (laminal). In France, for instance, both Northern and Occitan dialects prefer the latter.

The shift to dental articulation can be seen as the culmination of the fronting process, while a palatal or palatal-alveolar sound can be seen as a half-way house, resulting from a longer resistance to palatalization in the more conservative areas. The distinction between Rumanian reflexes exemplified in (42) above may support this hypothesis, in that the initial C+^{E,I} seems to have been more resistant than medial [kj].

Inconsistent developments

Similar inconsistencies, especially with Latin voiced consonants, are found elsewhere. This is particularly so in Italy, where different reflexes of the same word are often attributed to different regional developments:

(45)   MEDIU 'half' > *mezzo*/*meggio*, *GREGIU from GREGE 'herd, flock' > *grezzo*/*greggio* 'untreated cloth'.

Latin medial [dj], like [gj], had almost merged with [jj] in Late Latin, so that we expect to find parallels like:

(46)   MAIU 'May'/MEDIU: Rum. *maiu*/*miez*, Sard *maiu*/*meiu*, French *mai*/*mi*, Ptg. *maio*/*meio*.

Italian *maggio* and *meggio*, with [dʒ], thus appear anomalous, with the palatalized hardening that is found in strengthened word-initial position – see example (33) above. The [dʣ] of *mezzo* similarly recalls dental hardening of postconsonantal [dj] as in:

(47)   HORDEU 'barley' > Rum. *orz*, Dalmatian (Vegliot) *vuarz*, Ital. *orzo*, Sard *ordzu*, R-R (Engadine) *uerdi*, Cat. *ordi* (but see French *orge* with [dʒ] > [ʒ]).

French anomalous developments in, for instance:

Hardening, either towards the dental or the palatal, can occur also with [nj]:

(48)   LINEU 'linen' > Sard *lindza* [dz], French *linge*, Old [dʒ] (cf. LINEA 'line'> French *ligne*, Span. *liña*, with [ɲ]).

The 'dental hardened' reflex can have the same outcome as [ndj]:

(49)   VERECUNDIA 'shame' > Sard *birgondza*, Span. *vergüenza* (but Old Span. *vergueña*, Ital. *vergogna*, French *vergogne*).

French anomalous developments in, for instance:

(50)   *sage* < *SAPIUS for SAPIENS 'wise' / *sache* < SAPIAT 'that he know'

may likewise result from differential resistance to voicing of voiceless consonants in clusters threatened by palatalization.

If we turn to consonantal clusters that are prone to palatalization we can also attribute differential development to greater or less resistance to the process. The -CT- cluster palatalizes completely in the Western languages, resulting either as [tʃ] or as [jt] with the glide usually absorbed into the preceding vowel:

(51)   FACTU 'fact, doing' > Span. *hecho*, Occ. *fach* / French *fait*, Ptg. *feito*.

In more conservative languages, however, the velar completely disappears, or is transmogrified into a labial:

(52)   Ital. *fatto*, Sard *fattu* / Rum. *fapt*.

Thus the Romance languages have diversified in their more-or-less conservative reaction to the palatalizing processes they all share, and which differentiate them from Latin. There seems to have been some resistance in nearly all languages to the 'Proto-' or pan-Romance assimilatory palatalization that ultimately could result in the complete disappearance of functional distinctions. Later palatalizing processes will be discussed in 6.3.

(c)   Grammar: nominals

Whereas Latin inflections have survived to a considerable extent in the Romance verb, Romance nominal organization has changed more radically. Coseriu (see 1.1), in characterizing the Romance prototype, has framed this in terms of 'internal' and 'external' relationships. Anything more relevant to the (internal or psychological) semantic import of an item – as with tense–aspect–mood modifications of the reporting of an event – will tend to be expressed 'internally', or morphologically, whereas relationships in the real (external) world, like between participants in an event, will be expressed 'externally', or syntactically. On the whole, the Romance languages use 'internal' (morphological) marks for the verb system and 'external' (syntactic) marks for the nominal system. In this section, we shall look at the latter, comparing Romance with Latin.

(i)   Cases

The Latin nominal case system marked morphologically the grammatical relationship of nouns to the verb, or to other nouns, within the clause. The term **case** is based on the metaphor of 'falling' away from the 'straight' form – the **nominative**, marking the subject argument of the verb, and seen as the unmarked citation form of the noun. The term **inflection** 'bending' partakes of a similar metaphor. The non-nominative forms are, in the same spirit, usually termed **oblique**. Although even in Latin grammatical information conveyed by case inflections could be supplemented by other devices, like use of prepositions, in the prestige language the use of bare case forms was regarded as more elegant and economical.

> Suetonius reports that the Emperor Augustus preferred less ambiguous preposi-
> tional uses. In later Latin texts the use of prepositions became more frequent.

The inflectional case system has virtually disappeared from modern
Romance and has been replaced by word-ordering conventions (as with
subject–object relationships) or by use of prepositions (as with dative,
genitive or locative relationships).

Morphological case has remained more intact in the pronominal system. From a functional point of view this is explicable if we recognize that
the semantic (or theta) role of a lexical noun is often fairly predictable
from its inherent semantic features: for instance, an animate is more likely
to be an agent or an experiencer, and so on. Pronouns, on the other hand,
convey only grammatical, not lexical, information, and thus may need to
be more clearly marked for such information.

The Latin nominal system marked five cases (leaving aside the vocative,
used in forms of address, and the locative, of which there were only relics)
and two numbers. **Syncretism** of forms meant that a maximum of eight of
the possible ten forms were distinctively marked. In Romance the singular
is usually distinguished from the plural, but remnants of the case distinctions are few.

(ii)   Relics of the Latin case system

Old French and Old Occitan had a nominal case system which seems
clearly derived largely from the Latin, but which distinguished morphologically only two cases, nominative and oblique, almost exclusively in the
masculine. Here are some examples of forms.

Nominal case in Old Occitan and Old French

	Singular		Plural	
nominative	*murs*	MURUS	*mur*	MURI
	paire / pedre(s)	PATER	*paire /pedre*	PATRES
	senher / sire	SENIOR	*senhor / seignor*	SENIORES
oblique	*mur*	MURUM	*murs*	MUROS
	pairel pedre	PATREM	*paires/pedres*	PATRES
	senhor / seignor	SENIOREM	*senhors /seignors*	SENIORES

A non-etymological -*s* marking the nominative singular extended in
French to other masculine nouns (like *charbons* < CARBO), and even to
feminines (like *maisons* < MANSIO). This was fairly frequent in Eastern

texts in the late thirteenth century. By this period, however, word-final [s] had been lost in some varieties, and hypercorrection may have played its part in the graphical spread of -*s*. The vitality of the imparisyllabic stem-alternating pattern is evidenced by its use in Germanic borrowings (like *ber/baron*), but it is almost wholly confined to human reference.

The case marking seems to have had little functional value, as nearly always in texts it is possible to deduce the thematic role of nouns from other factors, like word order or lexical constraints. Starting with the Western varieties, French had lost its nominal case system by the fourteenth century, usually via the disappearance of the nominative forms, so that the -*s* came to mark plurality, rather than case. In Occitan, too, prose texts in particular show signs of disintegration of the case system from quite an early period, but it survived rather longer than in French, persisting through the fourteenth century.

In some Alpine Romance varieties there remain traces today of Latin nominal case marking. Apart from isolated lexical items, relics of case are found in predicative masculine singular adjectives which usually inflect like plurals. This is most evident in Surselvan Rhaeto-Romance, for which there is some evidence in the earliest (seventeenth century) texts of a system illustrated below:

Old Surselvan adjectival inflection

	Singular		Plural	
nominative	*sauns*	SANUS	*sauni*	SANI
	mes	MEUS	*mei*	MEI
	clamaus	CLAMATUS	*clamai*	CLAMATI
oblique	*saun*	SANUM	*sauns*	SANOS
	miu	MEUM	*mes*	MEOS
	clamau	CLAMATUM	*clamaus*	CLAMATOS

The modern Surselvan masculine plural forms reflect the old oblique for adjectives (e.g. *sauns* 'healthy') and the old nominative for participles (e.g. *clamai* 'called'). This distinction is not retained in other Rhaeto-Romance varieties. The varieties in Italy generalize, like Italian, what may be a nominative plural form (e.g. *debli* = Ital. *deboli* 'weak'), whereas those in Switzerland generalize the oblique plural forms. In the masculine singular Surselvan however distinguishes predicative (i.e. post-copular) adjectives from adnominal ('epithet' or 'attributive') forms:

(53)   *Quei gat ei alvs / in gat alv* 'That cat is white' (ALBUS) / 'a white cat' (ALBUM); *Il cavagl ei vegls / in cavagl vegl* 'The horse is old' (VETULUS) / 'an old horse' (VETULUM).

For some common adjectives the Latin origin of the distinction is not so clear, as the adnominal, but not the predicative, form shows umlauting, suggesting a distinction between etymological forms with a high (U) versus a mid (O) final vowel:

(54)   *bien/buns* 'good' (BONU/BONOS?), *gries/gross* 'big' (GROSSU), *niev/novs* 'new' (NOVU), *miart/morz* 'dead' (MORTUU).

These forms suggest that it is the oblique plural, and not the nominative singular, form that has invaded the territory of the singular predicative adjective. Some traces of this distinction are found in other Rhaeto-Romance varieties, especially with possessives, though usually a distinction is retained between singular and plural forms.

It has been suggested that the Surselvan distinction between 'inflected' predicative and 'uninflected' adnominal adjectives owes much to the influence of German. However, similar distinctions are found in modern Alpine Francoprovençal varieties, which have not been in close contact with German. The best evidence we have for this was collected in the mid-1950s in the Savoy Maurienne valley which leads to the Modane tunnel into Italy, but for other Alpine valleys there are similar data. In general a distinction is made between an unmarked masculine singular form used not only as an adnominal but also with non-count nouns and impersonals, and the marked predicative form which usually is identical with the plural:

(55)   Saint-Martin-la Porte (Maurienne) *D amo pa lo lae frejt / I tro frejt / Lo lae frejt e pas bõ / Lo laez e frej / Lo pla sõ frej* 'I don't like cold milk (LACTE FRIGIDUM?) / 'It's too cold' / 'Cold milk isn't good' / 'The milk is cold' (LAC EST FRIGIDUS?) / 'The dishes are cold' (FRIGIDOS?).

Regular patterning in this variety clearly points to the predicative adjectival form being identical with the plural.

> The *z* [ts] which appears on the nominative count noun *laez* in example (55) is not, it seems, a case marker but a word-final consonant that is regularly elided in preconsonantal position:

(56)   *ũ bez anez* 'a fine lamb' / *ũ be voez* 'a fine calf'.

However, in neighbouring dialects there is evidence of residual retention of a noun case distinction. For instance, older informants in reciting fables might distinguish:

(57)   nom. *korbjo, rejno* / oblique *korbe, rejnot* 'crow, fox' (French *corbeau* < *corbels, renard* < *renart*).

It has been suggested that the present-day Surselvan distinction can best be regarded as one of gender rather than of case, with the predicative adjective marking three genders (m./f./n.), rather than two. In 1.3 we argued that parallel distinctions in Asturian and Abruzzo might better be treated as of case, and that Romance is characterized by a two-gender (m./f.) system. The Alpine evidence clearly shows that the marking originates in case distinctions which have survived residually.

How far they are functional today is hard to judge: perhaps here we have an example of exaptation (see 7.5).

(iii)   Nominative or oblique?

Received wisdom has it that the Romance noun is normally derived from the Latin accusative form, the singular of which is usually cited as the etymon. It is usually assumed that the accusative form was unmarked in Latin, especially in the later period. The -M accusative mark is known not to have been 'fully' pronounced even in prestigious Golden Age usage: final -M did not count as separating syllables in metrics and it was frequently omitted in graphy in both early and late texts. It is assumed that it was, at most, a graphical representation for nasalization of the preceding vowel, and that the nasal quality was lost in the Romance languages.

In some monosyllables it hardened again to a nasal consonant:

(58)   REM, MEUM > French *rien, mon* (with subsequent vowel nasalization); QUEM > Span. *quien.*

In the first (A-) declension, there is no way of knowing whether the ancestral form is the nominative (in -Ā), the accusative (in -AM) or, because of the regular loss of vowel length with this vowel, the ablative (in -Ā). In the second declension, 'Western Romance' merger of Ŭ and ō means that we cannot tell whether the ancestral form is the accusative or the dative–ablative. Umlauting dialects often however seem to derive their masculine singular forms from an Ŭ form (nominative or accusative) rather than an ō form:

(59)   Span. dial. (Asturias) *guetu* 'cat' / *gatos* 'cats'; Ital. dial. (Lucania) *mwertu/morta* 'dead' (m./f.).

Note that in Southern Italian dialects the plural marker (< ī) triggers umlauting.

As we have seen, the count/mass distinction of Asturian and South-Central Italian varieties may stem originally from a case distinction, with count forms from the nominative–accusative in ŭ, and mass forms from the dative–ablative in ō. The differential development of these two final vowels is shown in:

(60)   Asturias *ibiernu* 'winter' < HIBERNU / *como* 'how' < QUŌMODŌ; Central Ital. dial. (Trevi, Umbria) *corpu* 'body' / *oto* 'eight' < OCTŌ.

The best evidence that Romance nouns do not normally derive from the nominative Latin forms is provided by the third declension, where very frequently, mainly as a result of sound changes that occurred in Latin, the nominative singular stem is shorter than that of the rest of the paradigm. Nearly always it is the longer (oblique) form that seems to survive into Romance (see e.g. (52) in chapter 1 for LACTE, PONTE etc.). Other frequent pan-Romance words include:

(61)   PES, PEDIS 'foot' > Ital. *piede*, French *pied*; FLOS, FLORIS 'flower' > Rum. *floare*, Ital. *fiore*, Sard *flore*, French *fleur*, Occ., Cat. *flor* (Span. *flor*, Ptg. *frol* are probably loanwords).

However, it is not always possible to tell from the Romance forms which the ancestral Latin form was (see e.g. Span. *pie*, Ptg. *pe* 'foot'). Moreover, it seems certain that some frequent words, in some languages at any rate, derive from the Latin nominative: these are often nouns denoting human beings:

(62)   SOROR, SORŌRIS 'sister' > Rum. *sor(a)* Ital. *suora* 'nun', French *sœur*; PRESBYTER, PRESBYTERUM 'priest' > Rum. *preot*, Ital. *prete*, French *prêtre*, Cat., Span., Ptg. *preste*.

Sometimes both nominative and oblique forms are found:

(63)   HOMO 'man' > Rum. *om*, Ital. *uomo*, French *on* / HOMINIS > French *homme*, Span. *hombre*, Ptg. *homem*.

In many North Italian varieties many forms appear to be derived from the Latin nominative, suggesting that the case system survived longer here than further south.

(iv)   Differential object marking

Some Romance languages differentially distinguish the object of the verb from the subject by a special particle usually derived from a Latin preposition. The **prepositional accusative** (PA) is best known in modern Spanish, where it is also called the 'personal accusative' because it is used normally with human objects, which are usually particularized. It was found sporadically in Old Spanish but it became grammaticalized at the time of standardization of the language in the sixteenth and seventeenth centuries. It seems to be used in all varieties of Spanish, though there is some dialectal variation in its scope.

The marker is derived from directional AD ('to'), which is also used as a dative marker. Traditional Romance philology sees it as an extension, during the medieval period, of dative marking. This is also generally found more often with animates, which figure more frequently as 'recipients'. In some varieties the dative is distinguished from the PA by a differentiated pronoun copy (dative *le* / accusative *lo*, *la*: see 4.3):

(64)   *Lo vimos a Juan* 'We see [him to] John' / *Le damos a Juan un libro* 'We give [to-him to] John a book'

but *leísmo* (see 6.5) varieties do not make the distinction.

> It has been suggested that the *a* is required to assign case to the noun object in sentences where the verb has already assigned structural case to a clitic object. It is, however, obligatory with personal names, for instance, even where there is no clitic copy:

(65)   *No conozco a Pepe* 'I don't know Joe'.

A plausible explanation for the development of PA is that it picks out, as an object of the verb, a noun which might otherwise be understood, by virtue of its animacy and definiteness, as an agent and topic, in a language where constituent order does not unambiguously signal grammatical relations. Potential ambiguity was given as a reason for prescribing the use of PA in early Spanish grammars.

The occurrence of PA earlier, and more frequently, with pronouns, which are morphologically or lexically marked for case, however, suggests that the disambiguation argument does not hold water. Besides, PA is particularly frequent in dislocated topical expressions, usually echoed by a clitic pronoun. These circumstances lead some investigators to postulate that PA was originally a stylistic device, used to highlight an argument of the verb. Its use has also been linked to increased concern with the individual in the early Christian era, and it is seen as a proto-Romance innovation, consequent on the decay of the inflectional case system, designed clearly to differentiate the sentence roles of human agent and patient.

Certainly parallel uses are found in other Romance languages, though not as consistently as in modern Spanish. In Portuguese, after an upsurge of popularity of the construction during the seventeenth century, it is limited in its distribution. It may be that the reaction against Spanish influence during the period of standardization of Portuguese discouraged its propagation in prestigious usage. Galician has not participated in the Portuguese reaction and makes full use of PA.

In Catalan, too, where regular use of PA is frowned on, as a Castilianism, it is frequent, not only in 'street language', but also, for instance, in more traditional use in Majorca. In Western Occitan, especially in Bearnese, the construction is particularly frequent in popular speech (and is transferred to regional varieties of French). It is also a feature of Sard and of Southern and Central Italian dialects, and of Engadine Rhaeto-Romance.

> In some Rhaeto-Romance dialects the agglutination of AD to the third-person clitic pronoun *til* etc., may explain its unusual form.

In all these areas some reflex of AD is used as the accusative marker: in Catalan a prevocalic form *an* suggests a conjunction of IN + AD, found also in Gascon *ena*, whereas in North Italian immigrant dialect islands in Sicily we find *da*, suggesting a combination DE + AD. Other prepositions can, however, perform the same function. In Rumanian *pe* (< PER 'through') is fully grammaticalized in much the same way as in Spanish; sixteenth-century texts also used *spre* (< SUPER 'above'). As Rumanian varieties south of the Danube do not regularly use PA, it is usually assumed that it was a comparatively late development in literary Daco-Rumanian. In Old Portuguese, and today in some creoles, *para* could be used to mark the object, and today Kristang (see 2.2) uses *ku* from *con*.

Everywhere the marker is used preferentially with tonic personal pronouns (often with **clitic doubling** – see 4.4), with personal proper names and with singular nouns designating specific human beings. It is less often used with plurals or collective nouns and in some varieties (e.g. Sard, Corsican, Bearnese, Rumanian) it seems almost mutually exclusive with the definite article. In Sard, use of PA (with *a*) is obligatory with all definite accusative NPs without a determiner:

(66)   *Connosco a Juanna* / *a issa* 'I know Joan/her'; *Istimo a frate meu* 'I love my brother'; but *Amus visto* (*a) *unu pastore* / *sos sordatos* 'We've seen a shepherd / the soldiers'.

The fact that PA is not found in French (except in some peripheral nonstandard varieties) is seen as linked to the medieval retention of an inflectional nominative-oblique case-system (which was mainly operative for nouns denoting human males). It is claimed that the Occitan case system was probably of Eastern dialectal origin, while the Western dialects favoured PA. Particularly striking is the contrast between neighbouring Rhaeto-Romance dialects, with Surselvan having retained an inflectional case system, and Engadine developing PA.

(v)   Oblique case

Leaving aside the marking of personal accusatives by a preposition, most modern Romance languages have for nominals a **direct/oblique** system, where nominative and accusative (direct cases) are grouped together in face of other (oblique) cases which are normally marked by a preposition.

The Rumanian system is, however, inflectional, with most inflections dependent on an agglutinated definite article (or pronoun? – see below) differentiated for direct versus oblique (dative–genitive) case. Some Rumanian cases, however, do not depend wholly on definite-article inflection. The vocative in *-le* m., *-o* f., and *-lor* pl.:

(67)   *Radule!* 'Radu!', *Ano!* (/ *Ană!*) 'Anna!', *mamelor!* (/ *mame!*) 'mothers!'

is thought by some to be influenced by Slavonic. In the feminine too the articleless oblique singular in *-e* is identical with the plural and not with the direct singular in *-ă*:

(68)   *mamă* (nom. sg.) / *mame* (other cases).

This ending may derive from the Latin genitive in -AE.

Otherwise traces are rare of the Latin genitive case (which marks relationships between nouns, and seldom between noun and verb). In Latin, already, the inherited genitive -S had been replaced in the first and second declensions by -Ī (AI > AE, OI > Ī) except for a few relics (PATER FAMILIAS 'father of the family'), and it has no reflexes in Romance. Some traces of the plural flection -ŌRUM (< OS-UM) are to be found: in Sard possessive *issoro* (/ *de issos*), and in pronouns and determiners Rum. *lor*, Ital. *loro*, French *leur*.

In very early Old French isolated nominals (quasi-adjectival) are found:

(69)   *gens Francor* 'people of the Franks, Frankish people', *tens ancienor* 'times of the ancients, old times'.

Everywhere, except Rumanian, the directional preposition DĒ is used to indicate possession; it is also used as a partitive marker in some languages (see 6.5). It is rivalled to some extent by AD, which tends to be used with personal possessors in many varieties:

(70)   French *le livre à moi* 'the book belonging to me' / ns. *le livre à Jean* 'John's book'; Rum. *tată a trei copii* 'father of three children'.

For family relationships flectional genitive marking survived into some medieval varieties:

(71)   Old French *li fils* (nom.) *le rei* (oblique) 'the king's son'.

Everywhere except Rumanian uses the preposition AD to mark dative (recipient) function, which is not consistently distinguished from locational goal. In some languages, however, there is some tendency to distinguish, by different pronominal reference, true datives (as in *donner à* 'give to') from lexically determined dative use (which can often be linked to PA), as in *obéir à* 'obey (to)' and directional movement, as in *aller à* 'go to'.

The agent in passive constructions is marked by a preposition derived from PER (French *par*, Span. *por*) or DE (+ AB) (Ital. *da*).

(vi)   Pronominal case

As elsewhere, Romance pronouns are more apt to distinguish case than are nouns. We have seen that discourse pronouns continue on the whole the differentiated singular nominative and accusative case forms of Latin, and that there is some tendency to create new distinctions in the plural.

However, disjunctive forms for persons 3 and 6 usually do tend to distinguish nominative and accusative. Some originally nominative forms like Span. *él, ella*, Ptg. *êle, ela* and Rum. *el, ea, ei, ele* are used both as subject and as object of a preposition (although in Rumanian, directional prepositions often govern oblique case). In Italian the nominative forms:

(72)   *egli* m. sg. < ILLĪ; *eglino* pl. (with plural verb inflection?), *esso* etc. < IPSU etc., and *ello* etc. < ILLU etc. (the preferred Tuscan forms)

have largely given way to *lui, lei*, which were originally dative (see also French *lui* (< dative) / *elle, eux, elles* (< acc.)).

Dative case is marked on Rumanian disjunctive person 3 pronouns (*lui, ei, lor*) and on clitic person 3 pronouns nearly everywhere. The clitic dative singular forms, which are not marked for gender, derive from Latin distal demonstrative m. sg. dat. ILLĪ:

(73)   Ital. *gli*, Old French *li*

or a refashioned form *ILLIAE (with addition of a feminine dative ending?):

(74)   Span. *le* (< [lje]), Ptg. *lhe*

or *ILLUI (on the model of CUI 'to whom'):

(75)   French *lui*.

Plurals derive from ILLĪS (dat. pl.):

(76)   Sard *lis*, Span. *les*, Ptg. *lhes*

or from ILLŌRUM (gen. pl.):

(77)   Ital. *loro*, Occ. *lor*, French *leur*.

Few languages, however, distinguish the dative from the accusative in non-third-person clitic pronouns. Rumanian does so consistently, in the singular:

(78)   *îmi/mă*; *îţi/te*

and Galician distinguishes from the person 2 accusative *te*, a dative *che* (often used as an ethic dative or 'solidarity pronoun'):

(79)   *O veciño tróuxoche estas cereixas* 'The neighbour brought you these cherries'.

            Note that *che* is not used as a reflexive:

(80)   *Comprouche un sombreiro* 'He bought you a hat' / *Compracheste un sombreiro* 'You bought yourself a hat'.

            Far Western varieties of Galician use only *che* and far Eastern varieties only *te* as the person 2 clitic, in all contexts.

Those Swiss Rhaeto-Romance varieties which today use only disjunctive pronouns also made a distinction between person 2 dative and accusative clitics in old texts.

(vii)   The definite article

Loss of the Latin case system has often been linked in the history of Romance with another salient occurrence: the growth of the **definite article**. Usually the definite article is seen as a device for inserting the bare noun into the sentence, just as case did in Latin. Whereas the Latin noun had no phonological shape not associated with sentence role, in Romance the morphological noun conveys only lexical content (and presence or lack of plurality). Syntagmatic strategies are used to code grammatical relationships.

The definite article seems to have been used initially less as a **specifier**, picking out the individuality of the object designated by the noun, than as a **topicalizer**, anaphorically marking a noun that is accessible to the hearer. As in other languages, the function of the definite article widened as time went on, as it was used with nouns denoting unique objects and with abstracts, and to show **inalienable possession**, through a generic use to denote type rather than an individual, to become almost merely a gender and number marker for the noun. It is as fulfilling the last function that traditionally Romance grammarians have characterized the definite article.

In modern Romance the definite article is used with very high frequency: in French, in particular, it is one of a series of virtually obligatory determiners that indicate **nouniness** and mark gender and number. In creoles, on the other hand, the Romance definite article survives sporadically only as an integral part of the noun. Other means (for instance, a locational adverbial) are used to mark specificity or noun phrase status.

The use of the definite article has never failed to strike observers as an outstanding difference between Latin and Romance. Latin grammarians frequently remarked on the absence of an equivalent of the Greek article in their own language. It has often been suggested that the article arose in Christian Latin as a transfer from Greek; however, evidence from early Latin translations of the Greek New Testament shows no consistent representation of the Greek article.

As elsewhere, the initially anaphoric article usually derived from a **deictic (demonstrative)** pronoun, which indicated the locational position of the targeted noun. In most Romance languages the demonstrative which gave rise to the article was the distal pronoun ILLE, which also forms the base of the distal demonstrative (in all the Romance languages), reinforced by a preposed ECCE 'behold!':

(81)   Ital. *quello*, Rum. *acel*, Span. *aquel*, Ptg. *aquêle*, Old French *cil*, Sard *kuddu*.

ILLE also survives in all the languages as a person 3 pronoun. One question that we should pose is how the pronoun relates to the article, in form and function; for the phonological relationship between determiners and their cognate pronouns see 7.5.

One difference between pronoun and article is that normally the latter does not inflect for case. This does not hold for Rumanian or for Old French. In Rumanian the enclitic article is clearly related to the inflected disjunctive pronoun:

Rumanian nominal inflection

      ('mother(s)'/'son(s)')

	Singular	Plural
nominative–accusative		
f.	*mama* (*mamă* + *ea*)	*mamele* (*mame* + *ele*)
m.	*fiul* (*fiu* + *el*)	*fiii* (*fii* + *ei*)
genitive–dative		
f.	*mamei* (*mamă* + *ei*)	*mamelor* (*mame* + *lor*)
m.	*fiului* (*fiu* + *lui*)	*fiilor* (*fii* + *lor*)

In Old French the masculine nominative article, unmarked for number, is etymologically related to, but not identical with, the corresponding pronoun:

(82)   ILLĪ > article *li*, pronoun *il*

whereas the modern surviving article forms are the same as the clitic object pronouns:

(83)   *le, la, les.*

The only way these latter differ from each other today is that articles, but not pronouns, fuse with preceding prepositions:

(84)   *du < de le, des < de les.*

This distinction was unknown before the fourteenth century.

In some Swiss Rhaeto-Romance dialects a dative definite article – identical with the dative person 3 pronoun – is still in use:

(85)   (Surmeiran) *Zhi kwit li màma* 'Say this to [the] mother'.

In Alpine Francoprovençal an accusative definite article is also distinguished:

(86)   (Valais) [i fwa] 'the fire'(m.) / [əm prẽjo ɔ fwa] 'I light the fire'; [i ʧla] 'the key'(f.) / [tiɲo a ʧla] 'I hold the key'.

In most of the languages (but for Sard see below) the article closely resembles the person 3 object clitic pronouns. In Spanish the masculine singular is identical (except for a graphical accent) with the subject pronoun *el*. Here, as with Italian *il*, the difference probably derives from a phonologically determined variant that has been standardized, rather than as a case distinction (see 7.5). The normal masculine (or in *leísmo* dialects 'non-animate') object clitic form *lo* is specialized in Spanish as the 'neuter article' (see 1.2).

Another way in which the person 3 pronouns differ from the articles is that the latter normally accompany nouns, whereas the latter are attached to verbs. This is, however, not always so: articles can be used with adjectives, where there has been apparent deletion of the noun:

(87)   *le livre blanc et le rouge* 'the white book and the red one'.

   In Italian a demonstrative, not an article, is used in this context:

(88)   *quello rosso*

   while in Rumanian both are used:

(89)   *cel roşul.*

Moreover, in all of the languages at an earlier period, and still in some, the article/pronoun form can be used as a pronominal:

(90)   Span. *la que buscas*, Ptg. *a que procuras* 'the [woman] you are looking for'; R-R (Engadine) *ils de Samedan* 'the [people] of Samedan'; Sard (Nuoro) *su ki keljo* 'the [thing] I want'; Old French *la sa mère* 'the [soul] of his mother'.

Thus the differences between article and pronoun are less pronounced than usually assumed, and it is no wonder that nearly all early Romance grammarians, and some present-day ones, see them as distributional variants. In particular, it is suggested that they fill the function of agreement markers, cliticized to noun or verb.

(viii)   IPSE as an article

Sard here seems to present a special case. The Sard article derives from the 'identifying' particle IPSE 'himself etc.':

(91)   *su, sa, sos, sas*

as do the disjunctive third person pronouns:

(92)   *issu, issa, issos, issas.*

Clitic object pronouns, on the other hand, continue, as in all other Romance languages, ILLE forms:

(93)   *lu, la, los, las.*

Some Catalan varieties also make use of both IPSE and ILLE article forms, but only ILLE pronominal forms. No Romance language uses an IPSE form as third-person non-reflexive clitic object pronoun; if they did, it would be likely to be confused with reflexive SE forms.

> There is evidence that IPSE article forms were once more widespread, though confined mainly to the 'central' Romance area, and popular in character. One factor that could have worked against the retention of IPSE articles elsewhere was their potential homonymy with SUUS 'weak' possessives. In modern Sard only 'strong', adjectival possessives (see 6.5) are found, but in Catalan varieties which use IPSE articles, the weak 'determiner' possessive, in the feminine singular form *sa* at least, can indeed be confused with the article. However, the weak possessive is in modern times restricted to use with the nouns denoting close kinship: the semantic difference between *sa mare* in its two possible senses ('the/his mother') is negligible.

We may well ask why IPSE should have been ousted in most of the Romance area. Such textual evidence as we have suggests that by the Late Latin period it had become the preferred adnominal identifying particle, and was ousting IS in its anaphoric function. ILLE , which had in classical times been less frequent, had become the deictic of choice, as the proximal HIC lost ground, but it was still used more often pronominally than adnominally.

It seems that IPSE became more identified with subject arguments and participant-orientated functions, while distal demonstrative ILLE referred more to third-person objects. Texts confirm that usually IPSE shows a more decided preference for nominative case. As modern Romance lexical nouns stem mainly from accusative Latin forms, it would not be surprising if they prompted a distal 'object' anaphor.

> What is puzzling is that some varieties prefer the IPSE forms for the definite article. Whether indeed this choice is accompanied by other relevant morphological or syntactic differences requires further investigation. In Sard we might look to such features as the use of the definite article in vocatives, the great frequency of clitic doubling, with left or right dislocation of the object NP –

which suggests that the NP may be syntactically detached from the sentence –
the tendency to non-use of the determiner in predicate nominals; and prepositional marking of object nominals.

(d)   Verbs

It is in the verbal system that Romance languages are said most clearly to
reflect their Latin origin, and their close relationship to one another. We
shall here examine some aspects of verb morphology which illustrate
these relationships.

(i)   Conjugation system

Latin regular verbs were organized into four conjugation types according
to the **thematic vowel** that linked the **root** (the lexical element) with the
inflection. The thematic vowels were Ā, Ē, Ĕ and Ī. Only the Ā-conjugation
remained truly productive in all the Romance languages, though the Ī-con-
jugation welcomed new words in earlier periods. The two E-conjugations
have tended to coalesce: reasonably well differentiated three conjugation
systems persist in Central Italian, Friulian and Bearnese-Aragonese.
Rumanian is the only language to retain four conjugations (a fifth in *î* represents a phonetic variant of the *i*-conjugation) but some of the forms that
make the distinction – like the **preterite** – are not in common use. The most
usual organization of the verbal system allows for two conjugations – *a*
and *i* most frequently – but French distinguishes them in comparatively
few forms. The **infinitive**, used as the citation form, is usually the most differentiated; person 5 forms come a close second. Latin Ĕ-verbs are among
the most frequent, and can survive as **irregular** forms or are incorporated
into another conjugation:

(94)   DĪCĔRE 'to say': French, Ital. *dire*, Span. *decir*; FACĔRE 'to do': French *faire*,
Ital. *fare*, Cat. *fer*.

Note that ESSE 'to be' seems to have been incorporated into this conjugation in
Proto-Romance.

The Ē-verbs figure prominently among auxiliaries and modals:

(95)   HABĒRE 'to have', DEBĒRE 'to have to'; also *VOLĒRE 'to want' for VELLE,
*POTĒRE 'to be able' for POSSE, *SAPĒRE 'to know' for SAPĔRE.

All the Romance languages make use of an -SC- infix, originally with inchoative force, in some verbs. In Spanish, Portuguese and Sard it is totally lexicalized and occurs through the relevant paradigms:

(96)   Span., Ptg. *fenecer* < FINĪRE 'to finish', *padecer* < *PATĪRE (PATĪ) 'to suffer'; Sard *albeskere* 'to dawn' < *ALBĪRE 'to whiten' (see Rum. *albí*).

         In Latin some inchoative forms were already lexicalized:

(97)   NŌSCŌ 'I come to know' / NŌUĪ 'I knew'.

In other languages the affix appears only in certain forms: the vast majority of verbs in the *i*-conjugation are affected, but the choice of verb is unpredictable:

(98)   French *finissons* 'we finish' / *finir* 'to finish', Ital. *finisco* 'I finish' / *finiamo* 'we finish'; Rum. *pătesc/pătim*, Cat. *pateix/patim* 'I / we suffer'.

         In Swiss Rhaeto-Romance the infix is also used in the *a*-conjugation:

(99)   Engadine *gratulesch* 'I congratulate' / *gratuler* 'to congratulate'.

         Another affix (< -IDIO, of Greek origin) is used in Rumanian, and in some Southern Italian varieties, in about half the verbs of the *a*-conjugation:

(100)   Rum. *lucrez/lucrează/lucrăm* 'I/he/we work(s)'.

The advantage of these affixes was that they facilitated regularization of paradigm stress placement. In the verbs affected the stress fell regularly on the syllable following the lexical root, which consequently showed no **apophony** (see 7.3). Compare:

(101)   French *meurt/mourons*, Ital. *muore/moriamo* '(he) dies / (we) die' (< *MORĪRE for MORĪ), alongside French *abolit/abolissons*, Ital. *abolisce/aboliamo* '(he) abolishes / (we) abolish' (< *ABOLĪRE for ABOLĒRE, ABOLESCERE); Rum. *omoară/omorîm* '(he) kills / (we) kill', alongside *uraşte/urîm* '(he) hates / (we) hate' (< HORRĪRE, for HORRESCERE, HORRĒRE, or ŌDĪRE, for ŌDISSE) for (< ŌDĪRE).

Thus, though the lexical material of the Romance conjugation systems is nearly all of Latin origin, the overall organization has changed considerably, mainly in the direction of simplification, but also of stem elaboration, of suppletion and of lexicalization. A consequence is that the Romance conjugation systems share a good many features not present in Latin, some of which may be Proto-Romance.

(ii)   Infectum and perfectum

As described by Varro (*c.* 116–37 BC), Latin verb morphology has as a basic feature the difference between the present (INFECTUM 'unfinished') and perfect (PERFECTUM 'completed') stem. The latter normally is an extension or modification of the former (as in AMA-/AMAU-, CRED-/CREDID- or FAC-/FEC-), though in some verbs there is **suppletion** (as in ES-/FU). The association of the forms respectively with **imperfective** or **perfective** aspect holds only to a certain degree: there is no distinct form equivalent to the Greek **aorist**, and its functions are filled by the present, or historic, perfect (AMĀUI) . The present stem has three finite **indicative** tenses – **present** (the timeless unmarked form), **future** and **past**. These two last both have a -B- affix (AMĀBO /AMĀBAM, VIDĒBO/VIDĒBAM) which probably derived from a form of the verb 'to be'. The Ĕ- and Ī-conjugations, however, have no -B- in the future (REGAM/REGĒBAM, DORMIAM/DORMIĒBAM): the asymmetry may be one factor that accounts for the complete disappearance of the Latin future from the Romance languages (see 4.5). The other two present-stem indicative forms – the present and the past imperfect – survive in all the Romance languages. Of the two parallel **subjunctive** forms the present survives everywhere; the imperfect subjunctive (AMĀREM) disappears, or perhaps develops as a **personal infinitive** (see 4.3). The imperative forms that survive in Romance usually mirror the equivalent indicative forms.

The perfect-stem forms have a more chequered career. The present perfect (AMĀUI) survives with **preterite** (punctual past) functions, especially in Western Iberian, Occitan and Southern Italian varieties, but only marginally in French, Catalan, Rumanian and northern Italy, being lost completely in Sard and some other varieties (see below). In its present perfect functions it is replaced nearly everywhere by **compound** forms (see below). The future perfect (AMĀUERO) merges with the perfect subjunctive (AMĀUERIM) and survives marginally as a future subjunctive (see 3.4). The pluperfect subjunctive (AMĀUISSEM) is used as a past subjunctive form in several languages, and in some areas is rivalled in this function by the pluperfect indicative (AMĀUERAM), which only marginally retains any pluperfect function, usurped in most places by a compound form. Some languages have kept a greater number of Latin verb-forms than others; for discussion of relative conservatism in Romance see 7.7.

Each of the active Latin forms had a passive equivalent. In the present-stem forms all were marked by an -R (possibly originally a nominalizing suffix). All of these were lost in Romance, which favoured the compound perfect forms (AMĀTUS SUM etc., but see 4.7).

Thus the Romance verb system, although using inherited material, is fundamentally different from that of Latin. It is usually assumed that the introduction of the new compound perfects and the loss of the Latin future and present-stem passives were effected at the Proto-Romance stage. Other changes are thought to have happened after the split-up of the languages, sometimes in parallel and sometimes as a result of inter-influence between the languages.

(iii)   The 'imperfect'

The Latin, and hence Romance, name given to the AMĀBAM forms is something of a mistranslation of the Greek equivalent (*paratatikós*), which implied not unfinished action, but an action on which no time limits are placed by the speaker. It survives in every Romance language (and even in some creoles) as a past tense, with unmarked semantic characteristics that allow for a range of discourse interpretations. Most usually it is seen as implying continuous or habitual action in the past, but it also takes on almost modal nuances, some of which hint at some distancing of the speaker from the action, as in indirect speech or conditionals. It can also be used as a conscious stylistic device to give an impressionistic tinge to narrative description. It is a tense that is comparatively little used in colloquial styles, and is found more often in subordinate than in main clauses.

The Romance forms of the imperfect are not, however, straightforward reflexes of the Latin forms. The A-conjugation endings from -ABA- are comparatively unproblematic, but the other conjugations have clearly not developed regularly. The I-conjugation in Latin was already out of line, with its -IEBA- endings; the -IBA- type endings of central Italian varieties (and of Aragonese-Bearnese and Friulian) may be survivals of a pre-classical type, or reformed to a three-conjugation pattern:

(102)   Ital. *cantava, vedeva, dormiva* 'he sang, saw, slept'.

Old texts support the latter hypothesis, but they may be influenced by other B-less varieties – Sicilian, for Italian, and Castilian, for Aragonese.

What is particularly odd, though, is the irregular loss of the Latin -B- in the E- and I-conjugations: a frequent pattern is of two endings -ABA- and -IA- (found in the Iberian peninsula, southern France and much of Italy):

(103)   Cat., Ptg., Occ. *cantava*, Span. *cantaba* / Occ. *vezía*, Cat., Span. *veía*, Ptg *via* /
Cat., Ptg., Occ., Span. *dormía*.

In northern France the one surviving imperfect ending (older *-oi-*, *-ei-*, modern *-ai-*) is assumed to derive from -EBA-, with irregular loss of -B- (earlier *oe-*, *-eve-* from -ABA- having fallen out of use):

(104)   *chantait, voyait, dormait.*

> The text-book story that the loss of -B- was by analogy with a postulated dissimilatory fall of the second -B- in HABEBAT never carried much conviction, and indeed originated only in a tentative suggestion.

A more promising line of enquiry may be to recognize that in early Romance intervocalic -B- (which merged with consonantal U [w] as [β]) tended to fall, as it did regularly in Rumanian and some other varieties:

(105)   Rum. *cîntá, videá, dormeá.*

We can then ask why it should have been retained (or restored) in some circumstances.

There is certainly a correlation between the maintenance of a three-conjugation system and -ABA-/-EBA-/-IBA- type endings. There is also some indication that the -B- mark may have been reinforced, in some languages, as an aspectual marker to distinguish the imperfect from the preterite. These are often languages in which the compound perfect coexists, in aspectual contrast, with the simple preterite.

In other cases, however, it seems that the preterite and the imperfect have tended to merge, as the temporal aspects of the forms were emphasized; in these circumstances the imperfect -B- marker would be more likely to fade away. Signs of merger are found in southern Italy and in older varieties in the Iberian peninsula and southern France.

Modern French may, as elsewhere, represent a special case. Here the formal homogeneity of the tense was reinforced by the analogical spread of a single marker through the conjugation system. In the spoken language the compound, originally perfective, form is the only other past tense. It is the quasi-modal, aspectual, and not the temporal flavour of the imperfect that comes to the fore. The 'fuzzy' passe-partout character of the French imperfect may well be reflected in its morphology, which stresses the homogeneity of the tense, rather than the morphological conjugation class of the lexical verb.

Another feature of the imperfect paradigms is that in persons 4 and 5 accentuation on the ending, as in Latin, is retained in Italian, French, Old Occitan and Sard, but elsewhere the accent has moved back on to the theme vowel, which is thus accented throughout the paradigm.

(iv)   The compound perfect

Nearly all the Romance languages make some use of a **compound perfect** consisting of the present tense of an auxiliary verb and an originally passive participial form (AMATUS 'loved' etc.). In traditional grammar this compounded form often has a name that implies a semantic import: in Italian *passato prossimo* 'near past', in French *parfait* 'perfect' or Spanish *pretérito perfecto* 'past perfect', in Portuguese *pretérito perfeito indefinido* 'indefinite past perfect'. But a name which refers to the form – implying the compounding of two verbs – is sometimes preferred: *perfectul compus*, *passé composé*. Everywhere the auxiliary also can appear with tense forms other than the present, with functions of, for instance, **pluperfect** or **future in the past** etc.

Some apparent ancestral constructions are attested in Latin. The transition seems to have been something like:

(106)   HABEO LITTERAS SCRIPTAS 'I have (got) letters written' > Ital. *Ho le lettere scritte* > *Ho scritto le lettere* 'I have written the letters'.

Originally this sentence could imply that the letters that I have, had been written by someone else. **Grammaticalization** of the sequence involves a reanalysis by which the subject of the finite verb is necessarily assumed to be the subject of the participle, which is interpreted as active rather than passive. The two verb forms thus amalgamate to the equivalent of a simple verb form, and come to be used with intransitive verbs; for the selection of a *HAVE* or *BE* auxiliary for these see pages 15–24.

The amalgamation is most complete in modern Spanish, where intercalation of elements between the auxiliary and the past participle is very rare. *Haber*, having ousted *ser* as the auxiliary of unaccusatives, has virtually lost its original lexical meaning of 'to have, to possess', in which sense it is replaced by *tener* 'to hold'. In many other varieties the retention of the *BE* auxiliary for certain verbs, and the possibility of agreement of the past participle with an expressed object, seems to indicate less complete grammaticalization (see 6.5).

In southern Italy and Western Iberian (including Latin America) the compound perfect is little used. In colloquial Portuguese (as in some Southern Italian varieties) *ter* < TENĒRE 'to hold' has completely replaced earlier *haver*, as an auxiliary as well as a lexical verb. The Portuguese compound does not in the indicative have the same present perfect functions as other Romance forms, but is used to indicate continuing, just completed or repeated actions in the recent past:

(107)   *Tenho feito muitas veces esse trabalho* 'I've done this work many times'; *Tenho*
         acabado o meu discurso 'I've got my talk over'; *Tenho estado doente* 'I've been
         ill (lately)'.

In the medieval varieties of both Spanish and Portuguese, TENĒRE reflexes competed with those of more frequent HABĒRE as perfect auxiliaries. Although the Spanish *tener* forms gained ground until the seventeenth century, they were not usually found in intransitive constructions, and the movement towards their grammaticalization was slowed down at the time of standardization of the state language, perhaps because arbiters perceived a difference of meaning between the competing forms. In the modern standard *tener* + *participle* constructions are not completely grammaticalized, usually involving participial agreement with the object, and they tend to be constrained lexically, appearing to retain some remnants of the semantic content of *tener*, implying possession or duration. In Portuguese, on the other hand, although *haver* forms were more frequent in the earlier texts, *ter* forms began to outnumber them by the early modern period, triumphing at the time of standardization. More or less simultaneously non-agreement with expressed objects became regular.

The Romance compound form was originally used only to indicate actions completed in the present, compared with the narrative simple past preterite form, which carries names like 'remote past', 'past definite' or 'past historic'. However, in many modern Romance varieties, the compound forms have replaced the simple past forms in colloquial speech. This can be seen as a shunning of the morphological complexities of the simple past (see 7.3), as part of a general drift towards analytic constructions, or as connected with the emphasis on the here and now in colloquial usage. It is assumed that the process was completed only comparatively recently as standard literary languages retain the older distinction.

In spoken standard Italian and Spanish the semantic distinction between the simple and compound forms persists. To some extent this distinction may be regarded as somewhat literary. In those varieties in which the simple form persists – for example, in Latin America and southern Italy – it is much more frequent and unmarked semantically, with the compound form tending to be reserved to refer to events in the immediate past.

> In the Spanish of the Andes the past tense of the compound form (pluperfect) seems to imply lack of personal commitment to the statement made, rather than past timing:

(108)   (Bolivia) *y en nada habían encontrado trabajo* 'and they haven't found work (apparently)'; *Habían sabido fumar* 'They *do* smoke (I gather)'.

> This usage is to be compared with that of the future or conditional perfect in some other languages:

(109)   French *Elle aura fait cela* 'She did that (apparently)', *L'accusé aurait tué trois personnes* 'The defendant (allegedly) killed three people'.

In some languages – in Occitan varieties and in the Oltenian dialect of Rumania, for instance – it is held that the compound is limited to reference to events that have taken place on the same day as the act of speech. Seventeenth-century French grammarians drew up a similar 'twenty-four-hour' rule for standard French, but it is not clear how far this was reflected in actual usage. Usually, however, the distinction between an event that took place in the past and one that was completed by the present has been lost in colloquial speech. Western Iberian and Southern Italian varieties, I repeat, cleave to the simple form, whereas most others use only the compound form for unmarked past reference. In modern spoken French and Northern Italian varieties, where the compound past has definitively triumphed, the preterite is nevertheless sometimes retained with stylistic force for certain types of narrative and so carries prestige as a quaint rarity.

> We should mention the use in some varieties of the *surcomposé* forms, like:

(110)   *J'ai eu fait* 'I have had done', for **pluperfect** *J'avais fait* or **past anterior** *J'eus fait* 'I had done'.

> In French the form is regarded as non-standard, although it has a respectable history. Similar forms are current in those other varieties that use the compound perfect.

(e)   Vocabulary

Although nearly all common Romance words are of Latin origin, we should note that not all common Latin words survived as popular forms into Romance. One count shows that 104 out of a list of some 5,000 'representative' Latin words disappeared completely from the inherited vocabulary. The following list gives some examples of common Latin words that were lost in Romance, and of their replacements.

Romance replacements for some common Latin words

AUXILIUM	'help': *ADJUTARE a derivative of IUVERE 'to help' gives nominal forms in all the languages.
DISCERE	'to learn': AD-PREHENDERE 'to get a hold of' gives most Romance forms. Ital. *imparare* is derived from PARARE 'to prepare'. Rum. *a învăţa* seems to be derived from VITIU 'vice' (presumably meaning 'to eradicate vice').
FIERI	'to become': the usual Romance word is from a derivative of 'to come' DE-VENIRE. It is possible that the Rumanian *fi* form ('to be') is from a corruption of FIERI.
HIEMS	'winter': the adjectival form HIBERNU is pan-Romance.
LOQUI	'to speak': FABULARE, NARRARE, PARABOLARE, RATIONARE are among the Latinate forms that have replaced the classical word.
MEMINISSE	'to remember': MEMORARE 'to call to mind' is the most widespread word, but formations from MENTE 'mind' and CORDE 'heart' are also frequent. SUB-VENIRE 'to come to aid' supplies, in reflexive form, Italian and French words.
PUER	'boy': French *garçon* is of Frankish origin, and has spread to Occitan. Span. *mozo*, *muchacho*, Ptg. *moço* are of uncertain origin: etyma proposed include words for 'young (of wine)', and 'close-cropped (of hair)'. Span. *chico* (also in Ital. dial.), *niño*, Cat. *nen*, *nin*, Ptg. *menino* may be playful in origin. Ptg. *rapaz* is from RAPACE 'rapacious', *mancebo* from MANCIPIUS 'slave'. Cat. *noi* and Ital. *ragazzo* are of unknown origin. Ital. *fanciullo* is possibly a derivative of *fante* < INFANTE. Rum. *tînar* is from TENERU 'tender'.
RUS	'countryside': most languages use some form of CAMPU 'field'. Rum. prefers *ţară* < TERRA.

Many of the lost words were replaced by other forms apparently of Latin origin, and most were reimported in some form as Latinisms:

(111)   French *auxiliaire* (AUXILIUM), *bellicose* (BELLUM), *civil* (CIVIS), *disciple* (DIS-CERE), *puerile* (PUER), *rural* (RUS, RURIS).

3.4   LATIN INFLUENCE

As we have seen, the legacy that Latin bequeathed to Romance is not limited to what is handed down from generation to generation by continuous transmission. Indeed what look to the superficial observer the most obvious shared features of the languages are sometimes quite late innovations. This applies to some apparent shared grammatical features, which may have become established in the standard languages by the work of grammarians schooled in the Latin tradition, but most especially to 'learned' vocabulary that was incorporated into each of the languages more intensively at some periods than others, and which supplemented or even displaced inherited lexical items.

(a)   Spelling

Even where differences of pronunciation mask the similarities between Romance languages, their similar spelling conventions usually enable speakers of one Romance language fairly easily to read another. All the Romance languages, even the Rumanian of ex-Soviet Moldavia (Moldova), use the Latin alphabet: Daco-Rumanian abandoned the Cyrillic alphabet in the nineteenth century, when it was asserting its individuality in face of its Balkan neighbours, and Moldavian switched only since the collapse of the USSR.

Each of the languages developed methods of representing sounds that did not exist in Latin. The letter *h* proved a useful diacritic, as the letter was not sounded in Latin: thus *ch* could denote [tʃ] or [ʃ], as in Spanish, French, Occitan and Portuguese (but [k] in Italian), and *lh*, *nh* could be used for [ʎ], [ɲ], as in Portuguese. *H* alone could be used for the new Castilian sound that developed from Latin F (probably originally [ɸ], then [h] until it became silent in the sixteenth century). It must have had a similar use in Old French in *hors* < FORIS 'outside' (cf. Ital. *fuora*), and it was also used for Germanic [h] as in *hâche* 'axe' < Frankish **hapja*. Today, in most varieties, this is, like Latin H, silent, but it prevents elision of a preceding vowel:

(112)   *la hâche* / *l'habit* < HABITUS 'style of dress'.

Other superfluous letters that are frequently brought into play are z and x, of Greek origin: the former is used for dental affricates [ts] or [ts] in Old French and Old Spanish, and [dz] or [dz] in Italian; the latter for *us* in Old French, and for [ʃ] in Catalan. Use is also made of *j* and *v*, graphical variants of I and U, to represent non-Latin sounds like [dʒ] and [v].

Usually spelling harks back to the Latin form, even when the pronunciation has changed, so Spanish or Catalan *ll*, Old French *ill*, and Italian *gl* should be read as [ʎ], reflecting generalization of spelling of ancestral forms. French shows vowel nasalization by postposition of *n*, whereas Portuguese superposes the tilde, which was originally an abbreviation for a nasal consonant. Other diacritics include a miniature *s* – *cedilla* – under the Latin etymological letter, to indicate assibilation, as in French *ç* or Rumanian *ţ*, and the Spanish tilde used in *ñ*, indicating an etymological geminate, pronounced as [ɲ].

Modern spelling reforms introduce other diacritics like the circumflex ˆ, which in French indicates the loss of an etymological letter, and in Rumanian the centralizing of *i* [ɨ]. (Note that the older graphy *â* is retained in the name of the language *român* to underline its 'Roman' status.)

The spelling, in the languages that used writing in medieval times, reflects the various conventions used in monastic scriptoria, which were more used to copying Latin texts than composing vernacular ones. Reforms, from the sixteenth century on, were usually designed to bring the spelling nearer to the spoken word, often by eliminating superfluous etymological letters and by standardizing the graphy for a particular phoneme.

Languages that saw rapid phonological change, like French or Portuguese, have been driven to make successive minor reforms, while others, like Spanish and Italian, retain more or less their Renaissance appearance. Always reforms have been bridled by the desire to retain a patent link with Latin, which, for all but Rumanian, remained the prestige language of religion and learning.

(b)   Grammar

It is easy enough to point to the controlling hand of Latin in Romance spelling. More difficult is to estimate the extent of Latin influence on grammar. Naturally, metalinguistic discussion was, until very recent times, wholly couched in terms of the Graeco-Latin tradition. Grammarians would talk as if the vernaculars had nominal case systems – though the manifestations would usually rely on prepositions – and verbal perfective and imperfective systems. They would emphasize the requirement of complete recitable paradigms and a whole array of tenses in the verb system.

Grammar would be seen as almost identical with morphology, and inflected forms would be seen as somehow superior, more elegant than analytic sequences with similar functions. There would be insistence on accurate agreement in number and gender, as necessary to signal relationships of units within the sentence – even though in Romance, unlike literary Latin, word order usually carries the burden of this function. When in doubt, traditional grammarians would turn to Latin models in order to describe, explain or even distort features of their vernaculars.

Most important, they sought, for their own languages, to recapitulate the prestigious status of Latin, incorporating into them the values associated with good Latinity – concision, elegance, clarity, musicality. In Dante's term, the *volgare illustre* (the illustrious vulgar tongue) had to aspire to the standing of Latin, in order to be acceptable as a language of culture.

How far, however, the grammarians influenced everyday usage is difficult to assess. In French, it is a commonplace to point to the wide discrepancy between standard *soigné* style and racy street idiom. This may have existed since the mid-seventeenth century. In Italian the standard is often said to have remained static since the sixteenth century or even earlier: it is usually contrasted with spoken dialectal usage. In Spanish the standard, firmly based on the innovating dialect of Castile, has been regulated since the late sixteenth century. Standard Portuguese asserted its independence from Spanish a little later. In the peninsula, though, other Romance varieties have remained vigorous to the present day.

The morphological similarities between Latin and Romance can, as we have seen, be regarded as consequential on uninterrupted development over time. In syntax, however, there are modern uses which one suspects might not have survived without the buttress of Latinate grammar. Let us examine three possible examples: use of the subjunctive, the 'accusative and infinitive' and negation.

(i)   Subjunctive

As we have seen, the forms of the Latin present subjunctive **mood** survive in all the languages – however, not without a good deal of syncretism with the indicative. In Rumanian it is marked mainly by the special complementizer *să* (< SI). Other tenses of the Latin subjunctive were less resistant. In spoken French, for instance, where the present subjunctive is differentiated from the indicative only in comparatively few forms, the 'imperfect' or past subjunctive has ceased to be used – though still learned as a written form.

In all the languages a 'past' subjunctive derives from the Latin pluperfect subjunctive:

(113)   (CANT)-Ā(UI)SSET > Rum., Span. -*ase*, Ital., Ptg. -*asse*, Old French -*ast*, modern -*ât*, Cat. -*és*, R-R (Engadine) -*éss*.

> In Spanish and Portuguese it is rivalled by forms deriving from the pluperfect indicative (see 7.5). In Catalan there is also a 'perfect' subjunctive compounded with the *GO* auxiliary. In some Francoprovençal varieties the etymological past subjunctive has virtually ousted present subjunctive forms.

In Portuguese, and in older Spanish (dying out in the eighteenth century), there is also a 'future subjunctive', deriving from what seems to have been a merger between the Latin future perfect indicative (e.g. -ĀVERO) and the perfect subjunctive (-ĀVERIM) – Span. -*are*, Ptg -*ar*. It can be questioned whether it does indeed refer to events in the future, or rather to those that could occur earlier than some specified reference point of time:

(114)   Ptg. *Quando chegar, eu vou sair* 'When he arrives, I'll go'.

> In Portuguese and Galician the future subjunctive is identical for regular verbs with the 'personal infinitive', which tends to replace it in uneducated speech (see 4.2). In Galician a present subjunctive would be used in (114), as in Spanish.

Some see the subjunctive as having essentially timeless reference, expressing the speaker's lack of commitment to the reality of the event mentioned. Others point to the emotive import of the subjunctive, expressing the attitude of the speaker to the event he reports, or conveying optative or volitive nuances. In any case, differences of tense form depend automatically on sequence conventions, and not on real time setting of the event reported. Use of the 'past' subjunctive can in some languages imply a greater distancing of the speaker with regard to the veracity of the report.

All the core Romance languages do show indicative/subjunctive distinctions, however minimally. Descriptions in traditional grammars, which particularly cherish the distinctions, usually claim that use, with **optative**, **voluntative** or **potential** semanticism, has remained virtually unchanged since Latin.

Romance now scarcely uses the subjunctive in main clauses, however. It survives best as an optative in person 3 'imperatives':

(115)   Ital., Span. (¡)*Venga*! 'Let him come!' (or polite 'Come!')

and in negative imperatives in the Iberian languages:

(116)   Span. *¡No vengas!*, Cat. *No vingui!*, Ptg. *Não venhas!* 'Don't come!'

In some languages person 3 imperatives are accompanied by a complementizer, in keeping with the intuition that they are governed by an underlying verb of command:

(117)   French *Qu'il vienne!*, Rum. *Să vină!*, Cat. *Que vingui!*, '[I command] that he
          come'.

In general, the Romance subjunctive is a form used principally in subordinated clauses, reflecting some Latin uses more faithfully than others. In
many cases it can be viewed as merely an agreement feature, a *servitude
grammaticale*, which serves to reinforce the semanticism of the governing
verb or conjunction, usually implying volition or the lack of certainty
inherent in anticipated events.

In other cases the choice seems one of style, with the subjunctive adding
a certain air of elegance to the subordinated postposition. This is particularly so, for some languages, after verbs indicating pleasure, anger, fear
and the like. Sometimes, where the choice of mood is prescribed by standard grammars, the actual verbs involved may differ:

(118)   Ital. *Spero che venga*, French *J'espère qu'il viendra* 'I hope he'll come'.

          In the Iberian languages *esperar* may be translated as 'to hope, to wait for' when
          followed by the subjunctive, and 'to expect' when followed by the indicative:

(119)   Span. *Espero que venga / vendrá.* 'I'm waiting for him to come,' 'I hope he'll
          come' / 'I expect him to come.'

          With verbs of saying and thinking, where Latin used the accusative and infini-
          tive construction, a finite verb clause is used in Romance, and choice of the
          subjunctive adds a nuance of doubt about the subordinated statement. In
          French, hesitation in usage, even at the time of standardization of the lan-
          guage, led to the formulation that the subjunctive be used after the negative or
          the interrogative (but not the negative interrogative). In the colloquial lan-
          guage only the indicative is used.

One construction where the subjunctive has semantic import is in restrictive relatives, where the antecedent is understood as non-referential when
a subjunctive follows:

(120)   Ital. *Cerco una ragazza che sappia (/ sa) il francese*; Span. *Busco una chica que sepa
          (/sabe) el francés*; French *Je cherche une fille qui sache (/sait) le français*, Rum.
          Caut o fată să (/care) ştie francez. 'I'm looking for girl who knows French'.

In French this sort of distinction is rarely made in the colloquial language, where the subjunctive is automatically used after volition verbs, but other-wise occurs rather erratically in the usage of uneducated speakers. In Italian there is, to a lesser extent, a tendency for the subjunctive to be avoided in many contexts. In these standard languages, it may be that the dead hand of Latin has forced the retention of a range of uses.

In the Iberian standards and in some non-standard dialects, on the other hand, the subjunctive seems to have retained more vitality in spoken usage, and it is difficult to say whether Latin has had the same sort of influence. In Rumanian, where Latin influence must be discounted, subjunctive finite complement clauses are used where other languages prefer an infinitive (see 4.3); here the influence of neighbouring Greek seems to be the culprit.

It can of course be maintained that the sort of context in which the sub-junctive is used – principally in elaborated discourse, with subordinate clauses – is in any case rare in unplanned everyday spoken usage. Certainly the subjunctive does carry with it an aura of refinement, which comes into play especially in more formal speech.

(ii)   Accusative and infinitive

In Latin, clausal complements of VERBA SENTIENDI and DECLARANDI, per-ception and saying verbs, had their subject in the accusative case and their verb as an infinitive. In Romance this construction survives with percep-tion verbs:

(121)   VOLUCRES VIDEMUS CONSTRUERE NIDOS: French *Nous voyons les oiseaux con-struire les nids*, Ital. *Vediamo costruire i nidi gli uccelli*, Span. *Vemos construir los nidos los pájaros* 'We see the birds build the nests'.

It has also extended to **factitives**, or **causatives**. Where Classical Latin used a subjunctive subordinate FACERE UT FACIAT later Latin developed a FACERE EUM FACERE construction, in the sense of 'to make him do'. This latter construction persists in the Romance languages (except in Rumanian, where a subjunctive clause or a supine construction is used):

(122)   Span. *Hace escribir a Juan*, Ital. *Fa scrivere Gianni*, Cat. *Fa escriure en Joan*, French *Il fait écrire Jean* 'He makes John write'.

When the complement clause contains an object, its subject has to be marked by a preposition:

(123)   Ptg. *Faz escrever a carta al por João* (not in Brazilian Portuguese), Span. *Le hace escribir la carta a Juan* (*por* is not used), French *Il fait écrire la lettre à/par*

Jean, Ital. *Fa scrivere la lettera a/da Gianni*, Cat. *Fa escriure la carta a en Joan* (not *per*) 'He makes John write the letter', 'He has the letter written by John'.

In Portuguese however it is possible to use two direct objects (see also 4.3 for the personal infinitive):

(124)   *Farei o José fechar a porta* 'I shall make Joseph close the door'.

Complements of saying verbs in Romance, however, normally take the form of a finite clause introduced by a complementizer, but in the modern Western standards a Latin-like infinitival construction can be used. As with the English equivalent, it is regarded as bookish and seems to date from the Renaissance period, when it was directly imitated from Latin.

When the subject of the complement clause is identical with that of the saying verb, the infinitival construction is reasonably frequent:

(125)   French *Je crois avoir raison*, Span. *Creo tener razón*, 'I think I'm right', 'I believe myself to be right'.

When the subject changes and is expressed as a pronoun, the subordinated verb 'to be' is omitted:

(126)   French *Je le crois intelligent*, Span. *Lo creo inteligente* 'I think he's intelligent', 'I believe him to be intelligent' (but see Ital. *L'aveva creduta essere pazza* 'He had thought she was mad').

Otherwise the construction in the modern standards is favoured only when the subject of the complement clause is extraposed:

(127)   French *la fille qu'il croyait être venue*, Span. *la muchacha que él creía haber venido* 'the girl he thought had come'.

In cases like these it is felt that the infinitival construction is more elegant than one with an accumulation of QU-conjunctions (see 7.4):

(128)   *La fille qu'il croyait qui est venue*; *La muchacha que él creía que ha venido*.

There can be little doubt that the extension of the accusative and infinitive construction to verbs of saying in the modern standards was directly influenced by the Latin model, in Romance as in English. However, it has remained, more so than in English, a literary, even precious, feature of the languages.

(iii)   Adjective placement

Language typology studies have shown that SVO languages tend to postpose adjectives to the noun, whereas SOV languages prepose them. Latin is, like other ancient Indo-European languages, a basically SOV language (though in main clauses surface word order is determined largely by pragmatic considerations) and the modern Romance languages are basically SVO. It is to be expected then that there would have been a change of adjectival ordering from prenominal to postnominal, in the transition from Latin to Romance.

Romance adjectives do normally occur after the noun they modify, though with some noteworthy exceptions, especially in the modern standard languages. In Classical Latin, however, as distinct from the earlier period, it is far from sure that prenominal adjective placement was the rule. In the grammar books a distinction is often made between determining (or 'emphatic') and attributive (or 'descriptive') adjectives, the latter appearing most frequently after the noun and the former before.

In the modern Romance standards, though much less so in non-standard varieties, a similar distinction is made. What is now a separate class of determiners normally occur before the noun, but otherwise adjectives can be preposed or postposed. In many cases there is a semantic difference:

(129)   French *familles nombreuses*, Span. *familias numerosas* 'large families' / *nom-breuses familles*, *numerosas familias* 'numerous families'; Ital. *un nuovo vestito* 'a new (i.e. different) dress' / *un vestito nuovo* 'a (brand-)new dress'; Ptg. *vários papéis* 'several papers' / *papéis vários* 'miscellaneous papers'.

In literary and pretentious official style, moreover, preposed adjectives have become very nearly the norm. The justification given for the different placement is that the preposed adjective is more subjective and emotive, enhancing the semanticism of the noun (French *doux miel*, Span. *dulce miel* 'sweet honey') whereas the postposed adjective is contrastive (*vin doux*, *vino dulce* 'sweet (not dry) wine'). The difference has been variously described in terms of restrictive and non-restrictive qualification, of predicative or attributive status, of intrinsic and extrinsic characterization, of reference and referent modification or of relative emphasis.

In most of the languages a few common adjectives always are placed before the noun, indicating usually common scalar or affective notions – 'good–bad', 'young–old', 'small–large', 'fine, beautiful' (BELLUS), 'pitiable, poor' (PAUPER), 'dear' (CARUS). They can be thought of as almost incorporated into their noun, and indeed suffixes express some of the same things in most languages. In modern usage lexical slippage can result in other adjectives being used in the same way (*Air France vous souhaite un agréable voyage* 'Air France wishes you a pleasant journey', perhaps influenced by the formulaic '*Bon voyage*'). Such usage has been stigmatized as an erroneous Anglicism.

Some adjectives can only with great manœuvring appear before the noun. This is true in general of past participles and of 'pseudo-adjectives' in phrases like *le discours présidentiel* ('the president's speech', not 'the speech which is a president'), or *un linguiste traditionnel* ('someone who does traditional linguistics', or 'a linguist who is traditional').

In the non-standard languages preposed adjectives, other than the half-dozen common ones, are rarely found (though it is to be noted that popular discourse is rather short on adjectives in general). In literary language, extensive use is made of the stylistic device of preposing adjectives. It is tempting to see the stylistic habit as arising from conscious imitation of Latin, rather than directly inherited from Latin.

In French there does seem to have been discontinuity in transmission, as Old French texts make much more use of preposed adjectives than modern French. The habit of preposing is maintained in Northern and Eastern dialects: influence from German is usually invoked. A similar influence may be felt in the literary Old French: see 1.2 for the suggestion that the language of the earlier texts may be related to a variety more Germanically orientated than the modern language, which has reverted more decisively to the Romance type. Nevertheless the influence of Latin on literary style was felt from the time of the Renaissance and of standardization, and preposing of the adjective became a device for tempering its qualifying characteristics, and especially for signalling figurative or emotive nuances.

In Rumanian, though preposition of common adjectives was found in early texts (*mare milă* 'great pity'), today this is so only in lexicalized forms: *bunăvoinţă* 'goodwill' (though 'poor, pitiable' can still appear before the noun, *biata ţară* 'poor country!'). However in the modern standard, presumably under French, rather than direct Latin, influence, preposition of other adjectives can be used with emphatic and affective import: *zi frumoasă* 'fine day' but *frumoasă casă* 'lovely house'. Note that in cases like these a definite article is enclitic to the adjective and not to the noun:

(130)   *marele profesor* 'the great teacher'.

The postposed adjective can be preceded by the so-called 'adjectival article':

(131)   *calul cel frumos* 'the [very] fine horse' ('the horse the fine one').

(iv)   Double negatives

Another development that seems to date from the time of standardization concerns **negation** (for a more general discussion of negation strategies in Romance see 7.4). The Latin distaste for **negative attraction** – by which a negative element sparks off a string of agreeing negatives – is reflected in the attitudes of most grammarians of Western vernaculars. In spite of widespread colloquial usage (as in *You ain't seen nothing yet*), grammarians go on insisting that two negatives make a positive as in mathematics, and that double negatives are ambiguous or downright incorrect.

In Romance, where many of the negative items stand also as **negative polarity** items, there is comparatively little argumentation along these lines and verb negation can be accompanied by a string of negatives:

(132)   Rum. *Nu dă niciodată nimic nimănui*, Span. *No da nunca nada a nadie*, Ital.
Non dà mai niente a nessuno, French *Il ne donne jamais rien à personne* 'He doesn't ever give anything to anyone' ('He not gives never nothing/ nothing never to nobody').

However, in standard Italian, Spanish and Portuguese, when a negative item is fronted the following preverbal negative *non*, *no* or *não* is deleted – a process called by some generative linguists **negative incorporation**. This is most usual when the negative item is the subject of the sentence (though the more usual construction relegates to post-verbal position):

(133)   Ital. *Nessuno è venuto / Non è venuto nessuno*, Span. *Nadie vino / No vino nadie*,
Ptg. *Ninguem veio / Não veio ninguem* 'Nobody came'.

It also, however, occurs when the object is fronted:

(134)   Ital. *Niente ho visto / Non ho visto niente*, Span. *Nada he visto / No he visto nada*, Ptg. *Nada tenho visto / Não tenho visto nada* 'I've seen nothing', 'I haven't seen anything'.

The negative incorporation rule seems not to operate in most Romance languages. In Catalan it is condemned as a Castilianism; in Sard and in central Italy, the use may be influenced by standard Italian. There are signs in sixteenth-century Rhaeto-Romance and Rumanian texts that the rule may have operated then, but little reliance can be placed on what are mainly translations.

In Spanish and Portuguese, usage without the rule is amply attested in earlier texts, though it roused the wrath of early grammarians. The present rule became firmly established in standard Spanish by the sixteenth and in standard Portuguese by the seventeenth century. Non-standard varieties tend not to observe it.

In Italian the picture is not so clear, but it would appear that the rule was established by the time of the great fourteenth-century writers, and examples can be found in earlier texts, mainly translations from Latin. It does not operate in Northern varieties, but there is evidence of its use in Central and Southern varieties.

Whether the construction persisted from the Latin period into Central Italian, or whether it was re-introduced under Latin influence is impossible to tell from the evidence we have. For the Iberian languages it seems clear that the rule was introduced by prescriptive grammarians only at the period of standardization, when both Latin and Italian were exerting influence on grammatical thinking. It is not surprising that non-standard varieties do not always observe the rule, and comparatively rarely use the (emphatic?) fronted constructions.

Another feature that seems to have been retained or restored by Latin influence is the so-called 'expletive negative' of the type:

(135)   TIMEO NE VENIAT 'I fear lest he come'.

This survives in French literary style as 'partial' negation:

(136)   *Je crains qu'il ne vienne.*

In older Italian (but more rarely in Spanish) *no(n)* was used with the subjunctive in complement clauses of this type, without an overt complementizer:

(137)   *Io temo forte non lo cor si schianti* (Dante) 'I fear my heart might (not) break'.

The use of a kind of negative concord, introduced by other 'semantically negative' verbs or conjunctions (including those expressing doubt) may have spread from this model and was particularly favoured by French. For the 'expletive negative' in clauses depending on comparisons of inequality, where Latin would use QUAM, often with a second comparative, see 7.5:

(138)   VERIOR QUAM GRATIOR POPULO 'more truthful than (more) popular'.

(c)   Vocabulary: Latinisms

The vocabulary of the Romance languages is not only inherited through smooth transmission from Latin (**popular** words), but also has been (as to more than about 30 per cent in some languages) borrowed from Latin during the course of the languages' history (**learned** words, **Latinisms**, *cultismos*). This is not true of Rumanian, which, except for the Transylvanian variety, had little contact with Latin through Church or learned sources.

In standard Italian it is hard to judge, on the basis of their phonological shape compared with Latin, whether lexical items are popular or learned. As we have seen, Italian has tended to retain, or restore, words with Latinate shape: the invention of the literary language in the fourteenth century, and its standardization in the sixteenth, constantly looked back to the past as the model. Clearly popular forms are more current in the non-literary dialects than in the national language.

To a lesser extent, the same is true of Spanish: one problem here is the proliferation of so-called *semi-cultismos*, which partake of some regular sound changes but resist others. The usual assumption is that they have been rebuilt, by association with the Latin equivalents heard continually in the Church services. This assumption depends, however, on a Neogrammarian model of sound change which holds that all items of a language are affected virtually simultaneously by a mechanical phonological shift: exceptions have to be accounted for within certain categories, one of which is that of loanwords. In some circumstances a Latin loanword is seen as contaminated with an existing popular word, the blend giving unexpected results: one much-quoted example is the word for 'church' from ECCLESIA (itself borrowed from Greek) which ends up in French as *église*, in Spanish as *iglesia* and in Portuguese as *igreja*. None of these looks like the Latin word, yet neither are they regular phonological outcomes, with expected palatalization (Italian *chiesa,* on the other hand, could be a regular form).

It is in French, where there was radical regular sound change, that it is easiest to measure the extent of learned vocabulary. Here the fashion for borrowing from Latin had passed its peak by the seventeenth century, after which time the Latin words borrowed tend to be international, like *laboratoire* 'laboratory' etc.

It would be a mistake to think that the term 'learned' implies that the relevant items are esoteric innovations. Indeed it is among the most common words in the languages that these items occur. For less frequently used items (for instance, in a dictionary like *Le Petit Larousse* covering some 50,000 items) the proportion of newer words is greater (about half of the current vocabulary entered the language after the sixteenth century), but these are not usually Latinisms.

The periods which most favoured Latin borrowing in French were the fourteenth century (when translations from Latin were commissioned by royal decree) and, to a lesser extent, the sixteenth century, when interest in classical culture was rekindled. But learned forms are found in texts from the very beginning of vernacular writing. It could be that the early attested Latinisms are merely an effect of graphical convention (with scribes writing as if the language were Latin but reading in vernacular). In Spanish and Portuguese the greatest influx of Latinisms seems to have occurred in the thirteenth century, when the vernacular started to be used for a new range of purposes, previously the province of Latin. It has been maintained that this was little more than a shift in writing practice, and that 'medieval Latin'– the written language of culture throughout the Middle Ages – was born of the change. Those writing in the new way, though, would probably have found the colloquial vocabulary inadequate for the more elaborated discourses, and so drew on the Latin sources that were readily available to them.

To give some idea of the extent of Latin borrowing in the most frequently used sections of the vocabulary, let us look at a sample of words in the *Français fondamental* dictionary of the 2,000 most used words in modern French. Taking words beginning with the letter *L*, and leaving out grammatical items, I find that 29 per cent of items are Latinisms, compared with 46 per cent of popular words inherited from Latin. Some of these Latinisms – like *labourer* 'to plough', earlier 'to work' < LABORARE – occur in the earliest texts. Others replace more popular forms – like *lac* 'lake', introduced instead of *lai* in the late twelfth century, or *légume* 'vegetable', a fourteenth-century substitute for *leün*. Post-sixteenth-century introductions are rare – one certain example is *litre* of 1793 – though some of the words changed their semantic scope in modern times.

We have already seen that Latin borrowings brought French more decisively into the Romance 'club' in the late medieval period: spelling conventions and revised pronunciation based on these (particularly frequent since universal education got underway) have prevented French from drifting off as a consequence of radical phonological change.

3.5   WHO KILLED LATIN?

The slickest answer to that question is the second Vatican Council meeting in 1962, which decreed that Roman Church services could henceforth be in the vernacular (but note that its proceedings were published in Latin). But it could also have been similar decisions of ecclesiastical councils in the ninth century, of which the most well known is the 813 Council of Tours, which decreed that homilies should be delivered in 'rustic roman' speech, so that the faithful could understand them.

The most conventional answer is that there is no culprit – Latin is alive and well and living in the Romance-speaking areas – that Romance is Latin, under another name. But we have already seen that, although the name Romance was used interchangeably with Latin for a long time, at some period the languages were recognised as different.

But when? Some say always – the spoken idiom was recognizably different from the written (which was presumably also a spoken form for an elite). Others say 'since the spread of Latin through the Roman Empire' as speakers of substratum languages shifted to Latin, bringing to it some of the features of their first language. Others say that the Latin language died, as a mother tongue, when Roman administration broke down in the fourth century, or with the influx of barbarian hordes into the Empire. Others will put the demise of Latin in the eighth century, when under Charlemagne there was a cultural renaissance which attempted to restore the written language to its former pristine purity, and so divorced it from the current colloquial use. Yet others will see the death of Latin as dating from the appearance of the first vernacular texts, which can be reliably dated to the tenth century at the latest. Feudal social and political organization could then be linked to the breakdown of communication between different parts of the Western Romance area. These questions will be discussed in more detail in chapter 6.

Certainly we can say that Latin went into terminal decline from the early Middle Ages, but it may still have been viewed as a more prestigious version of the language spoken by ordinary people. The educated still took pride in knowing Latin, and the signs are that Latin did not start being taught through the vernacular until later. In the twelfth century we start getting hints that Latin was being regarded as a foreign language, just as the different Romance languages were being seen as distinct one from the other. In the thirteenth century, administrative documents began to be written in vernacular, which previously had been used mainly for enter-tainment or religious instruction.

But Latin went on being used, in a diglossic situation, for more elevated purposes well into the sixteenth century. In some parts of non-Romance-speaking Europe, Latin was still used for administrative purposes in the nine-teenth century, when it remained everywhere a language of scholarship. In the sixteenth century, when there was another revival of classical standards, it may be that educated people were still able to follow sermons delivered mainly in Latin (their written versions were certainly in Latin). It is only in the twentieth century that Latin became virtually confined to Church func-tions (ending in the late 1960s), and was treated as an erudite sacred cow.

One question that can be asked is: when did Latin, in so far as it was dis-tinguished from Romance, cease to be anyone's first language? Recall that even for Erasmus, Latin was a second language: at the point of death he reverted to his mother tongue, we are told. The sixteenth-century French essayist Montaigne is usually quoted as the last first-language speaker. His father insisted (though with what success?) that even the servants should address him only in Latin during his early childhood. Montaigne himself, as a speaker both of Gascon and of French, claimed that, with his Latin as well, he could make himself understood in all Romance tongues (not including, of course, Rumanian). Later attempts to bring up children with Latin as their first language seem to have been doomed to failure – partly because of the difficulties in inventing new words for everyday objects.

Here we should mention the idea recently put forward by Roger Wright that Latin did not die (it is represented by the Romance languages today), but that in the eighth century a new Latin was created – Medieval Latin. This was a consequence of the Carolingian reforms under the aegis of the English scholar Alcuin of York, who is said to have introduced a new way of reading Latin, different from the Romance tradition, in which Latin was read as if it were the vernacular. The claim here is that it was only after this time that diglossia began, with Latin being recreated as a High language, and Romance as the Low. Before this, speakers were not con-scious of the difference between Latin and Romance, merely of that between written and spoken codes. This controversial view depends on ambiguous evidence about the nature of the Carolingian reforms, and about the causes of differentiation of Latin into distinct Romance idioms. It also does not adequately account for the salient grammatical differences between the Latin of the texts and the spoken vernaculars; even if speakers pronounced the Latin as if it were the local Romance variety, it is hard to believe that they were not conscious of the difference between the two.

Many scholars now agree, however, with views that were advanced first in 1929 by Henri Muller, but for a long time treated with scorn, that the birth of the separate Romance languages – if not the death of Latin – dates from a much later era than the one suggested by the political collapse of the Roman Empire. For a long time speakers continued to view Latin as the codified, fixed version of their own more homespun everyday usage, which they quite naturally accepted as varying from place to place and from person to person. Recognition by each community of the distinctness of its language presumably went hand in hand with the perception of its collective identity. Latin was killed, then, by Romance speakers who perceived it as dead, beyond their reach, and superseded by a new prestigious language that could adequately fulfil all the functions previously performed by Latin. The last blow then must have come from the Vatican Council, but the death had lingered on for many a century.

FURTHER READING

The first volume of Posner & Green eds. (1980–93) covers the main works on the Latin–Romance relationship up to 1980. The article about language in Jenkyns ed. (1992) gives a general introduction to the Latin legacy; see also Rohlfs (1984). On Latin morphology, Carstairs (1988); on Latin syntax and semantics, Panhuis (1982), Pinkster (1990); on Late Latin, especially Väänänen (1981, 1987), Herman (1990), Herman ed. (1987), Calboli ed. (1989, 1990). For the Romance–Latin interface, Wright (1982), Dahmen *et al.* eds. (1987), Wright ed. (1991). For the use of Latin in Europe, Burke & Porter eds. (1991). On accentuation, Pulgram (1975), Mayerthaler (1982). On word order, Bauer (1992), on case and nominal inflection, Gaeng (1984), Schøsler (1984), Blake (1994). On umlaut, Leonard (1978), Maiden (1991). On negation, Haegeman (1995), Rizzi (1982), Schwegler (1990), Zanuttini (1997). On Romance verbs, Vincent & Harris eds. (1982), Pountain (1983). On auxiliaries, Harris & Ramat eds. (1987), Heine (1994); on compound tenses, Harré (1991). On tense, Comrie (1985), Fleischman & Waugh eds. (1991). On the imperfect, Dauses (1981). On the subjunctive, Farkas (1982), Gsell & Wandruszka (1986), Palmer (1986). On the definite article Trager (1932), Abel (1971).

4

Convergence, interinfluence and parallel development

4.1   DRIFT AND METARULES

Where the Romance languages share idiosyncratic features classic methodology dictates that their origin is sought in Latin, or at any rate in Proto-Romance. It is true that shared morphological and lexical features can often be traced back to Latin sources, but non-universal syntactic features may stem from 'peripheral' morphological or phonological accidents. However, we should take into account the considerable interinfluence between the different Romance languages throughout their history, discernible most easily in the lexicon and in metalinguistic discourse, but also extending to syntax.

One little-understood process that may affect the history of related languages is **drift**, by which they independently develop in the same direction. An underlying, but often unstated, supposition here may be that the proto-language system was in some way unstable and that each language at its own rate, and in parallel but perhaps subtly different ways, sought to remedy any imbalance. An objection to this way of looking at things is that it seems to imply some sort of teleology, a striving for equilibrium, on the part of the language system. However, it can be claimed that 'drift' does not imply 'remediation' – for instance, the loss of noun-case morphology in English and French can be the result of non-functional drift (or 'slope', 'slant'), merely in the sense that at successive points of time there is less case morphology about.

Parallel developments, especially in phonology, can also be described by means of **metarules**, which are always potentially operational in the languages, but are sometimes in abeyance, perhaps because input has been 'bled' away by other changes, or because they are blocked by conservative social forces. The examples of palatalization, discussed in chapter 3, may

155

fit into this category – as a natural assimilatory process, it keeps popping up in a slightly different form all over the place from time to time.

The concept of drift is compatible with the functionalist view of language, and indeed with the **invisible hand** approach, originating in Adam Smith's view that individual attempts at maximizing advantage while minimizing effort can result in a collective directional shift. In similar circumstances it will be likely that the outcome in different languages will be alike, and that differences could be attributable to extraneous factors.

Is it also compatible with the view that new learners of a language, faced with excessively complex and degenerate input data, consequent on an accumulation of anomalies in the output of their seniors, utilize their **language acquisition device** (or **universal grammar**) to create a simpler, more elegant and consistent grammar that will incorporate the aberrant material? Presumably only when in all the related languages there are similarities in the less-than-systematic material in the adult output would the newly created grammars come up with the same solutions.

So we must again look to inherited peripheral phenomena, to the weight of tradition, to interinfluence and common external influences, to account for parallel developments. What all languages would have in common is the tendency to generalize and simplify rules to bring them into line with more basic principles, and probably to slough off tiresome features, especially arbitrary lexical constraints, that have hung on only through inertia and tradition. Universal tendencies may go deeper than that, though, perhaps targeting more **transparency** in derivation or more **iconicity**, relating surface forms more closely to underlying semantics.

Romance languages, like most other Indo-European languages, do seem to show a drift from heavily inflected **synthetic** word morphology towards more **analytic** structures with free units syntactically signalling grammatical relations. The progression has been viewed by theorists as either indicating decay and decadence from an earlier Golden Age, or as heralding progress in unravelling the parallel but tangled threads of form and substance.

I have already pointed out that in Romance the analytic process is carried further in the nominal system than in the verbal. But even here there is development of what are traditionally called **compound** ('composed') and **periphrastic** forms, especially to mark **aspectual** features. More conservative languages resist this trend which some see as an inexorable, though erratic, forging ahead towards a creole-like system of TAM marking (see 2.2). In this framework of thought, the term *français avancé* was introduced in the between-wars period to characterize a sort of French that had 'advanced' far along this path in the vanguard of Romance. It was seen as a popular colloquial variety untrammelled by reactionary traditional grammar and pointing the way to the future of Romance.

In this chapter I shall examine some of the possible candidates for the status of 'convergent' Romance developments. Except for lexical interchange, they are all controversial and are most often seen as having their roots in the proto-language. I shall be making the case for seeing them as one facet of 'the club effect', by which the Romance languages have stuck together as a federation. I shall pluck examples from the realms of phonology (diphthongization), syntax (the infinitive in complementation and subordination, and object clitics), morphology (periphrastic forms, paying special attention to the passive and the future) and lexicon (mutual borrowing between the languages).

4.2   DIPHTHONGIZATION

So-called 'Romance diphthongization' is almost universally believed to date from Proto-Romance. Differences between the languages are usually associated either with divergent early chronological ordering or ascribed to late developments in the individual languages. However, it is possible to postulate parallel rather than common development.

The type of diphthongization in question is that of Latin short Ĕ and Ŏ in stressed syllables. By the rules of Latin accent assignment (see 3.3) this covers the only accented vowel in monosyllabic or bisyllabic words, and the antepenultimate vowel in words liable to syncope. It will be recalled that classically it is assumed that, whereas in Sard all short and long vowels merged, and in Rumanian short and long o merged, in most of the rest of the Romance area Ĕ and Ŏ would be retained as the only short vowels that were distinct from their long counterparts (Ĭ and Ŭ having merged with Ē and Ō). They came to be, however, distinguished from their erstwhile long partners not by length, but by lower point of articulation.

> In traditional accounts the erstwhile short vowels are assumed to have become 'lax' in Proto-Romance. Labov (1994) argues, on the contrary, that Romance vowels are consistently 'tense' (or 'peripheral' in his terms). Thus, unlike Germanic 'non-peripheral' vowels, Romance vowels tend to rise during chain shifts. Moreover the 'escape route', by which high peripheral vowels may switch to the non-peripheral 'track', is blocked in Romance: thus Romance

high vowels (especially [i]) tend to remain stable in Romance, whereas in
Germanic they may diphthongize and lower. This would provide a partial
explanation for the apparent limitation of Romance diphthongization processes to mid vowels (but see also 6.4).

Proto-Romance [ɛ] and [ɔ] resulting from short Latin ĕ and ŏ are thought
to have tended to diphthongize under stress. Reflexes in Romance vary but
from some a diphthongized form can be reconstructed:

(1)   MĔL 'honey': Rum. *miere*, Ital. *miele*, French *miel*, Span. *miel*; NŎUU 'new': Ital.
        nuovo, Old French *nuef*, Span. *nuevo*.

Such diphthongization can be seen in terms of raising of the first mora of
the nucleus.

Diphthongization of ĕ is attested in spelling very sporadically in Late
Latin (e.g. NIEPOS for NEPOS 'nephew' in an inscription dated AD 120) and
is thought to date back to just after Sard lost contact with innovations in
Latin. It is impossible to tell whether the digraph represents a nucleus with
an onset glide ([je]) or change of point of articulation during pronunciation ([ie]), nor whether it was a heavy (two-mora) or a light (one-mora)
diphthong. Given parallels in some modern dialects (e.g. in Sicily), it has
been suggested that the diphthong was a phonetic variant of the short
vowel used in emphatic position.

Diphthongization of short ŏ is traditionally dated to a rather later period, partly because Rumanian did not apparently participate in the process.
The graphical form (*uo*), attested in a fifth-century inscription and then in
one of the earliest French texts (*buona* for BONA in the Eulalia poem of the
ninth/tenth century), suggests raising, perhaps closing to the glide [w], or
non-syllabic [u], at the beginning of the sequence.

The standard explanation of this type of diphthongization (usually
called 'spontaneous') dates back to Schuchardt (see page 4), who relates
it to later diphthongization of Latin ē and ō in French (see 6.4). It is
assumed that, with the loss of the phonological Latin quantitative system,
vowel length was determined by phonetic factors: stressed vowels in free
syllables were lengthened. The lengthened vowel could then suffer dissimilation ([ɛɛ] > [iɛ], [ɔɔ] > [uɔ] > [ue]). The assumption made is that *ie* and *uo*
were heavy rising (though down-gliding) diphthongs with stress on the
first element. This is rather puzzling as it is expected that the initial part of
the heavy diphthong would retain its original timbre, with the final part
tending to become a glide (a falling but up-gliding diphthong).

There is some evidence for the postulated stress patterning: in Old French verse *ie* and *uo* can assonate with *i* and *u*, and in some dialects today there is a (possibly metaphonic) ['iə] diphthong derived from Ĕ. But in most languages where the diphthongs persist they have an onset glide (/je/ or /ja/, /wo/, /we/ or /wa/; see also 7.2).

Another difficulty about the ('early') Schuchardtian explanation is that in some languages – notably Spanish – the diphthongization occurs in checked (blocked or heavy) syllables as well as in free (light) syllables:

(2)   HERBA 'grass': Rum. *iarbă*, Dalmatian (Veglia) *yarba*, Span. *hierba*, R-R
        (Surselvan) *jarva* / French *herbe*, Ital. *herba*; FORTE 'strong': Span. *fuerte*,
        Dalmatian (Veglia) *fuart* / French *fort*, Ital. *forte*.

This fact has to be explained away by appeal to analogical spread of the diphthong. It could, however, suggest that the diphthong was originally light (one mora) like the original vowel, and that the effect of stress was to favour a shift of articulation, rather than lengthening.

(a)   Metaphony

Another quite different explanation for Romance diphthongization (also originally proposed by Schuchardt) is that it originates as an assimilatory metaphonic (umlauting) phenomenon, sometimes called 'conditioned diphthongization'. This can be related to **breaking**, by which a short Ĕ or Ŏ is partially raised by a juxtaposed palatal consonant or glide. This type of diphthongization is well attested in French:

(3)   *vieil* '; old' (old [vjeʎ]) < VECLU (for VETULUS), *feuille* 'leaf' (old [fuɛʎə]) < FOLIA.

In Spanish and Italian, though, a palatal consonant sometimes has the effect of impeding diphthongization:

(4)   Span. *espejo* 'mirror' (Old [espeʃo]) < SPECLU (for SPECULUM), Ital. *meglio* 'bet-
        ter' < MELIUS, Span. *hoja* (Old [hoʒa]), Ital. *foglia* < FOLIA.

We have already mentioned the contention that Proto-Romance was an umlauting dialect, and the widespread Italian morphologization of umlauted forms, paralleled to some extent in Asturias in Spain. An ī, and sometimes a ŭ in the post-tonic syllable, could induce raising of the tonic vowel. Normally this means that [ɛ] becomes [e] or [i], and [ɔ] becomes [o] or [u]. However, sometimes the same features are realized by a transition ['iə], or [je], and [wɔ], less often ['uə] (not apparently [we]):

(5)   Ital. dial. (Chieti, Abruzzo) [bbiəjjə], [bbuənə], (Ischia) [bbjellə], [bbwɔnə]
            'beautiful, good' < BĚLLU, BŎNU.

This process seems to occur in both free and checked syllables, and, as vowel length is not clearly phonological in these varieties, there is no evidence that the resulting diphthongs are heavy.

This type of diphthongization could have been widespread in early Romance, though masked in some languages by later developments. For instance, it is possible to explain Portuguese tonic [e] and [o] < Ě, Ŏ, in syllables followed by [o], as due to levelling of early metaphonic [iɛ], [uɔ], or in terms of vowel harmony in more modern times. The anomalous Catalan [e] < Ě, compared with [ɛ] < Ē, in many dialects (an apparent phonological flipflop) may be described in terms of generalization of [iɛ] < Ě, permitting the lowering of [e] < Ē to [ɛ]. Once again there is difficulty in explaining the spread of the diphthong to all or nearly all lexical forms, in Spanish, for instance, or the restriction of the diphthong to Latin free syllables in French and Italian.

> For Asturian the metaphony may be independent of spontaneous diphthongization:

(6)   [gwinu] / [gweno] 'good' (count / mass) < BŎNU / BŎNO.

For French and Italian we have to postulate a process by which the light diphthong is reinterpreted as equivalent to a long vowel, which can occur only in a free syllable. In French this fits in well with other changes – like diphthongization of Latin Ē and Ō in free syllables (see 6.4), and with compensatory lengthening consequent on loss of syllable-final consonants or on diphthong levelling. In Italian it is less convincing, though here there is some evidence of vowel lengthening in stressed syllables (alternating with consonant gemination – see 6.3). Another alternative explanation advanced is that metaphonic raising originally occurred only in free syllables and then spread to all syllables in some varieties. This story seems to assume that the metaphonic diphthongs were originally heavy nuclei, and not, as I have suggested, light nuclei.

> In standard Italian the diphthong, especially *uo*, is often called 'mobile' – 'now you see it, now you don't':

(7)   *pruova/prova* 'proof', also *nuovo* 'new' < NOUU / *nove* 'nine'< NOUEM; *tiene* 'he holds' < TENET / *bene* 'well'< BENE, *leva* 'he raises'< LEVAT / *lieve* 'light' < LEVIS.

> This variation is usually explained in terms of dialect mixture, of morphologi-

cal levelling, or of learned versus popular development. It could, however, be related to the differential lengthening under stress, though with a good deal of subsequent lexicalization.

(b)   System pressures

Mention should also be made of the structuralist explanation of Romance diphthongization as a result of the imbalance in the vowel system consequent on monophthongization of Latin AU and AE. This would have triggered off a 'push-chain' reaction which had the effect of taking many reflexes of inherited Ĕ and Ŏ out of the simple vowel system and establishing a sub-system of complex nuclei. This works best for French, where the medieval language did have a whole set of diphthongs and triphthongs, most of which levelled by the modern period. It also accounts neatly for apparent non-diphthongization in languages where AU was not levelled, as in Rumanian, Portuguese, Occitan. On the whole the structuralist ideas about symmetrical systems, *cases vides*, functional load and push and drag chains are currently unfashionable (though see Labov 1994) and explanations in terms of internal systemic pressures are out of favour, as smacking too much of teleology. However, certain sound shifts can conceivably be seen as consequent on others, where potentially pathological phonological mergers threaten.

(c)   New approaches

In current multilinear phonological theory, explanations of diphthongization and diphthong levelling are sought more in terms of differential distribution of features at different tiers. Thus a heavy diphthong can develop from a long vowel as a result of divergence between the skeletal tier and the segmental tier, with delinking of the second mora from the skeletal tier and then raising:

$$
\begin{array}{cccc}
\mathrm{V} & \mathrm{V} & \mathrm{V} & \mathrm{V} \\
\multicolumn{2}{c}{\vee} & \multicolumn{2}{c}{|\;/\;|} \\
e & & e & i
\end{array}
$$

More catastrophically, it could become a light diphthong by merger at the skeletal tier and divergence at the segmental tier.

Features spelt out sequentially in a diphthong can also come to be concurrent in a single segment to form a new monophthong: thus [we] or [ew] can, as in French, be monophthongized to [œ], merging the labio-velar and the palatal elements into a new mid, or retracted front, vowel.

(d)   Why Ĕ and Ŏ?

Such changes can occur in any language and at any time, so that there is no need to postulate common origin for the parallels between Romance. What perhaps we could ask is why Latin Ĕ and Ŏ were particularly prone to diphthongization. Perhaps the answer is to be sought in the fact mentioned before: these were the only two short Latin vowels that survived as distinctive phonemes into most Romance languages. For these two vowels, which frequently occur in accented syllables in Latin, there was a certain mismatch between their inherent short quantity and their tendency to lengthen, especially in free syllables, under stress. In unstressed syllables, they everywhere merged with reflexes of their long counterparts. In stressed syllables, however, speakers may have tended to emphasize their differences from close [e] and [o], reflexes of Ē, Ĭ and Ō, Ŭ. Diphthongal variants may already have been familiar from metaphonic forms, and could have been extended to other contexts, perhaps not developing as distinct phonological units until well into the Middle Ages. That diphthongs were not wholly divorced from their monophthongal counterparts may be shown by the widespread medieval **apophony** that sometimes persists into modern verbal paradigms, differentiating stressed from unstressed vowels in the same lexical stem:

(8)   French *je lève* (Old *lief*) / *nous levons* < LĔVARE 'to raise', Spanish *muevo/movemos* < MŎVERE 'to move', Ital. *suono/soniamo* < SŎNARE 'to sound'.

Each language made use of the possibilities foreshadowed in Proto-Romance in different ways and the related but varied outcomes could have been arrived at independently.

4.3 THE INFINITIVE

The Latin infinitive was originally a verbal noun, but in some varieties it came to act as a substitute for a finite verb. In most Romance languages the infinitive has tended to extend its verbal functions, and to become the canonical verbal form – hence its use as an unmarked form in pidgin and creole. An apparently more colloquial Latin use of the infinitive of narration (**historical infinitive**) and of exhortation continues into Romance. The latter is found mainly in modern officialese, but also in negative person 2 commands:

(9)   Old French *Nel dire ja!*, Ital. *Non lo dire!* 'Don't say it!'

(a)   Complementation

We have already discussed the Latin *accusative* + *infinitive* construction (see 3.4). In some contexts (for instance, after verbs of wanting) this rivalled use of a finite clause introduced by a complementizer, like UT. What tended to happen, especially in poetic and later Latin, was the extension to such contexts of the use of the so-called **prolative** infinitive, in which the infinitival noun used as the object of a verb was understood as representing a completive clause whose unexpressed subject is identical with that of the matrix clause (so-called **Equi-NP** or **control** constructions). This contrasts in most Romance languages with the clausal complementation, introduced by a QU-complementizer, that is required when the subordinate subject is different from that of the main clause:

(10)   French *Je veux le faire / Je veux qu'il le fasse*; Ital. *Voglio farlo / Voglio che lo faccia*; Span. *Quiero hacerlo / Quiero que lo haga* 'I want to do it', 'I want him to do it'.

     For **clitic climbing** in such examples see 6.5.

In most Romance languages a prepositional complementizer (from AD or DE) can introduce a dependent infinitive:

(11)   French *apprendre à lire, oublier de faire*; Ital. *imparare a leggere, dimenticare di fare*; Span. *aprender a leer, olvidarse de hacer* 'to learn to read', 'to forget to do'; *aider quelqu'un à faire quelque chose, aiutare qualcuno a fare qualche cosa, ayudar alguno a hacer algo*, 'to help someone (to) do something'.

In most Romance languages an infinitive is preferred to a finite clause when the subordinate subject is the same as that of the main clause, or when the subject of the subordinate verb is the object of the main verb. Otherwise a finite clause, introduced by a complementizer, is preferred. Often the complementizer is closely related to a preposition, with the addition of, usually, a QU-form for a clause and, sometimes, DE for an infinitive:

(12)   French *avant* (*que*/*de*) / Ital. *prima* (*che*/*di*) / Span. *ante* (*-s de que* / *de*) 'before';
après (*que*), *dopo* (*che* / *di*) / *despues* (*de que* / *de*) 'after', *sans* (*que*), *senza* (*che*),
sin (*que*) 'without'.

(b)   Noun or verb?

The grammaticalized distinction between infinitival and clausal subordination appears to have become established quite late in the history of the languages. During the Middle Ages the infinitive still acted more like a noun. In the modern languages infinitival constructions are often in competition with subjunctive finite clauses, and are seen, especially in French and Italian, as a way of avoiding the subjunctive. Sometimes they are slightly bookish in flavour, avoiding clumsy morphological complexities associated with finite clauses:

(13)   French *Il lui faut le savoir* / *Il faut qu'il le sache* 'It's necessary for him to know
it'.

In modern Rumanian, on the other hand, the inherited infinitive form (e.g. *cîntare* 'to sing, singing') is used only as a noun, whereas a 'short' form has more verbal functions. This form is preceded for citation by a prepositional infinitive marker – *a cînta* – but is otherwise sometimes indistinguishable from person 3 finite forms:

(14)   *Face* 'He does' / *a face*; *voiu face* 'I shall do'.

In some types of complementation the short infinitive can be used in modern colloquial speech as an alternative to a subjunctive clause:

(15)   *Îţi pot spune* / *Pot să ţi spun* 'I can tell you'.

But on the whole Rumanian, like some Southern Italian dialects, has not favoured the more 'Romance' use of the infinitive in 'control' constructions, preferring a subjunctive clause introduced by a special complementizer (Rum. *să*, Southern Ital. dial. *mu*)

The older Rumanian evidence suggests that a long (nominal) form could be used in complementation contexts:

(16) *Au început a zidire biserica* (1574) 'They have begun to build the church' /
      (modern) *au început să zidească biserica* '. . . that they should build . . .'
      (cf. INCEPERUNT AEDIFICARE BASILICAM).

Whether the Rumanian reluctance to use the infinitive as a verbal form
continues colloquial Latin usage is disputable. Some see it rather as a
Balkan regional feature, perhaps influenced initially by Greek, which has
also lost the infinitive (see 8.6). The regional distribution in the non-use of
the infinitive lends support to this hypothesis, as dialects south of the
Danube seem to have carried the process further than more northerly
dialects. The Southern Italian dialects that make little use of infinitival
complementation could likewise have been influenced by neighbouring
Greek-speaking colonies.

All varieties of Rumanian differ from the other languages in preferring
other non-finite forms to the infinitive in constructions like:

(17) *uşor de făcut* 'easy to do' (French *facile à faire*, Ital. *facile a fare*, Span. *fácil de
      hacer*); *A terminat de scris romanul* 'He has finished writing the novel' (French *Il a
      terminé d'écrire le roman*); *maşina de spălat* 'washing machine' (French *machine à
      laver*); *Îl vă viind* 'I see him coming' (*Je le vois venir*, *Lo vedo venire*, *Lo veo venir*).

In modern literary use infinitival constructions appear where *să* clauses are
more colloquial:

(18) *Mi-e ruşine de a-ţi spune* / *să-ţi spun* 'I'm ashamed to tell you'; *Mai bine a munci*
      (/ *să munceşti*) *în loc de spune* (/ *decît să spui*) 'It's better to work (/ that you
      should work) instead of talking (/ that you should talk)'.

Such uses are usually viewed as influenced by the standard Western
Romance languages.

(c)   **The personal infinitive**

In Portuguese and Galician (also in some South-Central Italian dialects
and in Sard, and in older Western Spanish varieties) the 'infinitive' (and
indeed other non-finite forms) can take on verbal characteristics to such
an extent that it carries person inflections (though not for persons 1 and 3,
which require use of a pronoun). The **personal infinitive** (also designated as
'inflected' or 'conjugated') is in many contexts a social and stylistic variant
of the bare infinitive, principally used where there is a desire to emphasize
the subject of the action:

(19)   Ptg. *O livro é para as crianças lerem* 'The book is for the children to read';
            Galician *antes de chegarem os teus amigos* 'before your friends come'.

Standard grammar condemns the use of the personal infinitive after auxiliaries and modals, but popular usage in the Iberian peninsula sometimes flouts the prohibition:

(20)   *Podeis comerdes* 'You can eat'; *Vas a saberes o resto* 'You are going to know the rest'.

With causatives and perception verbs, the personal infinitive can be used when a lexical noun phrase precedes the infinitival form:

(21)   *Vi os cavalos correrem / Vi correr os cavalos* 'I saw the horses run'.

            Whether indeed such forms are truly infinitives, rather than finite subjunctive forms, has been disputed. The subject of an infinitive is also often expressed with an overt pronoun in Spanish:

(22)   *al llegar tú* 'at your arriving'; *¡Pagar yo por eso!* 'Me pay for that!'.

            In non-standard varieties of Brazilian Portuguese and Northern French we find also postprepositional infinitives with a disjunctive pronoun subject:

(23)   *para mim leer, pour moi lire* 'for me to read'.

(d)   Conflicting tendencies?

It is hard to discern in most of the developments described consequences of interaction between the languages. It looks more as if there were two conflicting tendencies inherited from Latin, one more archaic, by which the infinitive retained more nominal characteristics and verbal subordination was expressed in a finite clause (introduced perhaps by QUOD), and another more innovating one which stressed the verbal characteristics of the infinitive form. The Rumanian long infinitive and Portuguese personal infinitive, in this view, represent opposite poles. On the other hand, it is possible to view the indecision as a consequence of the 'squishy' nature of the infinitive, sitting somewhere on the continuum between noun and verb. Case-marked infinitives are attested in other Indo-European languages, so here we may view the hesitant behaviour of the Romance infinitive as perhaps derived from the properties of the category itself, rather than as a peculiarly Romance phenomenon.

Creole use of a single lexical verb form derived from the infinitive has resolved the conflict, coding verb person, tense, mood and aspect by use of detachable particles, and taking to the extreme the analytic tendencies that are less clearly discernible in the Romance verb. We have already an example of this in the development of the compound perfect. We shall also examine the morphological status of other Romance periphrastic forms – including the passive and the future – to try and unravel what is inherited, what results from interaction and reaction, and what can be attributed to 'drift'. But we shall first look at another 'hot topic' in Romance syntax.

4.4   OBJECT CLITICS

The syntactic question that has probably provoked more discussion in recent years than any other within the Romance sphere is that of object pronouns and their ordering relative to the verb. We have already seen that the 'discourse' pronouns derive mainly from their Latin counterparts, but **disjunctive** or full forms can differ from **conjunctive (weak** or **clitic)** forms in a way that usually can be related to rhythmic differences at an early period, when the development of stressed and unstressed vowels diverged. We have also seen that anaphoric third-person pronouns, derived from Latin demonstratives, can be related to the definite article. The only 'core' Romance language that uses only disjunctive pronouns is Surselvan Rhaeto-Romance, but there is evidence that the loss of clitics in that dialect is recent, possibly under German influence. Colloquial Brazilian Portuguese also prefers disjunctive pronouns to clitics; this is often seen as a sign of creolization.

> The Italian person 6 pronoun *loro* is always disjunctive; as a dative it is thought to be borrowed from French and substitutes in more formal speech for clitic *gli*, which does not distinguish singular from plural. *Loro* is sometimes interposed between auxiliary and participle (*Ho loro parlato* 'I have spoken to them').

What is most striking about Romance object clitics is not so much their form, but the fact that in most languages they precede the finite verb, whereas full lexical noun objects follow the verb (SVO being the normal ordering). It has been suggested that the clitic ordering represents a fossilized left-over from earlier Latin (and Indo-European) SOV ordering, in the clause. The historical evidence lends comparatively little support to the hypothesis, however. Within the 'Principles-and Parameters' framework there have been numerous attempts to account for the Romance data in terms of parameter setting, usually assuming different constraints on movement of the verb, or on agreement features.

> For Romance object clitic arrays, subject to strict ordering constraints in the standard languages, see 6.5.

(a)   Clitics as agreement markers

Romance philologists, from the beginning of the discipline, have favoured the idea that the object clitics represent agreement markers on the verb – echoing the person, and sometimes case and gender, of non-subject arguments. Diez (see pages 3–4) drew a parallel with Basque, and today many Romanists (some using the term **objective conjugation**) maintain that erstwhile clitics are today grammaticalized as verbal affixes. Proponents of this view point to the widespread occurrence of **clitic copying** or **doubling**, by which a full lexical object and a clitic can both appear in the same clause, and see the clitic as an agreement particle, rather than as a pronominal reduction of a lexical object.

(b)   Clitic doubling

This was condemned as repetitious and pleonastic by tone-setting arbitrators at the time of standardization of most languages (most strongly in French and Italian), and so it is attested mainly in non-standard and dialectal usage.

> Everywhere the 'expletive pronoun' is characteristically used with **left dislocation**, a frequent colloquial construction:

(24)   French *Jean, je l'ai vu*, Ital. *Giovanni, l'ho veduto* 'John, I've seen him'.

> In some varieties there is no intonational indication that similar sequences are indeed left dislocations, rather than simple clauses.

In standard Spanish grammar use of the 'redundant pronoun' is ruled obligatory with disjunctive pronoun objects:

(25)   *La vieron a ella pero no a mí* 'They saw her but not me'

and virtually so with definite objects introduced by *a* (including 'prepositional accusatives' – see 3.3):

(26)   *Le conviene a Juan* 'It suits John'; *Le puso un nuevo conmutador a la radio* 'He put a new knob on the radio'.

In some Latin American varieties (especially in Quechuan-speaking areas) non-gender-marked *lo* is habitually used to copy any noun object.

In contemporary Rumanian, clitic doubling is very frequent, and constructions which would be condemned as vulgar elsewhere are acceptable in the standard:

(27)   *Calul pe care l-am cumpărat* 'The horse that I bought [it]'.

In some varieties a proclitic can even be doubled by an enclitic:

(28)   Rum. (Transylvania and Moldavia) *L'am văzutu-l* 'I've seen him [him]' (cf. R-R (Friulian) *I a dit-i* 'I have told him [him]').

Clitic doubling is attested fairly rarely before the early modern period. In Portuguese today it is mainly confined to contexts where an emphatic disjunctive pronoun object refers to a human being:

(29)   *Disse-mo a mim* 'He said it to *me*'.

(c)   Other pointers

The non-pronoun status of clitics is also suggested by the various uses of the 'reflexive' clitics, for instance in middle/passive (see below), 'impersonal' (see 6.5) constructions and in 'inherent (or lexicalized) pronominals'.

These latter are found in all the languages (see pages 20–3). They are intransitive verbs with reflexive form but no discernible reflexive meaning:

(30)   *se souvenir, acordarse, recordarsi, a şi aminte* 'to remember'; *se battre, battersi, a se lupta* 'to fight' etc.

The pronominal status of the clitics is also cast into doubt by the tendency of popular speech to use a string of clitics, without any clear relation to arguments of the verb, especially as 'datives of interest' or 'solidarity pronouns'. The so-called 'adverbial clitics' in some languages (see 6.5) also are difficult to square with the equation of clitic with pronoun. Another possible indicator is the use of a neuter clitic as a substitute for a deleted or dislocated adjective (not usually in Portuguese or Rumanian):

(31)   French (*Jeune*) *il l'est*, Ital. (*Giovane*) *lo è*, Span. (*Jóven*) *lo es* '(Young) he is [it]'.

In non-standard varieties the clitic can mark gender in such constructions, so that, to a question, a female speaker might reply:

(32)   French (*Êtes-vous contente?*) *Je la suis* '(Are you happy?) I am [f.]'.

(d)   When did cliticization begin?

In tune with the received wisdom that all shared Romance features must originate in Latin colloquial usage, it has been maintained that an increase in the frequency of pronoun usage in the later Latin texts indicates that cliticization was already under way. However, the evidence can also be read as suggesting that the modern state of affairs dates from the late medieval period at the earliest.

In the older languages 'weak' and 'strong' pronouns were variants depending on difference of emphasis: the unstressed object forms were often attached enclitically to an initial-of-clause word – whether the verb, the subject or another stressed word – and could be, in these last cases, separated by other elements from the verb. This is a pattern familiar in other Indo-European languages, by which an atonic element cannot begin a clause (Wackernagel's Law is paralleled in Romance by the **Tobler-Mussafia Law**).

(e)   Portuguese enclisis

Enclisis to the sentence-initial finite verb, still marginally possible in literary style in Italian and Spanish, remains the rule in Portuguese (also in Galician):

(33)   *Disse-mo* 'He said it to me' / *Não mo disse* 'He didn't say it to me'.

Enclisis is regular even with auxiliary verbs in standard Portuguese:

(34)   *Tinho-o estudado a fondo* 'I have studied it thoroughly'.

> In colloquial Brazilian Portuguese, where subject pronouns are commonly used, such examples are regarded as characteristic of careful style, and the normative rule is often violated in speech.

In modern European Portuguese and Galician enclisis of the pronoun has been extended to any positive main verb preceded by a non-quantified definite lexical noun subject:

(35)   *Os rapazes ajudaram-me* 'The boys helped me' (but *Todos os rapazes me ajudaram* 'All the boys helped me').

Enclisis of this latter sort is sporadically attested in Old Portuguese (before the fifteenth century). It is usually assumed that the lexical subject in such constructions was emphatic, perhaps topicalized from an underlying postverbal position. Certainly in Old Portuguese VS ordering is frequent and in the modern European variety the linear position of the subject seems to be dependent on pragmatic, stylistic or rhythmic, rather than syntactic, factors.

> In modern normative grammar postposition of the pronoun is seen as prestigious, and examples of hypercorrection are frequent, especially in officialese:

(36) *Para que cumpra-se o contrato, não recusei-me às condições* 'In order to respect the contract, I did not object to the conditions'.

> It is also to be noted that in Portuguese the object pronoun is frequently altogether omitted in contexts where its reference is unambiguous:

(37) *Nunca vi* 'I've never seen (it)'; *Não gosta?* Don't you like it?

> In Spanish and Rumanian, too, there is normally no overt pronominal mention of objects that are non-definite. In most languages there is some tendency to omit direct object mention within a clitic array (see 6.5), but this is usually condemned by normative grammarians.

(f)   The change to proclisis

In the other Romance languages the atonic pronoun, frequently used in second position, between the subject and the finite verb, over time came to attach itself proclitically to the verb, and the ban on it appearing in initial-of-clause position disappeared. Proclisis seems to have been fully established in French by the fourteenth century, and Occitan and Catalan seem to have followed shortly after. The first Italian grammar (1495) still describes the medieval enclitic type, but possibly mainly as a literary device. In Spanish proclisis was normal by the sixteenth century. The earliest Rumanian texts of the sixteenth century use mainly tonic pronouns with usually postposed atonic pronouns, in ways that suggest Slavonic influence, but proclisis is attested sporadically in texts from the south-western Daco-Rumanian region of Banat from the seventeenth century.

> It is noteworthy that Greek also turned to proclisis rather than enclisis at about the same period as the Western Romance languages.

(g)   Why the change?

The traditional explanation for the switch in French was that there was a change of sentence intonation and accentuation, in the late medieval period, from descending to ascending, favouring rightwise cliticization, rather than leftwise. The hypothesis seems to square with the resistance to proclisis in positive imperative sentences (with assumed longer persistence of descending intonation), and the fact that sentence-initial atonic pronouns were first attested in early thirteenth-century texts in polar interrogative sentences (with assumed rising intonation). By the end of the thirteenth century, too, the old tonic object pronoun forms started to be used to replace disjunctive subject pronouns, while the atonic subject pronouns cliticized to the verb to become virtual inflections (see 1.2). It is assumed that it was around this time that word stress gave way to rhythm-group stress in French, so that the inherited tonic/atonic distinction no longer made phonological sense. What resulted was a wholesale reorganization of much of French morphology.

Even if this explanation works for French (and perhaps for Brazilian Portuguese), it is less plausible for the other languages, where there is little other sign of change of sentence rhythms. Another suggestion that could account for parallel developments is that, from Proto-Romance on, the pronouns increasingly tended to cluster round the verb, and with the growing rigidity of word order in the early modern period they became inseparable from their host.

(h)   Spread from French?

Comparativists, I repeat, shrink from postulating that common features stem from convergence, rather than from inheritance. But the chronology of the geographical progress of proclisis (or at least of preposing) of object pronouns through literary Romance does seem to point to diffusion from a French innovating centre. Any such influence must have begun at the turn of the twelfth and thirteenth centuries and could be linked with linguistic and cultural interchange during the Crusades. A text in the lingua franca believed to originate in 1204 during the siege of Constantinople has only preposed object pronouns, and may reflect to some degree spoken usage. Portuguese, out on a limb at this period and impervious to French prestige until a later period, seems to have fought shy of the trend, though Rumanian, where strong French influence was felt from the eighteenth century, did not. However, the Rumanian feminine (and neuter) pronoun *o*, thought to be Slavonic in origin, though normally proclitic, is still used enclitically with the participle and the gerund:

(38)   *O văd / am văzut-o la gară* 'I see / have seen her at the station'.

(i)   Imperatives

Each language has gone a different length along the road to proclisis. Modern French has gone furthest, but jibbing (unlike colloquial Brazilian Portuguese) at introducing proclisis into positive imperative constructions. Medieval French postposition of the pronoun to the imperative verb was regular only when the verb was in initial-of-clause position, but by the eighteenth century this ordering became characteristic of the imperative (though literary examples of older ordering can still be found even today).

In the modern language it may not be entirely accurate to describe the pronouns in imperatives as clitics. In the negative imperative we have the usual atonic proclitics, but in the positive they can occur in rhythmic group-final position which requires stress:

(39)   *Ne me le donnez pas! / Donnez-le-moi!* 'Don't / give it to me!'; *Ne le dis pas! / Dis-le!* 'Don't / say it!'

In the former example, conjunctive *me* is replaced by disjunctive *moi*, while in the latter the conjunctive form is retained, but with stress on the schwa that in other contexts can occur only in unstressed syllables. Some prefer to see it not as a schwa (*e instable*) but as a realization of the phoneme /ø/.

(j)   Infinitives

Other standard languages regularly postpose atonic object pronouns, not only to positive imperative verbs but also to non-finite verb forms – most generally to the infinitive. In Old French this was also a possibility, though more frequently a tonic pronoun was preposed to the infinitive, especially when the referent of the pronoun was human:

(40)   *pour garder le / pour lui garder* 'to keep him'.

A preposed atonic person 3 pronoun would be indistinguishable in most cases from an article introducing a substantivized infinitive, though occasionally both article and pronoun are used in the same construction:

(41)   *. . . au metre le en tere*

(*La mort le roi Artu, c.* 1230)

'...on burying him [at the putting of him] in the ground'.

By the fourteenth century use of the preposed tonic pronoun was unusual, but examples are found until the late fifteenth century. In modern French the erstwhile atonic form is always proclitic to the infinitive:

(42)   *pour le garder.*

In some other languages (for instance, in South-Western Occitan varieties) there are relics of a medieval distinction between preposed tonic and postposed atonic form.

In modern Sard, though the pronoun is often enclitic to the gerund, it is regularly preposed to the infinitive:

(43)   (Nuoro) *li nárrere* 'to tell him' / *nándelis* 'telling them'

though this was not so in older texts. The reluctance to use enclisis with the infinitive is probably connected with infinitival inflection in Sard. In Portuguese too pronoun preposing is obligatory with the personal infinitive:

(44)   *sem me verem* 'without them seeing me'.

(k)   Proclisis or preposing?

One difficulty in making generalizations about the Romance forms is judging how far they are indeed phonetically cliticized to their verb host. In Brazilian Portuguese, for instance, it is maintained that object pronouns retain a degree of individual stress and are not properly proclitic.

For older stages of the languages it is often impossible to tell whether a pronoun is incorporated metrically to a preceding or following word. Romance preposing of the pronoun to the finite verb is usually equated with proclisis, but in the medieval languages the pronoun was often enclitic to a preceding word rather than proclitic to the following verb.

More to the point, though, is the question of whether indeed the forms in question are 'syntactic clitics' – that is, reduced elements standing in for full forms that have gravitated towards the head of their phrase – or inflectional affixes that have become an integral part of the verb. It looks as if there has been a drift towards affixation in most of the languages, but that French has led the way, perhaps dragging others along with it.

4.5   PERIPHRASTIC ASPECTUAL FORMS

In Latin what are known as the **periphrastic** tenses are those composed of the verb 'to be' and the future participle or the adjectival gerundive:

(45)   AMATURUS/AMANDUS EST 'He is about to love' / 'He has to be loved'.

The former disappears altogether in Romance. The form with the gerundive (or perhaps the ablative of the substantival gerund) has to some extent survived, however, to signal progressive or continuous aspect, now with active rather than passive import. In most languages reflexes of ESSE have been replaced by other auxiliaries – most often STARE 'to stand' or verbs of motion:

(46)   Sard *Est ploendo* 'It's raining', but Ital. *Sta scrivendo*, Span. *Està escribiendo* 'He's writing', Old French *Va croissant* 'It's growing', Span. *Va disminuyendo* 'It's getting smaller'.

> Some believe that the Romance forms are grounded less in the Latin gerundival form than in an ancient Greek progressive periphrastic with a present participle, which is assumed to have penetrated into spoken Latin. In Romance the present participle (in -NT-) and the gerund(ive) (in -ND-) tend to merge. This process was completed in French (in *-ant* forms), while in Spanish and Italian the (possibly learned) present participle forms are lexicalized as adjectives.

The gerund in Latin was a neuter verbal noun in suppletion with the infinitive, which could not be used in contexts requiring oblique case marking. In Romance the infinitive has widened its scope to the detriment of the gerund(ive) forms and it provides the base for newer periphrastic forms. In French, for instance, the older *Va chantant* 'He is singing' progressive type was replaced in the seventeenth century by *Il est après chanter* 'He is after singing', which survives in Canada, the creoles and some metropolitan dialects. Condemned as vulgar, this was in its turn replaced in the eighteenth century by *Il est en train de chanter* 'He is in the process of singing'. The more archaic *Está escrevendo* 'He's writing' or *Ando procurando* 'I am getting', still used in Brazil, are similarly replaced in European Portuguese and Galician by *Está a escrever*, *Ando a procurar*.

(a)   Infinitival forms

We have already seen how the infinitive has tended in modern Romance to oust certain finite clauses. In many cases it also combines with (semi-) auxiliaries to produce what are virtually new tenses. The *GO* **future**, used to indicate the imminence of an event, for instance, today rivals the synthetic future in French, Spanish and Brazilian Portuguese:

(47)   *Il va chanter, Va a cantar, Vai cantar* 'He's going to sing'.

These forms, which are not yet totally grammaticalized, probably date from the early modern period.

Other Romance languages use only periphrastic future forms, with a variety of auxiliaries, but again these may be of fairly recent origin:

(48)   R-R (Surselvan) *El vegn a cantar* [he comes to sing]; Rum. *Va / a / o cînta* [he wants to sing]; Sard *Deppo cantare* [he ought to sing]; Ital. dial. *Ha (a) cantà*, European Ptg. *Há-de cantar* [he has to sing] 'He'll sing'.

In Catalan and Western Occitan varieties the *GO* + *infinitive* form functions not as a future but as a preterite:

(49)   Cat. *Vaig cantar* [baʃ kən'ta] 'I sang'.

Ambiguity of time reference for similar forms is detectable in the medieval French and Occitan texts, but grammaticalization to refer to the past is unusual. It does, however, occur also in the isolated (Francoprovençal?) dialect of Guardia Piemontese in Calabria, in southern Italy, which seems to have been carried from north-western Alpine Italy with immigrants in the late Middle Ages. This suggests that the germs of the change may have once been more widespread.

> Other periphrastic forms with the infinitive that are more or less grammatical-ized include the French recent past with the semi-auxiliary *venir de*.

(b)   Drift?

The variety of outcomes in Romance point to parallel development rather than common origin for many of the periphrastic forms. They are often used as an illustration of a drift towards analyticity which culminates in the creole verb systems. The opposite movement, illustrated by the history of the Romance synthetic future, lends support to the view that morphology and syntax interact in a cyclical manner, with synthetic forms withering away as they are replaced by syntactic combinations, which in their turn fossilize into new synthetic forms.

4.6 THE FUTURE

One Romance form that has not ceased to intrigue linguists is the so-called 'Romance synthetic future' and its partner, the **conditional** or 'future in the past'. These forms provide ammunition for those who maintain that 'today's morphology is yesterday's syntax' or that languages pass through a cycle which transforms analytic into synthetic forms, only then to replace them by new analytic forms.

(a)   A 'Romance' future?

In fact, as we have seen, most Romance languages today use analytic future forms, most of which are attested from about the fifteenth or sixteenth century. The 'Romance future' is confined to one part of the Western Romance area, and even there is threatened by elimination by periphrastic forms. This 'synthetic' future is exemplified as follows:

(50)   French *Il chantera*, Ital. *Canterà*, Span., Ptg. *Cantará* 'He will sing'.

The standard story about the Romance future is that there developed in Late Latin a periphrastic HABERE + *infinitive* form to replace the Latin future, which was vulnerable because of its inconsistency across the conjugations (AMABO, MONEBO / AUDIAM, REGAM) and because its most salient marker, the intervocalic B of two of the conjugations, was threatened by regular sound change, merging with the U of regular perfect forms.

Evidence for use of HABERE + *infinitive* forms functioning as a future tense is extremely doubtful in the Late Latin texts, which in any case make ample use of the Classical future forms. Such analytic forms were more often attested with imperfect than with present forms of HABERE, and more plausibly carried obligative meaning ('have to') than future tense reference.

> One seventh-century attestation, from Fredegar's Chronicles, is always cited. Here an apocryphal explanation for the place-name Daras occurs in an anecdote: to an interlocutor who protests NON DABO 'I shall not give', the Emperor Justinian replies DARAS. Given the jokey context, in a manuscript which dates from a rather later period, the example is dubious. But even if genuine it is more plausibly read as 'You have to give' rather than as a neutral future.

The next attested examples, in what is usually described as the first Romance text (the *Strasburg Oaths*, usually dated 842, but in an eleventh-century manuscript), *salvarai* and *prindrai*, can likewise be read as 'I have to save / take'. An obligative meaning can also be read into many of the medieval, and even some of the modern, attestations of the forms.

The relative positioning of infinitive and auxiliary, with stress on the latter, also raises questions. In most of the Western languages auxiliaries regularly precede the lexical verb, yet here a postposed auxiliary seems to have been agglutinated as an affix. This, for some commentators, proves that grammaticalization must have occurred early, in a Latin that still retained verb-final ordering.

In this perspective the fixed postverbal position could lead later to reanalysis of the auxiliary as an affix, as it did not fit into the usual pattern of auxiliary ordering. This story does not square well with the possibility, in Old Spanish, of the future auxiliary being preposed to the verb (though here deontic rather than future meaning may be intended), nor, in Old Portuguese, of a single auxiliary being used with two infinitival forms.

More impressive evidence that there was no such reanalysis at an early period is provided by the intercalation of object pronouns between the infinitive and the postposed auxiliary (**tmesis**). This suggests that the auxiliary was separable from the infinitive and not affixal (for object clitics with the infinitive see above). Such tmesis is occasionally attested in medieval Occitan, Catalan and Northern Italian, and in Spanish until the seventeenth century, but never in French. It remains obligatory for affirmative sentences in literary Portuguese to the present day:

(51)   *Responder-nos-à* 'He will reply to us'.

> In modern spoken Portuguese, which makes little use of the synthetic future, this rule does not hold, nor did it hold absolutely in Old Portuguese or Old Spanish.

It may be that in the medieval languages there were two constructions: a periphrastic *auxiliary* + *infinitive* which allowed tmesis, used when the infinitive began a clause, probably emphasizing its lexical content, alongside a synthetic future form. In the latter the lexical part of the verb tended to lose its identity as an infinitival form and to develop as a future stem, with an *r* marking futurity. In French the future stem early divorced from the infinitive (compare *venir* 'to come' with *viendra* 'will come'). In Spanish and especially in Portuguese, however, the distinctive future stems were rejected by language arbiters at the time of standardization, so that, for instance, Old Portuguese *salrei* 'I shall go out' was replaced by *sairei* (infinitive *sair*). In the modern language there are very few 'irregular' futures (like *farei/fazer* 'to do'). In Spanish the reform was not so thoroughgoing; frequently used forms retained their distinctive shape:

(52)   *habrá* 'he will have'(Old *avrá*) / *moverá* 'he will move' (Old *movrà*).

(b)   The French connection?

It has been plausibly suggested that the synthetic future was originally a Northern French innovation. The fusion of the two elements was perhaps connected with early radical sound shifts in that region, which meant that the unaccented stem became clearly differentiated from infinitive forms. During the Middle Ages French usage may then have influenced the development, in prestige varieties elsewhere, of a Proto-Romance inherited periphrastic form. Some languages, like Rumanian and Sard, would clearly have been beyond the reach of such influence at that period, while others, like Portuguese, resisted it. It has survived, sometimes marginally, in standard languages but it is rivalled everywhere in popular colloquial use by newer periphrastic forms.

4.7   THE PASSIVE

The Latin passive in the **infectum** forms, an innovation compared with most Indo-European languages, was formed with an R that was possibly originally a nominalizing affix:

(53)   AMOR, AMABAR, AMABOR 'I am / was / will be being loved'.

These forms are completely lost in Romance, though amply attested in Late Latin texts.

Most Romance languages do, however, continue the compound *BE* + *passive participle* of the Latin perfectum series. The form with the present tense of *BE* reflects more the present perfect than the aorist Latin meaning, and it is usually indistinguishable from the stative *copula* + *participial adjective*:

(54)   AMATUS EST: French *Il est aimé*, Ital. *È amato* 'He is loved' (rather than 'He is being loved')

except on those rare (and often dubious) occasions when the agent is expressed:

(55)   French *La maison est construite* (*par les maçons*), Ital. *La casa è costruita* (*dai muratori*) 'The house is built / is being built (by the bricklayers)'.

(a)   The *BE* passive

The *BE*-passive, like the *HAVE*-perfect, was probably not fully grammatical-ized in the medieval languages, and retained much more the character of an adjectival construction. In a few cases in the modern languages, there is a tendency to distinguish the participial form in the two senses, with the inherited 'strong' form used adjectivally, though there is much regional and individual variation:

(56)   Ital. *È veduto* 'he is (being) seen'/ *È ben visto* 'he is well regarded'.

In Spanish and Portuguese the distinction is made more clearly by use of different *BE* verbs (*ser* < SEDERE 'to sit' replacing some of the forms of *ESSERE, for ESSE / *estar* < STARE 'to stand'; see 7.5):

(57)   Span. *Es despertado* 'He is being awoken'/ *Está despierto* 'He is awake'; Ptg. *Foi corrompido* 'He was corrupted' / *Estava corrupto* 'He was corrupt'.

(b)   Other auxiliaries

The stative connotations of the *BE* passive can in some of the languages be surmounted by the use of other auxiliaries – especially verbs of move-ment – which convey a more dynamic aspect:

(58)   Ital. *Vengo lodato*, Cat. *Vaig lloát* 'I am being (come/go) praised'.

In the Swiss Rhaeto-Romance languages the normal passive auxiliary is the verb 'to come':

(59)   Engadine *E(a)u vegn ludò*, Surselvan *Jeu vegnel ludáus.*

(c)   The *SE* passive

In all the languages the *BE*-passive is frowned on by purists, though in cer-tain types of discourse (like journalistic or officialese) it is fairly frequent. More usually a **middle**, erstwhile reflexive, pronominal form is preferred when the agent is unexpressed:

(60)   French *La maison se construit*; Ital. *Si costruisce la casa*; Span. *Se construye la casa* 'The house is being built [is building itself]'.

Apparent examples with an expressed agent, although found in earlier stages of the languages, are now usually disputed.

This *SE* passive was already adumbrated in Latin and is thought by some to be the true Proto-Romance substitute for the Latin R forms, which were themselves originally more middle than passive. All the Romance languages have a *SE* passive, though it is less widely used in French than elsewhere. Its adoption in French by about the thirteenth century may be a consequence of direct influence from other Romance languages via Crusaders, who interacted through a pidgin-like lingua franca ('Frankish language') which drew elements from all the Romance languages, but especially from Italian.

In Rumanian, where the *BE* passive seems to be a fairly recent and book-ish introduction, imitated from the Western languages:

(61)   *Pachetul a fost trimis de el* 'The parcel was sent by him'

the *SE* passive is much preferred in colloquial use:

(62)   *S'a trimis pachetul* 'The parcel has been sent'.

The extensive use of the pronominal in Rumanian is often ascribed to Slavonic influence.

> The further development, from 'middle' uses, of an 'impersonal pronominal' in some of the languages, probably as late as the sixteenth century, is unknown in French (see 6.5).

(d)   Convergence or interinfluence?

Here again it is difficult to disentangle the threads of development of passive constructions. Do they all continue common Proto-Romance uses? Have they drifted in the same direction from a common base? Or has there been interinfluence during the course of history of each of the languages? Probably all three explanations are valid to some extent. The *BE* passive is most clearly derived from Latin, and so in certain types of discourse has carried some prestige, but in modern times it is often seen as clumsy and ambiguous. Consequently other strategies are favoured, probably developing in parallel, but helped on by interaction between the languages.

4.8   LEXICON

Whereas Romanists, as good comparativists, usually avoid seeking in convergence or contact the origins of common phonological, morphological or syntactic features, the same is not true for the lexicon, where, it is acknowledged, 'anything goes'. Loanword studies have always been a happy playground for the traditionalist, though dismissed as amateurish by more rigorous linguists. Purist normative grammarians meanwhile condemn or lament in vain the practice of borrowing and calquing foreign or regional words. True, loanwords are rarely found among the very basic vocabulary items, but at least 30–40 per cent (depending on the breadth of the lexicon under consideration) of the normally used vocabulary of any Romance language has originated from non-native sources.

(a)   Interchange between the languages

There is no denying that at the lexical level interchange between the Romance languages is of significant proportions, amounting to about 10 per cent of items in modern everyday usage. At the present time, and especially since the Second World War, the languages turn more to English for new vocabulary than to each other – much to the disgust of purists and nationalist politicians, especially in Francophone communities.

The extent to which each language is a lender or borrower has changed over time, and fashions rapidly fade, but it is probably true that French has been a perennial source of long-lasting loanwords for all the languages. During the Middle Ages the interchange was two-way between Italian and French, though in the thirteenth century, Italian was very much more the borrower. Here are some examples.

> *Interchange of vocabulary between Italian and French in the Middle Ages*
>
> Examples of Italian borrowing into French: *alarme, espion, magasin*
> Of French into Italian: *abbandonare, giardino, goiello, leggero, mangiare, omaggio, profitto, romanzo, sentiero, troppo, villaggio*

The apogee of Italian prestige came at the time of the Renaissance with floods of especially cultural and military words entering other languages (not only Romance) in the fifteenth and sixteenth centuries. Below are some examples of French borrowings which also penetrated often into other languages:

> Borrowing from Italian into French in the fifteenth and sixteenth centuries: *accoster, artisan, assassin, balcon, ballon, banque, bizarre (originally from Spanish), brave, briller, carton, campagne, cavalier, charlatan, esquisse, manquer, masque, numéro, parfum, risque, saucisson, valise*

In Spanish and Portuguese there was also some preference for Italian loanwords in the nineteenth and early twentieth centuries, when Rumanian also drew from that source.

Leaving aside Rumanian, which was deluged by Gallicisms after it attained national language status:

(63)   *cabinet* 'office', *plajă* 'beach', *menajă* 'household'

the peak of borrowing from French was in the seventeenth and eighteenth centuries. Spanish resisted this trend during its Golden Age, but succumbed again in the eighteenth century:

(64)   *botella, frambuesa* < *bouteille, framboise* 'bottle', 'raspberry'.

Portuguese, turning its back on Spanish from the seventeenth century on, has welcomed French loanwords in the modern period:

(65)   *duche, greve* < *douche, grève* 'shower (bath)', '(labour) strike'.

Until quite recently French was the favourite foreign language of most other Romance speakers: in Latin America, especially, this was to some extent a reaction against the *gringo*, but more generally it was a tribute to the rich French literary heritage. Today, however, French is losing its grip, even in Italy, Portugal and Rumania, the most loyal European admirers of French culture and diplomacy.

It was mainly through Spanish that Arabic and American words penetrated into the other Romance languages, usually accompanying new products or ideas (although a subsidiary source of Arabisms was via Sicily):

(66)   *naranja* 'orange', *azúcar* 'sugar' > French *orange, sucre*, Ital. *arancia, zucchero*;
              chocolate 'chocolate', *tabaco* 'tobacco' > French *chocolat, tabac*, Ital. *cioccola-*
              ta, tabacco.

The greatest influx of Spanish loanwords into all the languages occurred during the Golden Age, when Catalan was particularly subject to its influence, after having itself contributed substantially to Spanish vocabulary in the fifteenth century. Catalan, and then Spanish, invaded Sard vocabulary during its Aragonese period (1326–1718):

(67)   *barat, barato* 'cheap' > *baratu*, Cat. *treballar* 'to work' > *travallare*, Span.
              dichoso 'lucky' > *ditsosu.*

Catalan and Occitan otherwise had little impact on the other languages after the medieval period, when their literary prestige was supreme.

Portuguese was the channel for exotic words from Africa and the East to enter the other languages during the colonial period:

(68)   *bambú* 'bamboo', *acajú* 'mahogany, cashew' > French *bambou, acajou*, Ital. *bambù*, Span. *bambú*

but otherwise it seems to have been a net borrower rather than a lender. Admittedly its inherited vocabulary is so close to that of Spanish that it is not easy to distinguish it from borrowed vocabulary, but Span. *afeitar* 'to shave' and *enfadoso* 'irksome' are clearly of Portuguese origin. It appears, however, that Portuguese loanwords often entered other languages via French, rather than direct: one example is the word *creole*.

(b)   Borrowing from non-standard varieties

Until quite recently many, perhaps most, Romance speakers operated in at least two Romance varieties. With standardization, medieval Latin–Romance diglossia gave way to standard–dialect diglossia, which has only slowly been eroded by universal education. It is inevitable then that there has been seepage from one variety to the other. At some periods use of dialectal words in the prestige language was fashionable: this was particularly so in French during the sixteenth century. Some revival of this fashion came about in the late nineteenth century as more interest was shown in folk culture and literature began to take on a more populist tone.

But the transfer of words was made more in the opposite direction, with the standard variety tightening its grip on local dialects. However, as the dialects lose their autonomy, regional versions of the standard grow up, which typically incorporate some salient features of the dying dialects – this is particularly true of distinctive vocabulary, so that in Italy or Latin America, for instance, standard speakers in different regions have a whole range of different words for everyday objects and activities, each borrowed originally from their local dialects. In a similar way, words that were once kept underground, as popular or vulgar, begin to emerge into prominence in standard usage, as purist stances relax and literary style tolerates more social varieties. This is true particularly of French today, and the same tendency is discernible in European Spanish and Portuguese, as it long has been in Latin America.

4.9   CONCLUSION

What I have called the 'club' effect in Romance manifests itself not only by the common plundering of Latin sources that we described in the last chapter, but also in symbiotic interaction between the languages during their history. Each of the languages, except perhaps Rumanian and Sard, has had something to contribute to the common pool, but relative cultural and political prestige of any language at any time is correlated with the linguistic sway it holds on the others. It is in lexical borrowing that influence is most transparently exerted, but morphosyntactical interchange may also occur in situations, like the Crusades, where there is frequent interaction between the speakers of the diverse languages.

More difficult to assess are the parallel developments that have apparently occurred in the different languages, but at different rates and to different degrees. In so far as these represent quasi-universal tendencies, triggered by functional considerations, there is no puzzle: the replacement of synthetic by analytic forms, for instance, is widespread in all the Indo-European languages. But some of the Romance developments seem to be idiosyncratic – like the introduction of proclitic object pronouns, or the creation of a new synthetic future tense. Do we seek the origins of these features in a Latin variety for which we have little textual evidence? Or do we accept that each language is tracking at different speeds along tramlines that lead in the same direction from the same starting point? We wonder too whether the creoles represent a further staging point in this journey, or some sort of side-track.

So far we have looked at some of the many shared features of the Romance languages. But each language also has its own characteristics. Part II looks at the differences between the languages. In the next chapter we shall ask what delimits one language from another, and attempt to classify the languages into different groupings, and then we shall go on to discuss how the languages became different.

FURTHER READING

On diphthongization and on vocabulary interchange, see especially the articles by Purschinsky and Hope in Posner & Green eds. (1980–93), vol. I. On the infinitive, Joseph (1985); on infinitival complementation, Lamiroy (1984), Pearce (1990). On subordination, Dardel (1983). Calboli ed. (1989), Andersen & Skytte eds. (1995). On clitics, Nevis *et al.* (1994), Borer (1984, ed. 1986), Jaeggli (1981), Kok (1985), Wanner (1987), Jaeggli & Safir eds. (1989). On auxiliaries, Harris & Ramat eds. (1987). On the future, Fleischman (1982). On reflexivization, Everaert (1986). On 'middles', Fagan (1992). On the passive, Klaiman (1991). On noun phrase syntax, Giorgio & Longobardi (1991).

PART II

The differences

5

How many Romance languages?

5.1 HOW MANY ROMANCE LANGUAGES ARE THERE?

An answer to this question that has been slightingly labelled *sancta simplicitas* is that there is only one: the languages are all alike enough to be deemed dialects of the same language. Another equally disingenuous answer might be 'thousands' – of distinctive local varieties – or 'millions' – of individual idiolects. The usual textbook answer is 'ten, or possibly eleven', according priority to putative chronologically early differentiation from the common stock, allegedly linked to ethnic differences among the speakers.

(a) State languages

The layman has no difficulty in accepting as 'languages' the five that have 'armies and navies' (some of them several) – that is French, Spanish, Portuguese, Italian and Rumanian. Even then there is in some Latin American countries a reluctance to accept the names that refer to European states: 'Castilian' or 'national language' is preferred to Spanish, and in Brazil terms like 'Vernacular' or 'Expression and Communication' are sometimes used in educational institutions to avoid reference to Portuguese.

For French there appears to be less of a problem about nomenclature, but Suisse Romande or Belgian speakers sometimes resent the hegemony of Parisian French. Canadian French speakers are more immediately concerned with the challenge of English than with that of metropolitan ('hexagonal') French.

Rumanian is also associated with two separate states – in the ex-Soviet republic of Moldavia (Moldova) the majority of inhabitants use Rumanian, until recently written in Cyrillic script, and dispute continues to rage about separate language status.

Italian, on the other hand, is the language of a single state (leaving aside San Marino and the Swiss Tessin (Ticino) canton) but it overlays a host of different still lively dialects, with sometimes comparatively little in common. In origin it was basically a medieval literary language adopted by the Italian state unified in the nineteenth century, but it has yet to win over the hearts and mouths of all Italians.

(b)   Literary languages

Another two Romance 'languages' gain general recognition mainly because of their status as medieval literary languages, coupled with the militancy of linguistic propagandists. These are Occitan and Catalan.

Occitan is a modern name adapted from the older *langue d'oc* of southern France, distinguished from northern *langue d'oïl* (*oui*) on the basis of medieval words for 'yes'. In the nineteenth century it came to be known as Provençal, mainly to German linguists and partly because of the mid-century literary revival, whose main luminary was Mistral, which favoured the local varieties of Provence. Occitan is the name preferred by modern activists, whose local loyalties usually look further to the west. A standardized non-regional form is recognized in a limited way for French educational purposes, though modern spoken varieties can differ considerably, especially in Gascony.

One Bearnese variety of Occitan, spoken by the majority of inhabitants in the Val d'Aran, in the central Pyrenees, has official status, because the valley falls politically within the Generalitat de Catalunya (the regional government of Catalonia), which has a liberal language policy. The dialects of the extreme south-east coastal area of France, around Nice and Monaco, are closer linguistically to Italian Ligurian varieties than to Occitan: the zone was not drawn completely into the French political orbit until the mid-nineteenth century.

Old Occitan literature, especially the lyric poetry of the troubadours, is acknowledged as among the finest in Europe, before it was effectively stifled by the northern forces of the Albigensian crusade in the thirteenth century. The rediscovery of the literature during the Romantic revival was partly responsible for the growth of interest in Romance languages:

Raynouard (see page 113) virtually identified the 'language of the troubadours' with the postulated common *langue romane* from which all Romance languages have sprung, and a youthful Diez (see pages 3–4), on a pilgrimage to Weimar, was directed towards Romance studies by Goethe, who recommended troubadour poetry to him.

Literary Old Catalan was very close to Old Occitan, culturally and linguistically, and sometimes called by the same name *lemosí* (Limousine – from the Limoges region). It originated in the north-eastern buffer region of Catalonia carved out by Charlemagne from Moorish Spain, possibly as an innovating variety of Aragonese. Its prestige was great and it remained the chancery language of the Aragonese court until the union with Castile in the fifteenth century. The nineteenth-century revival of the language was aided by the prosperity of its main urban centre, Barcelona, and in spite of repression by the Franco regime (although even then it was the official language of independent Andorra) it has survived as a vigorously championed language, even achieving some degree of recognition within the European Union. Varieties of Catalan are used north of the Pyrenees in French Roussillon, in the Balearics and even, still actively, in Alghero, a fishing port in north-western Sardinia. There it survived from the time the town was resettled under the Aragonese occupation in the fourteenth century, almost unnoticed until its rediscovery by nineteenth-century Catalan archaeologists researching in Sardinian prehistoric sites. Algherian has since been drawn firmly into the Catalan orbit, with the keen support of the handful of now prosperous Catalan speakers in this attractive tourist resort.

Less enthusiasm for Catalan is shown in Valencia, where a Catalan variety was, until recently, spoken mainly by the less-privileged inhabitants, and where now the tone-setting intellectuals and politicians maintain that Valencian has separate language status, though objectively it differs little from other Catalan varieties.

> On the basis of an illustrious medieval literary tradition, Galician (Gallego), the Iberian language of choice for lyric poetry, should be counted as an additional Romance language. However, the textbook stance is that it is the same language as Portuguese – or rather Galego-Portuguese, associated with north-western pre-Romance Celtic population and post-Romance settlement by Swabians (rather than Visigoths, who occupied most of the rest of the peninsula). The language spread south with the Reconquest but split into two branches when Portugal became a separate state, leaving Galicia as part of Spain. (For standardization of Galician see 5.5.)

(c)   Linguists' languages

Two of the textbook Romance languages owe their status to the whims of a late nineteenth-century linguist, the Italian Graziado Ascoli (see page 4), voicing contemporary ideas about ethnicity and language. It was he who first mooted the idea of **Rhaeto-Romance** as originally a unified language, linked closer to French than to the North Italian dialects with which it is now intertwined. The name recalls the Rhaetians, who lived in the Alpine region in ancient times: the assumption was that their peculiar version of Latin survives today in the scattered Rhaeto-Romance dialects, which have been depleted by incursions by the Italian Lombard and Venetan varieties from the south, and by German from the north.

The view that they are really centrifugal varieties of North Italian dialects, whose prolonged contact with German sheltered them from innovations, is held particularly by Italian linguists, and was given official support under Mussolini. The Italian claim for the South Tyrol from Austria in the First World War was bolstered by the linguistic case. There, in the Alto Adige, amid a German-speaking population, the valleys of the Dolomites harbour a small number of speakers of idiosyncratic Romance varieties, known collectively to linguists as **Ladin**, and now officially recognized as a separate language. There were no written forms of these varieties before the nineteenth century. The Ladin speakers' loyalties went in the past to Austria rather than to nascent and impoverished Italy, and in the Second World War, following a pact between Hitler and Mussolini, most of them chose to throw in their lot with Greater Germany. The region, however, remained Italian after the war, a period of terrorism by German-speaking separatists being eventually ended by granting the region a degree of autonomy. This spectacularly beautiful region, particularly popular with German-speaking mountain-lovers, could then settle down to the lucrative tourist trade. Ladin is now taught in local primary schools, in a different version for each valley, and there seems to be no danger of its early demise, nor any desire for standardization and unification.

The Rhaeto-Romance varieties of the Graubünden (Grisons) canton of Switzerland had a rather different history. Mussolini's political threat persuaded the Confederation to grant to the dialects, in 1936, the status of 'national', but not of 'official', language; that means that it can be used for official purposes within the canton, but not elsewhere within the Confederation (unfortunate, today, when many speakers live in Zurich or

Geneva). Each commune, originally 120 in number, could decide whether its primary school uses the Romance variety; over the years more and more have moved to German, or sometimes to Italian. In those eighty-two communes that do adopt it, five different regional varieties are used. The 'school-taught' languages are based more on geographical regions than on linguistic affinities.

The most westerly variety, in the Upper Rhine valley, with the most numerous group of speakers, is known as **Romansh** (*Romontsch, roumanche*). Linguists call their language Sursilvan or Surselvan (*Oberwaldisch*). It was previously called *Churwälsch*, from the administrative centre Chur (Cuera) whose population in the fifteenth century was wholly (now only 10 per cent) Romance-speaking. The dialect area has shrunk over the last few hundred years as German spread its tentacles, and the Surselvan dialect is clearly heavily influenced by German. Early texts date from the sixteenth century – mainly Bible translations and religious commentaries. The area was riven asunder by the Reformation, and different orthographical systems were devised for Catholics and for Protestants. A smaller, and shrinking, dialect grouping Sutselvan (*Nidwald*) is quite closely related to Surselvan, which was until quite recently often used as a school language in the region. The Surmeiran (*Ober-* and *Unterhalbstein*) grouping embraces heterogeneous varieties, some of which are quite remote from the school-taught language. In all these regions bilingualism with Swiss German is general.

Further easterly varieties, just south of western Austria, have long been known to the mountaineer and skier. In the Inn valley, the Engadine is split between Upper and Lower dialects (*Ladin puter* and *vallader*), while the Val Müstair (Munster) version is often classed separately. These varieties are closer to Italian dialects south across the mountain passes than are the Western varieties. Influx of German-speaking population has in the last half-century reduced radically the proportion of Romance speakers, who often number among the less prosperous of their communities.

Recently a new unified standard form embracing all the varieties has been elaborated (see 5.5) in an attempt to save a language which the Swiss claim to be proud of, but do little to sustain.

Friulian (or Friulan), a third group of dialects associated by Ascoli with the Rhaetians, is much closer to Italian than the others, as West Friuli has been closely associated with Venice since the sixteenth century. East Friuli, though, had, until after the First World War, closer contact with German (not to mention Slovenian to the east). Friulian has had a flourishing literature from the sixteenth century and communication between the different varieties is relatively easy. It is not recognized as a separate language by the Italian state, and most speakers operate freely with the Veneto koine as well as in Friulian and Italian. Friulians, like Galicians, have in the past emigrated to other parts of the world, often retaining their distinctive speech habits. There is even in the Danube delta region of Rumania an active community of Friulian speakers, implanted there in the nineteenth century. The link between Friulian and the other Rhaeto-Romance varieties is slender and many linguists deny any connection, pointing to the features it shares with surrounding dialects of Veneto.

The other Romance language that Ascoli wished on us is Franco-Provençal. Today it is recognized by most linguists as a distinctive set of South-Eastern French dialects, bordering on Occitan, and the compromise name 'Francoprovençal' is used. Some would prefer to see the dialects as basically Occitan into which French has made earlier and even greater inroads than further west; certainly the vocabulary is close to that of Occitan, but that may reflect the archaic character of the dialects rather than genetic affinity. Others point to the similarities between Rhaeto-Romance and Francoprovençal, postulating a common Alpine ancestor that had French-like features. Yet others relate Francoprovençal features to those of other 'outpost' French varieties in the north and east, which, it is assumed, retain more archaic characteristics. In France the dialects, which once embraced Lyon, Grenoble and the Jura, have all but disappeared, but they have endured better in Switzerland and Italy. They are today spoken mainly in mountainous regions in eastern France (Savoy) and western Switzerland (Vaud, Neuchâtel, Valais) as well as over the Alps in the Val d'Aosta (*valdôtain*). Wartburg associated them with Burgundian settlement, though it has since been shown that this was not coterminous with the Francoprovençal area. Although the language of some medieval texts shows signs of provenance from this area, the culture language is French (though Mussolini temporarily imposed Italian on his side of the Alps). There has never been a koineized version, nor any substantial literary output. For the relationship of these varieties with German see 8.6.

(d)   One-off

The inclusion of **Sard** as a separate Romance language is agreed by most Romanists, on the ground that the island was cut off early from the rest of the Romance area. How Romanized the island was is doubtful: excavations in the interior to find traces of ancient roads may cast light on that question. Fever-ridden (until American armed forces sprayed the mosquito swamps at the end of the Second World War), it was used as a penitentiary for hardened criminals by the Romans, and it was part of the Byzantine Empire and then under Saracen rule. In the ninth century independent townships were established, under the authority of Pisa, before it succumbed to the Aragonese. Yielded to the Austrians in 1714, it was soon handed over to Savoy in exchange for Sicily. It thus was fully integrated into Italy at the time of Unification.

The dialects spoken within the island are not all, however, classified as Sard. The Northern dialects, of the western Sassari area or eastern Gallurian, lack the Sard distinctive features, like the IPSE-derived definite article (see 3.3). It is thought that they are in fact Corsican in origin, brought by refugees from vendettas in that island (for Corsican, usually classed as a Tuscan dialect, see 5.6).

It is the central mountainous and, even today, relatively inaccessible part of the island which is supposed to harbour the prototypical Sard (Logudorian), while the Southern Campidanian group of dialects are seen as more heavily influenced by Italian. Although Sard is attested in charters from the late eleventh century, it never was standardized, and intercommunication between the dialects is minimal. In the nowadays semi-autonomous region, the authorities encourage development of the language, but much of the island has remained poor, depopulated and bandit-ridden, with high emigration rates, so that there has been little popular pressure for standardization.

(e)   A thoroughly dead language

Another language that sometimes rounds off the textbook score is Dalmatian, now totally extinct. It is seen as bridging the gap between Italian and Rumanian, and representative of a whole host of lost Romance languages that must once have existed. We know that a Romance language was once spoken along the Dalmatian coast, and that Ragusa (now Dubrovnik) still used the language in governmental functions in the sixteenth century, before Croatian took over completely. It is difficult to tell how different the language was from that of Venice, which controlled ports along the coast for centuries. The only evidence we have of a living version of the language is that collected from the last surviving speaker, who was killed in 1898 by a landmine in the island of Veglia (Krk), off the Istrian peninsula. He seems to have been a garrulous, but not necessarily reliable, witness. He had never been an active communicator in the language, having picked it up from private conversations between his parents, who used it as a secret code. His own toothless condition, at the time of the investigation, may have played havoc with his articulation, and the transcriptions are in any case probably rather hit or miss.

The fact that the informant had worked alongside Friulians (whose conversational exchanges he said he could follow easily), and had frequent contact with Venetian, may render his evidence a little suspect. Nevertheless the information we can glean does suggest that the variety he used differs in some respects from other Romance varieties. In the Istrian peninsula nearby, some other tiny pockets of Romance remain – some of these are labelled 'Istriot' by investigators who see them as another distinct language, but others claim they are versions of North-Eastern Italian dialects, whereas Ascoli linked some of them with Rhaeto-Romance. There are also isolated localities using 'Istro-Rumanian', which appears to be more closely related to the Daco-Rumanian of the standard language than to other varieties, but infiltrated through and through by Serbo-Croat. Their origin is lost in the mists of time, but the communities are thought to have fled the Ottomans at an early period, and they have no folk-memory of Rumanian culture.

(f)   More languages?

Other Romance varieties lay disputed claim to 'language' status: some of these will be discussed under Standardology (5.5) and others under Language and Dialect (5.6).

5.2   GENETIC CLASSIFICATION

Although there is comparatively little doubt about the membership of the Romance family, there is considerable disagreement on sub-grouping within the family. Classically, sub-grouping is based on historical and geographical criteria. Assuming a past-time unified language, the **Stammbaum** (family tree) model looks for successive innovations, shared by more than one daughter language. Each diagnostic innovation creates a new unified proto-language differentiated from its siblings, which then may be further split by later innovations among some of its members. As each sub-group is envisaged as a real-life language it must occupy space (geographical or social) as well as time. Causes of the innovations are usually sought in ethnic or social factors, but breakdown of communications between far-flung areas also takes pride of place.

The earliest Romance split postulated by traditional sub-grouping is that involving the loss of Latin vowel quantity (see 3.3). The merger of Ĭ/Ē and Ŭ/Ō is seen as an innovation that affected 'Western Romance' (or 'Vulgar Latin', see 3.2), eluding those regions that had become isolated from trendy innovations at earlier periods – like Sard, Rumanian and Southern Italian varieties.

Within the Stammbaum model usually in Romance only phonological criteria for diagnostic shared innovations are considered valid. George Trager in 1934 also introduced, as a check, some morphosyntactic criteria like the use of the two-case system in Gallo-Roman (French and Occitan). Nevertheless he grouped case-free Catalan more closely with Occitan than with French. On the basis of non-palatalization of Latin /k/ before front vowels, Dalmatian is grouped with Sard (as 'insular' Eastern Romance, as distinct from the 'peninsular' variety represented by Italian and Rumanian).

The now most widely accepted version of the Romance Stammbaum is that of another American, Robert Hall Jr, who, having split off the isolates (first Proto-Sardinian, then Proto-Eastern Romance) from 'Proto-Italo-Western Romance' using vocalic criteria, then proceeds to use only criteria of consonantal changes to effect further sub-grouping. Proto-Italian is distinguished from Proto-Western on the basis of the treatment of clusters like /kt/ (assimilated in Italian but palatalized in Proto-Ibero- and Proto-Gallo-Romance; see 3.3). Then Proto-Western Romance is sub-divided further mainly by reference to palatalizing innovations. The end-result looks suspiciously like areal grouping.

Lexicochronology adopts similar assumptions to traditional Stammbaum theory but uses the criterion of shared basic vocabulary for sub-grouping. The most recent revisions of the method point to subgrouping on areal lines, with Rumanian and French at the poles, Portuguese and Spanish very closely related, and Catalan more loosely associated with the same group, while Friulian is more closely bound with Italian than with the other Rhaeto-Romance languages. Lexicochronologists are less con-

cerned to establish a Romance classification than to justify the validity of
their methodology: therefore they are pleased that their sub-grouping, and
the associated time-depth, closely resembles traditional areal ones.

A more radical but committed American reconstructionist relying on
phonological criteria, Clifford Leonard, insists on consistent use of only
vocalic changes, seeing the most important split off as that between
'heterochronic' versus 'isochronic' Romance languages. The former distinguished, at an early stage, between free and blocked syllables in their
treatment of stressed vowels, sometimes lengthening the vowel in the free
syllable (see 4.2). A sub-grouping along these lines would class the dialects
of north-east Italy and of Abruzzo and Apulia with French and
Francoprovençal, but Venetian and Occitan with Spanish and Portuguese.
This areal distribution would suggest that the heterochronic varieties are
innovating, leaving a margin of more conservative areas.

This grouping is consistent with a 'wave' model that, since Schuchardt
(see page 4), has always been more widely favoured among European
Romanists than the Stammbaum model. It accounts better for the apparent catenation of interintelligible varieties, with few distinct dialect boundaries, across the Romance area.

A widely favoured distinction between central innovating areas and the
conservative rim is based largely on lexical criteria. For instance,
Spanish/Portuguese and Rumanian seem to share certain more archaic
items that are lost elsewhere, like FORMOSUS rather than BELLUS 'beautiful',
MAGIS not PLUS 'more', or FERVERE not BULLIRE 'to boil':

(1)   Span. *hermoso, más, hervir*, Ptg. *formoso, mais, ferver*, Rum. *frumos, mai, fierbe* /
         French *beau, plus, bouillir*, Ital. *bello, più, bollire*.

Another distinction along similar lines, but using a range of criteria,
most notably verbal morphology and lexical translation equivalents,
would distinguish **Romania continua**, running from the Atlantic along the
Mediterranean, from the two outposts, in northern France and Rumania
(with Portuguese on the Atlantic rim also showing idiosyncratic features,
and Castilian acting as a bit of a maverick).

Other historical classifications are equally areally based. The most generally accepted is the east–west divide, most consistently advocated by
Walther von Wartburg, who drew a dividing line across Italy from La
Spezia to Rimini. Wartburg's criteria, curiously for a scholar best known
for his lexicological work, were phonological – the west retains Latin final

-s and voices intervocalic voiceless consonants – but they were linked to social factors (see 6.2). The conservative retention of -s, important for morphology, was seen as due to the influence of schools, whereas the retention of intervocalic surds and of geminates in the east was a popular conservative feature. Sard conserves both features, having escaped the popular innovation of loss of final -s as a consequence of early isolation from the rest of the Romance area.

Another less widely accepted areal grouping sees the Mediterranean as the centre of 'Romanceness', continuous intercommunication having presumably been maintained by sea transport.

(a)   Classification on the basis of historical data

In the post-Second World War period other attempts were made at quantitative classification with a historical perspective, using various criteria, but without specific reference to proto-stages. They arrive at different groupings, or more often rankings. Mario Pei in 1949 measured seventy-seven 'change-points' in Latin stressed vowels and came out with a ranking that placed French at one pole with 44 per cent of the points and Sard at the other with 8 per cent. Unusually, Portuguese by this measure was not grouped with Spanish. Joseph Grimes and Frederick Agard's 1958 quantitative classification of phonological changes from Latin did place Portuguese nearest to Spanish, and French, showing most changes, at the opposite pole from Sard, but linked, through Catalan to the Iberian languages.

(b)   Mixed historical/synchronic classification

Žarko Muljačić's classification of twelve languages mixes diachronic and synchronic data, using forty plus-or-minus parameters from different levels (of which sixteen concern phonological changes familiar from Stammbaum classifications). Many of these are chosen because they differentiate one language from the others, either as innovations or as archaisms – like the use of an IPSE-derived definite article (see 3.3) or of two forms of negative NON in Sard, and the enclisis of the definite article, or the use of nominal case forms (see 3.3) in Rumanian. Nasal phonemes (see pages 24–9) differentiate French, Francoprovençal and Portuguese from the others, whereas the existence of central vowels characterizes

French, Occitan, Francoprovençal and Engadine Rhaeto-Romance. In Catalan, Spanish and Portuguese, there is a three-term set of demonstratives (corresponding to the three persons of the verb –'here by me', 'there by you' and 'over there'), while a prepositional accusative (see 3.3) is used in Rumanian, Sard, Engadine Rhaeto-Romance, Spanish and Portuguese.

A pairwise comparison of shared features, unsurprisingly, reveals that French and Francoprovençal, and Spanish and Portuguese, are very close one to the other. More controversially, Catalan comes out closer to Occitan and to French than to Spanish, while Friulian is closer to Engadine Rhaeto-Romance than to Italian, which is quite far removed from most other languages, especially French.

But how far is this grouping dependent on the choice of criteria rather than on real-life communicative factors? Giovanni Pellegrini, using virtually the same measures, but including in his purview some Italian (and from his standpoint more significantly, Rhaeto-Romance) dialects, demonstrates that the category 'Italian dialect' makes little linguistic sense: there are more differences between standard Italian and a Lucanian dialect than between that dialect and Spanish or even Rumanian. The Rhaeto-Romance of the Dolomite Val di Fassa may be nearer, on these criteria, to Friulian than to Italian, yet, Pellegrini asserts, a Friulian finds it easier to read a newspaper even in Spanish than one in Dolomite Ladin.

5.3   TYPOLOGY

Typological classification of the Romance languages is less commonly practised than genetic grouping. The languages are, it is often argued, very similar typologically, and indeed fit into patterns that are familiar in European languages. Whether there is indeed a Eurotype, and what its distinguishing characteristics are, is currently under investigation in a large-scale inter-European project under the auspices of the European Science Foundation. Certainly there are many formal resemblances between the Romance languages and the Germanic languages, even leaving aside the substantial resemblances that date back to their common Indo-European ancestors, or that have arisen since through communicative interaction.

A 1963 study, by the Chilean Heles Contreras, applied to seven Romance languages the now classic morphosyntactic indices devised by Joseph Greenberg (measuring, for instance, the relative degree of synthesis versus analysis, of agglutination, derivation and compounding etc. in constructions). Portuguese was shown, by this count, to be the most, and French the least, synthetic of the modern languages, while in other respects Sard most resembles Latin. No clear classification emerged from the exercise, but it appeared to bunch together first French and Catalan, and then Spanish, Italian and Rumanian, with Portuguese and Sard as isolates, loosely associated to the first and second main groupings respectively.

More recently the German Karl-Hermann Körner has proposed that the Romance languages be split typologically into two groups. One, including French and Italian, makes use of the partitive article and agreement of the past participle in the compound tenses with preposed objects (see 6.4), as well as the 'predicative relative' (or 'tensed complement', see 7.4) and the 'nominativus pendens' (that is, topicalization in preference to left dislocation with clitic doubling; see 4.4). Only languages in this first group may be 'non-pro-drop' (though many of them are not). The other group, including Spanish, Portuguese, Sard, Rumanian and Engadine Rhaeto-Romance, uses a 'prepositional accusative' (see 3.3), left dislocation with clitic doubling, the infinitive as a noun and with an overt subject (see 4.3), as well as a dative as subject of the infinitive in causative constructions (see 3.4). The data adduced are hotly disputed, especially for Italian, where Northern varieties seem to be privileged in the analysis. Körner, however, insists that he is looking for preferences rather than absolute distinctions, and that the division does not apply to the past, when the features he selects as diagnostic for typing the modern languages were admittedly more widespread over the Romance area.

The Principles-and-Parameters version of Government and Binding (GB) theory has also led to the postulation of a whole host of potential typological distinctions within modern Romance – of which the most fruitful has been that correlated with the 'pro-drop' parameter (see 1.2). Other candidates for parametrization have concerned head government (manifested, for instance, in adjectival and determiner placement, see 3.4), verb raising (with evidence from, for instance, negative placement; see 7.4), the status of reflexive pronominals (see 4.7, 6.4), and hosts of others. In more recent 'minimalist' theory, parametrization has been more closely linked to morphology than to syntax; approaches along these lines have been made to features like the 'Romance future' (see 4.6) and placement of object clitics (see 6.5).

Typological distinctions based on surface ordering of elements in the

sentence are now somewhat out of fashion in Romance studies, but did
have some vogue among Romanists for a while. The putative passage of
Latin SOV to modern SVO ordering was assumed to have passed through
a stage where the Topic, rather than the Subject, took pride of place.
Modern languages like French with consistent SVO ordering have also
been distinguished from those with pragmatically determined freer word
order. It has been proposed that Spanish, for instance, is basically a VSO
language, and that French is heading in the same direction, with grammaticalization of subject clitics as person markers (see 1.2).

5.4   DIALECTOMETRY

The greatest problem about such comparisons is that the data used are
disparate: the findings of even the most meticulous dialect description are
not directly comparable with the prescriptions of an official standardized
language, backed by educational and administrative institutions. In parts
of the south of Italy or in Sardinia, no dialect koinai have become established and nearby local varieties can differ considerably, with only the
standard being used for intercommunication between localities. In north
Italy, on the other hand, purely local varieties are ousted by regional
koinai that tend to be sharply delimited one from the other. The diverse
dialects are 'Italian' only in the sense that they are spoken in Italy: their
linguistic relationship to the standard arises from interaction rather than
any deep-seated and ancient affinity. The classic model of Italian dialectology, championed by Ascoli (see page 4), was that the standard, based
on the Tuscan dialect, represented the continuation of a Latin relatively
uncorrupted by contact with other ancient Italic dialects (allegedly
because the substratum Etruscan language was so far removed from Latin
that interference was minimal). It therefore was taken to represent most
nearly the common denominator from which all dialects were historically
derived.

What was neglected in this classic account is the apparent closer linguistic affiliation of some 'Italian' dialects to non-Italian Romance. Indeed
everywhere Romance non-standard varieties share features and tendencies
not always reflected in the related standards. Support is thereby lent to the
Schuchardtian contention that at the level of folk usage, before the imposition of standards, there were, within the Romance area, few, if any, boundaries (substantial bundles of isoglosses). Therefore classification other

than on a geographical basis was deemed impossible. However, modern 'dialectometry' attempts to measure the linguistic distance between the local varieties, taking into account degrees of interaction.

Dialect studies in the Romance area have a long and respectable history, dating back to the eighteenth century. Before that there were informal references to regional variants, as well as works explicitly composed in dialect, usually for comic effect or with political motives. The earlier more serious traditions favour the dialect monograph (often by a native speaker and usually concentrating on phonological changes from Latin, and highlighting differences between the local dialect and the related standard), and the questionnaire about non-standard usage, circulated to local dignitaries (the first being that of Abbé Grégoire, during the French Revolutionary period, which sought information for sociopolitical purposes). In the twentieth century priority has gone to the dialect atlas, which presents in spatial terms local variants of lexical items and common phrases. The first was the 1902–10 *Atlas linguistique de la France* (*ALF*), under the direction of Jules Gilliéron, a maverick linguist, who is best known for his opposition to Neogrammarian sound-laws and his championship of the atomistic 'Each word has his own history' slogan. The atlas initiated the use of amateur fieldworkers (specifically an ex-shopkeeper, Edmont) cycling between localities and registering the responses of chosen 'good speakers' (usually elderly) to a predetermined set of questions.

The prestige of the *ALF* encouraged official support for a massive new series of more professionally executed French regional linguistic atlases in the postwar period. The 'ecological' aspect of this type of study is paramount: fear that doomed rural dialects would not be recorded for posterity triggered the attempt to preserve part of a national heritage that no longer served social or economic goals.

The equally prestigious Italian linguistic atlas of 1928–40, *Sprach- und Sachatlas Italiens und der Südschweiz* (*AIS*), edited by the Zurich University professors Jaberg and Jud, was conceived in the 'Word and Thing' tradition, seeking to link traditional culture with the language used to convey it. The fieldworkers included future luminaries of Romance linguistics like Max Leopold Wagner and Gerhard Rohlfs, and its data remain an invaluable record of interwar dialects in Italy, Sardinia and southern Switzerland.

The tradition of linguistic atlases has been continued in the other Romance countries though, given the expense of carrying out and publishing such projects, they have not always seen the light, except when they have received, as in France, substantial government subsidies.

It is the dialect atlas that fostered the idea of measuring the distance between dialects – partly because isoglosses traced along the boundary between alternative forms rarely coincided with meaningful frontiers between sets of dialects. In France a bundle of phonological isoglosses do mark, in the west, the switch from French to Occitan, but the isoglosses fan out unpredictably in the east. The Western clearcut division may in any case be misleading, as there is evidence that it is there that Northern varieties have since the Middle Ages encroached heavily on Southern varieties, pushing perhaps some of the diagnostic isoglosses further south to form a more compact bundle. In the east, mainly in more mountainous terrain, incursion of Northern dialectal features may have been less consistently triumphant (though see 5.1 for 'Francoprovençal', as fundamentally a French rather than an Occitan variety).

In Italy, too, a bundle of isoglosses appears to silhouette the central dialects, which were for centuries under papal rule. It is assumed that their separation from the prosperous north and the indigent south was accompanied by communication barriers. It is noteworthy that regional dialect koinai, which are an important feature of the northern Italian linguistic scene (see 8.4), failed to develop in the Papal States.

Typically, however, Romance dialects form a chain of mutually intelligible varieties (leaving aside, of course, Rumanian). There are few insurmountable natural barriers to communication within the Romance area: the Pyrenees and the Alps have accessible passes; rivers and seas can be crossed in boats. Traditionally villages would group round the market town and the diocese, but young people could still, with a little more effort, go courting in less familiar neighbourhoods. It has been claimed that in the Middle Ages forests posed more of an obstacle to intercommunication than other natural features: Old Walloon's distinctiveness compared with other Northern French dialects has been attributed to a densely wooded dividing belt, rather than to the later political separation of the Walloon area in Belgium. In modern times the area, assumed previously to be thickly forested, forms a transitional dialect wedge between Picard and Walloon, with some features of both.

> In any case there were fewer settlements in remote areas in the Middle Ages. As population expanded and protection against aggression improved, more isolated localities were settled, sometimes by people coming from far afield.

Dialectometrists are concerned mainly with the confines of areas of possible intercommunication. Nowadays, of course, speakers rarely even attempt discourse in their local dialect with strangers from other localities, resorting immediately to a version of a standard, or at least of a regional koine. Besides, intelligibility depends on the goodwill and co-operativeness, as well as the range of experience, of interlocutors, more than on linguistic factors.

Jean Séguy, when in charge of the regional atlas of Gascony, noted that often there would be more differences between two close-by dialects than between those further off. Each locality diifferentiates itself from near neighbours (not only by language, but perhaps by wearing a hat in a different way and other such markers). This does not hinder communication, though it is, as speakers will be fully conscious of the dissimilarities, often a butt for mockery in the privacy of in-groups. Séguy maintained that it was not phonological variants (which merely produce unheeded surface noise) but lexical differences that make for loss of intelligibility. Positing that a 50 per cent difference in vocabulary would render a foreign dialect impenetrable, he traced across Romance dialectal space the lexical representation of a hundred everyday concepts randomly chosen from atlas material, finding that there was a fairly constant relationship between lexical differences and geographical distance within the same umbrella 'language'. On an imaginary walk across southern France, from Biarritz on the west coast to Menton in the east, there is no intelligibility frontier in the 700-odd kilometres covered, but going from south to north from the eastern Pyrenees to Liège in Belgium, a frontier has to be crossed at about half that distance. On his journey north through Italy from Apulia to the Alps he encounters an intelligibility frontier after some 850 kilometres, but then things do not get much worse during the next 200 or so kilometres covered. To illustrate his point more sharply he pinpoints the sudden increase of lexical differences as he passes from his home-base in Gascony, east to Catalan (Roussillon) and west to Basque territory.

Séguy and his successors, most notably Henri Guiter and Hans Goebl, also use more sophisticated quantitative techniques and a wider range of criteria, though still culled from atlas data, in order to trace the boundaries between dialect groupings. Sub-dialects, dialects and languages are defined in terms of the concentration of differences or similarities of linguistic features over geographical space. Transitional areas and hybrid languages nevertheless still exist, and there are gaps in frontiers at points where intercommunication between the different groups is more frequent.

Nevertheless a perception of what constitutes a dialect grouping may be related to a real or imaginary prototype. For instance, the most prototypically Gascon of the dialects or south-west France is Bearnese, hard up against the Pyrenees. From there in every direction dialects display fewer emblematic Gascon features as they retreat from the Pyrenees, with particularly intense de-Gasconization around large centres of population.

5.5   STANDARDOLOGY

If dialects merge into each other on the ground, each modern standard is, on the other hand, almost consciously defined in contradistinction to the others and usually covers a defined territory. Within each area local usage nowadays adjusts to a greater or lesser degree to the standard (reacting sometimes by setting up its own rival standard).

A type of classification known as 'standardology' distinguishes the **Abstand** ('stand-off') from the **Ausbau** ('built-up') language, each embracing a range of related varieties, social or regional. The former may on linguistic grounds (but which?) be distinguishable from its neighbours, but it is conscious elaboration that establishes the clearly delimited standard. The Abstand can be described in terms of a distinct **diasystem**. The dialects it covers usually shelter under the 'roof' (a better metaphor might be 'are within the orbit') of an elaborated form of one of the dialects, or of the fruit of **accommodation** between the dialects (a **koine**). In some cases the 'roof' may be provided by a totally distinct language: the Germanic dialect of Alsace operates, for political and cultural reasons, within the orbit of standard French and not of standard German.

(a)   Abstand

The diasystem can manifest itself spontaneously as a koine, used for intercommunication between speakers of related dialects who have some sense of solidarity. Such koinai grew up, as we have seen, in northern Italy, and perhaps in medieval northern France. In southern France a degree of koineization between local dialects was effected after the Revolution. Compulsory military service, which grouped young conscripts by region, helped to create an underground barracks Occitan, along with a comradeship that distanced them from the French-speaking officer class.

The more radical levelling (or perhaps non-differentiation) of (Daco-) Rumanian dialects may be different in character. It has been suggested (by, among others, Hungarians who still smart from the secession of Transylvania in 1918) that the lack of dialect diversity in the Rumanian state is evidence that the language was imported at a comparatively late date from south of the Danube (where isolates are much more diverse – see 5.6) by Vlach migrant herdsmen. Other possible explanations are that feudal organization and its consequent fragmentation of early medieval social grouping never hit that corner of Europe, or that the Ottoman strategy of Balkanization (dividing the Empire into small satellite states the better to exercise control) had the effect of ensuring for Wallachia and Moldavia more internal linguistic unity.

(b)   State standards

The codification of the four Western Romance standard (Ausbau) languages can be dated back to the Renaissance, though vernacular literary and administrative texts are numerous from the twelfth and thirteenth centuries. The desire for a unified state language is associated with the threatened demise, in the sixteenth century, of Latin as the vehicle of culture, law and government. At the same time there were being fashioned in Europe large states with more absolute power than had been possible in the feudal era. The adoption of an authoritative state language could, it was thought, bolster external prestige, manifested by cultural brilliance and military conquest, as well as internal control, enabling the raising of the resources to finance the prestige. There was no need, though, for it to be imposed as a spoken idiom on those whose only role in government was to supply tax revenue and cannon fodder: indeed there was advantage in restricting access to the language of power. Why, therefore, frown upon a codified elitist or regionally restricted language that was far removed from the speech of the masses?

(i)   Spain

In almost the first of the European unified states, Moorish occupation confined the early medieval Christians to the far north, with their Galician, Asturo-Leonese and Aragonese dialects strung out from west to east. In the south, a koineized Spanish Mozarabic was allegedly used by

Moors, and especially by Jews and the small part of the population remaining Christian (most of whom eventually went north to resettle conquered areas).

Castilian was probably originally an innovating Leonese variety, mingled perhaps with Mozarabic and Basque, developed by the settlers of the first reconquered territories (the land of the forts, *castillas*). It eventually took over most of the peninsula, as it swept down, widening its territory as it proceeded south. A series of alliances, as well as military successes, meant it engulfed first (from the thirteenth century) the Leonese and then (at the end of the fifteenth century) the Aragonese territories, and flooded the south, with the capture of Granada, the last Moorish bastion, in that famous year 1492, when the quest for the New World was launched, and the Jews were expelled. The Reconquest resembled what is now called 'ethnic cleansing', with expulsion and extermination of undesirable elements, and resettlement of depopulated zones by more congenial immigrants, making for more homogeneous language use the further south it penetrated. The imposition of Castilian as the official language of the state dates, however, only from the early eighteenth century, on the advent of the Bourbons to the Spanish throne.

The result has been that, except in the north, where original dialects persisted, Castilian became not only the administrative, but also the spoken, language of Spain (though in the west, Portuguese first asserted its political independence in the twelfth century, and in the east, Catalan was the chancery language of Aragon until the union with Castile). Royal patronage, obsessed with glory and its holy vocation, aimed to render the language of Castile, as perfected in Toledo, worthy of the kingdom and its religious mission, and fit to be spread through the country, and eventually round the world, with the empire-building forces: the first grammar was ceremoniously presented to Queen Isabel in that illustrious year of 1492. The Spanish grammatical tradition has remained until recently one of intolerant purism. Yet the Castilian dialect is deviant phonologically and innovating morphologically, and far from a koineized compromise between Iberian varieties. It nevertheless constitutes the official language of the whole of the Spanish state, which all Spanish citizens have the duty to learn.

Today racier Southern versions of the language, which resemble in some phonological respects the Latin-American varieties, have been acquiring more prestige than what is often perceived as the rather stiff and harsh idiom of Castile itself. In Spanish America the nineteenth-century Venezuelan statesman and grammarian Americo Bello sought to codify the language for the new states freeing themselves from the colonial yoke, but by perfecting and rationalizing tradition, not by breaking with it. Thus differences of the American standards from European Spanish are more phonological and lexical than grammatical (see 8.7).

In twentieth-century Spain, after a brief period in which Catalonia enjoyed some autonomy, the Franco era, with its 'España una' policy, marked suppression of other languages in the peninsula. In 1978, however, new legislation established semi-autonomous regions throughout Spain and encouraged the protection within the regions of local 'modalities', as part of cultural patrimony, while still insisting on the role of Castilian as the language of the whole state. Standard forms of some of the regional idioms have since been accepted (see 8.3).

(ii)   Portugal

The European standard is based on the variety characteristic of the capital, Lisbon, where phonological development was idiosyncratic. Even though the Brazilian variety, phonologically more conservative in some ways, differs considerably, European Portuguese speakers have no difficulty in understanding it (indeed Brazilian television soap operas are very popular in Portugal). But it should also be noted that the Portuguese, who regard themselves as adaptable, quick-witted and easy-going, readily comprehend both spoken and written discourse in Spanish (though the understanding is not reciprocated). By most objective standards, it is almost only the phonological (and orthographical) differences that set the two languages off from each other (though the Portuguese point proudly to their distinctive future subjunctive and personal infinitive – see 4.3).

In the Middle Ages, the two varieties were conventionally used for different literary genres, the 'softer' Western pronunciations being seen as more suitable for lyrics and the 'virile' Castilian for epic. In the sixteenth century even writers of the standing of Luis de Camões or Gil Vicente alternated between the languages, and by this time Portuguese was regarded as less prestigious. Hostility between the two states is deep-rooted, and it was really only in the seventeenth century, after a period (1580–1643) under Spanish rule, that Portuguese shook itself free of Spanish and created a standard almost deliberately in counterpoint to its neighbour. (For *fronterizo* see 8.5.)

As a poor and backward maritime country which looked out more to the wider world and to emigration than to its internal development and education, Portugal did little until recently to encourage adoption of the standard by all its population, so that the diversity of dialects still persists, and literacy spread very slowly. One difficulty posed to codifiers by the phonological deviance of the standard was that of orthography. Reform followed reform, in some cases negotiated with Brazil.

The devising of a standard 'educated Brazilian' has recently prompted extensive investigations into the forms actually used by the relevant speakers. Subservience to the older established standard is no longer well regarded among the elite, who nevertheless are antipathetic to the more 'creolized' Brazilian varieties.

(iii)   France

French is also usually seen as directly derived from the dialect of the capital city, or at any rate of the Ile de France region in which Paris stands. Its adoption as the state language was a purely political move dating from the sixteenth and seventeenth centuries. In the early Middle Ages other 'dialects', especially those of the west (Normandy), the north (Picardy) and the east (Champagne), were more regularly used for literary expression. However, it is sometimes claimed that the so-called dialectal differences manifested in the medieval texts are more a matter of the orthographical tradition followed by the scriptorium in which the manuscript was written than a reflection of local spoken usage.

From the thirteenth century the vernacular replaced Latin in charters, and the chancery language used in different northern regions can be related to later attested spoken dialects. However, dialect traits usually are in the minority in such charters, and it is possible that in the whole of the north there existed a koine with attenuated dialect features. It was this koine that came to be identified with the metropolis to which people flocked from all regions, rather than with the more distinctive Central dialect that evidence suggests was used by the longer-standing Parisian populace. It was this koine too that ousted dialect in literature by the fourteenth century.

Strengthening of state functions required the use of a common language and it was, under François I, a 1539 edict (of Villers-Cotterêts) that is usually cited as marking the triumph of French as we know it. However, the wording used gave rise, even at the time, to legal wranglings: *langaige maternel francois* 'French mother tongue' was taken by some to imply 'the mother-tongue that I, as a subject of the French king, speak', rather than 'the vernacular of the Ile de France'. Whether the edict was directed mainly against Latin or against dialect is disputed. What is certain is that the spoken usage of the illiterate masses would be largely unaffected by such a move.

In the sixteenth century, intellectuals, backed by political power, exerted pressure for a state language to aspire to the prestige and the international acceptance of Latin. Debate raged about what vernacular form it should be based on, and especially about codification of its orthography and grammatical rules. No doubt one motivation for seeking to replace Latin was the advent of printing, which potentially would spread literacy to consumers who had not the leisure nor the patience for classical studies. Another was the Reformation, which sought to spread the word in a vernacular accessible to all – just as Luther is sometimes said to have virtually invented German, so Calvin was an important figure in the creation of French.

Sixteenth-century polemicists on the whole preferred a 'polynomic' standard that would not sacrifice to bland uniformity the picturesque contributions of dialects, but would tolerate regional variation. Parisian cultivated middle-class usage was, moreover, favoured over that of the Italianized court. The seventeenth century saw a switch in emphasis, especially after Louis XIV sought to curtail the influence and provincial affiliations of the turbulent nobility, by gathering them around his court, and by fostering centrally controlled administration. The language imposed on the country, and the vehicle for a new literary blossoming, was that of the 'most sensible part of the Court'. The middle classes were quick to ape fashionable courtiers, in language as in other respects, but there is little indication that the adoption of the standard affected the mass of the population, whose duties of devotion and dumb obedience required minimal verbal skills. Commentaries on dialect usage from this period took the form of comic parodies or admonitions to misguided speakers.

By the time of the Revolution, though, it is quite likely that in much of northern France (especially in the towns where literacy rates were high) lower-class speakers did not think of their usage as different regionally, as distinct from socially, from that of their betters. In the south, and in marginal and rural areas, however, dialects persisted as strongly as before. The Jacobin doctrine, that a common language was necessary to permit all citizens of the 'nation' (in the sense, here, of all whose loyalty is willingly given to the state) to take a full part in democratic processes, has been condemned as destructive of the local dialects. It was, however, more the nineteenth-century expansion of education, conducted exclusively in French, especially after the introduction of compulsory primary education in 1882, and the increase in mobility, both social and geographical, that effectively led to the virtual death of most North French dialects. It is only after the Second World War that local languages spoken within France gained a degree of recognition.

(c)   Nation–state standards

The nineteenth-century 'nation–state' era of nationalism was initiated by the French Revolution. The ideology decreed that the state should be legitimized not only territorially (with 'natural frontiers' and a 'threshold size') but also by the ethnicity and language loyalty of its citizens.

(i)   Italy

Italian, although dating, as a standard, from the same sort of period as Spanish, French and Portuguese, was originally a written culture language with little governmental backing. It was fashioned from a sanitized literary version of the Tuscan dialect, gaining prestige from the earlier writings of the *Tre Corone* – the 'three crowns' of Florence, Dante, Petrarch and Boccaccio – whose usage was taken as a model by sixteenth-century arbiters (notably Cardinal Bembo). It was Rome, at the centre of the Papal States, that promoted the literary language as the common language of the peninsula, but local dialects remained dominant, as they still continued to do after the Risorgimento and Unification. This latter was virtually completed by 1860, at the height of nationalist fervour.

Although the new King of Italy, and his court, were, as northerners, more at home in French, Italian was adopted as the 'national language' to mould the very diverse regions of Italy into one cohesive polity. The doctrine adopted was that dialects of Italy must be 'Italian dialects', with close historical and cultural affinity. 'We have made Italy', said one statesman, 'now we must make Italians'. Objective criteria for the affiliation of dialects were ignored: for instance, the justification offered for surrendering Nice to the French in 1860 was, surprisingly, that Niçois was remote from Italian. Linguistically, however, it is closer to the neighbouring dialects of Liguria than to those of Provence.

Today about 60 per cent of Italians (compared with 2.5 per cent in 1860) do claim the standard language as their first tongue, but regional variation is great. Monolingual dialect speakers are rare nowadays, but even when they still existed the majority could with an effort usually understand Italian (but, note, so can Spanish speakers). Many Italians, especially in the north, with a tradition of dialect literature, control at least three related languages: a local dialect, a regional koine and a regional standard (see 8.4). In some urban centres, like Florence and Rome, some speakers may think of their dialect as 'bad Italian', rather than as a separate idiom, but more often loyalty and affection are bestowed on the dialect rather than the standard. However, interdialect communication is rare: television viewers claim that popular theatrical representations in dialect from regions other than their own are incomprehensible to them, and southern immigrant workers in the northern industrial centres often feel excluded by their ignorance of the Northern local dialects.

Recent political developments have seen support for separatism among northerners, but the 1946 regional legislation did much to defuse feeble cries for separate standard languages, and dialects, however diverse linguistically, remain within the orbit (or under the roof) of a standard that is tolerant of variation.

(ii)   Rumania

Codification of the Rumanian language was carried out, largely with French encouragement, with the aim of differentiating it maximally from its non-Romance neighbours. The basis of the standard was the Daco-Rumanian educated usage of the capital Bucharest, but, as we have seen, there was comparatively little dialectal diversity among Rumanian speakers within the state. Latin orthography was imposed and many Western loanwords were introduced to replace, or supplement, older Slavonic words. Although Rumania has always had substantial minorities of other language groups (including Gipsies – see 8.6), the establishment of the Rumanian state in 1862 (and its enlargement by the incorporation of ex-Hungarian Transylvania after the First World War) was conceived in the 'nation–state' spirit of the time, which modified the 'nationality' requirements by those of economic viability. A state which filled the 'threshold size' requirements of nationalist ideology would inevitably in the Balkans include subordinate national groups.

Irrespective of the size of the state, the between-war period brought little prosperity and much conflict to Rumania; emigration of intellectuals and artists was particularly intense. Postwar, when language questions were at first enthusiastically pursued, early hopes of a well-ordered, prosperous and tolerant future were soon to be dashed, and today Rumania remains in a sorry state, with, once again, many of its intellectuals seeking refuge abroad, and ethnic and social conflict barely held in check. What does seem to have changed is that now the other Romance languages hold less attraction for Rumanians than, say, English or German. But there is at present little in the way of coherent discussion of the role of the standard in the new Rumania.

(d)   Small-nation standards

Newer Romance standards have been developed in the mode of the 'small-nation' doctrines of Woodrow Wilson, but with the added incentive of the promise of European integration and federation and the dissolution of the large European nation–state. Some groups of dialects have sought to free themselves from the orbit of the state language to which they have unwillingly been subordinated (on language conflict see 8.3). Standardization is seen by activists as a means of breaking with the parish-pump associations of dialect and fitting their mother tongue for the modern world, by increasing its scope both in catchment area and in subject matter. (For fear of language death see 8.3). Earlier associations of the assertion of national language rights with irredentism and separatism evaporate, as new standards look for validation to Brussels, rather than to Paris, Rome or Madrid.

(i)   Spain

Since 1978 there has been official encouragement for standardization of local languages within the Spanish state. Standard Catalan, a success model for other small nations, is based on Barcelona usage, but taking into account other varieties. Nineteenth-century codification was purist and archaizing, but in the twentieth century more liberal doctrines developed by Catalan activists have strongly influenced other national language movements. Today the processes of **normalization** or 'status planning' (fitting the language for a wider range of social roles) and **normativization** or 'corpus planning' (codifying the language) are handled sensitively and professionally, with moral and financial support from the regional government.

Standard Galician, even though it is spoken by a larger proportion of the local population, has had a rather harder time than Catalan, partly because of disagreements about the shape standardization should take. Unlike industrialized, go-ahead Catalonia, Galicia has long been a backward, impoverished part of the country, reliant on agriculture and fishing (though from very early on a centre of tourism, with the popular pilgrimage centre of Santiago de Compostela). The local language was suppressed by the political and religious authorities and spurned by the local middle classes, so that the nineteenth-century revival of national languages was not so successful in this region as elsewhere. However, the very poverty and neglect of Galicia helped to preserve the traditional dialects and also created some sense of national identity, in that the masses of enterprising Galicians who emigrated to the New World to seek their fortune, nostalgic for their verdant homeland, kept the local language alive and gave moral and financial support for its rescue. Language activists, however, were split between those who advocated standardization along the lines of Portuguese, and those who preferred to go it alone. Post-Franco liberalization of language policy has allowed the Galician regional Xunta to encourage use and diffusion of the language, but opinion is still split on how far the sway of Castilian, as the language of the Spanish state, should be challenged.

For other Spanish languages, Valencian, Asturian and Aragonese, where support for standardization is less strong, and the language debate is often animated, see 8.4.

(ii)   France

In France, the medieval literary language of the south was a skilful blending of the Poitou dialect with other varieties. How close it was to spoken language in the area is hard to tell, but as an artistic language it was fairly unified. After the violent crushing of southern cultural individuality by the north in the thirteenth century, the language continued to be used for a while for literary purposes in the south and in Catalonia, and, indeed, it was codified at this time. But by the seventeenth century it had been degraded to a mere set of low-status *patois*, roundly condemned by language arbiters. Although the dialects were still in use as the first language of most Occitans in the nineteenth century, French language and education policy has since succeeded in reducing their scope and status. They declined rapidly till the middle of this century and were confined mainly to older users in rural communities. The literary revival led, from 1854, by the Félibrige did seek standardization, but only locally based (specifically the Provence varieties), and attempts to devise a standard language that would serve the needs of speakers across the region were left till the mid-twentieth century to militants inspired mainly by principles enunciated by the Catalan standardizers. Standard Occitan has had a degree of success since 1951, when it was admitted as a subject for school examinations: the result has been a noticeable slowing down of the decline in its use among young people, and an increase in use in urban environments. However, there is no success commensurate with that of Catalan standardization, and a great deal of disagreement about how many Occitan speakers remain (estimates ranging from about 1 million to an unlikely 10 million).

The dialects spoken in Corsica are usually classed as Tuscan, but influence from French, and decreasing contact with Italian, since the island's incorporation into the French state in 1769, has given them a more sharply silhouetted profile. Attempts to standardize the language have aimed at the 'polynomic' approach favoured for Occitan, which does not force speakers of different dialects to abandon their own usage, yet allows them to participate in a wider linguistic community. It remains to be seen whether a standardized Corsican will catch on, now that the island has a significant proportion of non-Corsican residents, especially since the settlement there of refugees from Algeria after independence. The island, moreover, is a holiday centre for both French and Italian speakers. Unjustifiably linked by opponents with a more violent separatist movement, the Corsican language cause attracts little official support.

(iii)   Switzerland

Although moves have been made from 1880 to devise a standard to accommodate the diverse Swiss Rhaeto-Romance dialects, a common language did not get going until 1982. Inevitably, as the largest number of speakers use Surselvan, it is based largely on that set of dialects, but great (some say too great) efforts have been made to take in Engadine features. The codified koine *Rumantsch Grischun* is welcomed especially by those 40 per cent of speakers who now work outside the Grisons canton, who fear that their children will have no proper access to the language, but within the canton there is comparatively little support for it to be used in schools. Given the quite wide differences between the local varieties, for instance in ways of negating the verb, it would be preferable to allow some leeway within the standard for variants, rather than imposing a single norm. It has yet to be seen whether the creation of a standard will halt the erosion of use of the dialects.

5.6   LANGUAGE AND DIALECT

Grouping of European Romance 'dialects' is usually done on the basis of genetic classification and of the 'roofing' language. They are nearly always contiguous territorially and usually derive their names from the area in which they originate (for discussion of the social status of dialects see chapter 8). Only in the Balkans, in southern Italy and in Sardinia are there pockets of Romance speakers of varieties that differ radically from those that surround them.

In the south of Italy and Sicily there survive isolated Northern Italian (Gallo-Italian) dialects in immigrant settlements, attracted there by royal patronage, mainly during the twelfth and thirteenth centuries, partly to repopulate areas after expulsion of Saracen dissidents. They have not accommodated to their neighbours' Romance dialects sufficiently to have lost all their distinctive dialect features. In northern Sardinia, influxes of Corsican refugees to what were presumably unpopulated areas also constituted dialect groupings distinct from the indigenous Sard dialects.

The Balkans harbour some Romance varieties surrounded and intermingled with non-Romance. These include a sprinkling of Arumanian dialects in Albania and Macedonia. Although the earliest inscriptions date from the eighteenth century, they are thought to date back to Roman times and to be more archaic in character than the Daco-Rumanian varieties of the Rumanian state. A smaller pocket of different Rumanian dialects – called Megleno-Rumanian – precariously survives in the north-east of Macedonia. Some of the Macedonian Rumanian speakers settled in

Rumania after the Second World War, escaping from the conflicts between Slavs and Greeks. The tiny groups of Rumanian speakers in the Croatian Istrian peninsula, on the other hand, feel no affinity with the Rumanian state, even though their dialects are closely related to Daco-Rumanian. (For Friulian speakers in Rumania see 5.1.) Some Judeo-Spanish dialects (see 8.7) also survive in the Balkans and in Turkey, carried there after the 1492 expulsion from Spain.

(a)   Dialect and regional standard

A distinction is usually made, by linguists though not necessarily by speakers, between the dialect of a locality and the regional version of the standard within whose orbit the dialect is drawn. A dialect is assumed to have descended directly from Latin, whereas the regional variety is seen as a modification of the imported 'roofing' language. This is one of the reasons why the dialect usage of monolingual elderly rural inhabitants is regarded as more 'authentic' or 'purer', in that it is more archaic and less likely to have been contaminated by contact. However, as we have seen, the degree of mutual intelligibility between different Romance varieties has probably meant that they have always interacted. On the other hand, use of some local dialect features may be regarded as a community membership badge (see 8.3). The consequences of accommodation between different Romance varieties are discussed in chapter 4.

(b)   Overseas dialects

When a Romance-speaking community has established itself in a far-off land, its usage over time will differ from that of the metropolitan variety. The degree to which this happens is related to the amount of contact with the metropolis, and to the social attitudes of the speakers. We shall be examining American Spanish, Portuguese and French in 8.7, and considering how closely they are related to metropolitan dialects or standards. Their linguistic distance from the home languages is sometimes described in terms of creolization by contact with other languages. Here we shall consider in what ways we can distinguish between a non-European 'dialect' and a true 'creole' which, although still a member of the Romance family, no longer conforms to the Romance type, and has resigned from the Romance club (see page 95).

5.7 CREOLE AND DIALECT

The difference is not always clearcut, especially in those regions in which varieties that span the two are used. I shall not here go into the general problem of coverage of the term 'creole', as it is one that originated as a Romance word and, within Romance, refers only to those language varieties that arose between the fifteenth and eighteenth centuries following contact of European Romance-speaking adventurers, traders (especially slave-traders) and colonists with non-European populations. These varieties have some common features, but also differ widely among themselves.

Not all Romance creoles are so called by their speakers: French Caribbean varieties are often called *patois*; other varieties receive a name that means, sometimes pejoratively, 'language' (*papia(mentu)*, *lengua*, *chabacano*, etc.) or that refers to the name of the region. 'Creole' in French was a name originally given to French colonists, so that in Louisiana, for instance, it referred to a variety close to standard French, whereas the creole was known as 'Negro-French', or, pejoratively, 'gumbo', the Bambara word for 'okra'. Just as the designation differs, so does the association between different Romance languages and their related colonial offshoots: some of the overseas varieties may be more profitably regarded as 'dialects' than as creoles, retaining many of the grammatical features of their lexifier languages.

(a) Spanish

It has been argued that this may be true of Spanish-based varieties. Little reliable data exist for Philippine Spanish, which has been seen in any case as a relexified Portuguese creole. *Papiamento*, spoken in Curaçao and neighbouring islands, is also sometimes thought to be originally Portuguese, and is regarded as an atypical creole (see 1.3). *Palenquero*, spoken in an originally maroon (runaway slave) settlement in Colombia, has only recently been classified as creole, and even then is seen as heavily 'decreolized', as its 3,000-odd speakers all speak Spanish (*kateyano*). It is better then not to use these Spanish varieties as examples in our quest for 'creolity'.

(b) Portuguese

Portuguese-based creoles are a different matter, as there is a long documented tradition of *lingua do preto*, 'black's language', of the pidgin that was used by mariners and traders throughout the world. However, the creoles found in Africa differ from Asian varieties (which in any case are now obsolete or obsolescent), especially in that they are still in close contact with Portuguese, and also, in some cases, with African languages. In Cape Verde, *crioulo* is the national language of a mainly mixed-race population; variants range from something very like colloquial Portuguese to a version that is more like that of Guinea-Bissau, where *crioulo* is widely used by Africans as a second language. Gulf of Guinea (São Tomé, Principe, Annobon) creoles grew in social conditions that were more similar to those of New World creoles – slavery in a plantation agricultural system – with more infiltration of African features and lexicon, distancing the languages more decisively from Portuguese.

Asian Portuguese speakers – usually Christian and of mixed race – identify, on the other hand, more closely with Portuguese: intermarriage and assimilation were encouraged by the metropolitan authorities. In so far as their languages survive, they vary widely; Macao Portuguese could be equated with popular metropolitan and Brazilian varieties, while that of Batticoloa in Sri Lanka is now penetrated by Tamil grammatical features. Popular Brazilian has itself been called a 'semi-creole', in that inflections are much reduced compared with the standard, and periphrasis is favoured. However, many non-standard metropolitan Romance varieties show similar tendencies. Indeed the term *français avancé* for popular varieties of French (see 8.2) implies the view that Romance's future lies in simplification of morphology and greater reliance on syntactic devices.

(c)   French

It is the French-based creoles that most closely approximate to the more traditional idea of what a creole is. They are all the product of importation of African slaves for plantation (tobacco, cotton, sugar) agriculture, during the seventeenth and eighteenth centuries, and they all have similar grammatical features, even though they are geographically as far apart as the Caribbean and the Indian Ocean. It is easy to imagine that they could have been created from an amalgam of French lexicon and African grammar; there are difficulties, however, in tracing the precise African origins.

(i)   Caribbean

The French creole which deviates most radically from the Romance pattern is that of Haiti, spoken by some 6 million people, most of them monolingual, in a country that won its independence, after slave revolts, in 1804. Many of the other French creoles have been used continually alongside French since their creation. Indeed, until recently they were often not perceived as other than a variety of French: comments on the 'otherness' of creole mainly date from the eighteenth century. Today, in the French Caribbean Départements d'Outremer (DOMs – Guadeloupe and Martinique), creole is widely used among all sections of the population, with functional differentiation and frequent code-switching between creole and French. Regional popular French varieties are tending to disappear as standard French and creole polarize, so that the 'creole continuum' that has been described for New World English-based creoles is not so evident. In islands where English is the official language – like St Lucia and Dominica – the creole seems to be less influenced by French, and is threatened with extinction (as in Grenada and Trinidad). On the coast of Dominica facing Guadeloupe the creole survives better, presumably because contact is maintained with Guadeloupian creole.

There are, however, some cases in which French 'dialects' and 'creoles' are said to exist side by side and are not clearly demarcated: in the Caribbean, the Indian Ocean and in North America.

(ii)   St Barth and St Thomas

A curious linguistic situation is reported for the tiny, dry, rocky Caribbean island of St Barth(olomew) in the DOM of Guadeloupe, which has an almost wholly white population, reputedly descended from Norman immigrants in the seventeenth century. In the west of the island French varieties that some characterize as 'Norman' are used, while in the east there is a creole that is readily interintelligible with that of Guadeloupe and Martinique. Each part of the island was said to practise endogamy, at least until the 1970s. Few precise linguistic or sociolinguistic details are yet available, although investigations are in progress: the fact that the island is now an exorbitantly expensive winter resort for the international smart set cannot help research. Certainly the 'dialect' is much closer to French than the 'creole' (however, as all education is in French there is likely to be contamination). Examples from the verb morphology of each variety illustrate the French of the dialect compared with the creole:

(2)   Dialect [jekimãʒ] / [jetekimãʒe] / [imãʒra]; creole [ikamãʒe] / [itekamãʒe] /
         [ikemãʒe] 'he is eating / he was eating / he will eat' (= French *il mange* [*il est qui*

mange] / *il mangeait* [*il était qui mangeait*] / *il mangera*). Dialect (like French) *Je te le donne*; creole *Mwē ka ba ou li* 'I give it to you'.

More is known about the 'dialect' that was reportedly imported in the nineteenth century from St Barth by fishermen immigrants to Carenage in St Thomas, now part of the US Virgin Islands (and, incidentally, the birth-place of the impressionist painter Pissarro). There is little that differentiates their French from other non-standard American varieties. A farming community of St Barth origin at Northside in the same island is said, however, to use creole, but it has not been studied. In both communities English is reportedly currently in use, but the respective French varieties are said to be mutually intelligible.

It is possible that the St Barth / St Thomas creole was imported from Guadeloupe by refugees during the Revolutionary period, but it has also been suggested that it was an indigenous creation, at a period (late seventeenth / early eighteenth century) when apparently slaves formed about 40 per cent of the population of St Barth.

(iii)   Indian Ocean: Réunion

This volcanic island (originally called Bourbon), a French DOM and part of the Mascareignes group in the Indian Ocean, uses what is locally called 'creole'. This is spoken, with a wide degree of variation, by a poor white population mainly in the mountainous interior, descendants of eighteenth-century immigrants, by communities largely descended from maroon slaves in inaccessible localities in ex-volcanic craters, as well as by the racially even more mixed population on the coast. Most commentators agree that these varieties have evolved from an archaic popular French; some would deny they are creoles, rather than dialects. Their relationship to the undisputed creoles of Mauritius (earlier called Ile de France) and the Seychelles is hotly disputed. The creoles of these last two island clusters are closely related, and are more decidedly creole in character. Probably the Seychelles varieties were originally, in the nineteenth century, imported from Mauritius, when, on to the previously unpopulated archipelago, liberated slaves were disembarked from ships intercepted by the British. In both the Seychelles and multi-ethnic Mauritius, English is the official language but creole, the spoken language of all, is gaining ground and prestige. In Mauritius there is still some influence from French, via the wealthier Francophone community, mainly of European origin, and private educational establishments.

(iv)   Louisiana

French varieties of Louisiana also can be divided into dialects and creoles (leaving aside the approximation to standard French that was once used by plantation owners). The *cajun* dialects are derived ultimately from the language of those immigrants who eventually ended up in western Louisiana after their expulsion from Acadie (now part of New Brunswick and Nova Scotia) by the British in 1755, supplemented by Francophone settlers from the Mississippi valley. Modern speakers include other ethnic origins, including German immigrants and Amerindians, while some of the more prosperous descendants of original *cajuns* identified with English-speaking plantation owners in the nineteenth century. *Cajun* shares many of the features of modern Acadian and other Canadian varieties (see 8.7). It is usually contrasted with 'Negro-French', *nègre*, characterized jocularly as *mo gain* (French *moi gagne*) 'I have', or *mo couri mo vini* 'I'm going to come' (French *moi courir moi venir*). It is reported that this creole variety could still be heard on the streets of New Orleans in the prewar period. Nowadays no sharp contrast between *cajun* and creole can be drawn, and doubt is not absent about whether they were ever clearly differentiated. Creole characteristics may have been reinforced in some localities by the influx of refugees from Haiti during the slave revolts, when masters brought some of their slaves with them, but there is evidence of the existence of Louisianan creole before then.

Black Louisianans nowadays show preference for English, and indeed many are descended from the English-speaking slaves brought in from the north during the early nineteenth century to work the sugar plantations. However, in the western *bayou* and prairie regions in which French survives, somewhat precariously, sharp differentiation between the language of blacks and whites is not evident. Some localities, like Lafayette or Avoyelles, use more *cajun*-like varieties, others, like St Martin, use a fairly conservative creole that has nevertheless Haitian-like features. Where it is claimed that there are two distinguishable varieties, as at Vacherie (St James), the *cajun* tends to be penetrated by creole, with frequent code-switching and bilectal exchange, even within the family circle. Since the mid-nineteenth century, when *cajuns* tended to be treated as 'white trash', there has been some sense of identification of all local French varieties with under-privileged social status. The distinction between 'white' and 'black' French can well have been exaggerated in the post-Civil War accounts that we have, which not infrequently have racialist overtones.

In cases like these it is often claimed that two originally quite distinct languages have with time intertwined: the dialect has 'creolized' and/or the creole has 'decreolized'. Incidentally, attempts to introduce standard French into the Francophone regions of Louisiana, through the COD-OFIL programme, have not been conspicuously successful, especially as speakers of the local varieties find the language taught almost as alien as English. At present there has been instituted a major research programme, under the direction of Albert Valdman, to investigate Louisianan French, in particular *cajun* varieties, which seem to be in danger of extinction, and about which we have little firm information.

5.8   CREOLIZATION AS CREATION, OR AS CATASTROPHIC CHANGE?

Identification of a creole is intrinsically bound up with ideas about creolization. The most prevalent theory about the way creoles are formed is that they are mixed languages that draw their lexical substance from one language – in our examples a Romance language – and their grammatical structure from another. One difficulty with this theory is often in identifying the source of the grammatical structures, and in tying together the linguistic and the historical evidence. Creoles are often also seen as originating in simplified 'babytalk' used in limited exchanges between speakers with mutually unintelligible languages. The way in which such 'pidgins' can in modern times become fully fledged languages is matter for the developmental psycholinguist, but we have little evidence about such processes in the past. The creoles that arose during the slave-trade period are thought by some to result from relexification of the Portuguese slavers' pidgin, by the simple replacement of Portuguese items by those of another language. This would account for the surprising similarity of structure between many of the relevant creoles.

The most interesting recent hypothesis, by Derek Bickerton, that seeks to account for such similarities suggests that, when children have to create a language from incomplete and distorted linguistic data, in conditions which preclude the more normal language acquisition processes, a language 'bioprogramme' is at work. In the slavery context, it is assumed, the children would be exposed to *ad hoc* pidgins composed of lexical items culled from the master's repertoire and used by adults who shared no common language. With no normal access to a fully functioning natural language, the children will use their innate language capacities to create for themselves a new language, using the lexical material at hand.

In this perspective, a true creole would be the one that adhered most closely to the bioprogramme and had least input from the master's language. Communities descended from runaway slaves (maroons) would be more likely to have more authentic creole features. None of the Romance creoles fits well into this pattern (though for Angolar and Saramaccan see 2.3). Yet some varieties are more 'imperfectly creolized' than others. The creoles of Haiti and São Tomé are more radical than those of Réunion or Louisiana, not because the African input is greater, but because contact with the model language was less intense. The distinction between a dialect and a creole could similarly depend on the degree of continuity of transmission from one generation to the next: a creole would be a new creation, whereas a dialect would be the result of an evolution, a handing down of tradition.

Another view of creolization, much favoured by Romanists, is that it is an extreme and rapid version of linguistic change, brought about in social conditions in which there was a break in continuity of transmission. Simplification of inflectional morphology, loss of redundant distinctions, like that of gender, reliance on word order to signal grammatical relations and use of analytic constructions are apparently merely extensions of tendencies that are observable in the history of all the Romance languages. Some languages, like French, have gone further along the line; others, like Rumanian, have held back. In this view the creoles have rushed forward at a breakneck pace, some even faster than others. There would therefore be no qualitative difference between a dialect and creole, merely a quantitative one, which would depend on such things as difference in social conditions, geographical position, language contacts and so on. Creoles would take their place towards the bottom of a continuum of Romanceness which would include at different points on the scale the rest of the Romance family.

5.9 CONCLUSION

The answer to the question that we posed in this chapter must be an indecisive 'It depends what you mean . . . ' The Romance languages, dialects and creoles can be seen, from one perspective, as an unbroken continuum, in which certain sectors are brought into focus by standardization or koineization for particular social purposes.

In the next two chapters we shall examine how some of the linguistic features that differentiate one sector of the geographical continuum from another could have arisen over time. In the final chapter we shall glance at the social factors that add other dimensions to the relationships of variants.

FURTHER READING

The works already mentioned in the Further Reading for earlier chapters give ample bibliography to supplement this chapter: consult especially Harris & Vincent (1988) for a succinct description of the main languages and of the creoles, and Posner & Green (1980-93), vols. II, III and IV for dialectology, standardology, 'smaller languages', overseas Romance and creoles. On classification the most recent substantial work is Mańczak (1991); Embleton (1986) gives an up-to-date account of lexicochronological findings for Romance. On dialectometry, Goebl (1984), and on dialect variation, Lang (1982), Sankoff (1986), Fisiak (1988), Roberge & Vinet (1989). Benincà ed. (1989). On Romance typology, see Manoliu-Manea (1985), Raible ed. (1989), Körner (1987). The most general recent synchronic or diachronic linguistic works on individual languages include the following: on Catalan, Hualde (1992); on French, Jones (in press), Lodge (1993), Battye & Hintze (1992), Ayres-Bennett (1996), Posner (1997); on Italian, Lepschy & Lepschy (1989), Muljačić (1991), Maiden (1995); on Portuguese, Teyssier (1984); on Rhaeto-Romance, Haiman & Benincà (1992); on Rumanian, Mallinson (1986); on Sard, Jones (1993), Blasco-Ferrer (1986, 1995); on Spanish, Penny (1991), and on American Spanish, Lipski (1994). On Louisana, Valdman ed. (1997). For Eurotype, see Auwera ed. (1998), Bernini ed. (1998), Dahl, Ö. ed. (1998), Feuillet ed. (1997), Hulst ed. (1998), Plank ed. (1998), Riemsdijk ed. (1998), Siewierska ed. (1997), Vincent ed. (1998).

6

When did the Romance
languages differentiate?

6.1 INTRODUCTION

The question of the split of a uniform Latin into several distinct languages
has always formed the main subject matter of Romance historical linguistics.
Older thinkers, like Dante (see page 2), took for granted that languages, like
all things human, change and decay, and saw the differentiation as an
inevitable consequence of the passage of time. The geographical spread of
Latin over a large Empire was also seen as causing inexorable disintegration
and disruption of language unity; thus the seeds of development of each
Romance language were there from the beginning in each region, but masked
by the apparent steadfastness of the written language. Classic nineteenth-
century Romance philology looked mainly for the sources of differentiation
in the Dark Ages, between the administrative breakup of the Empire and the
appearance of the first Romance texts at the start of our millennium. In more
modern times there have been suggestions that the differences stemmed not
so much from negative forces – like organizational chaos, breakdown of communications, terrorization by marauders – but from relatively positive social
and cultural developments which affected some areas earlier than others –
like Christianity's solicitude for the salvation of the humble and the growth
of concern for individual welfare. It is even possible that the perception of
gulfs between the languages may date from much later, possibly not emerging
into popular consciousness until the Renaissance period, hand in hand with
the idea of the modern state and political society.

6.2 EARLY DIALECTALIZATION?

But what degree of differentiation was there in Latin before it spread
beyond the Italian peninsula? In 3.2 we saw that it has been claimed that

the Romance languages derive from a sociolect of Latin, or from a related Italic dialect, rather than from the language of the classical texts. Some see the language of Rome itself as a hybrid between different Italic dialects, and as it was imposed, by about 270 BC, on the rest of the peninsula, over-laying numerous other tongues, it must, in its spoken form, have acquired a degree of flexibility. But we have comparatively little evidence for dialec-talization of Latin within the peninsula, and we are unsure how long the other languages continued in use.

(a)   The influence of Greek

The literary language of the Golden Age, however, is thought to have been profoundly influenced by Greek, to which it looked for prestige and style. The Greek-orientated education of the Roman aristocratic classes could not fail to penetrate the high style of serious literature and especially poet-ry. We have already mentioned the possibility that the metrical use of quantity, rather than stress, was not so much a native Latin development as an imitation of Greek, and borrowings from Greek into the literary lan-guage are numerous. Grammatical writings are also clearly inspired by Greek grammarians; one has the impression, though, that the more methodical and disciplined Romans were readier to codify and conform to a standard usage than their Greek subjects. One effect of these tendencies may have been greater sociolectal differentiation, as the spoken language developed untrammelled by the rigid requirements of high style.

Influence from Greek came also from another direction, in the shape of the numerous Greek slaves, who were among the first to adopt Christianity. Some Greeks, as freedmen, also acquired considerable wealth and influence in the later period. Such Romance developments as the creation of a definite article or of the compound perfect are often linked to the impact of Greek on later spoken Latin.

(b)   Social differences

That there were differences in language use among different sectors of the Latin-speaking population is not doubted: we have enough direct and indirect testimony from classical times. What is in doubt is how far such differences account for divergence between the Romance languages. In his classic study of Romance differentiation, Wartburg (see 5.2) distinguished eastern and western areas, with the dividing line drawn across Italy from La Spezia to Rimini. One hypothesis he advanced was that the eastern part of the Latin-speaking Empire continues a lower-class variety, whereas the Western Empire was more subject to the linguistically conservative influence of schooling. In most of the eastern part Romance has not survived to the present day: the evidence adduced relates mainly to southern Italy and to Rumania, with some reference to Dalmatian. It is held that Dacia was settled by veterans from the legions, who would not be expected to use high-flown Latin style, while in the south of Italy a popular Latin may have survived unscathed since ancient times.

One feature that Wartburg picks on in his east/west distinction is the treatment of Latin word-final -s. All the inscriptional and textual evidence points to the tendency of this sound to disappear in colloquial usage, and in early literary Latin it did not 'make position' (see 3.3) before a word-initial consonant – a feature that was regarded as rustic in classical times. It is usually assumed that in Late Latin -s was no longer pronounced in colloquial usage: the collapse of the Latin case system can be linked with the disappearance of the distinction between nominative and accusative inflections S/M.

In Romance, however, the -s persisted (at least at first) in the west, here including Sardinia, while disappearing in the east, though after a stressed vowel it seems to have vocalized to [i] or [j]:

(1) TRĒS 'three' > Rum. *trei*, Dalmatian (Veglia) *tra*, Ital. *tre* (earlier *trei*)/ Sard (Logudorian) *tres*, R-R (Engadine) *trais*, French *trois*, Occ., Cat., Span., Ptg. *tres*.

   More plausible is a development that involves lengthening and diphthongization ([treː] > [trei]).

In the east the accusative plural forms for most nouns thus would be identical with the singular, whereas in the west the [s] clearly marked the plural. The Rumanian and Italian plural forms are thus often assumed to be derived from the nominative rather than the accusative (see 3.3):

(2) *capre* 'goats' < CAPRAE / Sard (Logudorian) [kraβas], French *chèvres*, Span. *cabras* < CAPRAS.

However, in Italian (unlike Rumanian) this plural marker -*e* has not, unlike the regular reflex of Latin AE, provoked palatalization of preceding [k]:

(3) *amiche* [amike] 'friends' / *Cesare* < CAESARE.

This suggests that it may have levelled from a diphthong [ai] < -AS. Similarly the *i* which serves as masculine plural marker and the person 2 verbal marker (and which in Rumanian is realized phonetically by palatalization of the preceding consonant) is more plausibly derived from -ES, rather than -Ī:

(4)   *cani, cîini* 'dogs' < CANES; *vedi, vezi* 'you see' < VIDES.

The word-final *s* of the western languages not only marked the nominal and pronominal plural and the person 2 verb endings, but in Old French and Occitan was the mainstay of the nominal case system (see 3.3). Nevertheless it has tended to weaken and disappear over time in many of the varieties.

Even in Sard we find assimilation of *-s* before voiced consonants:

(5)   *sar dentes* 'the teeth', *sa mmanos* 'the hands' for *sas dentes/manos*.

In Occitan and North Italian varieties the *-s* has frequently weakened to a palatal glide in similar conditions:

(6)   Gascony [eraj duoj rodos]' the two wheels' < ILLAS DUAS ROTAS.

In French word-final *-s* began to be lost in the twelfth or thirteenth century, and had virtually ceased to be pronounced by the seventeenth century. Today it is used only in liaison contexts, usually in tightly knit syntagmata:

(7)   *les arbres* 'the trees' [lezaʁbʁ] / *les petits arbres* 'the little trees' [leptizaʁbʁ]; *ils portent* 'they carry' [ipɔʁt] / *ils aiment* 'they love' [izɛm].

          Thus it can be argued that plural marking can be effected in speech by a morpheme-initial [z] marker, rather than by the word-final *-s*, indicated in the graphy.

In Spanish, too, syllable-final *s* tends to open to [h] and sometimes to fall; there is evidence of this change from the sixteenth century. It is particularly noticeable in the south of the peninsula and in many American varieties, especially on the Pacific coast. Some trace of the marker of the plural is usually retained within the noun phrase, though not on every word:

(8)   *los hombres* 'the men' [lohombre], *las manos* 'the hands' [lahmano].

Elsewhere, however, as in eastern Andalusia, the *s* is completely lost and the burden of marking the plural falls on the preceding vowel:

(9)   *bolo* [bolo] / *bolos* [bɔlɔ] 'skittle(s)'.

> In some varieties of Colombia [s] is aspirated in other than word-final positions (e.g. *necesario* [nehesario], *una señora* [unaheɲora]).

The glottalization of -*s* has been linked to the 'Western' palatalization (laminalization) to [ʃ], which occurs sporadically in other positions:

(10)   Old Span. *xabón* 'soap'< SAPONE, Ptg. *baixo*, Old Span. *baxo* 'low' < BASSU

(where *x* represents the spelling for [ʃ], the modern Spanish [χ] being written as *j*). Evidence for the standard European Portuguese palatal pronunciation of syllable-final -*s* dates back to the thirteenth century (though modern Galician uses an apical sibilant, and Brazilian, outside Rio, a dorsal sibilant).

6.3   SPREAD OF ROMAN RULE

It seems obvious that as the Roman Empire, and its Western official language Latin, spread, regional variation would increase. Little reference to variation was made by contemporary commentators, and such remarks as have been preserved are ambiguous. Much effort by modern scholars has been devoted, without great return, to the meticulous study of 'errors' in late texts and imperial inscriptions from different areas, in the hope of uncovering information about such variation. Almost ineluctably, only phonological evidence is available; searches for early signs of some of the differentiating features of the languages we know – like voicing of intervocalic consonants or merger of mid vowels – have so far yielded only meagre rewards.

Yet vernacular texts from the early years of our millennium already show clear marks of phonological regional differentiation. The common assumption is that the Late Latin texts continued spelling conventions that masked pronunciation changes. Classic doctrine has it that two codes were current in the Romance area during the first millennium: one an approximation to Latin, represented by the written texts and used by the educated for certain purposes, and another underground spoken vernacular in more general use, which, at first sporadically and then consistently, broke into the written form.

Another view is that an evolved form of Latin, represented distantly by the texts, continued to be spoken and written until the Carolingian spelling reforms of the eighth century, which divorced the written from the spoken form and triggered experiments in writing the vernacular. A variation (see

3.5) on this view is that the 'Latin' texts were indeed conventional representations of the spoken vernacular until reforms of Latin pronunciation, under Charlemagne, re-invented a learned Latin that henceforth was in a diglossic relationship with the vernacular.

The differences – especially phonological – between the different regions are often attributed to transference from the languages with which Latin was in contact. This is plausible enough; difficulties arise largely from chronological and sociolinguistic considerations, and from our paucity of knowledge about the source languages. One would expect that phonological transference would be accompanied by a considerable degree of lexical borrowing and morphosyntactical influence, but this is more difficult to trace. I shall look in the following sections at some of the Romance features attributed to language contact. A distinction can be made between **substratum, superstratum** and **adstratum** influence.

The first type of interference – from the first language of a subjugated people who shift to their masters' language (here Latin) – is so familiar that it needs no explanation. It has seemed obvious to most past Romanists that differentiation of Latin spoken over the Empire must owe a great deal to the languages of different pre-Romance populations. Unfortunately, most of these languages are now extinct, and our knowledge of them is defective. We can hazard guesses about possible phonetic interference but little else. There are also difficulties about the chronology of the interference phenomena. One would expect these to operate during a period of bilingualism, but to fade as the pre-Roman languages died out. We still have little knowledge about how quickly the populations embraced use of Latin (which they seem to have done fairly enthusiastically) or about regional variation in Imperial Latin. It does seem to be true that such variation was so superficial that it did not impair communication across wide spatial areas, even after the institutional collapse of the Western Empire; hence scepticism among many modern Romanists about the validity of the substratum theories advanced.

The second type of interference is more problematic. At the end of the Western Empire period, some Germanic-speaking 'barbarians', though dominant militarily, appear to have respected Roman culture enough to have adopted a form of Latin, so that today a Romance, not a Germanic, variety is spoken in, for instance, northern France, northern Italy and Spain. The hypothesis advanced, especially by German Romanists, is that the 'Latin-speaking' population adopted some of the features of the 'faulty' speech of their overlords, so differentiating their varieties from that of other Latin-speaking areas. We are on firmer ground here about the sort of features that may be affected, as the Germanic languages are well known to us – though we do not always know so much about the individual varieties involved. It is suggested in particular that Northern French shows interpenetration of many Germanic characteristics taken from the Franks, but we are uncertain about the Frankish variety, about the number of German speakers settled in the area, and indeed about how long they continued to speak a Germanic language. It has been claimed, for instance, that about half the Frankish loanwords in French date from the Imperial period.

Other superstratum languages that may have had an influence on the development of post-Imperial Romance varieties include Arabic – on the Iberian and South Italian varieties in particular (Romance seems to have been swept away from North Africa by the Arab incursions). Here lexical borrowing is evident, but other types of influence are more doubtful. The same may be said of Slavonic influence on Rumanian – though here it is difficult to distinguish between 'superstratum' and 'adstratum' influence.

By the latter, we mean the influence of languages with which Romance is in contact geographically and socially. Again it is the lexicon that most clearly shows such influence, but other levels may also be affected. Rumanian, surrounded by Slavonic, Hungarian, Greek and Albanian, and part of the Ottoman Empire for a long time, was particularly subject to such influence. Elsewhere in Europe adstratum influence is detected in the Romance varieties along the frontiers with Germanic (though in modern times there seems to have been strong resistance to such interpenetration of features). Linguistic isolates, like the Rumanian of the Croatian Istrian peninsula, of Macedonia or of Albania, the Judeo-Spanish of the Near East, or the Romance varieties in southern Italian Greek-speaking areas, almost inevitably show contact influences. Non-European Romance varieties, in the New World, in Africa and Asia, can be seen as particularly under siege from other languages – at the extreme, creoles may be viewed as 'non-Romance' from some points of view (see 2.2).

I shall reserve further discussion of adstrata for chapter 8. In the next sections I shall review some of the main hypotheses about how substratum interference may have caused differentiation in the early history of Romance, first in phonology and then in vocabulary. In 6.4 we shall turn to the question of superstratum influence.

(a)   Phonology

(i)   Celtic lenition

One of the criterial features for Wartburg's division of the Romance area is the lenition in the west of Latin intervocalic consonants, which regularly remain intact in the east. The voicing and weakening of intervocalic consonants can be seen as a 'natural' assimilatory process, with the voiced and open qualities of the surrounding vowels spreading to the intervening consonant; note that following voiced /r/ or /l/ has the same effect as a vowel on a preceding consonant. Some maintain that voicing was a (phonetic?) feature of some Latin varieties from early on, and some evidence is found in Pompeian graffiti – in an area where today intervocalic voicing is not found.

It is possible that lenition was a general Indo-European tendency that surfaced most conspicuously in Celtic. Perhaps voice was not a distinctive feature in the Latin consonantal system, for which a tense/lax distinction was more fundamental. The opposite tendency to fortition, lengthening or doubling intervocalic consonants, was generally regarded as a popular expressive means of securing emphasis; it is found in Southern Italian varieties today (see below).

In the Western Romance languages word-initial consonants were usually treated like geminates: a link could be made with the postulated early Latin word-initial stress.

> Spanish reflexes of initial L [l] and N [n] (rather than [ʎ] and [ɲ], form an exception. In Catalan, on the other hand, initial L does become [ʎ], like the intervocalic geminate; initial N gives [n], whereas NN > [ɲ] in the standard (but [n] in many dialects).

In intervocalic position geminates are, however, normally simplified and voiceless obstruents are voiced, while voiced obstruents tend to open to fricatives (and in some cases eventually to fall):

Intervocalic voiceless obstruents in Romance

RĪPA 'riverbank': Rum. *ripă*, Ital. *ripa*, Cat. (older), Ptg. *riba*, Span. [rriβa], French *rive*;
VĪTA 'life': Rum. *vita* ('livestock'), Ital. *vita*, Cat. [viðə], Ptg. [vidɐ], Span. [biða], French *vie*;
AMĪCA 'female friend': Ital. *amica*, Cat. [amiɣə], Ptg. *amiga*, Span. [amiɣa], French *amie*.

> In Tuscan, and to a lesser extent in standard Italian, there is sporadic (usually lexically determined) voicing: this is particularly found with sibilants (for instance, in the suffix *-ese*). The voicing is sometimes explained in terms of

dialect borrowing (in northern Tuscany it is more frequently found) or of accent placement (occurring more frequently after the accent, as in *fègato* 'liver' < FICATU). However, the words that are affected do not fall within any obvious category, semantic or stylistic, and it has been suggested that in Tuscan the process can be related to the spirantization known as *gorgia toscana* (see below for 'Etruscan spirantization').

Voicing or lenition has been described in terms of a chain shift, triggered initially in the Late Latin era by the simplification of geminates. It must be assumed in this scenario that the Rumanian loss of geminates dates from a later period.

Geminate obstruents in Romance

CŬPPA (alongside CŪPA) 'cup': Rum *cupă*, Ital. *coppa*, Span., Cat., Ptg., *copa*, French *coupe*;

GŬTTA 'drop': Rum. *gută* ('gout', perhaps from French), Ital. *gotta*, Span., Ptg., Cat. *gota*, French *goutte* [gut];

BŬCCA 'mouth': Rum. *bucă* ('cheek'), Ital. *bocca*, Span., Cat., Ptg. *boca*, French *bouche* [buʃ].

The lenition process has also been ascribed to Celtic substratum influence, even though word-initial consonants in intervocalic sentence position are not usually affected, in the way that they are in Celtic.

Intervocalic sonorants are not usually affected by lenition. In Portuguese, however, N and L are lost:

Portuguese loss of N and L

MANU	*mão*	MALU	*mau*
SONU	*som* [õo]	SOLU	*só*
PANE	*pão*	SALIRE	*sair*
PANNU	*pano*	CABALLU	*cavalo*

This loss is attested in the earliest texts (though in the case of N the graphical tilde may have been an abbreviation for a pronounced nasal consonant, rather than denoting nasalization of the vowel).

The Celtic substratum theory is eroded somewhat by the presence of some of the more conservative Sard varieties in the Western 'leniting' group, even though there is no evidence of Celtic populations in the island. Though some central varieties, like those of Bitti and Nuoro, do retain Latin intervocalic voiceless consonants, this is not so of most dialects.

Perhaps lenition here is of more recent origin. Indeed in modern Logudorian and Campidanian Sard varieties, as in south-central Italy (including the Roman dialect), it seems that a productive lenition rule operates, by which voiceless consonants tend to voice and open in all intervocalic positions, including in word-initial position.

In the Italian dialects affected, the consonants may be lengthened (or doubled) especially in word-initial position, perhaps as a reaction against lenition. A process in the standard language known as 'syntactic reinforcement' or 'doubling' (*rafforzamento* or *radoppiamento*) ensures the protection of word-initial consonants from lenition, especially after a stressed vowel and certain prepositions. Sometimes the gemination is lexicalized and represented in the orthography:

(11)   *davvero* 'truly', *soprattutto* 'above all, especially', *frattanto* 'meanwhile', *addio* 'farewell', *neppure* 'yet', *diciassette* 'seventeen'.

In other cases, it is more or less obligatory in pronunciation:

(12)   *Perchè no?* [nn] 'Why not?', *Così fu* [ff] 'Thus it was', *Più volte* [vv] 'More times', *Dove sei?* [ss] 'Where are you?', *Come mai?* [mm] 'how on earth?'

The doubling can be distinctive in some cases:

(13)   *lodato* [lo.dato] 'praised' / *L'ho dato* [lod.dato] 'I have given it'.

        Northern speakers, whose dialects fall within the 'western' area, do not habitually use double consonants in colloquial use of standard Italian and may omit to reinforce in this way.

Explanations for doubling include the suggestion that it originates as consonant assimilation, with loss of a final consonant:

(14)   [am.me] 'to me' < AD ME, [soprat.tutto] 'above all' < SUPRA-AD TOTTU.

This sort of gemination seems to be regular in many Southern Italian dialects. Another suggestion is that the lengthening is effected by the preceding accent. In some cases, as we have seen earlier, a stressed vowel is lengthened, and sometimes diphthongized:

(15)   [laːto] < LATU; *nuovo* < NŎUU.

However, in proparoxytones, the vowel lengthening is less evident in the stressed syllable, and sometimes, regularly in some dialects, there is consonant gemination instead:

(16)   *pècora* (not **piecora*) 'sheep', but *màcchina* < MACHINA.

There are examples of gemination even in some paroxytones, lending credence to this theory:

(17)   *succo*/*sugo* 'juice'< SŪCU; *brutto* 'ugly'< BRŪTU.

We do not know whether the sort of lenition/fortition found in southern Italy and Sicily dates back to Proto-Romance, or whether it is a modern development. What it seems to show is some sort of neutralization of the length and voice distinctions in consonants. Sometimes there is alternation between devoicing and gemination:

(18)   Salento [krassu] 'fat' / [kkjuggrassu] 'fatter' (Ital. (*più*) *grasso*), [tetʃi] 'ten' / [kuddetʃi] 'with ten' (Ital. (*con*) *dieci*).

'Western' lenition, on the other hand, is envisaged as a chain shift, which avoids merger between long and short consonants, even at the risk of merging voiced and voiceless counterparts (and, at the extreme, of eliminating them altogether from the relevant lexical forms).

One problem about postulating an east/west dichotomy on the basis of voicing is that in dialects straddling the central Pyrenees (Aragon on the Spanish side and Béarn on the French) Latin voiceless consonants are regularly retained. Some suggest that these conservative varieties resisted Western innovation, whereas others see the influence of Basque in a postulated early merger of geminates with single consonants, which precluded the chain shift.

(ii)   Celtic fronting

Another feature that has been attributed to Celtic substratum influence is French front rounded [y], as the regular context-free reflex of Latin Ū. It is assumed that the Latin sound was a high back rounded vowel [u], like the reflexes in all the other major languages.

We note, however, that Greek υ ([y]) in some (early?) loanwords into Latin appears with the graphy U : short Ŭ, as shown by later Romance developments: e.g.

(19)   BURSA > Ital. *borsa*, Span., Ptg. *bolsa*.

Elsewhere the accepted graphy (*y*) and pronunciation imitated the Greek, but in colloquial speech [i] was presumably pronounced:

(20)   GYRARE > Ital. *girare*, French *girer*.

> It is just possible that Latin ū was in some varieties pronounced as [y], but in others as [u]. One could then conceivably view the [y] pronunciation as a feature that persisted from Latin to some Romance varieties.

The [y] pronunciation is not confined to Northern French, but is widespread in Occitan and North Italian dialects, as well as in some Portuguese varieties. It is absent from some Northern French varieties, in particular Belgian Eastern Walloon and some Francoprovençal dialects, where it is assumed that there was regression to [u] under the influence of neighbouring Germanic dialects. However, the existence of [y] pronunciations in some Germanic varieties has led some to see it as an areal feature and even to postulate a connection with genetic factors.

The connection with Celtic is somewhat tenuous, especially as we know little about Gaulish Celtic. The evidence adduced points to Latin loanwords into insular Celtic (e.g. Welsh) in which ū appears as [i]. Those who uphold the Celtic substratum hypothesis maintain that Gaulish continued to be spoken for some considerable time under Roman occupation, and that interference from the subject language produced a regional pronunciation in Gallo-Roman. We have little hard evidence about the persistence of Gaulish, nor indeed of the widespread use of Celtic throughout Roman Gaul.

> Breton, we recall, is generally thought to have been imported from Britain in the fifth century, although some do believe that it may also have some connection with a Gaulish Celtic that may have survived in the far west.

Moreover, we are uncertain about the chronology of the fronting of [u] to [y]. As in French the graphy *u* was always used, and as there was no contextual differentiation, we have little information about pronunciation before sixteenth-century commentaries, which sometimes call it 'Gaulish *u*' and liken it to the Greek, German and Scottish sounds, commenting on its affinity with [i]. In the sixteenth and seventeenth centuries there was frequent confusion with *eu*, which was still diphthongal in some varieties in the earlier period, but then levelled to [ø] in the standard.

In English, French loanwords are pronounced with [ju]:

(21)   *pure < pur.*

The English grammarian Palsgrave (1530) still likens French *u* to the sound in *mew*, though sixteenth-century native-speaker teachers of French to the English condemn this pronunciation, emphasizing that the lips should be rounded, without movement of the tongue. It is usually thought that the [ju] always represents an English mispronunciation, with fission at segmental level, delinking of the labial element from the palatal. It is possible, though, that French *u* was originally diphthongal (in tonic free syllables but later spreading to pretonic and to blocked tonic syllables?). It would then have levelled to [y] in the same way as [eu] > [ø].

> The differential development of PŪLICE (> PUL'CE with syncope) 'flea', in French (*puce*) and Old Occitan (*piuce*) suggests that the French, and not the Occitan, fronting may have taken place after the vocalization of preconsonantal [l] to [u], thus dating it to after the twelfth century. However, if the French graphy *u* did at one time represent [ju] there would be no significant difference from the Occitan form. Besides, in the preconsonantal sequence [il] in e.g. *fils* < FILIUS, the *l* fell, so perhaps the same was true in the sequence [yl]. Note that Norse loanwords, presumably dating from the tenth century, also show the fronting, and that [y] did not trigger at an early period palatalization of preceding [k].

One postulated effect of the fronting is that it triggered a 'drag' chain shift by which Gallo-Roman [o] was raised to [u] whenever it was not diphthongized :

(22)   ŪRSU > *ours*, *TŌTTU > *tout*.

The graphy *u* is found in eleventh- and twelfth-century texts, *ou* being introduced in the twelfth century (presumably after diphthongal [ou] had differentiated to [eu]). Another suggestion (in 1949, by Haudricourt & Juilland, who compare similar changes in Greek, Swedish and Portuguese) is that the fronting was conditioned by the existence of four degrees of aperture in the vowel system, which placed a burden on the back series (owing to the asymmetry in the articulatory space available at the front and at the back of the mouth). The fronting of the high back vowel is part of a 'push' chain shift that originated in the greater differentiation between [ɔ] and [o], resulting in [o] raising to the [u] slot.

Another effect of vowel fronting in Northern French is less often ascribed to Celtic influence, but deserves mention here. In French (but not the more northern dialects) Latin velar consonants palatalize before A (and also before AU, even though this eventually levels to [ɔː]). This wave of palatalization is not found in other Romance languages, except Western Rhaeto-Romance varieties, and has a different result from the 'pan-Romance' palatalization of velars (see 3.3). In French the *velar* + A palatalization yielded [tʃ] and [dʒ] (or perhaps [c], [ɟ], usually written *ch*, *j*), becoming [ʃ], [ʒ], by loss of the delayed release feature, in the thirteenth century:

(23)   CANTARE > *chanter* [ʃɑ̃te] 'to sing'; GAMBA > *jambe* [ʒɑ̃b] 'leg'.

(Compare the dental affricate, usually written *c* or *z*, resulting from a voiceless *velar* + E, I.)

> In Francoprovençal varieties dental affricates result from both waves of palatalization. In French, German and Arabic loanwords in *velar + e, i* participate in the second wave of palatalization:

(24)   **skina* > *échine* 'spine'; *meskin* > (Old) *meschin* 'young man', with [tʃ] > [ʃ]

> (cf. Occ. *esquina*, Ital. *meschino*, both with [k], the latter borrowed into French in the seventeenth century as *mesquin* 'shabby, paltry').

The second wave of palatalization seems to imply that French *a* at the time was a front vowel, whereas in the other languages its counterpart was a mid or back vowel. In tonic free syllables French *a* gave *e* by the time of the earliest texts, perhaps by diphthongization via [ae] or [aj] (see below).

> The affinity of French [a] to [e] was still stressed by sixteenth-century commentators. By the eighteenth century there is evidence, however, that lengthened [aː] had backed to [ɑ], and the distinction is still maintained in some varieties:

(25)   *patte* [pat] 'paw' / *pâte* [pɑt] 'paste, pastry'.

Although accepting that there must have been fronting of *a* to give the necessary phonetic conditions for palatalization in French, Haudricourt & Juilland maintain that the sufficient condition for the phonological change lies elsewhere. They point to the resolution in French of the Latin QU [kw] before A:

(26)   *quand* [k] / Ital. *quando*, Span. *cuando* [kw] 'when'

as provoking a push-chain shift that resulted in the palatalization of C ([k]) in the same environment. It is, however, uncertain when the [w] element was lost in [kw]: in AQUA 'water', for instance, traces remained for a long time (see Old French *eve*, *eue*, which eventually yields *eaue*, modern *eau* [o]). Certainly secondary [kw], like that of COAGULARE > *cailler* 'curdle', seems to behave in the same way as Latin QU. In modern French some words in *qua-* can still be pronounced with [k] or [kw]: these are usually Latinisms, like the thirteenth-century borrowing *quadruple*. Some sixteenth-century spelling reformers, however, advocate the omission of *u* in words usually spelt with *qu*.

Perhaps we should look elsewhere for the causes of the phonologization of the allophonic variation [tʃ]+ *a* / [k]+ *o*. The levelling of the *au* diphthong, probably to [ɔː], is attested in the graphy of the earliest texts, though these provide no evidence for palatalization (e.g. *cosa* < CAUSA), and probably by this period there had been raising or diphthongization of inherited central back vowels, so that the earlier allophony was no longer transparent. Moreover, the influx of loanwords in *ca-* began early (e.g., from Occitan in the twelfth century, *cabrer* 'to rear up', and *cadeau* 'gift, present', originally meaning 'capital letter') and it was soon to become a flood. This may be a sign that [tʃ] was no longer at that time analysed as an allophone of [k]: the sequence [tʃe], we recall, had become current with the fronting of tonic free *a* (as in *chez* < CASA), though the sequence [tʃi] was not well established at an early date.

(iii)   Etruscan spirantization

I have already mentioned the localized Tuscan spirantization of intervocalic consonants, which some believe to be in some way related to the lenition of more northerly Italian dialects. Its geographical distribution has prompted some to make a link with the extinct (and as yet undeciphered) Etruscan language – even though much of the area known to have been inhabited by Etruscans in classical times does not participate in spirantization. Usually the relative conservatism of Tuscan dialects, which form the basis of the Italian standard, is ascribed to the local population having learned Latin as a totally foreign language, and thus being less apt to introduce colloquial elements from their own tongue. Today, though, in Tuscan intervocalic voiceless plosives are pronounced as spirants, a feature that has acquired a degree of prestige. The process affects /k/ in particular, which is pronounced as [h] (which falls altogether in Lucca and Livorno):

(27)   *dico* [diho], *poco* [pɔho], *la casa* [lahaːsa].

The sounds /p/ and /t/ are also affected in some dialects: thus *rapa* is pronounced [rapʰa] or [raɸa], and *stato* as [statʰo], [staθo] or [staho]. In rapid Florentine speech all three voiceless plosives may be dropped altogether.

Spirantization of /k/ is attested since the sixteenth century (for instance, in the spelling of the surname *Cecherelli* as *Ceheregli*), though this does not necessarily mean it was not current in popular pronunciation earlier. It has been claimed that Dante's remark about the 'turpitude' of Tuscan speech refers to this unprestigious pronunciation. Some also believe the early spelling *ch* for [k] may signal a pronunciation [χ] (but we recall that *ch* is normally used in Italian before *e* and *i*). In any case, although it is believed that Etruscan consonants were aspirated, there is no evidence of spirantization, nor of differential treatment of intervocalics in that language. Nevertheless the Etruscan substratum hypothesis still has advocates.

(iv)   Spanish /f/ > /h/

Equally speculative, and now almost wholly discredited, is the association with an Iberian substratum of the Castilian change of Latin F to [h], nearly always, though not exclusively, in word-initial position. This change appears to have been originally confined to the region of Old Castile, but spread with this dialect to the standard. In the modern language the [h] has disappeared but it is still marked in the graphy:

(28)   FERIRE > *herir* 'to injure', FACIES > *haz* 'surface', FUNDU > *hondo* 'deep'.

Although the modern standard pronunciation of *f* is a labial dental fricative, a regional pronunciation [ɸ] is frequent and possibly original. It has been suggested that this sound had the features [continuant], with weak approximation, and [round], and can be realized in some dialects sequentially rather than simultaneously, as [hʷ], as in some varieties today:

(29)   Peruvian Amazon *juacil* for *fácil*, also *Fan* for *Juan*.

Some credence is lent to this suggestion by the fact that in standard Castilian the change does not occur before a diphthong:

(30)   FESTA > *fiesta* 'feast', FOCUS > *fuego* 'fire'.

In these cases the delinking of the [round] feature may have been inhibited by its not being able to form a diphthong with the following nucleus. In some dialects, though, the feature is lost before a rounded vowel:

(31)   *juego* for *fuego*.

Perhaps in the Castilian change, too, the split [round] feature was lost first before a rounded vowel, with subsequent generalization of its loss.

> In some older graphies it seems that *f* may have represented [h] whereas *ff* was used for [f]: the graphy *h* was introduced only in the late fifteenth century.

It is quite possible that the feature splitting occurs most frequently in the acquired speech of those whose first language has no [ɸ] sound: this seems to be true of Latin American varieties. That Basque does not have an /f/ phoneme is adduced as evidence that this was also so in pre-Roman Iberian (though in Basque, Latin F is usually represented in loanwords as [b] and not as [hʷ]). It has also been pointed out that the F > [h] change is attested in some Southern Italian dialects, where Iberian influence is implausible, and indeed it is not unusual for [ɸ] to open to [h]. Moreover, as some later loanwords are affected, it is assumed by some that the change occurred long after Iberian had ceased to be spoken. It has been suggested that the Spanish phonemic split can be dated as late as the twelfth or thirteenth centuries, when there was an influx of French and Occitan speakers into Spanish territory.

(v)   Rumanian 'vowel centralization'

Rumanian has a neutral central vowel *ă* [ɐ] or [ə] < Latin unaccented A, a development found in many Romance varieties. In Rumanian (as in European but not Brazilian Portuguese) it is also found in some accented positions:

(32)   *păr* 'pear-tree' < PIRU, *țări* 'lands' < TERRAE.

There is also another central unrounded front vowel, *î* (also written as *â* in older graphy and in certain contexts today). This is sometimes described as a high central vowel [ɨ] or as a fronted back vowel [ɯ]. In some words the two central vowels are interchangeable, with colloquial speech preferring the former, but some minimal pairs testify to their distinct phonemic status:

(33)   *văr* 'cousin' (*ver* in dialects south of the Danube) < (CONSOBRINUS) VĒRUS / *vîr* 'I insert', of Slavonic origin.

The provenance of the *î* vowel seems to be due to a whole range of more or less sporadic processes. These are said to include the raising and centralization of non-high Latin vowels before a nasal, and the retraction of front vowels following so-called 'velarizing' consonants, especially /rː/:

(34)   *lînă* 'wool' < LANA (see Ptg. *lã* [lẽ]), *rîpă* 'ravine' < RĪPA.

Some seek the origin of *î* in Slavonic influence, as it occurs in a number of Slavonic loanwords. Others prefer to see the 'velarizing' tendency of Rumanian as stemming from the pre-Roman Thraco-Dacian substratum. There is little evidence to support this hypothesis, however, and it may be preferable to view the central vowels as defaults to which other vowels revert when their context induces loss of distinctive features.

What may also be possible is that *ă* and *î* continue a former short [a] and [i], whereas modern [a] and [i] represent former long vowels. These latter could have resulted from coalescence of two like vowels:

(35)   *casă* 'house' / *casa* 'the house', where the latter incorporates definite article [*ʎ*]*a* (see Ptg. *casa* (*azul*) [kazɐ] / [kazazul]); *Cîntăm* 'We sing' / *Cîntam* 'We were singing' / CANTAMUS, CANTA[B]AMUS (see European Ptg. present tense ending [ɐmuʃ] < -AMUS / past tense ending [amuʃ] < -AVIMUS).

In other cases the long vowels could have resulted from lengthening in tonic syllables, a process that may have been inhibited by a following nasal or in some cases a preceding labial, sibilant or long *r*. The metaphonic effect of a following palatal glide seems sporadically to have provoked the change *a > ă*:

(36)   *mare* sg. / *mări* pl. 'sca(s)' < MARE(S) (but *mare*/*mari* 'big' < ?(MAS), MARE(S))

Chronologically, spatially and morphologically there is some alternation between *i* and *î*, which is not incompatible with the view that the former was a longer version of the latter:

(37)   Old *şî* / modern *şi* 'and' < SĪC; dial. *zîc* / standard *zic* 'I say' < DĪCO; *vînă*/*vine* 'vein(s)' < VĒNA(E), *vînd*/*vinde* 'I/he sell(s)' < VENDO /VENDIT.

> The fact that the *r* had an effect on retraction of a front vowel may indicate that it once had retroflex or perhaps uvular articulation (as it has today in some varieties, allegedly influenced by French). For the genesis of uvular *r* in other Romance languages see below.

(b)   Borrowing from substratum languages

The proportion of any Romance lexicon that can be firmly derived from pre-Roman languages is very small, though some scholars have a tendency to ascribe a pre-Roman etymon to any word of unknown origin. Celtic supplies a number of common words to the Western languages: some of them may have already been borrowed into Latin (like the word for 'cream', CRAMA, which survives in France and north Italy). Most, however, are not attested in texts before the twelfth century at the earliest. Occitan seems to have retained the largest stock of allegedly Celtic words: *clot* 'pit, grave', *lausa* 'roof slate', *comba* 'valley', for instance, which also are known to

Catalan; *borne* 'milestone', *caillou* 'pebble' seem to be confined to the north of France, but cognates of *boue* 'mud' are found in the Alps, of *creux* 'hollow' also in Occitan, and of *mouton* 'sheep' also all over the north of Italy and in Catalan. French *berceau* 'cradle' still has cognates in Occitan, Catalan and Portuguese, but the Old Spanish forms are no longer used.

The Iberian languages have some everyday words unknown elsewhere, which are assumed to be of pre-Roman origin. One is the word for 'butter': Span. *manteca*, Ptg. *manteiga* (which has been borrowed by Catalan, Occitan and Italian dialects). Another is the word for 'left hand' (*izquierdo*, *esquerdo*), which is clearly related to a Basque word and which is also found in Catalan and Occitan. Portuguese appears to keep more of these words than Spanish: Ptg. *carvalho* 'oak-tree' remains, whereas Span. *carvajo* has been ousted by *roble* < ROBUR.

If it is hard to assign substratal origins to words in the Western languages, it is even more hazardous in Rumanian, as we have little knowledge of Thracian and Dacian. Normally it is assumed that where Albanian and Rumanian share common vocabulary of unknown origin, it must have survived from the pre-Roman era. Quite a few common words in modern Rumanian fit into this category:

(38)   *abur* 'steam', *brad* 'fir-tree', *brîu* 'belt', *bucura* 'to rejoice', *buză* 'lip', *cioc* 'beak',
         copac 'tree', *copil* 'child', *fărîmă* 'crumb', *ghimpe* 'thorn', *groapă* 'pit, ditch',
         rață 'duck', *vatră* 'fireplace'.

Very often the words that we believe emanate from the substratum languages are commonplace, but rather quaint, words to do with traditional rural life. These words add a certain exotic flavour to each of the languages, but proportionally they are so insignificant that they do not constitute any sort of communication barrier to speakers of the modern languages.

6.4   BREAKUP OF THE ROMAN EMPIRE –
           SUPERSTRATUM

(a)   Germanic influence on French

The most widely accepted theory about superstratum influence provoking differentiation in Romance concerns the role of the Franks in northern France. Within the present European French-speaking area different Romance varieties underlie the standard: the linguistic line between the North (*oïl*) and the South (*oc*) is unusually sharp, though in the East ('Francoprovençal') the isoglosses fan out in a fairly unpredictable manner (see 5.1). The linguistic divide is paralleled by several different traditional cultural patterns – for instance, in house-building, in agricultural techniques and in legal practice. The north is seen as influenced profoundly by Germanic cultural features.

The Oc(citan) dialects are much linguistically closer to their Romance neighbours, and form part of Romania continua (see 5.2), and indeed, as we have seen (page 3), it has even been suggested that they are nearest to a postulated unitary *langue romane* from which all the Romance languages were deemed to have sprung. The Northern dialects, on the other hand, show radical differences, which have even, in the past, led to doubts about their Romance character. The Northern linguistic area has, since the Middle Ages, encroached on the Southern, especially in the West, where the isoglossic boundary plunges south to encompass Saintonge in the Oïl orbit. Elsewhere in the south Occitan varieties survive, if somewhat precariously, even though French has been dominant since the sixteenth century, and today there are no adult monolingual Occitan speakers.

(i)   Phonology

Some of the distinctive characteristics of French date, as we shall see, from the later Middle Ages. But the first French texts (from the ninth or tenth century) indicate that, phonologically at least, French had already developed in a different way from most other Romance languages. The specifically French phonological transformations are usually linked to a postulated 'heavy' word stress that had the effect of reducing atonic and lengthening tonic syllables. Thus, for instance, all vowels in atonic final syllables except *a* were lost. The sound *a* appears to have been reduced in preliteracy times to [ə], usually spelt *e*. This weakened further in the course of Old French and was virtually lost by the modern period (though the *e instable* or 'mute *e*' does re-appear in some contexts).

In the more conservative areas, central and southern Italy, Rumania and Sardinia, word-final *e* is maintained in some form, but elsewhere it usually falls:

(39)   LEVARE 'to lift': Sard *leare*, Rum. *luare*, Ital. *levare*, Occ., R-R, Ptg. *levar*, Cat., Span. *llevar*, French *lever*.

However, there is more general retention of the distinction between final *o* and *a*, morphologically so important for gender marking (see 1.3), and also to mark the distinction between persons 1 and 3 in many common verb paradigms (see 1.2). In many Romance varieties [a] eventually weakens to [ə]; [o] often closes to [u], and it is regularly lost in Catalan, Occitan and Rumanian in absolute final position.

Old French words thus were frequently monosyllabic, ending in a consonant; word-final obstruents seem to have been devoiced as in modern German:

(40)   NOUE > *neuf* 'nine', GRANDE > *grant* 'big', TRABE > *tref* 'beam', LONGU > *lonc* 'long'.

The most salient effect of the postulated strong accent was, however, felt in the tonic syllables. It was only in the Northern French varieties that the Proto-Romance vowels [e], [o] and [a] were subject to regular diphthongization (for the pan-Romance diphthongization of [ɛ] and [ɔ] see 4.2). In the centre of the area only vowels in free syllables were affected: some seek to relate the process to Open Syllable Lengthening in Germanic languages. In some more peripheral varieties, however, especially near the frontier with Germanic (here we include also some Northern Italian and Rhaeto-Romance varieties), diphthongization can take place in both blocked and free syllables. The relative chronology of French sound changes places this wave of diphthongization later than the pan-Romance wave, as words in which syncope of unstressed vowels occurred, thus blocking the relevant syllable, are not affected by the second wave:

(41)   DĒBITU > *dette* 'debt' but TĔPIDU > *tiède* 'lukewarm'.

The specifically French diphthongization process can plausibly be linked to lengthening of the tonic syllable, producing a falling diphthong: [ee] > [ej], [oo] > [ow], spelt in early texts *ei*, *ou*. The effect on [a] is less clear: a diphthongal graphy appears only before a nasal (a context which blocks diphthongization in other cases):

(42)   MANU > *main*, modern [mɛ̃], AMAT > *aime*, modern [ɛm] (but CANE > *chien*, modern [ʃjɛ̃], with 'Bartsch's Law' breaking under influence of the preceding palatal < *chen*).

Elsewhere the graphy *e* is found:

(43)   TALE > *tel* modern [tɛl], GRATU > *gre* modern [gre] (where the modern difference in vowel quality is recent and depends on syllabic structure), CARU > Old *chier* (with breaking), modern *cher* [ʃɛʀ].

It is usually assumed that a diphthong [aj] or [ae] had rapidly resolved to a simple vowel, by mutual assimilation.

> Unlike the 'pan-Romance' diphthongization process, this French one does not seem to affect Latin checked monosyllables:

(44)   IAM > *ja* 'already' (see REM > *rien* 'thing, nothing', MEL > *miel* 'honey').

The Old French *e* < A does not rhyme or assonate with other *e* vowels in the twelfth century, but is coupled with the *e* of loanwords: it is usually assumed to be longer than the other *e* sounds. 'Bartsch's Law' breaking of this *e* to *ie*, however, suggests a [ɛ] quality, whereas [e] < Ē in similar contexts seems to be raised to [i]:

(45)   CĒRA > *cire* 'wax'.

The *ei* and *ou* diphthongs soon became *oi* and *eu* in most dialects and contexts, by flip-flop differentiation of the nuclear vowel from the glide, though in the west the glide tended to be lost, perhaps indicating a shortening of the stressed syllable. Differentiation, which is attested from the eleventh century, is associated, in traditional studies, with retention of syllable length and the heavy accent which was thought to characterize more northerly and easterly dialects.

(ii)   Morphosyntax: German influence on French word order

It has been implausibly suggested that certain features of French syntax – notably the obligatory use of subject pronouns (see 1.2) and postverbal negation (see 7.4) – are due to influence from German. Chronologically this is unlikely. More acceptable is the suggestion that some aspects of Old French word-order owe much to Germanic influence.

In Old French, in declarative main clauses, the verb normally appears as the second constituent (verb-second or V2), an ordering which is current in Germanic languages. Where the subject occupies the first position, there is little difference between Old and modern French, which prefers SVO ordering. When, however, another element of the clause is topicalized by placing it first in the clause, then the lexical subject is inverted – that is, placed after the verb – while a pronoun subject is usually left unexpressed:

(46)   *Longtemps fu ly roys Elinas en la montaigne* 'For a long time was King Elinas on the mountain'; *Iteuses paroles distrent li frere de Lancelot* 'Such words uttered Lancelot's brothers'; *Atant regarda contreval la mer* 'Then (he) looked down at the sea'.

Although in the other early Romance languages examples of V2 ordering can be found, it is more regular in Old French. To invoke the influence of Germanic seems reasonable, though there are doubts about whether the relevant Germanic dialects were themselves V2 at the time of most influence (between the fifth and eighth centuries).

> In Surselvan V2 ordering is regular, but here it is likely that influence comes from close modern contact with German.

By early modern French the V2 ordering became less frequent and stylistically marked: the language arbiters decreed in favour of direct, logical (i.e. SVO) ordering. One question we could ask is whether indeed in Old French the V2 ordering was not also a literary artefact, and whether less formal usage, for which we have little evidence, may have preferred a less Germanic-type ordering.

Another word-order feature of Old French which may owe something to Germanic influence is interrogative inversion in polar questions, where the verb often occurs as the first constituent in the sentence (V1) with a postposed subject:

(47)   *Durrad li fiz Ysaïa vus tuz chanps e vignes?* 'Will the son of Isaiah give to you all the fields and vines?'

In fact, use of a lexical subject in such cases was quite rare, but a postposed pronoun was more frequently overtly expressed than in declarative V2 sentences. By the fifteenth century inversion of a lexical subject in polar questions was apparently archaic; for modern so-called complex inversion see 7.4.

In the other Romance languages, V1 ordering is not uncommon, so much so that some claim that the basic order is V1. Usually, however, this ordering implies not so much interrogation, as a degree of topicalization. We may assume that intonation has always been, as now, the principal means by which a polar question is distinguished in Romance from a statement. It is quite possible that French borrowed from Germanic the association of V1 ordering with interrogative function.

(iii)   Germanic vocabulary

In the Western languages there is a not negligible proportion of common words of Germanic origin that have survived from the Roman and post-Roman periods. French, as one might expect, has the largest share, and Portuguese the least, with Italian high on the list of recipients. Some words were borrowed into Latin and spread through the Empire: the word for 'soap' SAPONE is pan-Romance, and hints at the washing habits of Romans and Germans. Others are widespread but did not reach Rumania: the words for 'war', 'to win', 'to guard, ward', 'to equip' all speak of the military prowess of the Germanic invaders:

(48)   **werra:* French *guerre*, Ital. *guerra* (probably borrowed into the other languages); **waidanjan:* French *gagner*, Ptg. *ganhar*, Ital. *guadagnare*, Span. *guadañar.* ; **wardon* 'to ward, guard': French *garder*, Ital. *guardare*, Span., Ptg. *guardar*; **warnjan:* French *garnir*, Ital. *guarnire*, Span., Ptg. *guarnir*.

In other cases French is differentiated from the other languages by its choice of German word rather than Latin:

(49)   *choisir* 'to choose' (**kausjan*) / Ital. *scegliere* < **EX-ELIGERE*, Span. *escojer* < **EX-COLLIGERE*, Rum. *alege* < ALLEGERE; French *sale* 'dirty' (*salo*)/ Ital. *sudicio*, Span. *sucio* < SUCIDU; *saisir* 'to seize' (**sakjan*) / Ital. *cogliere*, Span. *coger* < COLLIGERE etc. (see French *cueillir* 'to pick, to pluck').

However, the Germanic input into the French vocabulary remained marginal, and mainly confined to more specialist terms, so that they do little to alter the overall configuration of the lexicon.

It has been maintained that the relative paucity of Germanic loanwords in Rumanian is evidence that the language originated south of the Danube, and migrated north to present-day Rumania during the Middle Ages. However, others claim that there is a considerable number of such words that have survived the centuries from the earliest period: for most of these the etymological origin is contested. *Nasture* 'button' is one of the few that is generally recognized as Germanic, but it could have been borrowed via Italian *nastro* 'ribbon'.

(b)   Arabic influence in Spain and Portugal

The contact with Romance of the Moorish conquerors of most of the Iberian peninsula, from the eighth century until their final defeat in 1492, was quite different from that of the Germanic invaders of the Romance Empire. For one thing, Arabic culture was far in advance of that of Dark Ages Western Europe, and the invaders were not so eager to adopt the language of the conquered people. That they did do so to some extent is shown by the evidence of the Romance refrains (*harǧa's*) of *muwaššah* poems, written in both Arabic and Hebrew, of which we have evidence from the eleventh century. However, some scholars cast doubt on the linguistic authenticity of some of these refrains: because of the difficulties of transcription from Arabic and Hebrew script, interpretation is often hazardous, and it is possible that some of them are little more than Romance-like 'hey-diddle-de-dee' nonsensical refrains.

In the past, there has been a resistance on the part of Spanish and Portuguese writers to admitting any profound linguistic influence on the Northern dialects that spread south with the Christian Reconquest. Many of the characteristics that the layman may associate with Arabic, like Spanish velar fricative *jota*, are of comparatively recent origin. Very little in the modern languages, apart from borrowings, can reliably be attributed to Arabic: one exception is the suffix -*í*, as in *alfonsí*.

More recently, politically correct attitudes prefer to envisage a symbiotic, rather than a conflictive, relationship between the medieval languages of the peninsula. It is quite probable, on historical grounds, that Portuguese was less long in contact with Arabic than Spanish varieties were. Certainly we know that the Spanish Jews, an influential and cultured group until their expulsion in 1492, were proficient in Spanish, and often acted as interpreters between Arabic and Spanish speakers. There is some doubt, however, whether the Muslim *moriscos*, mainly farmers, who were in their turn expelled in the early seventeenth century, did ever know much Spanish.

Before the Reconquest, a conservative Romance language was used in Moorish Spain, by Christians, Jews and possibly by Muslims of Iberian stock (*muwalladat*). This variety is sometimes known as Old Andalusian, or more often as *mozarabic*, from the name (*musta'ribun*) given to Christians under Muslim rule, though there may have been very few of these left by the twelfth century.

Certain features of this variety were conceivably influenced by Arabic, and it has been suggested these have survived into modern Andalusian Spanish. These concern mainly the pronunciation of sibilants and dental fricatives. In Castilian /s/ (s mainly < Latin s) is apico-alveolar, while /θ/, earlier [ʦ] (*c*, *ç* < Latin+^{E,I}) is dental (and usually coronal): for devoicing of former voiced fricatives see 7.2. In Andalusia by the fifteenth century the two series seem to have begun to merge, with the spelling *ç* (*ceceo*). It is assumed that /s/ had dental articulation in this area. In coastal areas today a sound similar to [θ] is used for both series, whereas elsewhere, including Seville, a dental [s] (*seseo*) is current. This is the pronunciation which was purportedly exported to the Canaries and America. In much of Galicia and Portugal, though not in standard Portuguese, a distinction is maintained between the two series. There is no good reason, however, to link the merger of the two series with Arabic influence, as northern France underwent the same change, probably by the thirteenth century.

More reliable evidence of the influence of Arabic on the Iberian languages is found among loanwords. Many Arabic words, as we have seen, entered the rest of the Romance languages via Spanish, usually accompanying some cultural innovation. There was some reaction in early modern standard Spanish against the use of such words, so that more have survived in the Portuguese basic vocabulary than in the Spanish, though in both languages the proportion remains small:

(50)   Ptg. *alfaiate* 'tailor' / Spanish *sastre*, borrowed from Old French *sartre* < SAR-
         TOR (but Old *alfayate*).

Most of the common words that are different from those of other Romance languages are shared by both languages:

(51)   Span. *aceite*, Ptg. *azeite* 'oil'; Span. *aldea*, Ptg. *aldeia* 'village'; Span. *almacén*,
         Ptg. *armazem* 'store'; Span. *hasta* (Old *fata*), Ptg. *até* 'until'.

(c)   Slavonic influence on Rumanian

By the seventh century there was extensive Slavonic settlement in former Eastern Romance territory, and it is claimed that the newcomers north of the Danube adopted the local Latin, with a long period of bilingualism. It is certain that loanwords and cultural history provide evidence of close contact, but there is dispute about how far Slavonic influence accounts for the idiosyncratic features of Rumanian.

I have already discussed, as a possible substratum phenomenon, the centralization of Rumanian vowels that some attribute rather to Slavonic influence. The frequent palatalization of Rumanian consonants may more plausibly thus be linked, especially in the case of the realization of the masculine noun plural ending, and the person 2 verb ending, *i*, as palatalization of the preceding consonant. In many Rumanian dialects, too, there is Slavonic-like jodization of initial vowels.

Some attribute to Slavonic pronunciation the *ea* result of Proto-Romance [e] when *ă* (or sometimes *e*) appears in the final syllable:

(52)   *neagră* < NĪGRA 'black', *ceară* < CĒRA 'wax'.

However, the parallel diphthongization of *o* is less likely to be due to Slavonic:

(53)   *poartă* < PORTA, *coadă* < CAUDA, *floare* < FLŌRE.

Moreover, the diphthongization is found also in dialects south of the Danube, suggesting an early date for the change. It is possible that it is connected to the metaphonic changes of tonic vowels discussed earlier as a possible Proto-Romance development. In Rumanian, as in Portuguese, there may have been raising and closing of a metaphonic diphthong under the influence of a following high vowel, but lowering in other cases:

(54)   Ptg. *porco* [o] / *porca* [ɔ]; Rum. *porc*/*poarcă* < PORCU/-A 'boar'/'sow'.

In Rumanian the lower vowel, perhaps lengthened under stress, seems then to have opened further, anticipating at the end the timbre of the following low vowel. The stem alternation frequently marks nominal gender distinction and so is firmly rooted in the grammar.

Other phonological features of Rumanian are clearly Slavonic in origin, in particular the sounds, like *h* ([h] or [χ]), and sound sequences, like *sl*, that are found mainly in Slavonic loanwords:

(55)   *hrană* 'food', *a se odinhi* 'to rest', *slab* 'poor'.

Other features often linked to Slavonic are the abundant use of reflexive forms and the frequency of clitic doubling. These are, however, found in other Romance languages (see below), though Slavonic influence may have reinforced them in Rumanian.

There is no doubt that there has been copious borrowing from Slavonic into Rumanian, though the vocabulary of any text still remains preponderantly Romance. We have already mentioned the influence of Slavonic on the composition of Rumanian numerals; similar loan-translation effects are found in, for instance:

(56)   *lume* < LUMEN 'light' and 'world', *față* < FACIES 'face' and 'person'.

Slavonic derivational suffixes like *-ac*, *-nic*, *-uş* are particularly common. Examples of everyday words of Slavonic origin include:

(57)   *boală* 'illness', *bumbac* 'cotton', *ceas* 'hour', *ciocan* 'hammer', *clopot* 'bell',
         coborî 'to go down', *coş* basket', *deal* 'hill', *drag* 'dear', *gata* 'ready', *găsi* 'to
         find', *hotărî* 'to decide', *lovi* 'to hit', *mîndru* 'proud', *nevastă* 'wife', *omorî* 'to
         kill', *prost* 'stupid', *război* 'war', *scîrbă* 'disgust', *trăi* 'to live', *veac* 'century',
         zimţ 'tooth'.

         We may mention here common words that penetrated into Rumanian from
         Magyar:

(58)   *gînd* 'thought', *fel* 'manner'

         and from Turkish:

(59)   *chel* 'bald', *duşman* 'enemy'.

6.5   SYNTACTIC DIFFERENTIATION IN THE EARLY MODERN PERIOD

In chapter 3, we considered the question of the timing of the death of Latin, and I suggested that this was intimately bound up with the question of when the Romance languages differentiated. As long as the vernaculars were viewed as merely variants of the prestige language, Latin, then there was no clear perception of the separateness of the Romance languages. We have already seen that nonstandard regional varieties of Romance tend to merge into one another in a spatial continuum, with catenate mutual intelligibility. The standards, on the other hand, are clearly demarcated, and indeed often deliberately emphasize differences between themselves and their neighbours. Thus we may wish to date the definitive differentiation of the Romance language to the period of standardization, which in most cases coincides with the era of the Renaissance, which, by its own lights, was innovative and forward-looking. It can be claimed that there was at the time a new insight into history and the processes of change which arose primarily from the consciousness of language change over time, as distinct from that of spatial and social variation. The perception of the vernacular, on which intrastate communication depended, as labile and shifting was disconcerting, and so every effort was made to elaborate standard, fixed codes.

Many of the differences between the early Romance varieties that we have already discussed in terms of stratal influences were phonological, and probably even, initially, merely phonetic. They may not have seriously hindered comprehension between Romance speakers, as superficial, natural and easily formulable variation. Vocabulary also varied from region to region, but often less frequent synonyms persisted in one area that made the usage of another area understandable. There was less variation in grammatical structures before the post-medieval period.

We have ample evidence of medieval writers operating in different Romance varieties, as well as in Latin, and little inkling of any serious communication barriers. Even though feudal society confined much of the population to one place, there were always pedlars and strolling minstrels, who presumably had to be proficient in a number of local varieties, and who could spread features from one to another. We must not forget either that the Crusades meant that speakers of different Romance varieties mingled together and, apparently, forged a common lingua franca of clearly Romance character.

It is true that by the thirteenth century we become more and more convinced that many Romance speakers found learning Latin a hard task, and that recourse had to be made to the vernacular to ensure comprehension (especially in official documents). As we have seen, it is about then that different language names began consistently to be applied to different regional varieties. That translations from the Latin into French were commissioned on royal authority in the fourteenth century is surely evidence of the growing perception that these were substantively different languages, as well as of a deliberate attempt at status planning (normalization). Codification (corpus planning or normativization) did not really get going till the sixteenth century, when the new technology of printing was set to make the written word more accessible to a wider public. By the seventeenth century in Western Romance-speaking Europe, individual vernaculars, now linked to state power, were replacing Latin in nearly all its functions. But Latin still retained prestige as a cultural and religious language.

I have suggested earlier that in some cases the very recourse to Latin and to other Romance languages for new vocabulary may have hastened phonological differentiation by introducing new phonological contrasts where previously there was merely allophonic variation. Against this may be placed the consideration that Latinized forms may have re-introduced, at the synchronic level, into speakers' consciousness the morphological link between forms that were related etymologically, but whose phonological relationship had become obscured by sound changes.

Another source of early differentiation in the texts may be an effect of the differing prestige of competing varieties within a Romance-speaking community. For instance, it can be argued that early Old French literary texts exhibit more Germanic-like traits than later ones. The very earliest texts appear in bilingual contexts or originated from bilingual areas (like England). It may be that the more Germanic syntax that is detected in these texts is not characteristic of Old French as an entity, but of a certain prestige variety. The changes that apparently took place during the Middle French period may reflect, then, not a change over time, but a switch in prestige between different varieties. Similarly, in Italy an early prestige Sicilian variety gave way to a more Tuscanized version represented in the great fourteenth-century writers, and the Galician variety used by medieval Spanish lyric poets was ousted by more politically prestigious Castilian. A parallel can be drawn with modern Rumanian, which opted more towards Romance models than towards Slavonic, in the process of standardization.

Some of the syntactic changes that differentiated the Romance languages in more modern periods will be discussed in the next section. Here we should emphasize that it is not always only standard varieties that participate in these changes, but also sometimes non-standard varieties. It is difficult in these cases to unravel the influences at work, but one must assume that nonstandard varieties tend in the modern era to be drawn into the orbit of their 'umbrella' or 'roof' language (see 5.5). This is particularly so in the last century, with the advent of universal education, which is almost exclusively conducted in the state standard language. Also to be taken into account is the koineization of regionally grouped dialects, in tune with assertion of separate identity: this is most evident in northern Italy and, to a lesser extent, in southern France. For more discussion of bilingualism in Romance-speaking countries see chapter 8.

Many of the syntactic structures differentiating the modern Romance languages date back only to the early modern period, when a choice seems to have been made between earlier variants, with each language opting, presumably, for the most common, or the most prestigious, in local usage. In the next sections I shall concentrate on some aspects that have received particular attention from linguists because of their theoretical interest. These concern past participle agreement, clitics and determiners.

(a)   The compound perfect and past participle agreement

In the Introduction we considered auxiliary selection in the compound perfect, and in chapter 3 the genesis of this form. Here we shall consider in more detail the question of agreement of the past participle with the argument of the verb in such forms. Everywhere when a *BE*-verb is used, as in the passive and with unaccusative or pronominal verbs, the past participle can show gender and number agreement with the subject, just like any predicative adjective with a copula:

(60)   Ital. *Maria è amatalandata*; French *Marie est aiméelallée*; Span. *Maria es querida* (but *ha ido*) 'Mary is loved / has gone'.

Even though the standards decree that such agreement is obligatory, it is to be noted that spoken varieties not infrequently ignore the ruling, especially when the participle precedes the subject, or when they are at some distance one from the other. Non-agreement is attested in medieval texts, especially with coordinated subjects:

(61)   ... *où les hystoires et li fait de touz les rois sont escrit* ' ... where the histories and the doings of all the kings are written'.

(*Grandes Chroniques de France*, *c.* 1270)

In some North Italian dialects agreement occurs only when a subject clitic is used:

(62)   Cremona *La roba e rivat* / *La roba l'e rivada* 'The stuff has arrived'.

In those languages in which a *BE* auxiliary can still be selected for the compound perfect there can also be agreement of the participle with the object when a *HAVE* auxiliary is selected. In those Catalan varieties that do not retain the auxiliary selection feature, there is still limited and optional past participial agreement.

In all the languages for which we have medieval evidence, past participle agreement with the object of the verb is attested, although somewhat irregularly. This possibility ceased at about the same period (between the fifteenth and seventeenth centuries) as the possibility of selection of the *BE* auxiliary in Spanish and Portuguese. We must assume that these two features are related and that the process of standardization led to the fixing of usage which had previously been variable.

In Spanish it is tempting to see the features as bound up with the specialization of *haber* as an auxiliary, and the comparatively tight cohesion between the finite and the participial forms in the Spanish compound past.

In standard Catalan, where there is similar cohesion, the retention of optional agreement may be connected with the concern of nineteenth-century language arbiters to differentiate their language from Castilian, and to embrace as many dialectal varieties as possible. In modern Portuguese, where *ter* has virtually replaced *haver* in its auxiliary function, the compound tense is little used and not strictly comparable with that of the other Romance languages (see 3.3). There is comparatively little cohesion between the auxiliary and the participle, however. The pronoun object can be intercalated, even though there is no agreement:

(63)   *Tenho-as escrito* 'I have written them'.

As already pointed out (page 20), a link has been made between retention of the adverbial clitic (< INDE 'thence') and of the possibility of auxiliary selection. These can be seen as conservative features (see below).

In the medieval languages past participial agreement is understood as a remnant of an original construction in which the *HAVE* functioned as a full lexical verb and the participle as a passive (adjectival) form qualifying the object noun phrase (see 3.3):

(64)   HABEO LITTERAS SCRIPTAS 'I have letters written'.

In some more conservative Romance varieties today such agreement is still possible with a postposed object:

(65)   Occ. (Western Languedoc) *Ai venduda / o la vaca* 'I have sold the cow'; Balearic Cat. *He vista la mare* 'I have seen the sea'.

          Agreement is normal (though not always found in colloquial use) in Spanish and Catalan with the verb *tener* 'to have', which is distinguished from the auxiliary *haber*:

(66)   *Tengo escritas las cartas; Tinc escrites les cartes*.

In the medieval Romance languages the object noun phrase was frequently, but not invariably, intercalated between the finite form and the auxiliary. Agreement usually was marked, though not always. Attempts to formulate watertight rules on the basis of medieval attestations have not succeeded: one must assume that there was variation in usage, and that non-agreement tended to signify grammaticalization of the *auxiliary + participle* sequence, or, possibly, as in some modern uses, emphasis on the action rather than on the goal of the action.

In modern standard Italian agreement is obligatory only with a third-person pronoun object, which must be proclitic to the auxiliary, but it can be found in other contexts:

(67)   *Le ho scritte / Ho scritto le lettere* (infrequently and very formally *scritte*) / *Le lettere che ho scritto* (rarely *scritte*).

In dialectal usage agreement is not infrequent with a following object, but most often a pronoun copy is inserted before the verb:

(68)   *Hai vendute le uova / Le hai vendute le uova* 'You have sold the eggs'.

In Italian child language, we note, the participle tends to be acquired early with past reference and often agrees with its object:

(69)   *Messa la palla* 'put the ball', i.e. 'He/I put the ball' or 'the ball was put'.

Agreement is also possible, in the standard, with the adverbial pronoun *ne*, but rarely found with first- and second-person pronoun objects:

(70)   *Ne ho scritte due* 'I have written two of them (letters)' / *Mi ha veduto* 'He has seen me (female)'.

Standard Italian also has agreement of the participle, in an absolute construction, with a postposed object noun phrase:

(71)   *Conosciuta Maria . . .* 'Mary known . . .'

In modern standard French the schoolbook rule states that the participle agrees with any preposed object – not only the clitic but with a fronted lexical noun phrase:

(72)   *Je les ai écrites; Les lettres que j'ai écrites; Il m'a vue.*

However, grammarians are uncertain about agreement with the adverbial pronoun *en*, and usually advise against:

(73)   *J'en ai écrit(es) deux.*

The rules were first formulated in the sixteenth century, and refined in the seventeenth, after heated discussion. The principle followed was, on the whole, that only a preposed direct (accusative) object could trigger agreement. Much depends on the analysis of such pairs as:

(74)   *les belles années qu'il a vécues / les soixante-quinze années qu'il a vécu* 'the happy years' / 'the seventy-five years he lived'

where the latter, as distinct from the former, is seen to involve a temporal expression rather than an argument of the verb. In pairs like:

(75)   *Elle s'est servi(e) de la soupe*

the form with agreement would be an inherent pronominal verb (*se servir de* 'to use') which, controversially, can be said to have an obligatory direct object *se* (absorbing accusative case), whereas, without agreement, the *se* is interpreted as an indirect (dative) object ('She served soup to herself'). Even more contentious is the status of agreement in verb sequences. To trigger agreement the noun phrase has to be the object argument of the participle, rather than of another verb in the sequence. Thus:

(76)   *la fable qu'il a eu(e) à réciter*

with agreement, is interpreted as derived from *Il a eu la fable à réciter* 'He had the fable to recite', and without, from *Il a eu à réciter la fable* 'He had to recite the fable'.

> For most verbs modern spoken French has no overt mark of participial agreement, and violation of the schoolbook rule is so frequent that even the education authorities 'tolerate' non-use of agreement.

In standard Catalan agreement is found optionally with the clitic pronoun, including the 'adverbial' *ne/en*:

(77)   *Jo n'he menjada una* 'I have eaten one of them'.

Number agreement is less frequent than gender agreement, with other clitics.

In some Rhaeto-Romance varieties (mainly those of the Engadine), in some Gascon Occitan varieties and in the Bastia dialect of Corsica agreement can also be triggered by a dative clitic object:

(78)   Lower Engadine *Je tilla n'ha dit(ta) co chi sta* 'I told her how things are'.

The version with agreement is interpreted as calling more attention to the addressee.

If we view the present-day Romance usage from a historical standpoint, we can easily account for differences in terms of relative inertia and resistance to simplification: the more conservative varieties retain some relics of the adjectival status of the participle modifying the noun phrase which was the object of the *HAVE* verb. Even in the medieval languages agreement with a preceding noun phrase was more frequent than with a following one: in general, agreement is more regular from left to right than vice versa. What is interesting is that agreement with a preceding clitic is more persistent than with a full noun phrase. It is tempting to see this as due to pragmatic considerations, in that the antecedent of the object clitic is not always easily recuperable without additional grammatical information. It may also be connected with a restructuration which turns the clitic into a morphological affix to the verb.

At a synchronic level it is rather more difficult to account for all the vagaries of Romance past participle agreement within a single model. Most often links are made to agreement in the passive and unaccusative constructions: the object can be seen as underlyingly attached to the participle, and raised first to the participle's subject position and then further leftwards, leaving a trace in the preparticipial position, which can trigger off agreement in the participle, similar to subject–verb agreement.

(b)   Clitics

(i)   Adverbial clitics

Some of the modern Romance languages use clitic forms for locative reference. The most usual are derived from Latin IBI 'there' and INDE 'thence', to give:

(79)   Ital. *vi, ne*, French *y, en*, Occ. *i, en/ne*, Cat. *hi, en/ne*, Sard *bi, nde*, R-R (Friuli) *i, ind/-nt.*

Similar forms were found in Old Spanish and Portuguese, but ceased, except in Aragonese, to be used by about the sixteenth century, when stressed locative adverbials were preferred. The [j] of Spanish *hay* 'there is', and perhaps of person 1 forms like *soy* 'I am', is a relic of the IBI clitic. Relics are found in other Romance varieties, but there is no evidence for the clitics in Rumanian (the preposition *înde* 'between, towards' probably derives from IN+DE).

In the Italian of Tuscany these forms began to replace the persons 4 and 5 object pronouns *no* and *vo* from the earliest period. In the standard, *ci* replaced *ne/ni* with person 4 reference by the seventeenth century. It is thought that the *ci* form, which also has locative meaning almost interchangeably with *vi*, is also originally an adverbial, perhaps for ECCE-HIC 'behold here' or HINCE 'hence'. The equivalent in Sard is *nke*, which lends credence to the latter etymology.

From the earliest texts the adverbial clitics could refer not only to location but also to prepositional phrases that were only vaguely directional, typically with AD 'at, to' or DE 'of, from'. The earliest Romance occurrences of both IBI (*iv*) and INDE (*int*) reflexes are attested in the (ninth century?) Strasburg Oaths:

(80)   . . . *in nulla ajudha . . . nun li iv er* ' . . . in no help . . . to him in that respect I shall
         be'; . . . *neuls cui eo returnar int pois* ' . . . no-one whom I can turn back from it'.

The Romance reflexes of INDE increased in importance with their reference to the partitive, which typically was compounded with DE, and gained ground in some languages in the modern period (see below). It has been claimed that with unaccusative verbs in Italian *ne* can function as a subject pronoun:

(81)   *Ne arrivano* 'Some arrived'; cf. *Ne arrivano quattro* 'Four of them arrived'.

Reflexes of IBI and INDE used pronominally in the modern standard languages tend to be confined to reference to inanimates. Nevertheless dative pronouns are frequently replaced by IBI forms, especially in nonstandard varieties, while INDE forms may displace prescribed DE + disjunctive pronoun sequences.

> In some varieties (as in East French dialects) IBI forms can be used as neuter
> accusative pronouns.

(ii) Animate and inanimate pronouns

Language standardizers tend, in relation to pronominal reference, to emphasize the semantic distinction between animates and inanimates. The specialization of adverbial clitics in the latter role is an example of this. In standard French, for instance, a distinction can be made between:

(82)   *J'y pense / Je pense à lui* 'I think of it / of him'; *J'en attends la fin / J'attends sa fin*
         'I await its/his end'.

There are, however, inconsistencies in usage.

Another notable example of the animate/inanimate distinction is that of Spanish *leísmo*, which can be linked to the 'prepositional accusative' (see 3.3). Here an originally dative pronoun *le* is used for the accusative in reference to a human referent, while the originally accusative forms *lo*, *la* are reserved for nonhuman referents. American Spanish varieties (with the exception of those of the Ecuador highlands and of Paraguay) rarely make use of this distinction, nor is it found much in southern Spain, but it is widespread in the north of Spain. There is evidence, too, of use of Portuguese *lhe* in the same way, in Brazil as well as in Europe. In some

parts of northern Spain the dative form is extended to refer to all animates, and sometimes to inanimate count nouns. In the Madrid area there
is (nonstandard) extension also of the specifically feminine accusative
form *la* to use as a dative in reference to human females. This tendency
suggests that gender differences override case distinctions in this variety.

Similar uses are attested in medieval texts, though because of the frequent reduction of all the singular third-person pronouns to *l* it is not easy
accurately to judge how common it was. In the modern Spanish standard
language, on the other hand, the forms *lo*, *la* and *le* are clearly differentiated. Some early grammarians have attempted to prescribe modern use by
reference to etymology and to traditional case distinctions, and have therefore condemned *leísmo*. However, in the modern standard, it is accepted as
a feature of prestigious, polite usage (even though the Spanish Academy is
still wary of use of the etymological dative plural *les* as an accusative).

There are traces in the other Romance languages of a tendency to
equate pronominal dative case with animate reference. This has been
explained in terms of relative involvement in the activity denoted by the
verb: an animate participant of an action is more likely to play the role of
recipient than of patient, and so typically the dative form will more often
refer to an animate than will the accusative.

(iii)   Clitic climbing

Reduction, over time, in the frequency and range of past participle agreement in the compound tenses seems to have involved an increase in cohesion between the relevant verb forms. The opposite trend may be discerned
in another type of two-verb construction, where the second verb is an
infinitive.

We saw, in 4.3, that there has been, in all languages except Rumanian, an
increase over time in the use of infinitival complementation. In resultant
finite verb + *infinitive* sequences, where the two verbs share the same subject, a clitic pronoun object of the infinitive often attaches clitically to the
(higher) finite verb: this process is called **clitic climbing** or **promotion**. It is
assumed that this is an effect of the close cohesion (**clause union** or 'matiness') between the two verbs, which are treated syntactically as a single
unit.

Clitic climbing is found from the earliest period in the history of
Romance, and it is, in most languages, still a more colloquial construction

for some sequences. With causatives ('factitives') and perception verbs (where the clitic can refer simultaneously to the object of the finite verb and the subject of the infinitive) climbing is the rule nearly everywhere:

(83)   Ital. *L'ho fatto fare / Gliel'ho fatto fare / Lo vedo venire*; French *Je l'ai fait faire / Je le lui ai fait faire / Je le vois venir*; Span. *Lo hice hacer / Se lo hice hacer / Lo veo venir*; Ptg. *Fi-lo fazer / Fi-llo hacer / Vejo-o vir* 'I had it done' / 'I had him do it' / 'I see him come'.

Although Rumanian does not use an infinitive in these constructions, the clitic still attaches to the higher verb:

(84)   *Am facut-o / Am văzut-o să vină* 'I made/saw her come'.

          In the modern languages, the clitic can attach to the infinitive when its subject is different from that of the higher verb, so that a semantic distinction is possible:

(85)   Span. *Hizo decirmelo* 'He had them tell me it' / *Me lo hizo decir* 'He made me tell it'.

          Sometimes too a clitic (especially the reflexive) can attach to the infinitive when there is a close semantic connection between the two:

(86)   French *Nous l'avons fait se laver*, Span. *Lo hicimos lavarse* (but Ital. **L'abbiamo fatto lavarsi*) 'We made him wash (himself)'.

          Note that in older French texts a reflexive pronoun would not be used in this context.

With modals, most languages prefer climbing, but permit the attachment of the object clitic to the infinitive:

(87)   Ital. *La posso vedere / Posso vederla*; Span. *La puedo ver / Puedo verla* 'I can see her'.

In modern Portuguese non-climbing is preferred, but in Brazilian the clitic can attach proclitically to the infinitive, rather than enclitically to the finite verb:

(88)   (European) *Pode-me dizer? / Pode dizer-me?* (Brazilian) *Pode me dizer?* 'Can you tell me?'

Rumanian, which permits an infinitive construction with *putea* 'to be able', always shows climbing in this construction:

(89)   *O pot vedea* 'I can see her'.

     Climbing in French was usual until the seventeenth century, when it was ruled out by grammarians, largely on the grounds that it is more logical to attach the pronoun to the verb which governs it. In the modern language the object pronoun is proclitic to the infinitive:

(90)   *Je peux la voir* / older *Je la puis voir*.

         In older French texts only a tonic pronoun could appear before the infinitive:

(91)   *Le roy veult soy acquitter envers toy* 'The king wishes to acquit himself towards you'.

         Encliticization to the infinitive was rare.

Climbing is found with other sequences, with much variation between languages, and even between individuals. The differences have provoked much discussion, within various theoretical frameworks. The evidence points to a hierarchy of preference for climbing among verbs that take the infinitive, with modals and aspect auxiliaries high on the list, followed by conative (e.g. 'try'), motion (e.g. 'come') and raising (e.g. 'seem') verbs.

Given the variation in usage, it is not perhaps surprising that in non-standard varieties we sometimes find clitics doubled up and attached both to the finite verb and to the infinitive:

(92)   Occ. (Gascony) *Qu'o me va portar-o-me* 'He is going to bring it to me'; popular Ital. *Ti posso assicurarti* 'I can assure you'.

This can be seen as an effect of hypercorrection where climbing is older and more popular and non-climbing is more modern and prestigious.

         Note that in Spanish, *leísmo* (see above) is found less frequently with climbing:

(93)   *No puedo ir a ayudarle* / *No lo puedo ir a ayudar* 'I can't go and help him'.

Where there is more than one consecutive infinitive, which one attracts the clitic will be subject to some variation:

(94)   Span. *Te lo quiero permitir hacer* / *Quiero permitírtelo hacer* / *Quiero permitirte hacerlo* 'I want to allow you to do it'. Galician *Comenzo-o a aprender a fazer* / *Comenzo a o aprender a fazer* / *Comenzo a aprendêlo a fazer* / *Comenzo a aprender fazélo* 'I am beginning to learn how to do it'.

Again we sometimes find repetition of the clitic on consecutive infinitives:

(95)   Occ. (Gascony) *aqueth pan qu'o vau poder-o anar-o-te portar* 'that bread that I am going to be able to go and bring to you'.

In the early history of Romance, clitic climbing seems to have been regular, not only with causatives and perception verbs, but also with modals, which are normally followed by a bare infinitive. One assumes that there was considerable cohesion between the sequential verbs, so that they filled a single verb slot. The climbing pattern seems sporadically to have spread by analogy to other *finite verb* + *infinitive* sequences, even where the infinitive is introduced by a preposition (or complementizer). However, in the modern period there has been some reaction against climbing, with a tendency, prompted by logical and semantic considerations, to cliticize the object pronoun to the verb to which it most closely relates. This process is most advanced in French, where climbing with modals is no longer permitted in the standard, following the intervention of language arbiters.

(iv)   Clitic arrays (or clusters)

One effect of the abundant use of clitic pronouns in Romance is that it is possible, theoretically at least, to have a whole sequence of clitics before or after the verb. In practice, it is quite rare to have an array of more than two clitics, and virtually unknown to have more than three, though seemingly superfluous clitics may appear, usually to involve participants in the discourse (typically persons 1 and 2 datives of interest or 'ethic datives').

Each modern standard has set rules on how the clitics should be ordered in an array. Most of these rules do not reflect medieval usage, which was more flexible (though it is not always certain from the textual evidence whether or not the pronouns were clitics and which pronouns received special emphasis). On the whole the rules favour orders that, in proclisis, place first-, second-person and then third-person reflexive clitics before other third person clitics, dative clitics before accusative, and adverbial clitics after all others. After the verb sometimes the same ordering is maintained and sometimes a mirror ordering is preferred. In some languages frequently used clitic groupings have special forms, often involving coalescence morphologically. This is especially so for dative–accusative sequences:

(96)   Rum. *i-l* for *îi îl*, Ital. *glielo* etc. for *gli lo*, Span. *se lo* etc. for *le lo*, Ptg. *llo* for *lle lo*, Sard *liu* for *li lu*, Cat. *li'l* for *li lo*. (In these last two cases a sequence with the adverbial clitic, *bilu* and *l'hi*, is often preferred.)

There is also a tendency to avoid the ambiguity that would arise from using clitics for both accusative and dative first- and second-person reference, as most of the languages have no distinctive form for these cases (see

3.3). Even where there is a separate form, as in Rumanian, the accusative tends not to be used in arrays. Not infrequently, too, there is a tendency to omit third-person accusative reference from the clitic array.

Beyond that there are curious differences of convention between the different languages – though it should be noted that nonstandard use does not always conform to the set conventions. Discussion abounds on the ways to account for the differences, which sometimes are described in terms of surface filters that have no underlying validity, of the case marking on the clitics, or the degree of activity or prominence of the participants in the activity denoted by the verb. Among the ordering puzzles most discussed is the French third-person accusative–dative ordering (*le lui, les leur* compared with dative–accusative in *me le* etc.), the French ordering of adverbial clitics (*y en*), Spanish 'spurious' use of an apparent reflexive *se* (in *se lo* etc.) and the anomalous treatment of impersonal *si* in Italian.

In the first case, the modern third-person ordering seems to be a leftover from the medieval regular ordering of accusative third-person pronouns first in the array, when there was encliticization to the first element in the clause:

(97)   *Jel vos di*, modern *Je vous le dis* 'I say it to you'.

This ordering was found before the thirteenth century, not only in French but also in Occitan, Catalan and some Northern and most Central Italian varieties. The change seems to be coeval with the change from enclisis to proclisis: in French the modern ordering is found from the fourteenth century but was not mandatory till the eighteenth, after much dispute among grammarians, first being codified in 1640. In Old French the sequences *le li, le leur* were rare, and the dative form *li* may have been interpreted as *l'y*, with the adverbial clitic playing the role of dative pronominal, as in Cat. *l'hi*, Occ. *loi*. From the fourteenth century the masculine tonic form *lui* began to replace *li*, ousting it completely by the end of the fifteenth century. With longer dative forms prefixation of the [l(ə)] of the masculine accusative, in particular, appears more natural. Modern non-standard usage often omits the accusative clitic, as was normal until the seventeenth century, but language arbiters insist on the overt mention of each argument of the verb.

In written Occitan the new (*mi lo*) order was adopted from the eighteenth century, probably under French influence, but the old order is still found in some varieties, and in the Francoprovençal of the Swiss Valais. Standard Catalan has adopted the Spanish ordering, though some varieties retain the French. Tuscan abandoned its older ordering, usually enclitic (e.g. *lo mi*), by the fifteenth century (modern *me lo*, both proclitic and enclitic), owing, it is thought, to penetration from other dialects, where dative–accusative ordering was the norm. The change of vocalism in *mi > me* etc. may be influenced by the growing use of the adverbial *ne*, which has from the fifteenth century, now nonstandard, functioned as a third-person accusative clitic: *me ne* for *mi ne* was a common sequence from the thirteenth century. With third-person sequences like *lo li* there had been vowel assimilation from the thirteenth century (> *lili*): the form *gliele* (for *lele*) is attested from the fourteenth century, with *glielo* found from the fifteenth century.

As for the French ordering *y en* (which now virtually never occurs except in *il y en a* 'there is some of it/them'), this was imposed by the mid-seventeenth-century grammarians, even though until the sixteenth century *en i* had been usual:

(98)   *XXX en i ad* = *Il y en a trente* 'There are thirty of them'.

Perhaps we can ascribe the change in order to the loss of syllabic status of *y* (*il y a* [ija]). In Italian the equivalent sequence is *ci ne*, and in Sard *bi nde*, but in Catalan the opposite ordering, *n'hi*, is preferred.

The Spanish 'spurious *se*' is usually seen as due to a sixteenth-century re-interpretation of Old Spanish dative–accusative sequences, e.g. *gelo* (with regular early development of [lj] in ILLĪILLU > [eljelo] > [ʒelo], and subsequent regular devoicing to [ʃelo]). The [ʃe] form seems to have been identified with reflexive *se*. In the modern Iberian standard languages the *se* form, whatever its function, heads all clitic arrays: this has been explained in terms of its comparative neutrality in relation to case, animacy and deixis.

In standard Italian so-called 'impersonal *si*' (see below) always appears later in clitic arrays than reflexive *si*:

(99)   *Lo si compra* 'One buys it for oneself' / *Se lo compra* 'He buys it for himself';
cf. Ital. *Non mi si asculta* / Span. *No se me escucha* 'One doesn't listen to me'.

When two *si*'s are juxtaposed in the standard the adverbial or person 4 *ci* form is substituted for the first one: this is usually seen as due to a surface constraint on repetition of the same form. It was not found before the sixteenth century and was not ruled obligatory until the nineteenth century. Note the relationship between the 'impersonal' and person 4 (*ci*) semantics and that *ci* is the normal reflexive form in some dialects. In the standard the impersonal *si* is not used when there is already a *ci si* sequence:

(100)   *Uno ci si avvicina* / *Vi ci si avvicina* 'One approaches there'; see R-R (Friulian)
         Si consolasi 'One consoles oneself'

         where in the first sequence *ci* is the adverbial and *si* the inherent reflexive, and in the second, with adverbial *vi*, *ci* is reflexive and *si* impersonal. In the Friulian example the first *si* is interpreted as the 'impersonal'.

The rules for the use of impersonal *si*, which appears not to have developed at the start of the modern period (see below), are complex and subject to variation, especially when agreement phenomena are involved. Note especially variation in past participle and auxiliary agreement:

(101)   *Ci si è comprati due penne* / *Ci si è comprate due penne* / *Ci si sono comprate due penne* 'One bought two pens for oneself'.

A complicating factor is that for some speakers impersonal *si* appears to act functionally as a subject pronoun, and that in modern usage it is often equivalent to *noi* 'we' (see below).

(v)   Impersonal (indeterminate) *se* and *on*

French differs from most Romance languages which make use of an 'impersonal', or rather 'indeterminate human', *SE* construction, preferring the use of *on*. This usage is traditionally associated with Germanic influence.

(102)   Ital. *Si mangiava il cioccolato* = *On mangeait le chocolat*, 'One was eating chocolate'; Rum. *S'a găsit băiatul* = *On a trouvé le garçon* 'One found the boy'; Span. *Se quemó el dulce* = *On a brulé le dessert* 'One burnt the pudding'; Ptg. *Vive-s bem aqui* = *On vit bien ici* 'One lives well here'.

There are some similar *se* uses in formal French style, but they are subject to strict constraints, especially as regards the definiteness of the object noun phrase, and the lexical status of the verb.

(103)   *Il se pense plus de choses qu'il ne s'en dit* 'One thinks more than one says'; *Il se mange beaucoup de spaghetti en Italie* 'A lot of spaghetti is eaten in Italy'.

In French the Romance *SE* passive (see 4.7) has never known quite the popular success that it enjoys in the other languages. The sixteenth-century growth in the use of this construction, usually ascribed to fashionable imitation of Italian and Occitan, was condemned by purists, who preferred, for instance, *On mange la soupe* to *La soupe se mange* 'Soup is eaten'. It was at about the same period that in other languages the impersonal construction developed out of the passive.

The distinction usually made in Italian between the passive and the impersonal constructions concerns verb agreement. 'Agreeing' constructions:

(104)   *Si mangiano i dolci* / *I dolci si mangiano* 'Sweets are eaten'

are labelled as 'passive pronominals', where the 'derived subject' ('logical object') triggers agreement. 'Non-agreeing' constructions (sometimes condemned as nonstandard):

(105)   *Si mangia i dolci* 'One eats sweets'

are viewed, on the other hand, as active impersonals, with *si* playing the role of an indeterminate agent, acting as an argument of the verb. These latter constructions seem to be acquired earlier by Italian-speaking children.

> A distinction is made by some analysts on the basis of word order, so that where the 'logical object' precedes the verb, in thematic position, it has become a 'derived subject' – as in passive constructions. Where the 'logical object' is in postverbal focus position, the *si* is regarded as the subject (or as co-indexed with an empty subject slot), and the 'agreeing' and the 'non-agreeing' constructions can be seen as stylistic variants. Alternatively, the 'agreeing' construction is regarded as ambiguous between 'passive' (with stylistic inversion) and 'impersonal'.

One question that puzzles grammarians is how both 'agreeing' and 'non-agreeing' constructions can coexist synchronically. What is their relative status? How did they arise diachronically? It is in Spanish and Portuguese that there is most disagreement – even about the raw data. Some purists deny the existence of the non-agreeing constructions, or, at any rate, condemn them either as solecisms or as hyperurbanisms. Others see the agreeing constructions as anomalous ('acceptable' but 'ungrammatical') and the (admittedly less frequent) 'non-agreeing' constructions as basic.

It is tempting to suggest, with some, that in some Romance varieties – Rumanian, for instance – the apparent 'impersonal' is merely a 'slovenly' version of the 'passive', with neglect of verb agreement. Non-agreement is attested from the fourteenth century in Spanish and Portuguese, but apparent examples may result merely from a scribe's omission of the tilde that would conventionally distinguish third person plural from the singular form. It is really only in the sixteenth century that undisputed examples begin to abound.

It can be suggested that the impersonal *SE* construction results from a re-interpretation of an inverted (*SE* VS) construction as non-inverted (SVO). The difference in semantics between an agentless passive and an indefinite agent construction is often so slight that one merges into the other. Whether indeed a new construction arose at the beginning of the modern era, or merely that the semantic range of the old construction widened, is a matter for debate.

In Spanish and Italian, at least, however, the 'impersonal' *SE* acts syntactically in different ways from 'reflexive', 'passive' or 'middle' *SE*. How and when did the differences arise?

In Spanish, the appearance of the object marker *a* before human patients (the 'prepositional accusative'; see 3.3), in *SE* constructions with human-agent transitive verbs, seems to mark a change in interpretation.

(106)   *Se mataron los cristianos*

was ambiguous between a two-participant and a reflexive interpretation: 'The Christians killed themselves / each other', or 'The Christians were killed (by unspecified persons)'.

(107)   *Se mató a los cristianos*

on the other hand, can have only the latter interpretation. The not infrequent 'agreeing form':

(108)   *Se mataron a los cristianos*

is often condemned as illogical and ungrammatical.

> Historically the more or less consistent use of the 'prepositional accusative' dates from the fifteenth century; from the sixteenth century it became part of standard usage (though even today there is regional and social variation).

Spanish pronominal usage with intransitives, sometimes labelled as anomalous or as a Gallicism, is attested from the sixteenth century:

(109)   *Se vive feliz* 'One lives happy'.

It is found principally with verbs that can have a 'cognate object', and with the *BE* verbs, *ser* and *estar* (see below). Although an adjectival complement, as in:

(110)   *Se es bueno* 'One is good', *Se vive tranquilo* 'One lives quietly'

appears in the masculine singular form in the standard, when reference is made to a human female (usually the speaker), the feminine singular is widely acceptable. Plural agreement is less acceptable, though not always rejected.

In contrast, similar forms in standard Italian require a masculine plural agreement, as in:

(111)   *Si è contenti* 'One is content'.

This seems to be connected with the interpretation of *si* as *noi* 'we', an allegedly Tuscan feature that gained widespread popularity in the nineteenth century. The masculine plural agreement is seen as indicative of an impersonal usage, whereas, for female speakers, a feminine plural agreement would imply a first person plural subject.

Unambiguous examples of 'impersonal *si*' are hard to find before the fourteenth century (one difficulty is caused by the non-differentiation in the older graphy between *sì* and *si*). The construction with unaccusative verbs:

(112)   *Si parte* 'One departs'

postdates this period.

In Spanish, Italian and Portuguese 'impersonal *SE*' was a post-medieval development which grew up when the grammars of the standard languages were being codified and when the vernacular was being used to treat of 'serious' topics, which lend themselves more to depersonalized, objective statements, focusing on the activity rather than the agent. The 'morphological' passive, which in Romance has stative or resultative overtones, was overtaken for this function by the more dynamic pronominal construction.

French possibly developed earlier than the other languages a lexical means (*on*) of expressing the notion of 'indeterminate agent', though it is not the only language in which the pronoun is found. However, in Occitan and Catalan, at least, it is less popular than the 'impersonal *SE*' construction.

Nearly all the languages in their earlier stages seem to have had access to a

HOMO, HOMINEM 'man, human being' form, cognate with French *on*, which could be used to designate an unspecified human participant in an event. In most Western standards this fell out of use at the beginning of the modern era. It has been suggested that one of the reasons for the demise of HOMO forms was that they were popular in flavour and associated with first-person semantics, both singular and plural. They tended to be replaced by the more formal, less personal and unambiguously singular, reflexes of UNUS.

When the HOMO forms came to be interpreted as an indeterminate human ('anyone') rather than as an indefinite ('man, a man, someone') is hard to say. The widely accepted suggestion is that from the beginning in French *on* had indeterminate meaning. Usually the evidence of the Strasburg Oaths (*om*, used in parallel with German *man*) is thought conclusive, but in that text *om* is separated from its verb, in a manner that suggests that it is not an unstressed pronoun, but a full lexical noun. The 'indeterminate' meaning of *on* was well established, but not categorical, by the twelfth century; by the fourteenth century it flourished, but even then there was still a possibility of full lexical interpretation.

> One feature of French that favoured the differentiation of the indeterminate pronoun from the full lexical noun was the medieval retention of a two-case system (see 3.3), so that nominative HOMO > *on* (*en, an*) was formally distinct from HOMINEM > *homme* (*omne, ome*) – even though the case distinction between the two forms was not consistently adhered to. The use or non-use of the definite article with the two forms was not a diagnostic feature: even today *l'on* can be used as an elegant variant of *on*, and dialects often have a similar form as their only variant.

Perhaps the question, of when *on* came to denote an indeterminate human, should be approached from a different direction, asking when *on* was grammaticalized as an indeterminate agent clitic. It is noticeable that in many of the earlier examples *on* appears postverbally; at the same period subject pronouns were usually omitted in inverted declarative constructions. The regular spelling-out of *on* would seem to indicate that it was not unequivocally equated with subject pronouns. Later, when the subject pronouns were obligatorily proclitic to the verb in finite declarative clauses, *on* could be ranged among the other subject clitics. We know that French had definitively made this change by the seventeenth century.

> Another pointer to the grammaticalization of *on* may be found in the pronominal forms with which it is co-indexed. Until the sixteenth century the third-

person pronouns *il*, *le* and *lui* could refer back to *on*, but in modern French *soi* is reserved for reference to *on* and a few other 'indefinites', while *se* is the object pronoun used for cross-reference within the clause (*nous* or *vous* sometimes being used over longer stretches of speech). This usage was standardized in the seventeenth century.

It is therefore possible to see modern French *on* as the subject form of *se*, a non-referential clitic, of which the disjunctive equivalent is *soi*. In this perspective, the difference between French and those languages which prefer the impersonal SE construction in a similar function is indissolubly connected with its 'non-pro-drop' character (see 1.2). In French *on* 'absorbs' its *se*, except in true reflexive constructions, and with inherent pronominals; in the other languages SE refers back to an empty *on* slot.

The French 'impersonal' constructions exemplified at (103) above may also be seen in the same light, with *il*, not *on*, as the overt subject. *On* in modern times has taken on first-person semantics, with more 'involvement' in the discourse situation. More formal objective styles have consequently turned to the impersonal construction with *il* to emphasize the indeterminateness of the agent. Colloquial styles, on the other hand, prefer to use the familiar second-person form *tu* for indeterminate reference.

(c)   Determiners

(i)   Partitives

Modern French differs from the other Romance languages by its reluctance to use determinerless noun phrases. The so-called **partitive** articles *du*, *des* etc. replaced, by the seventeenth century, constructions without an article in examples like:

(113)   *Donnez-moi* (*du*) *vin* 'Give me (some) wine'; *J'ai vu* (*des*) *chevaliers* 'I saw (some) knights'.

These determiners are clearly derived from DE + *definite article* sequences (*de le > del > du* originally preconsonantal; *de les > dels > des*). They can be related to the pan-Romance prepositional partitive construction with a quantifier:

(114)   *beaucoup des chevaliers* 'many of the knights'

and to what is sometimes known as the **pseudo-partitive**:

(115) *beaucoup/pas de chevaliers* 'many/no knights'

where the *de* may be regarded as a case marker.

Constructions like these were quite frequent in French by the twelfth century, and partitive articles began to be used in the thirteenth century. A similar chronology seems to be valid for Italian, but here the standard language does not absolutely prescribe use of the partitive article. It is more characteristic of spoken use, and of northern regional varieties, than of formal language.

The definite-article component of the partitive-article forms must have generic, rather than specific, meaning: the generic use of the definite article was not found in the early medieval texts, so it is not surprising that the partitive-use article developed quite late. The *de* component of the partitive article can be analysed as a case marker, with a function similar to the partitive genitive of Latin.

It is usual to describe the French singular partitive article, subject to certain lexical and syntactic constraints, as determining non-count nouns. The plural partitive is usually seen, on the other hand, as the plural of the indefinite article, which is identical with the numeral 'one' (UNUS).

Some languages, like Spanish, Catalan, Portuguese and Rumanian, make use of a plural form of the indefinite article, translatable as a quantifier 'some'. In Portuguese it is little used and conveys the meaning of 'approximately'; in medieval French and Italian similar forms referred mainly to collectives, like 'a pair', and died out at the start of the modern period. Normally, however, the Romance indefinite plural has no overt determiner. There are syntactic restrictions on the use of determinerless noun phrases, which tend not to occur in preverbal (topical) subject position.

Examples of partitive determiners, similar to those of French, are attested for medieval Spanish, and there remain relics in some dialects, but the modern standard language gives preference to determinerless constructions, with indefinite reference.

I have already suggested a possible link between the partitive and the adverbial INDE. In Catalan and Sard, where the adverbial survives, the partitive noun phrase, as in early French and Italian, is marked by (preposition or case marker) *de* without a determiner:

(116) Sard *Bimus abba* / (*De abba*) *nde bimus* 'We drink water' / '(Of water) we drink some', Cat. *Tenia gossos* / *En tenia* (*de gossos*) 'He had dogs' / 'He had some (of dogs)'.

French determinerless noun phrases were virtually banned from the language at the time of standardization. Constructions like:

(117)   *J'ai faim* 'I am hungry' ['I have hunger']

tend to be treated in the modern language as single units, rather than as *verb + noun* sequences. For instance, *faim* in this sentence cannot pronominalize: see

(118)   Spanish *Tengo hambre* / *?La tengo*, Ital. *Ho fame* / *?Ne ho*, but French **Je l'ai,
J'en ai.

Standard Italian is more tolerant than French, with the north tending to prefer the radical French solution, and the south the more conservative Catalan/Sard one.

(ii)   Possessive and demonstrative determiners

Modern French, I repeat, eschews determinerless noun phrases: apart from the definite and indefinite articles developed by all the Romance languages, French, in the early modern period, also introduced possessive and demonstrative determiners that are formally and functionally different from the related pronouns.

We have already seen (3.3) that pronouns and determiners are historically related: Latin did not have overt determiners but sometimes used, for emphasis, pronouns in adnominal position. It has been suggested by modern theorists that the relevant pronouns are determiners (heading a DP) with an empty noun slot, or that they occupy the noun slot in a structure in which there is no determiner slot. For Latin the latter description seems appropriate, but as, over time, adnominal (appositional?) use of the pronouns increased there was reanalysis and the determiner slot came into being. In French this slot nearly always has to be overtly filled; in the other languages, as we have seen, non-topicalized, non-specific nouns can appear with a zero determiner.

A formal distinction arose in Romance between stressed and unstressed pronouns, as a result of differential phonological treatment. In Old French the distinction was particularly salient, because of the radical effects of diphthongization under stress and reduction of atonic syllables. In the case of possessive and demonstrative pronouns, the atonic (weak) forms were often used adnominally; one assumes they carried less emphasis than their tonic counterparts. At the end of the Old French period, when there appears to have been a change in the stress patterning of French, the old phonological distinction became opaque, and there was a redistribution of forms, by which, by and large, the weak forms were specialized as determiners, while the strong (tonic) forms were the basis for the creation of modern pronouns. This distinction was not made so clearly in the other Romance languages.

Possessives

Let us look first at Romance possessives (see 2.2). In most modern languages the Latin forms survive as adjectives requiring the addition of a determiner, while the modern pronominals have identical forms, usually with a definite article and a deleted lexical noun:

(119)   Ital. *il mio (cavallo)* / (more literary) *il (cavallo) mio*, Rum. *calul meu / al meu*,
          Sard *su (caddu) meu*, Span. *il (caballo) mio* (see also 'neuter' *lo mío*), Ptg. *o meu*
          (cavalo), Cat. *el (cavall) meu / el meu (cavall)* 'my horse'.

In most languages the determiner with the adjectival form can be omitted in certain circumstances – for instance, when family relationships are referred to, or when the possessive is used predicatively. In some languages, particularly Italian, the possessive tends to be preposed to the noun, whereas adjectivals most often follow (see 3.4).

In French the old use:

(120)   *le mien cheval*

was condemned as archaic in the seventeenth century. The pronominal form can be used in the modern language only with the definite article, *le mien*, and adjectival use of the erstwhile strong forms is no longer allowed.

In Rhaeto-Romance the strong forms are used as determiners without an article

(121)   Engadine *mieu chavagl*, Surselvan *miu cavagl*.

It is thought they are modern substitutes for earlier weak forms.

Weak forms are found in most of the early Romance languages, used sometimes enclitically (see 2.2) but mainly proclitically to the noun phrase. They have disappeared in most modern languages, but survive as determiners in French and Spanish (also in North Italian dialects):

(122)   *mon cheval, mi caballo*.

The differentiation between forms with and without a determiner in the older languages is not easy to understand. Sometimes weak forms were accompanied by an article, but usually it was the strong form. Use of the demonstrative was not infrequent, as in modern Spanish:

(123)   *este caballo mío* 'this my horse'.

It is possible to see the so-called article forms which accompany the possessive as originally pronominal, used for emphasis. The change in the modern languages is that they have become determiners. In French and Spanish the weak possessives also became determiners, rather than adjectives, and so a functional distinction arose to match the formal distinction that had originally been phonologically motivated.

Another way in which French, here accompanied by Rumanian, standard Italian, Swiss Rhaeto-Romance, Occitan and Catalan, differs from other Romance languages is by developing, at a very early period, a person 6 possessive from the genitive plural of the Latin distal pronoun ILLORUM. Sard uses a similar form derived from IPSORUM. In Rumanian *lor* takes the form of a case flection of the personal pronoun (see *casa lor* '[the] their house' / *caselor sale* 'of his houses'). In the other languages, except Sard and Italian, similar possessives are not accompanied by the article:

(124)   Ital. *la loro casa*, Sard *sa domo issoro* / R-R (Engadine) *lur chesa*, French *leur maison*, Cat. *llur casa* 'their house'.

French alone inflects this possessive form for the plural to agree with the following noun.

> French *leur* and Italian *loro* are used as person 6 dative pronouns; although originally a stressed form, it is cliticized in French. In Italian, where it is characteristic of the modern standard rather than of colloquial speech, it is used disjunctively (see 4.4).

The other Romance languages use the original reflexive SUUS as possessives for both persons 3 and 6. As Romance third-person possessives do not distinguish the gender of the possessor, a *preposition + strong pronoun* sequence is often substituted, or added, where there may be ambiguity:

(125)   Ital. *la di lei casa*, Sard *sa domo de issa*; French *sa maison à elle*, Span. *su casa de ella* 'her house' (cf. Rum. *casa lui, casa ei*, with the inflected pronoun, used frequently for *său căsa* 'his/her house', also *casa lui Jon* 'John's house' etc.).

Demonstratives

We saw (3.3) that Romance definite articles derive from Latin demonstrative pronouns, usually the distal ILLE. Latin has three grades of demonstrative, which match the three persons of the verb. The Latin proximal HIC did not survive in its simple form anywhere. The second-person demonstrative, ISTE, took on the proximal role in most languages, usually reinforced by (AC) ECCE/U 'behold':

(126)   Rum. *ăst*, Span. *este*, Ptg. *êste* / Rum. *acest, cest*, Ital. *questo*, Sard *custu*, Cat.
         aquest, R-R (Surselvan) *quest*, Old French *icest*, Occ. *cest.*

The distal demonstrative was always an extended form of ILLE:

(127)   Rum. *acel, cel*, Ital. *quello*, Sard *cuddu*, R-R (Engadine) *quel*, Span. *aquel*, Ptg.
         aquêle, Cat. *aquel*, Old French *icel.*

A middle-distance demonstrative survives in some languages, though it is not as vigorous as the other two:

(128)   Ital. *codesto* < ECCE TI ISTU; Span. *ese*, Ptg. *êsse* < IPSE; Sard *cussu*, Cat. *aqueix*
         < ECCE IPSE/U.

         In Spanish the demonstrative can be still be used as an adjective, as well as as a
         determiner:

(129)   *el caballo ese* 'the horse over there'.

Modern French differs from the other Romance languages in two important respects:

1   There is no difference between the forms of proximal and distal demonstrative,
         so that the semantic distinction must be conveyed by the addition of a locative
         particle (*ci* 'here' < ECCE HIC / *là* 'there' < ILLAC).

2   There is a formal difference between determiners and pronouns, whereas the
         other languages use the same form for both:

(130)   determiners *ce(t), cette, ces* / pronouns *celui, celle, ceux, celles.*

The determiners are seen to be derived from the old proximal demonstrative, while the old distal demonstrative has specialized as a pronoun. There are, however, some difficulties raised by the masculine singular preconsonantal form *ce* which has neuter pronominal status in some contexts: e.g.

(131)   *ce qui* 'that which':

and which seems to be a continuation of the old neuter pronoun *ço*

(< ECCE HOC). Moreover, synchronically it is possible to analyse the pronoun as a *determiner* + *strong third-person pronoun*: *ce+lui, ce+elle* (*s*), *ce+eux*: making it a full noun phrase (or DP).

What is relevant for our present discussion is that these changes in French took place at the end of the medieval period, when there seems to have been a radical upheaval of the morphological system and when closed sets of determiners, distinct from the related pronouns, were created. The other Romance languages do not as clearly distinguish determiners, adjectives and pronouns.

6.6   CONCLUSION

In trying to answer the question 'When did the Romance languages differentiate?' I have also obliquely addressed the more difficult question: Why?

The examples I have examined in this chapter, and in previous chapters, of differences between the languages have pointed to early differentiation (or rather variation) in phonology and lexicon, but later splits in morphology and especially syntax. Many of the differences that modern theorists pay so much attention to arose in the modern period, and often only in the standard forms of the languages. Nonstandard varieties often preserve remnants of old uses that have been discarded by the prestige languages. The standards themselves have often been codified partly with the aim of differentiating clearly between the languages. It is to morphology and syntax – grammar – and to elaborated written style that the language codifiers paid most attention. Phonological differences, which loom so large in the work of traditional Romance philologists, were comparatively little considered by those who sought to illustrify the vernaculars in an attempt to rival Latin. Thus it may be that the differentiation is as much a result of the different representations that prestigious users had of their languages as of external influences or of internal processes.

In chapter 4, I emphasized the forces for cohesion within the Romance linguistic world. Here I have been considering forces for dispersion. The two forces have always been in conflict, but at different times one would win out over the other. In the next chapter I shall consider the 'How?' question. I shall thus be concerned with the more general problem of how languages change, illustrating my discussion with examples from Romance, whereas in this chapter my concern has been more parochial, starting from differences within Romance and considering when, and why, they came about.

FURTHER READING

For a general introduction to some of these questions, Posner & Green eds. (1980–93), vol. I. On substratum and superstratum, especially Kontzi ed. (1982); on German influence, Rohlfs (1983). On intervocalic stops, Barbarino (1981). On weakening of /s/, Seklaoui (1989). On clitics, Eckert (1986), Wanner (1987). On determiners, David & Kleiber eds. (1986).

7

How did the Romance languages differentiate?

7.1   PROCESSES OF CHANGE

Assuming that the Romance languages were once one language, differentiation may be compared with speciation in evolution. With isolation of one linguistic group from another, one would expect that they would each select and develop different variants in their parent language, or, in addition, that each group would produce its own variant. As, over time, each group favoured internal interaction at the expense of communication with other groups, one would expect the differences between the groups to become accentuated. Thus each group would develop its own distinct language, which could be cherished as an emblem of its identity, and therefore be to some extent fossilized.

This story raises problems for the Romance languages, as, except for Rumanian, they were never isolated from each other, commercially or culturally, and state frontiers have been mobile, even in the modern period. It also raises questions about the dimensions of the linguistic group that breaks away from its fellows. Are we talking of a family, a village, a region, or a country? It was only in the early modern period that the state came to be regarded as a linguistic domain; even today in more geographically inaccessible areas, as in the Alps, southern Italy or central Sardinia, each village retains its own linguistic identity, having to communicate with its neighbours in an alien language. Yet even here there has always been some intercommunication, involving either bilingual exchange or more often the use of a common interlanguage (now usually the official state language). In the Middle Ages it is assumed most Romance speakers were more or less captive territorially and that the Church diocese or the catchment area of a market town would form the domain of a linguistic grouping. This, however, was only partly so, and there were always pedlars, strolling players, mercenaries, itinerant friars who linked one community with another. Even though the everyday language of one region may have been barely intelligible to inhabitants of another, there was probably no consciousness of a gulf between the languages. Western travellers in Rumanian-speaking regions in the fourteenth century described the language as a variety of Italian, and indeed the differences between Rumanian and other Romance languages were probably not perceptibly greater than those between modern 'Italian dialects'.

So our question should cover both real and perceived differentiation. We saw in chapter 5 that the perception of difference came to prominence from the early modern period, when language began to be associated with nationhood. Codification concentrated on written language, and tended to ban variation, so that orthography and syntax were strikingly differentiated during the process of standardization.

'Natural' processes must, however, have been giving rise to real differentiation long before that, as phonological and lexical variants were adopted and generated differentially by communities. We have already seen that in many cases the path followed by a Romance language is familiar from other language families. There is usually no need to make appeal to, for instance, contact phenomena as a necessary or sufficient cause of changes discussed in chapter 6: at best, stratal influences may have done little more than slant the course in one direction.

Yet we should, I think, resist the temptation to write off all change as random, and therefore uninteresting. What is remarkable in Romance is, as we saw in Part I, just how much has *not* changed, how stable the languages have remained over two millennia, so that they can still in some senses be considered as a single linguistic unit. It is a puzzle why a language should fall into stasis, comparative stability, in spite of the potent pressures for change that must be exerted through daily use by diverse individuals and communities, and by the hazards of the acquisition process. Universal grammar, constraints imposed on language in general, may account for the narrow restrictions in possible syntactic change. Phonetic factors, articulatory and acoustic, must place a limit on what phonological changes can succeed. But it is, I claimed in Part I, in Romance morphology and lexicon that we find most stability.

Here is not the place to discuss in detail theories of change: I shall merely refer to Roger Lass's inspiring forthcoming work on *Historical linguistics and language change*. In particular, I pick up the insightful image of language (or at least the 'grammar' without the semantics) as a dynamical system in which apparently swirling movement tends to gravitate towards 'attractors' or 'sinks', and there to settle until a jolt is administered to the system. In language, grammaticalization and lexicalization may represent sinks of this sort. The morpheme or word allows economical transmission of information and is readily acquired: in a social environment that favours smooth transmission of knowledge from one generation to another, language-specific conventions like morphology and lexicon may resist the attrition and distortion that inevitable phonetic variation must occasion.

In Romance, accepted wisdom sees the first millennium as a period of apparently rapid change, followed by comparative stability during the Middle Ages, with again a transition leading to the apparent immobility of the modern standard languages. It is disputed how far the periods of stability are illusive, merely 'artifacts of textual conservatism' (to quote Lass). The medieval texts on which we base our knowledge of language use at the time may be carefully crafted and may conceal, rather than reveal, linguistic reality. The modern standard languages, I repeat, have been subject to conscious manipulation and codification, deploring variation, rigidly dictating standards of correctness, and condemning socially unprestigious usage.

It is often assumed that under the protective superstructure of a stable written language, underground forces were mining away at the foundations of real-life speech, which then would emerge (more or less) triumphant when there was a switch in prestige or of perception. It is also often claimed that the periods of apparent stability depended on the solidity of transmission of tradition, usually among the educated elite, but with the implicit support of a deferential majority. Social upheaval, war, famine, ideological or cultural revolution, and the like could, however, shake up the system and start it swirling around again.

In chapter 8, we shall discuss some of the sociological factors that should be considered in a discussion of the Romance languages. We have already considered in chapter 6 the chronology of differentiation of the languages: in the rest of this chapter we shall look at a few phonological, morphological, syntactic, lexical and semantic differences. Fitting individual developments into a classificatory Procrustean bed is not always profitable, as multiple causation and contradictory tendencies are in play in most cases. However, it may be illuminating to place some Romance events in the context of more general processes of linguistic change. These processes are of course not peculiar to Romance, and examples may seem commonplace to historical linguists. What is of particular interest is how some processes have had a free run in some languages and have been blocked or reversed in others. This raises the question of measures of relative conservatism (or reaction) and innovation within Romance. Taking for granted that language is a dynamic and not a static system, in what senses have some varieties been less open to change than others, and what linguistic, ideological or cultural factors could account for the differences?

7.2   PHONOLOGICAL CHANGES

It seems obvious that the level of language most subject to variation is that of phonetic realization. The Principle of Least Effort can operate most freely in allegro informal speech, where phonetic short-cuts are normal, and where psychological, social and communicational constraints operate least. Much linguistic change is therefore most usually seen as originating in phonetic variation: historical linguistics is concerned with how, over time, the variation takes a definite direction and triggers a change in the phonological system, and how the phonological changes interact with requirements of the meaningful side of language.

Romance phonological changes are readily paralleled from other languages. The significant thing here is the divergent directions the regional varieties have taken, and how far the differences draw the line between one language and another. Some of the features we shall examine involve differential evolution of those we have discussed in other contexts – like lenition and fortition or cluster and diphthong resolution. Within the confines of this survey, the minute details of every change cannot be listed. I have chosen only those that are salient, and which illustrate striking differences between the languages. Most frequently, the most variation and rapid change occurred in the earlier periods, while with standardization variation was reduced in the prestige variety.

(a)   French accentuation and sandhi

We have already mentioned the suggestion that a prime reason for the difference between French and the other languages is its accentuation. In Old French there was allegedly a 'strong' word stress which clearly demarcated each lexical unit and favoured the loss of unaccented syllables, hence the shortening of the word. In modern French, on the other hand, stress falls regularly only on the last syllable of the rhythmic group and words within the group run into each other. The change is assumed to have occurred in the Middle French period, probably between the fourteenth and the sixteenth centuries: some link it to the troubled times, with wars, the plague, economic depression, population decline, internal strife. A host of other related changes can be related to the accentual change, some of which we discuss elsewhere. These include levelling of diphthongs, truncation of word-final consonants and vowels, phonologization of nasal vowels, weakening of the noun case and of verbal person inflections, with consequent recourse to other strategies, the use of syntactic means to secure topicalization (dislocation, clefting, etc.), pronoun cliticization, strengthening of forms of negation and interrogation.

Some of these phenomena are, however, found elsewhere in Romance, where the word accent is kept: sandhi features, such as Spanish *sinalefa*, Italian *rafforzamento sintattico*, French *liaison*, elision and assimilation everywhere are found within the 'cursus', a syntagmatic sequence often identified with a syntactic constituent. It is to be noted, however, that normally, except in Sardinia and southern Italy, sandhi phenomena affect only word-finals.

In French the erosion of word-finals threatened, in the early modern period, pathological homonymy: one consequence has been that final consonants have not infrequently been restored in pronunciation.

(1)   *chef* [ʃɛf] / *clef* [kle]; *finir* [finiʁ] / *porter* [pɔʁte].

Usually the consonant restored is represented in the graphy, though there are non-standard examples of final epenthesis with no etymological justification:

(2)   [isit] for *ici*; [finit] for *finie*.

> Incidentally modern French also seems to show a preference for consonant-final English loanwords.

Reaction against the reduction and elision of the only Latin atonic final vowel to survive into French ([ə]) must have begun earlier, as the feminine singular definite-article form in central French is, irregularly, [la]. In Picardy, where the masculine and feminine forms more regularly fall together as [lə], an originally demonstrative determiner very often replaces the article, perhaps to preserve gender agreement (see 1.3). However, curiously, the masculine possessives *mon, ton, son* replace, in modern French, the feminine forms *ma, ta, sa* in prevocalic position. Until the fourteenth century elided forms (*m', t', s'*) were used. A similar 'disagreement' is found in Spanish, when the definite article is used before a word-initial accented *a-*: here the masculine form *el* is used, instead of a feminine *l(a)* (for the distribution of article forms see below).

(b)   Levelling of diphthongs

If diphthongization can involve feature splitting within a vocalic nucleus, then monophthongization, on the contrary, may result from the simultaneous, rather than the consecutive, realization of features: this is often the process that is more traditionally known as levelling by mutual assimilation. More often one element of the diphthong disappears or, as a glide, becomes part of the onset or coda. For instance, from the putative Proto-Romance diphthong [i̯e] in north-east France, [i] results from loss of the second mora, whereas in the Central French, Italian and Spanish outcome [i̯ɛ] the first mora approximates to become a glide.

In the Central varieties (and hence the standard) the rich array of Old French diphthongs usually levelled by the process of mutual assimilation, allegedly as a consequence of change in the accentuation system. Confusion of the Old French diphthongs [uɛ] (< [uɔ] < tonic free Latin ŏ) and [eu] (< [ou] < [eu] < tonic free Latin ō) is attested by graphy (written *eu*) and assonance in the twelfth century. In modern French the result is /ø/ (with [œ] as an allophone): intermediate stages [uø] and [øu] are usually assumed, and seem to have persisted in some varieties into the seventeenth century. Similarly Old French [ai], as in:

(3)   *fait* 'deed' < FACTU, *mais* 'more, but' < MAGIS

levelled to [ɛ] (via [ɛi]?) by the twelfth century, to be followed in the same direction by the later, but similar, early modern French complex nucleus, as in:

(4)   *plaie* [plɛ] < [plaj] <[plajə] 'wound' < PLAGA.

In the latter case, however, the glide pronunciation was defended by sixteenth-century arbiters, and remnants survive:

(5)   *paie/paye* [pɛ] / [pej] 'he pays' < PAGAT.

Inherited [au] < Latin AU also levelled to [ɔː] very early in French; the same course was followed by the Old French diphthong resulting from vocalization of *l* (see above), though here in the sixteenth century there is evidence of diphthongal pronunciation in some varieties. In the modern standard [ɔː] has shortened and closed to [o].

One feature of French diphthong levelling is worth a closer look. This concerns the modern pronunciation of *oi* as [wa], as in

(6)   *moi* < *mei* 'me' < MĒ; *toit* < *teit* 'roof' < TĔCTU.

Old French [ei] differentiated by backing and rounding of the first mora. Conventional wisdom has it that there was also lowering to and jodization to [ɔj], differentiated in twelfth-century verse texts from [oj], found, for instance, in:

(7)   *noix* [nojts] 'nut' < NŬCE.

Certainly the two soon merged apparently as [oj]. In North-East French there was simplification to [o], but in Central French the second mora lowered and opened to [ɛ], while the first raised and closed to approximant [w].

Thus, as earlier [wɛ] (<ŏ) backed to [wø] in the twelfth century, its place was taken by a very similar complex nucleus, which in its turn seems to have levelled to [ø] in some varieties. In the central area, however, it took two divergent directions: either it simplified to [ɛ] (buttressed by the earlier western lowering and simplification of *ei*, [ei] > [ɛi] > [ɛ], parallel to the *ai* levelling), or the second mora lowered to [a].

This latter process was probably initially conditioned by a following [r], as early as the thirteenth century (graphy *oa*), but generalized to become a feature of Parisian popular speech by the sixteenth century. Italianate court pronunciation favoured the monophthongal variant, but seventeenth-century grammarians strenuously sought to reimpose [wɛ]. In the eighteenth century, owing largely to Voltaire's intervention, the [ɛ] variant, for instance in the imperfect endings, was written *ais/ait*. The [wa] variant was accepted into prestigious use at the Revolution, but continued to be written *oi*. Today there subsist lexicalized variants, including doublets like:

(8)   *Français* 'French' / *François* 'Francis'.

Shift of syllabicity from one mora of a diphthong to the other is not unusual. The history of French *oi* is of interest, not only as an example of social and regional variation and of conscious intervention but also because it invites comparison with the development of some other Old French diphthongs. That of:

(9)   *nuit* 'night' < NŎCTE

for instance, seems to have been:

(10)   [ɔj] (perhaps via [uɔj] breaking) > [uj] > [yj] > [ɥi].

Presumably it was at a late stage that there was western simplification of [oi] to [i] and central absorption of the rounded approximant by the preceding labial:

(11)   *vide* 'empty' < *vuide* < VŎCITU

In North-Eastern dialects simplification to [u] or [y], on the other hand, must have happened at an earlier stage, [uj] or [yj].

It has been suggested that the development of French *ie* (< tonic free Ĕ or < tonic free A, with Bartsch's Law diphthongization under the influence of a preceding palatal) was parallel to that of *ui*. Initially stressed on the first mora, in the North-Eastern dialects it was simplified to [i]. In the centre and west (beginning in the twelfth century) there would have been jodization > [jɛ]. In the west this simplified to [e] and in the centre the jod was absorbed by a preceding palatal:

(12)   *cher* < *chier* 'dear' < CARU.

> There was some tendency in the modern period, especially in versification, to resyllabification, treating the two elements of the diphthong as nuclei in hiatus. This was especially evident in Old French monosyllables:

(13)   *hier* 'yesterday' < HĔRI (see Ital. *ieri*, Span. *ayer*).

> In modern French there are hesitations about the syllabic status of some *ie* sequences, which do not continue Old French diphthongs:

(14)   *lier* 'to bind' [lije] /[lje] < LIGARE.

> Note that there is doubt about the phonemic status in the modern standard of the [i]/[j] distinction which seems to be licensed by very few minimal pairs, like:

(15)   *abbaye* [abei] (older *abbadie*) 'abbey' < ABBATIA / *abeille* [abɛj] (older [abeʎə]) 'bee' < APICULA.

(c)   Prosthetic and paragogic vowels

Word-initial consonants and clusters are usually in Romance strengthened in comparison with their counterparts in medial or final position. It is not unusual, either, to find vocal onsets to geminate word-initials like [rr]. A striking case concerns so-called 'impure' *s* followed by an obstruent, where a prosthetic vowel is attested from second century texts. In the early history of the languages of the Iberian peninsula and of France, as well as in Sard, a vowel regularly was inserted, forming the nucleus of a new syllable with *s* as its coda:

(16)   SCALA 'ladder': Sard (Logudorian) *iskala*, French *échelle* (Old *eschele*), Occ., Cat., Span. *escala*; SPERARE 'to hope': Sard *isperare*, French *espérer*, Occ., Cat., Span., Ptg. *esperar*.

This type of prosthesis, due to the phonotactic constraint that forbids [#sC], remains productive in the Iberian languages, so that loanwords also acquire an initial vowel:

(17)   *esnob* < English *snob*.

In French syllable-final *s* was regularly lost during the course of the Middle Ages, leaving the initial [e] stranded; however, in many words the *s* continued to be pronounced, allegedly through learned influence, and in later loanwords there was no prosthesis:

(18)   *étable* 'cow-shed' < STABULU / *stable* 'stable' (adjective) < STABILE; *estomac* 'stomach' (thirteenth century) / *squelette* 'skeleton' (sixteenth century).

In Rumanian the initial *s* may be pronounced [ʃ] in non-standard speech, and prosthesis is not common; indeed a 'mobile' *s* may itself be prefixed to a word-initial consonant:

(19)   (*s*)*coborî* 'to go down' (Slavonic); (*s*)*tufiş* 'bush' (< TUFA).

In modern standard Italian, prosthesis is limited to postconsonantal contexts:

(20)   *in iscuola* 'in school', *per istrada* 'by road'

and it is not popularly used outside Tuscany and Corsica. However, what may be in question here is apheresis of an earlier vowel parallel to:

(21)   *Spagna* < HISPANIA; *storia* < HISTORIA.

This is particularly common in Italian, Rhaeto-Romance and Rumanian, where the *s* continues an earlier prefix:

(22)   EXCADERE: Rum. *scădeà*, R-R (Surselvan) *scader*, Ital. *scadere* 'to decline'.

On the other hand, the striking predominance in Italian of vocalic word-finals and of open syllables may result from insertion, rather than from retention of Latin atonic finals: certainly in Sard paragogic vowels are frequent after word-final consonants, usually echoing an internal vowel:

(23)   *bator/batoro* 'four' < QUATTUOR (Ital. *quattro*); *tempus/tempusu* 'time'< TEMPUS.

It has been suggested, then, that Italian final vowels (other than *a*) are paragogic, as in:

(24)   *sale* 'salt'< SAL; *cuore* 'heart'< COR.

The question, then, is how it is they so often reproduce the lost Latin vowel rather than a mere default [e] or [ə]. Here Catalan provides a partial parallel. In plurals of nominals in which the final vowel is lost in the singular, earlier epenthetic [ə] has been replaced, since the fifteenth century, by [u] (*o*) in masculine nouns:

(25)   *braç(os)* 'arm(s)' < BRACCHIU; *mes(os)* 'month(s)'< MENSE.

The same epenthesis is found in words of Germanic origin:

(26)   *bosc(os), fresc(os)*

'Incorrect' restitution of apocopated final vowels is also found in North Italian dialects:

(27)   Genoa *kamižu* 'shirt'< CAMICE, *śu(v)enu* 'young' < JUVENE; *füme* 'smoke'<
              FUMU, *kwante* < QUANTU.

Re-introduction of the final vowel is particularly frequent in Lombardy, and indeed in all urban dialects, where presumably hypercorrection plays its part. It may be that, here, as with the French definite article, the difference between masculine and feminine final vowels was reinforced comparatively recently, partly aided by etymological spelling.

In cases like these, differences between the modern languages may very well have been the consequence of a modern discarding of an earlier variant in some languages, which is retained in others.

(d)   Consonantal clusters and epenthesis

We saw, in discussion of palatalization (3.3), that in Romance consonantal sequences tend to be reduced. This is particularly so when there is a syllabic boundary between the consonants. On the whole Romance prefers free syllables, so that a syllable-final consonant is often weakened or lost: this has been illustrated in connection with French nasalization, and French and Spanish opening of syllable-final sibilants. But already in Latin there was a tendency towards regressive assimilation of the syllable-final consonant to the syllable-initial, resulting in a geminate:

(28)   DORSU > DOSSU 'back' (Dalmatian *duas*, Ital. *dosso*, Sard (Logudorian) *dossu*, French, Occ., Cat. *dos*); MENSA > MESA 'table' (Rum. *masă*, Dalmatian *maisa*, Span., Ptg. *mesa*, Old French *moise*).

This tendency has continued most strongly in central and southern Italy.

Syllable-final *r* is the most resistant of the consonants (but even this sporadically falls or > [l], sometimes being restored by learned influence):

(29)   French *arbre*, pronounced in the seventeenth century as [aːbr], now frequently as [aʁb] (see Ital. *albero*, Span. *arbol*).

Syllable-final [l] (presumably with a velar tinge) frequently vocalized to [u] and then usually merged with the preceding vowel:

(30)   ALTERU 'other': Span. *otro*, Ptg. *outro*, French *autre*.

The vocalization of syllable-final *l* is a feature of modern Portuguese varieties. Sometimes, however, the resultant [w] is fronted to [j], usually by dissimilation:

(31)   MULTU 'much' > Ptg. *muito*, Span. *mucho*.

In some Sard varieties syllable-final [r] replaces etymological *l*, whereas in standard Italian and Rumanian *l* usually survives:

(32)   ALTU 'high' > Campidanian *artu*, Rum. *înalt*, Ital. *alto*.

Syllable-initial clusters ending in *l* frequently palatalize (see 3.3), but *obstruent* + *r* clusters usually persist. In Portuguese, *r* is substituted for *l* in those clusters which escape palatalization:

(33)   *branco, fror* 'white', 'flower' / Span. *blanco, flor*.

Given the resistance to retention of consonantal sequences, it is perhaps surprising that syncope (see 3.2) should have operated to create even more unfamiliar sequences, often heterosyllabic. In French, with frequent loss of atonic vowels, this process has been reversed to some extent by epenthesis of so-called *e instable* [ə], which breaks up consonantal sequences (in an operation usually known, inexactly, as the *Loi des Trois Consonnes*, which implies that three-consonant sequences are regularly affected by epenthesis). Whether the [ə] is present in the underlying morpheme structure, or is merely a surface lubricant, is a matter for dispute. In favour of the latter solution, the non-standard insertion of non-etymological [ə] in sequences like:

(34)   *ours blanc* [uʁsəblɑ̃] 'polar bear'

is usually cited. It is to be noted that in modern spoken usage one frequently hears non-etymological [ə] supporting a final consonant:

(35)   *Agnès!* [aɲɛzə].

I have already suggested (see 3.2) that there may have been similar epenthesis in Italian *sdrucciole* (with antepenultimate stress). In morphological forms where syncope has brought consonants into contact there is frequently regressive assimilation in Italian:

(36)   *vorrà* < VOLERE+AT, *verrà* < VENIR+AT.

In the other modern languages there is a tendency to consonantal epenthesis in similar conditions, creating a syllable-initial cluster:

(37)   Span. *saldrá, vendrá,* French *voudra, viendra.*

Spanish seems to have less distaste for consonantal sequences than other languages, but frequently regularizes them in radical ways, showing particular preference for syllable-initial C*r* clusters:

(38)   HOMINE > *hombre* 'man', SEMINARE > *sembrar* 'to sow'.

Indeed epenthesis, or metathesis, of *r* after a syllable-initial obstruent is sporadically found with consonant sequences in all the Romance languages:

(39)   French *trésor,* Cat. *tresor,* Old Span. *tresoro* (modern *tesoro*) 'treasure' <
         THESAURU; French *fromage* / Ital. *formaggio* 'cheese' < FORMATICU; Sard
         (Campidanian) *braba* 'beard' < BARBA; Span. *milagro* 'miracle' < MIRACULU.

In the earlier periods there was no clear-cut geographical differentiation between the ways in which consonant sequences and clusters were handled in Romance. While gemination or vowel epenthesis could be seen as 'conservative', palatalization, *l*-vocalization, nasalization or consonantal epenthesis were viewed as 'innovatory'. Within each area one or other of these tendencies prevailed, though not uniformly over all levels of the language. In Spain and France the prestige languages were on the whole more innovating, whereas in Italy and Rumania it was the more conservative reaction that was usually preferred.

(e)   Uvular *r*

One feature of French that does not fail to strike the most casual observer is the character of the *r*-sound in the standard. In some contexts it is a uvular vibrant, and in others a velar flap or fricative. The other standard Romance languages use an apical [r]: in Spanish the distinction between rolled initial and geminate [r] and intervocalic retroflex flap [ɾ] is salient. Commentaries about the pronunciation of R in Latin leave no doubt but that it was a rolled apical sound. Non-Parisian varieties of French also frequently use such a sound, and it is still generally used by singers, though the uvular version has gained ground rapidly. It is known that before the Revolution the non-apical *r* (*grasseyé* 'greasy') had been, for at least a century, seen as an unprestigious Parisian middle-class feature, but it was accepted by the national language during the Revolutionary period.

As uvular *r* is found in other European languages, it has been suggested that there may be some genetic distribution that would correlate with its use. Other explanations for its spread have emphasized the fashionable prestige of French.

One suggestion, advanced by André Martinet, is that the uvular pronunciation derived from that of the geminate (paralleled by word-initial use) generalized to all positions within the word. A parallel can be drawn with some Occitan and Portuguese varieties, where indeed a distinction is drawn between apical simple *r* and uvular geminate *rr*:

(40)   Ptg. *caro* [karu] 'dear' / *carro* (ns.) [kaχu] 'cart'.

In French we have ample evidence that in popular central usage in the sixteenth century simple *r* had weakened to a flap or dental fricative or even sibilant [z]: the doublet

(41)   *chaise/chaire* 'chair (furniture/symbol of office)' < CATHEDRA

is a remnant of this variation. Much scorn was poured by contemporary commentators on local pronunciation of *Paris* as [pazi], and it was probably then that the Parisian bourgeoisie began to react by using the 'strong' equivalent in intervocalic as well as in initial position. It was only when this same class itself acquired prestige during the Revolutionary period that the uvular pronunciation became smart, and began to oust more conservative rustic variants.

(f)   Devoicing of Spanish sibilants

Modern standard Spanish differs from the other Romance languages in having no voiced fricative phonemes. The voiced fricatives [ß], [ð] and [ɣ] are allophones of the voiced stops, occurring mainly in intervocalic position. In some varieties a voiced affricate [ʤ] is found for [j] < standard [ʎ], as in:

(42)   [ʤußia] *lluvia* 'rain' < PLUVIA

but its phonemic status is uncertain.

Medieval voiced sibilants [z], [ʣ] and [ʒ] were phonemically distinct from their voiceless counterparts in intervocalic position, as shown by the following minimal pairs:

(43)   *espesso* 'thick' < SPISSU / *espeso* 'expense' < EXPENSU; *deçir* 'to go down',
          derived from DESCENSUS / *dezir* 'to say' < DĪCERE; *fixo* 'fixed' < FĪXU / *fijo*
          'son' < FĪLIU.

The voiced reflexes devoiced by the seventeenth century, and [ʃ] took on velar articulation (at first identified with the *h* reflex of Latin F: see 6.3), while [ʦ] became interdental [θ].

It has been suggested that the devoicing of sibilants was due to the influence of Basque, which has no voiced sibilants, and that it was current among the bilingual population of the newly reconquered Castile area from an early period. It would, however, have remained underground, owing to the more conservative usage of prestigious varieties, until the shaping of the innovative standard in the sixteenth century. It has alternatively been claimed that the devoicing of intervocalic sibilants stems from a generalization of regular devoicing in word-final position.

Another possibility is to view the feature [voice] as redundant in the modern Spanish consonant system: in the stop series the contrast is between [tense] and [lax], with the latter having context-determined voiced stop or voiced fricative allophones. In the fricative series, the medieval lax members were used infrequently, and nearly always in intervocalic position. In the radically innovating standard language, the old distinction could be dispensed with. Sometimes forms that showed it were abandoned (as with *espeso* and *deçir* above). Sometimes, other differential marks were developed:

(44)   *fijo* 'fixed' / *hijo* 'son'.

But quite frequently homonyms were kept:

(45)   *hozes* 'sickles'/'gorges' < FALCES/FAUCES; *cojo* 'lame'/'I collect' <
             COXUS/CŎLLIGŌ; *oso* 'bear'/'I dare' < ŪRSU/AUSŌ.

The fronting of [ʦ] to [θ] and the backing of [ʃ] to [χ] is seen also to be connected with a conscious attempt in the standard to differentiate the sibilants, which in medieval Spanish were sometimes confused.

7.3   MORPHOLOGICAL CHANGES

I have maintained (chapters 1 and 3) that one of the diagnostic features for Romanceness is morphological similarity. Within the 'sameness', however, there is room for differences. Here we shall look at irregularities in verb morphology and how they differ between languages.

(a)   Morphological irregularity

Irregular verb forms in Romance, as elsewhere, are a bugbear for the foreign learner, especially as they differ between the languages. Many of the so-called irregularities have arisen from phonological developments in the early periods of development. In some cases they may appear to have little synchronic patterning and even require analysis in terms of suppletion, but in others they conform to a limited range of alternative templates. Some languages appear to tolerate a wider range of templates than others.

    It is usually assumed that morphological irregularities place a burden on the acquisition process, involving separate memorization of the irregular items, rather than the formulation of more general rules. That they are maintained, except in the case of very frequent items, is often attributed to acculturation processes, by which the child learns that some regularized forms are unacceptable in the community. One might expect therefore a non-standard language to tolerate fewer irregularities than a standard, which asserts greater social pressures. Alternatively it is not unlikely that in dying languages (like many Romance non-standards today) irregularities are imperfectly learned by new speakers who have insufficient access to fluent, prescriptive language use, and so analogical levelling is frequent. Neither of these explanations covers all cases, and the degree of irregularity is different in different paradigms within the same language. In the present tenses, for instance, it has been shown, from a sample of standard and non-standard Romance varieties, that Catalan, Occitan (Languedoc) and Italian have the most allomorphic variation, and French, Francoprovençal (Vaud), North Italian (Piedmont), South Italian (Lucania) and Rumanian have least.

Some languages have been more radical in regularizing by analogical remodelling; some retain more accidental irregularities without change; others have incorporated more verb forms into regular templates, or have spread the use of regularized inflections. Here we focus on differentiation and analogical relevelling in the roots of present indicative and subjunctive (which are pan-Romance), and on the simple past, or preterite (which has fallen out of spoken use in a number of languages). Examples will be cited mainly from the standard languages.

(b)   Stem alternation in the present tense

Allomorphy in the Romance present tense stems historically principally from accent shifts within the paradigm, with differential vowel changes, or from different treatment of consonants depending on their position within the word. Virtually all the Romance languages contrast rhizotonic persons 1, 2, 3 and 6 forms with persons 4 and 5, which are stressed on the thematic vowel. In many cases today the quality of the vowels of the accented (e.g. p. 3) and unaccented (e.g. p. 4) stems differ in a fairly predictable way:

(46)   Rum. *tace* [a] / *tăcem* [ə]; Ital. *teme* [ɛ], *temiamo* [e]; French *il lève* [ɛ]/ *nous levons* [ə]; Cat. *passa* [a] / *passem* [ə]; Ptg. *corta* [ɔ] / *cortamos* [u].

Moreover, the stem-stressed forms in some languages still today reflect the effects of earlier diphthongization (see 3.2, 6.4):

(47)   Rum. *doarmă*/ *dormim*; Ital. *possiede*/*possediamo*, *muove*/*moviamo*; French *il acquiert*/*nous acquérons*; *il meurt*/*nous mourons*; Span. *cierra*/*cerramos*, *cuenta*/*contamos*.

In French there was extensive remodelling of paradigm apophony of this type in the early modern period, so that, except in comparatively few verbs, there is uniformity of stem throughout the paradigm: the choice of model for remodelling seems pretty random. In Spanish, on the other hand, though there has been levelling, there has also been some extension of the alternating pattern to verbs which were not originally affected by diphthongization:

(48)   *piensa/pensamos* < PĒNSARE 'to think'; *cuela/colamos* < CŌLARE 'to filter'.

Spanish also has another template for vocalic alternation in -*ir* verbs, which involves the raising action of [j], with analogical spread to other parts of the paradigm:

(49)   *pide/pedimos* (see Ptg. *sigo/seguimos, durmo/dormimos*).

Yet another Spanish template involves a three-way variation, *e/ie/i, o/ue/u*, with the high monophthong appearing in the present subjunctive ending-stressed forms:

(50)   *siente/sentimos/sintamos; duermo/dormimos/durmamos*.

Even more striking are some of the effects of consonant changes on the verb paradigm. In French where consonants were lost in final position we have alternations like:

(51)   *dort* [dɔʁ] / *dormons; veut* [vø] / *voulons; boit* [bwa] / *buvons*.

Palatalization of velars by following front vowels (see 3.3) also makes for alternation, as in:

(52)   Ital. *dico, dica* [k] / *dici* [ʃ], Span. *digo, diga* / *dices* [θ]; Ital. *leggo, legga* [gg] / *leggi* [dʤ].

     Note that in the present subjunctive Latin E does not trigger palatalization:

(53)   Ital. *paghi*, Span. *niegue*

One feature worth special mention is the 'hardening' of [j] to a velar:

(54)   VENĪŌ > Ital., Span. *vengo*, Cat. *vinc* [biŋ] / Old Ital. *venho*, Ptg. *venho* [ɲ]; Ital. *salgo* < SALĪŌ / Old *saglio*, cf. *voglio* < *VOLĒO.

     Here there may be analogical influence from forms with etymological *g* like:

(55)   Ital. *colgo/cogli* [ʎ] (COLLIGERE).

     However, in Catalan, for instance, we have *collo* [ʎ] not *colc*.

In Catalan, Spanish and, to a lesser extent, Italian the patterning with a velar in person 1 of the present indicative and in the present subjunctive paradigm has spread to other verbs where there is no etymological motivation:

(56)   Ital. *sciolgo* (*sciogliere*, older *solvere*), Span. *pongo* (PŌNŌ), *traigo* (older *trayo*)
         (TRAHŌ), Cat. *caic* (CADŌ), *crec* (CREDŌ), *escric* (SCRĪBŌ).

In Spanish some verbs have been incorporated into the pattern, whereas others have left it:

(57)   Old *oyo* / modern *oigo* (AUDIŌ); Old *fiergo* / modern *hiero* (FERIŌ).

The effect of analogical reformations, although increasing the predictability of morphological patterning in each language, often reduces the similarity between languages. Before standardization of the languages, there was more variation in each of the languages and overlap between them, but in the modern period usually only one of the variants is regarded as correct, and different languages tend to opt for different patterns. French on the whole has preferred levelling of the paradigm with little distinction made between persons, whereas Catalan makes greater use of stem alternation within the paradigm; Italian and Portuguese are comparatively conservative (that is, they favour inherited forms), whereas Spanish is comparatively innovative, though not consistently so, in adopting newer templates.

(c)   Irregularity in the preterite forms

The Romance preterite (simple past) forms are another example of the differential action of sound change and analogy in the different languages. Here though, unlike for the present tenses which are in current use in all the languages, there is also the added complication that in some languages the tense forms carry a distinct stylistic aura, which may help them to retain exotic morphology.

The Romance preterite (*passato remoto*, *passé historique*, *passé défini* etc.) is derived from the Latin present perfect, which incorporates the Indo-European aorist. Its descendants have distinctly perfective meaning to some extent only in Portuguese: there is some evidence that this represents a modern reaction, rather than simply a survival of the Latin use. Elsewhere it is replaced in perfective function by the compound perfect (see 3.3). Where it survives it is used mainly as a punctual, or as an inceptive, past tense. It has fallen out of use in north Italy (including Rhaeto-

Romance) and Sardinia, and is not used in spoken Rumanian, Catalan or French, though still used in formal written style. In more colloquial Catalan it was replaced from about the seventeenth century by a periphrastic form composed of the verb 'to go' and the infinitive, which in the medieval period had ambiguous time reference (see 4.6). In the other languages, including the Catalan of Alghero in Sardinia, it has been replaced by the compound perfect, which has extended its use to refer also to past punctual events.

There were many irregularities in the Latin perfect stem, most of which were inherited from Indo-European. The personal inflections, on the other hand, are predictable:

(58)   -Ī, -ISTĪ, -IT, -IMUS, -ISTIS, -ĒRUNT.

In Italian these endings develop fairly regularly, though there is some contraction in the regular stems, and a paragogic [o] is added to the person 6 ending:

(59)   -ĀVIT > [aut] > [o]; -ĀVIMUS > *-ammo*: -ĀVĒRUNT > *-arono*.

In Spanish and Portuguese the putative person 3 [aut] ending is extended to regular verbs in the other conjugations (which are merged in this tense) and in Spanish also to irregular verbs:

(60)   Span. *durmió*, Ptg. *dormiu* 'he slept' < DORMĪVIT, Span. *dijo* / Ptg. *disse* 'he
          said' < DĪXIT.

Italian also has a few verbs with theme vowel [e] which have optional endings that are apparently derived from the perfectum of STARE 'to stand' (STĔTĪ):

(61)   *vendetti* /*vendei* < VENDĪDĪ 'I sold'.

Rumanian and Catalan have extended the [r] of the Latin person 6 to all plural inflections. In Catalan there is extension of the velar element used in the present subjunctive (see above) to many preterite stems:

(62)   *rigui, volgui* (pres. subj. p. 1) / *riguí, vulguí* (pret. p. 1) (*riure* 'to laugh' < RĪDĒRE,
          voler 'to want' < *VOLĒRE, for VELLE).

Latin common 'strong' verb perfect stems tend to survive, enhancing the degree of synchronic irregularity in the modern Romance preterite. In Spanish and French metaphonic raising of the stem vowel by the person 1 ending ī is extended through the paradigm:

(63)   Span. *hice, hizo, tuve, tuvo*; French *fis, fit* (older *fist*), *tins, tint* < FĒCĪ, FĒCIT, TENŬĪ, TENŬIT / Ptg. *fiz, fêz, tive, teve.*

In Spanish high stem vowels [i] and [u] are sometimes seen as almost markers of the preterite:

(64)   *hube* < HABŬI; *estuve* (Latin STĚTĪ), *puse* < POSŬI, *vine* < VĒNĪ, *di* < DĚDĪ 'had', 'was', 'put', 'came', 'gave'.

The greatest degree of irregularity among the reflexes of the Latin strong perfects is found in Italian, where there is stem alternation in the paradigm, between stem-stressed and ending-stressed forms:

(65)   *conobbi, conoscesti* 'I, you knew' (< COGNŌVĪ, -ISTĪ), *scrissi, scrivesti* 'I, you write' (SCRIPSĪ, -ISTĪ), *misi, mettisti* 'I, you put' (MĪSĪ, -ISTĪ), *feci, facesti* 'I, you did' (FĒCĪ, -ISTĪ); *ebbi, avesti* 'I, you had' (HABŬI, -ISTĪ).

Whereas Portuguese alternation can be called conservative, the Italian alternation is an innovation and is sometimes explained as analogical to the alternation induced by regular phonological change in, for instance:

(66)   *tenni, tenesti* (TENŬĪ, -ISTĪ)

where the ending-stressed form of the stem is identical with the present stem. Others claim that the present-stem resemblance is merely accidental, and that it is the stem-stressed preterite forms that have most resisted the levelling which had already affected the Italian imperfect subjunctive:

(67)   *facessi* (FĒCISSEM) / Span. *hiciese*, Ptg. *fizesse.*

Only a few strong preterite forms do not fit into the usual alternating pattern:

(68)   *fui, fosti* 'I was, you were' (FŪĪ, -ISTĪ), *diedi/detti, desti* 'I, you gave' (DEDĪ, -ISTĪ), *stetti, stesti* 'I, you stood' (STETĪ, -ISTĪ).

These happen to be the verbs that do not use the present stem in the imperfect subjunctive:

(69)   *fossi, dessi, stessi.*

Here, even more than in the present, then, the interaction of sound change and analogy has increased the distance between forms in the modern languages.

7.4   SYNTACTIC CHANGES

Syntactic structures are fairly uniform across the Romance languages. It is usually possible to isolate the small differences that exist, and relate them to morphological, or eventually phonological, differences. Here we shall examine some deviations in the syntax of negation, relativization and interrogation that single out French as different from mainstream Romance.

(a)   Negation

In Latin traditional grammar, sentential negation is seen as effected primarily by the 'negative adverb' NON. This survives as a negator in all the Romance languages; where it is used in sentence negation, it normally occurs, as in Latin, in preverbal position. A N(E) prefix also serves to negate other elements, such as (N)UMQUAM '(n)ever', (N)ULLUS 'none/some'. The former of these survives in Spanish and Portuguese (*nunca*) and perhaps in Arumanian (*ningă, ni(n)că*) and the latter, with rather literary flavour, in a number of languages. In Walloon *nuk* is used for 'nobody' (as distinct from [rẽŋ]); the neuter plural form NULLA is used for 'nothing' in Dalmatian, Sard and Friulian Rhaeto-Romance:

(70)   Veglia *Jal non kapua nolla al majo diskurs* 'They didn't understand anything I said'; Sard *Es tantu tontu ki non inde gela nudda* 'He is so stupid he doesn't understand anything about it': Friuli *Nol ves sintut nuje di nuje* 'He had heard nothing at all'.

NIHIL 'nothing' probably survives nowhere. NEMO 'nobody', which was already defective in Latin, has modern reflexes only in Sard (*nemmos*) and Rumanian (*nimeni* < NEMINE). More usually, new morphologically negative pronouns are formed by prefixing a negative element:

(71)   'nobody': Ital. *nessuno* < NE-IPSE-UNU; Rum. dial. (Arumanian) *niţiun*, Span. *ninguno*, Ptg. *nenhum*, Old French *niun*, Occ. *degun* < NEC-UNU; 'nothing': Ital. *niente*, French *néant* (now used only as a lexical noun) < NEC-ENTE or NEC-GENTE; Rum. *nimic* < NE-MICA.

What is striking, though, is the number of Romance negative items that are derived from etymologically positive ones. This is particularly so in French, which has lost most of the inherited negative items. Originally polarity items associated with NON in sentence contexts, they have often taken on negative semanticism when used alone. Today they can still be used with NON, but the effect is of negative concord, rather than of double negation. These items often derive from nominals and include:

(72)   Span., Ptg. *nada* 'nothing' (originally from (RES) NATA, 'thing born', cf. also
         Span. *nadie* 'nobody', earlier *nadi*); French *personne* 'nobody' / *une personne* 'a
         person', *rien* 'nothing' < REM 'thing', *pas, point* 'not' / *un pas, un point* 'a step, a
         point'; Ital. *mica* 'not at all' / *una mica* 'a crumb'; Cat. *gens, cap* 'none' < GENS
         'people', CAPUT 'head'.

Negative adverbs like Italian *mai*, French (*ja*)*mais* 'never' (< MAGIS 'more') developed in the same way, but we shall consider only the development of the nominals.

Acquisition of negative meaning by such items results historically from their very frequent use in postverbal position in the scope of a preverbal negative NON. The process is of course well known from other languages, like Germanic. Nominals originally designating some insignificant item (as in 'not a jot') were frequently used to reinforce the negative in the medieval languages. Among those that survive as negative elements in Romance are:

(73)   GUTTA 'drop', BECCU 'beak', CORNU 'horn'.

Optional use of postverbal reinforcers is known to all the Romance languages and was particularly common in the Middle Ages.

> When the reinforcing element is fronted in modern standard Italian, Spanish and Portuguese it 'absorbs' the NON reflex (see 3.4).

By early modern French the use of such reinforcers had become virtually obligatory, and *ne* < NON was cliticized to the finite verb. Some languages, notably non-standard French, Occitan and some Rhaeto-Romance and Northern Italian varieties, have gone further and lost the NON reflex in preverbal position, leaving the old 'reinforcer' (called in French the *forclusif*, marking the scope of negation) as the only negator:

(74)   R-R (Surselvan) *Capesch buc* (BUCCA) 'I don't understand'; North Ital. dial.
         (Turin) *Lu saj neng* (NEC-ENTE) 'I don't know it'; Occ. (Gévaudan) *Be pa*
         (PASSU) 'He isn't coming'.

Usually this is connected with phonetic weakening and cliticization of NON, which tended to favour obligatory use of the reinforcer, which in its turn led to the neglect of the weakened preverbal negator, which became redundant. There is direct evidence of the loss of the preverbal negative element in southern France and Switzerland from the sixteenth century, and it may be that in colloquial French seventeenth-century use, the *ne* was already regularly dropped in negative sentences, though the standard continues to dictate its use. In northern Italy loss of the preverbal negative may have occurred more recently; in some dialects reliance on the postverbal negator is more complete than in others, and is subject to a variety of constraints (for instance, the subjunctive sometimes requires 'weaker' negation, without a reinforcer, than the indicative).

> A not dissimilar process is found in some modern Portuguese varieties, where negation is marked by *não* at the end of the clause, representing a simplification from the widespread emphatic echoing of preverbal *não*.

It has also been suggested that the shift in placing of the negator to postverbal from preverbal position foreshadows a typological change from OV to VO ordering, and that non-standard French, in particular, has taken this process furthest. In Surselvan Rhaeto-Romance, a V2 language, the influence of German is plausibly suggested.

Current conventional wisdom among generativists is that negation can be represented as a (universal?) non-lexical functional projection, which is ordered hierarchically above the T(ense) projection. The head of this projection would be the negator (NON), but in specifier position there would be an 'operator' (the *forclusif*, e.g. *pas*). When the (finite) verb raises to receive (or to 'check') tense and agreement features, the head negator raises with it (and may cliticize to it), whereas the operator remains in postverbal position. The difference between, say, Italian and French negation could therefore be resolved simply by postulating that in Italian the NON element can negate on its own, and the operator can be non-overt (i.e. absent in the surface representation), whereas in French the *ne* needs the overt presence of an operator (e.g. *pas*) to fulfil its negative function. In some languages (e.g. non-standard French) it is the negative head (*ne*) that is nonovert, so that the whole burden of negation falls on the postverbal operator.

This hypothesis does not adequately account for the similarity in distribution between the *forclusif* elements and adverbials, nor for the intuition that it is these elements that are the true negators in some languages. Note that in the French creoles the *pas* reflexes serve as preverbal negators (see 2.2), whereas in standard French a sole *ne* element seems little more than a decorative expletive, in complement clauses dependent on some verbs or introduced by a conjunction with 'negative semantics' (see 3.4).

It also leaves us with the old-fashioned problems of explaining how the 'head' negator lost overt expression in some languages, and why others prefer (as was normal in Latin) non-overt expression of the operator. Loss of the NON reflexes is not always preceded by phonological weakening and/or cliticization, but it appears to be correlated in many varieties with subject cliticization and with use of the 'adverbial' clitic INDE (see 6.5), which often takes on a form easily confused with the NON reflexes.

The modern timing of the change from preverbal to postverbal negation in the affected languages suggests comparison with the syntactic changes discussed in chapter 6. In the early modern period, while some languages clung to more archaic patterns, others opted for innovating variants. Here there is also a discernible difference between the standards and non-standards. The latter, on the whole, tend to eliminate redundancy, but tolerate variation. Thus in the dialects of north Italy either NON or the *forclusif*, or both, may be permissible, according to context. The conservative standards tend towards economy when this squares with etymology, so the preverbal NON negator is preferred but may be absorbed by a fronted negative element, and the use of 'unnecessary' *forclusifs* is frowned on.

The innovating standard, French, on the other hand, insists on the overt expression of both elements, whenever the verb is present. Comment has often been made about the 'hypercharacterizing' tendency of standard French, with its insistence on clarity and overt expression of semantic elements. In most French usage omission of *ne* is variable, depending much on region, register and socio-economic factors, but especially on degree of education. Small children seem to learn the use of the negative without *ne*, but incorporate it into their usage, as a stylistic variant, at a late stage of acquisition.

> Note too that whereas older French often used a clitic *ne(n)* with a pronoun as a 'no!' answer to a question (*nen-il*, *ne-jo* 'not-he', 'not-I' > *nenni*), the modern language uses only the full stressed form *non* (or even, since the sixteenth century, *non pas*, with simply *pas* as a possibility in modern colloquial usage).

(b)   Relatives

Another example of hypercharacterization in French is the distinction made between subject and object relative pronouns *qui* and *que*, whereas in the other Romance languages (including non-standard French) one form is used for both.

(75)   French *la femme qui est* (ns. *qu'est*) *venue* / *que j'ai vue*; Ital. *la donna che è venu-*
             ta / *che ho visto*; Rum. *doamna care a venit* / *care am văzut*; Span. *la mujer que*
             vino / *que vi* 'the woman who came / whom I saw'.

             There is a case difference in Engadine Rhaeto-Romance between [t͡ʃi] and [t͡ʃa],
             the former identical with the interrogative 'who?' and the latter with the com-
             plementizer. In standard Catalan *qui* may be used as a subject relative after a
             pronoun referring to a person, but in the colloquial language non-case-marked
             que, identical with the complementizer, is current. In Sard, as in many creoles,
             a non-case-marked [ki] form is used as relative pronoun and complementizer.

There was a tendency to merge the Latin relative pronouns QUI, QUAE,
QUOD and the interrogatives QUIS, QUIS, QUID. In the Romance interrogatives a distinction is usually made between human:

(76)   QUI > Ital. *chi*, Sard *kie*, French, Cat. *qui*; QUEM > Rum. *cine*, Span. *quién*,
             Ptg. *quem*

and nonhuman reference:

(77)   QUID > Ital. *che*, Sard ([ɣ])*itte*, French *que*, Rum. *ce*, Span. *qué*, Ptg. (*o*) *que*.

No such distinction is usually maintained for the relatives.

The dative pronoun (< CUĪ) survives in Rumanian as an interrogative
and in Italian as a postprepositional relative form. In modern French it
merges with *qui* in this latter function, with human reference:

(78)   *l'homme à qui j'ai donné le livre* / Ital. *l'uomo a cui ho dato il libro*, Span. *el*
             hombre a quien di el libro.

In Spanish and Portuguese gender- and number-marked reflexes of the genitive singular CUIUS survive as both relative and interrogative pronouns:

(79)   *cuyo, -a, -os, -as; cujo, -a, -o, -as*.

Alternative forms of the relative have been developed from QUĀLIS 'of
what kind?', preceded, in the west, by the definite article which allows
expression of gender and number:

(80)   Rum. *care* / Ital. *il quale*, R-R (Engadine) *il quêl*, French *lequel*, Span. *el cual*,
             Ptg. *o qual.*

Central French relative *qui* is often seen as a mere surface variant of *que*,
which is used as a universal complementizer in other dialects, and
increased its scope in texts between the thirteenth and the sixteenth centuries. *Qui* is sometimes used only as a masculine animate subject pro-

noun, with *que* preferred elsewhere. The triumph of *qui* as a subject relative has been linked with the non-pro-drop character of modern French (though, except for the Engadine, there is no parallel in other non-pro-drop Romance languages). The *que* > *qui* change (sometimes known jocularly as *mas-QUE-rade*) occurs not only when the relative functions as a subject, but also in examples with subject extraction, like:

(81)   *l'homme que j'ai dit qui est venu* / Ital. *l'uomo che ho detto che è venuto* 'the man that I said came'; *Qui as-tu dit qui est sorti de bonne heure?* / Span. *¿Quién dijiste que salió temprano?* 'Who did you say went out early?'

Here the *qui* seems to stand for *qu'il*, which indeed is found in this position in early modern French texts and in the non-standard today; in older texts *que* was usual. As *il* was usually pronounced as [i], it could be that the spelling *qu'il* merely represents a mistranscription. However, there are parallel examples with the feminine pronoun (*qu'elle*), which suggest that it is perceived as a combination of the complementizer *que* and a pronoun. This type of construction was condemned by seventeenth-century grammarians, who preferred infinitival complementation (as in *que j'ai dit être venu* see 3.4). In modern written style a different construction is advocated:

(82)   *l'homme dont j'ai dit qu'il est venu* 'the man of whom I said that he came'.

A similar curious use of French *qui* is found with the so-called 'attributive relative' as in:

(83)   *Je vois les enfants qui sortent de l'école* / Rum. *Îi văd pe copii că ies dîn sçoală*; Ital. *Vedo i ragazzi che escono dalla scuola*; Span. *Veo a los niños que salen de la escuela*; Ptg. *Vejo os meninos que saem da escola* 'I see the children come out of school'.

Here the *qui* acts more like a complementizer than a relative:

(84)   *Je vois que les enfants sortent de l'école* 'I see that the children come out of school'.

Medieval texts in the languages other than French also show sporadically nominative case-differentiated relative pronouns, but it may be that the written usage was influenced by Latin. In the late medieval period in French there were signs of the spread of the use of relative *que* to subject function, but this was blocked at the time of standardization.

(c)   Interrogative markers

One consequence of the specialization of French relative *qui* as a subject is that interrogative *que?*, used for inanimates, cannot comfortably in the modern language be used as a subject.

(85)   **Que vous ennuie?* 'What is worrying you?'

has to be rendered:

(86)   *Qu'est-ce qui vous ennuie?* 'What is it that is worrying you?'

where the inanimate interrogative *que* has to be bolstered by case-marked relative *qui*. Even with *que?* as an object the periphrastic form is more normal in colloquial style:

(87)   *Que faites-vous? / Qu'est-ce que vous faites?* 'What are you doing?'

This can again be regarded as an example of hypercharacterization.

Modern *est-ce que?* can be analysed as an interrogative marker [ɛsk], rather than an inversion of *c'est que*, which normally is used with senses like 'That's the reason that . . . ' or 'It's the situation that . . . '

> In non-standard French *qu'est-ce que*, *qui est-ce que* can also be used as relatives.

The development of the interrogative marker [ɛsk] in French can be seen as an example of exaptation, by which use is made of an old form for new functions. It dates from the sixteenth century, when, as we saw (6.4), the Old French use of inversion of lexical subject and verb in polar interrogatives had fallen into disuse. In WH- (QU-) questions such 'stylistic inversion' can still be used (except with *pourquoi?* 'why?'), but is less usual than, and sometimes carries different implications from, so-called 'complex inversion', in which the lexical subject appears to be copied by a pronoun:

(88)   *Quand votre fils est-il mort? / Quand est mort votre fils?* 'When did your son die?'
        (in which the latter would be insensitive, seeming to take the death for granted).

Use of interrogative inversion of lexical subjects in polar questions was infrequent in Old French, while inversion of pronouns was usual. In such cases, unlike declarative sentences with inversion (triggered, for instance, by the V2 requirement), overt expression of the pronoun was frequent in questions. There are a few cases in the earlier period of dislocation of a lexical subject in a polar question, with a pronoun copy in postverbal position, but it is not till the fourteenth century that such 'complex inversion' became dominant. In modern spoken French, as in most other Romance languages, polar questions differ from declarative sentences mainly by their intonation, but the standard language still dictates inversion of the subject pronoun, and, when a lexical subject is present, complex inversion. Non-inverted questions were rare in Old French texts (and difficult to distinguish from emphatic statements), but they increased in frequency from about the fourteenth century.

> When the subject pronoun is *je* inversion is no longer used with -*er* verbs, and uncommon with others:

(89)   (older) *Porté-je . . . ?* [pɔʁtɛʒ] / *Est-ce que je porte . . . ?* 'Am I carrying . . . ?'

The change from use of simple to complex inversion can be seen as part of the trend to 'direct' (SVO) ordering in the early modern period. By the sixteenth century, an epenthetic -*t*- was inserted before inverted third person pronouns in interrogative and similar constructions: in popular usage the [ti] element (-*t-il*) became an interrogative marker. This remained in common use in popular French until recently, and is still used in Canada (especially in *c'est-i. . . ?* 'is it . . . ?', for *est-ce . . . ?*). In Canada the modern pronunciation is [ty], possibly from confusion with personal pronoun *tu*. In more formal French the [ɛsk] interrogative marker with no inversion is much used, though it is regarded as emphatic and rather clumsy in written style.

The Latin interrogative markers NE, NONNE, NUM left no trace in Romance. The WH- forms survive better, usually with no distinction between interrogative and other forms; besides QUI and QUID (see above), QUANDO 'when', and UBI? or UNDE? 'where?', 'whence?' have reflexes in most languages:

(90)   Rum. *cînd*, (Old) *iu, unde*; Ital. *quando*, (*d*)*ove*, (Old) *onde*; Sard *kando*, (Logudorian) *ube*, (Campidanian) *undi*; French *quand, où*, (Old) *ont*; Span. *cuando*, (Old) *o*, (*d*)*onde*, Ptg. *quando*, (Old) *u*, (*d*)*onde*. (Swiss R-R *cura?* 'where?' is a derivative of HORA 'hour'.)

CUR?, QUARE? 'why?' are replaced in most languages by new derivatives:

(91)   Rum. *pentru ce*, Ital. *perché*, Sard (Logudorian) *proittu*, French *pourquoi*, Span. *porque*, Ptg. *porquê* 'for what?'

QUOMODO? 'how?' survives everywhere in some form (in Sard and French with the adverbial suffix MENTE (see 2.3)). QUANTUS? 'how much?' is general, except in modern French, which has created a new compound *combien?*, from BENE 'well', used as a quantifier (see *bien des choses* 'many things').

> Some non-standard languages have also developed new interrogative markers
> for polar questions: in Sard, for instance, sentence-initial [a], and in the
> Occitan of Gascony [e] (in this latter set of dialects declarative clauses are also
> usually introduced by a particle [ke]). In many North Italian and Rhaeto-
> Romance varieties interrogative markers have developed from enclitic pronoun
> forms (see 1.2). All of the Romance languages frequently use tags (usually
> 'yes?' or 'no?') to emphasize polar questions.

7.5   HYPERCHARACTERIZATION, SIMPLIFICATION AND EXAPTATION

Simplification and elimination of redundancy seem to proceed in the opposite direction from hypercharacterization, which tends to increase redundancy, which in its turn may be reduced (as in the case of the dropping of French *ne* in non-standard usage, which relies on *pas* to convey negation). Alternatively it may favour functional differentiation of the redundant variants. **Exaptation**, or as Roger Lass graphically puts it, 'making things out of junk', is found in the history of every natural language. The term in evolutionary theory was coined to refer to the co-optation, for new purposes, of structures that were developed for other purposes but then became redundant. In this section we shall examine some examples of how these processes have helped differentiate the Romance languages.

(a)   Spanish imperfect subjunctive forms

A remarkable feature of Castilian Spanish is the retention of two separate imperfect subjunctive forms (in *-se* and in *-ra*) for one function. The two forms in the standard language are stylistic variants, though the *-ra* form is preferred in some areas, especially America, and in expressions of politeness (like *quisiera* 'I'd like'). In very formal written Spanish the *-ra* form can also be used with pluperfect indicative meaning (which was normal in Old Spanish, but archaic by the seventeenth century).

The Latin imperfect subjunctive (e.g. CANTAREM) apparently survives only in Sard and Portuguese (see 4.3 for the 'personal infinitive').

Normally the pluperfect subjunctive (e.g. CANTA(VI)SSEM) moves into its slot as a past subjunctive, though in Rumanian it is used as a pluperfect indicative, and a compound form with *a fi* 'to be' is used for the past subjunctive (see page 17). In Rhaeto-Romance varieties the forms are used as 'conditionals', a function that in other western languages is filled by future-in-the-past forms, apparently grammaticalized from *infinitive + habere* forms in the imperfect or imperfect (see 4.6):

(92)   French *chanterait*, Span., Ptg. *cantaría* < CANTARE + HABEBAT; Ital. *canterebbe* < CANTARE + HABUIT.

In Rumanian the origin of the auxiliary in the conditional suggests a form of *VOLERE, as in the future, or a past subjunctive of HABERE:

(93)   *cîntaraş -ai, -ar / aş, ai, ar cîntă.*

However, the Latin pluperfect indicative (*-ra*) forms (CANTA(VE)RAM) appear early to have taken on modal functions, especially in conditional clauses. This latter use survives especially in southern Italy, but it is also found in Old Tuscan and Old Catalan and Occitan texts. In modern standard Catalan some forms of common verbs can still be used instead of the more usual conditional:

(94)   *fora, haguera* for *seria, hauria* 'I would be, have'.

In non-standard Argentinian Spanish, on the contrary, the conditional form can substitute for the *-ra* subjunctive.

In the other Iberian languages *-ra* forms moved further into the territory of the subjunctive. In the Catalan of Valencia they ousted, by the eighteenth century, the *-se* subjunctive forms. Whereas in standard Spanish both forms subsist as equivalents, sociolinguistic surveys show that, in Seville for instance, the *-ra* forms are far more frequently used. In Castile, on the other hand, the *-se* forms are current.

For the pluperfect indicative the CANTAVERAM forms are usually replaced in Romance by the past form of the 'compound past' (see 3.3), with the auxiliary in the 'imperfect' tense. They survive precariously in modern formal written Portuguese, and even more marginally in Spanish (see above). There are examples in old texts, especially in Sard, and the very earliest French texts seem to use cognate forms as a past punctual tense.

(b)   *Ser* and *estar*

The Iberian languages show an interesting instance of hypercharacterization that is unknown to the other Romance languages. This is the development of two separate words for the copula ('*atributivo*') / auxiliary 'to be'. The distinction between *ser* (*ésser* in Catalan) and *estar* forms causes some confusion to speakers of other Romance languages, especially as their use is not identical in the three languages.

In all the medieval Romance languages there was some tendency to confuse the inherited 'to be' (ESSE) forms with those of SEDĒRE 'to sit', in particular in the future and the present subjunctive forms. In Spanish and Portuguese older *seer* completely merged, in the early modern period, with *ser*, and a derivative of SEDERE (*sentar*) provides the modern word for 'to sit', but in Catalan *seure* (< *SEDĚRE?) is clearly distinguished in the modern language from *ésser*.

Although (*es*)*ser* remains the most common BE form, there has been invasion of its traditional territory from medieval times by STARE 'to stand'. In 4.5 we saw that this verb is widely used with the present participle to convey the present progressive ('is doing'); it is also used in a periphrastic immediate future 'to be on the point of':

(95)   Span., Ptg. *estar para cantar*, Cat. *estar per cantar*, Ital. *sta per cantar*.

Participial forms, in particular, of STARE are frequently incorporated suppletively into the ESSE paradigms:

(96)   French *étant* < STANTE, Ital. *stato* < STATU

while as a full lexical verb in its Latin meaning it is often replaced by other expressions.

> In Rumanian *a sta* can mean 'to sit' as well as 'to stand', whereas the usual word for 'to sit' *a sedea* can mean 'to stay', like the STARE forms in other languages.

In the Iberian languages, the two BE forms are differentiated, except in the Catalan past participle:

(97)   *estat* / Span. Ptg. *sido, estado*.

Although their function was not always clearly distinguished before the modern period, in the modern standard languages they are said to differ semantically broadly along the lines of 'permanency' versus 'changeability', reflecting, it is claimed, the etymological distinction between 'sitting' and 'standing'. Individual uses do not always, however, fit smoothly into this pattern, and there is considerable variation lexically, regionally and between speakers. This is particularly so in Catalan.

The morphological passive requires the (*es*)*ser* auxiliary, whereas the use of *estar* with the past participle implies stative, resultative adjectival function. (*Es*)*ser* is used with noun complements and *estar*, with locative adverbial complements (in Portuguese and Catalan, and probably in early Old Spanish, only with animate subjects). With adjectives it is not always easy to predict the choice of copula: sometimes *ser* and *estar* are optional alternatives and sometimes they signal different uses of the adjective.

Castilian seems to have been most consistent in the spread of *estar* to more contexts, at the expense of *ser*. The late and hesitant movement of Catalan in this direction suggests influence from Castilian, though it is also argued, because of parallels in Occitan, that the development was early and independent of the other Iberian languages. Portuguese does not show evidence of influence from Castilian, except in so far as the early development of both languages went hand in hand. Modern Portuguese also uses *ficar* (originally 'to fix'), apparently as a substitute for *estar*; a similar use of *fincar* (modern *hincar*) was found in older Spanish, replaced today by *quedar* 'to stay'.

It is tempting to link the creation of two *BE* verbs with the loss of the use of *ser* as a perfect auxiliary in the Iberian languages during the early modern period, and with the reduced use of the *BE* passive in these languages (see 4.7 for the *SE* passive). Another factor that may have played a part is early loss in the Iberian languages of full lexical meaning of *estar*, whereas in Old Italian and Old French texts the cognate form is used for 'to stand' and 'to stay'. Yet another factor is the extreme irregularity (with suppletion) of the (*es*)*ser* forms, whereas *estar* fits into familiar morphological templates and may therefore have extended its distribution. We have already seen that Catalan and Spanish tend particularly to favour analogical remodelling.

> Note here that in Gascony the *estar* stem has been introduced even into the simple past of the 'to be' verb:

(98)   *estèi/estoui* for *houi* < FUĪ.

(c)   Comparatives

Reduction of redundancy can lead to differentiation between languages that choose to perpetuate different alternative forms. An example can be found in expressions of comparison of inequality in Romance. In Latin a nominal complement (or target) of the comparison could be introduced by the conjunction QUAM, or it could appear in the ablative case. In the latter ('phrasal') construction the nominal can be interpreted as the location from which the comparison starts ('from A, B is -er'). In the former case it looks more as if there has been ellipsis of the verb phrase in a complement clause, with the QUAM acting as a link particle, or pivot, like English *than* ('B is -er than A is –').

In later Latin the genitive case sometimes replaces the ablative in the comparative phrasal complement. All the Romance languages continue to some extent this use, with the preposition DE acting as a case marker. The clausal introducer QUAM survives as a distinct particle in some Romance languages (especially in older texts), but the comparative clausal link is most often effected by what looks a WH- (QU-) complementizer, apparently introducing a subordinate clause. This coincidence of forms suggests that there has been movement, as in relative clauses, of part of the complement clause, rather than ellipsis. In virtually all the languages, at some time during their history, the QU- complementizer was used regularly to introduce a complement clause with an overt finite verb.

> In Romance, analytic constructions for most adjectives replace the Latin synthetic comparative forms (MAGIS used in the Iberian peninsula and Rumania, and PLUS elsewhere).

In most languages both introducers (DE or QU-) are found in old texts, sometimes apparently interchangeably. There is also some limited extension of the QUOMODO particle used in comparison of equality into the realm of comparison of inequality. Though the complementizer normally introduced a complement clause, it was, however, sometimes omitted in older texts, in the presence of an 'expletive' or 'pleonastic' negative element, used perhaps to accentuate the difference between the two comparands ('B is -er than A is not –'). Omission of the complementizer was most frequent with an overt verb in the subjunctive ('B is -er than A may not be –'). In Old Italian we find examples like:

(99)   . . . *più suave dorme non faccia Signore* '. . . he sleeps more sweetly than a
            Nobleman would do'

where *che* would now be required. These can be paralleled by French examples without the subjunctive like:

(100)   *. . . plus frois ne fu.* '. . . colder than it was'.

Such examples may, however, possibly stem from poetic licence, and are absent from the very earliest texts. A parallel may be drawn with the not infrequent medieval omission of the complementizer, when the combination of the negator and the subjunctive unambiguously signals subordination.

It would appear that in the earlier texts in some languages use of the subjunctive and of negation in the complement clause were alternatives: possibly the former implied a more tentative judgement of comparison. In some languages, though, the negator has become almost a marker of clausal comparison. From early Old French negation in the complement clause was regular, except when there was already negation in the principal clause, and the subjunctive was infrequent. In Italian, however, use of the negative and subjunctive became complementary, though some variation persists:

(101)   *Maria è più intelligente che non sia Gianni* 'Mary is more intelligent than John might [not] (be thought) to be'.

In modern standard French the use of the 'expletive negative' *ne* in complement clauses of comparatives is regarded as elegant but optional. In older French a full negative was frequent, and even in the seventeenth century we find examples like:

(102)   *Vous avez plus faim que vous ne pensez pas* 'You are hungrier than you [don't] think'.

          Note that whereas today a pro-adjective is virtually mandatory in standard French:

(103)   *Elle est plus intelligente que Jean ne l'est* 'She is more intelligent than John is [not so]'

          this was not true in older French, where ellipsis, rather than pronominalization of the adjective was regular.

In Spanish texts, too, before the seventeenth century, a negative could be used in a finite complement clause depending on a comparative, though this usage appears to have been less frequent than in French or Italian. A negation marker appears in the modern standard only when the link particle *que* would be followed immediately by complementizer *que*:

(104)   *Más vale que vengas que no que quedes* 'It is better that you come than [not] that you stay'.

In less prestigious speech *no* is also found in phrasal complements:

(105)   *El perro es más feroz que (no) el gato* 'The dog is fiercer than [not] the cat'.

Catalan, on the other hand, optionally uses *no* (*pas*) after a *que* introducing a finite verb:

(106)   *Dona més que (no) promet* 'He gives more than he [doesn't] promise(s)'.

        It appears that the negative is not normally used after a DE introducer. In Rumanian there are, however, examples of polarity items being used in the older language:

(107)   *ma dişteptu di nîs* / modern *mai deştept decît dînsul* 'more intelligent than no-one/anyone'.

        In modern Italian there has also been analogical spread of the negator from *che* to *di quanto* constructions (see below).

In modern French the link particle *que* has spread to most comparative constructions at the expense of *de*, which lost ground in the early modern period, and is now confined to very few types of comparison. In modern Spanish and Catalan, too, the *que* particle is used with a nominal complement, where modern standard Italian prefers *di* (though *che* is usual in Northern varieties, and a sequence of both forms is also attested):

(108)   *plus haut que moi*; *más alto que yo*; *més alt que jo* / Ital. *più alto di me*, Sard (Nuoro) *prur artu 'e mimmi* 'taller than me/I'.

Portuguese in the same context may use *que* but prefers a combination *do que*, with *de* followed by a pronoun and relativizing complementizer:

(109)   *mais alto do que eu.*

    The same sort of sequence introduces a finite clause preferentially in modern Spanish and Portuguese, and more optionally in Catalan:

(110)   *más alto de lo que parece*; *mais alto do que parece*; *més alto del que (/que no) sembla* 'taller than he seems'.

In Italian (though apparently not in Sard) similar sequences of *di* + *pronoun* / *quantifier* + *relativizer* are preferred in modern colloquial speech to introduce a finite complement:

(111)   *più alto di quanto (non) creda / di quel che pensavo* 'taller than he believes / than
          I thought'.

The Italian *di quanto* sequence is etymologically cognate with the standard
Rumanian link particle *decît*:

(112)   *mai înalt decît mine* 'taller than me'.

In phrasal, though not clausal complements, on the other hand, some varieties of colloquial Rumanian prefer the complementizer-like introducer *ca*.

The differences in usage between the languages seem to have developed
Thus what originally looked like a contrast between a phrasal and a
clausal complement of the comparative, the former introduced by DE and
the latter by a QU-complementizer, has been obscured in the modern languages, which have generalized along different lines. The QU-option has
been most widely generalized in French, and the DE option most in Italian.
In the Iberian languages the use of the nominative pronoun, as in (108)
and (109) above, hints at reduced sentential status for the target of the
comparison, as distinct from the phrasal status in French, Italian, Sard
and Rumanian, where a postprepositional pronoun form is used. Yet in
modern Spanish a clausal comparative complement is not usually introduced by the simple complementizer *que*, but rather by DE + *pronoun* + *relativizer que*.

The differences in usage between the languages seem to have developed
only during the modern period: the evidence of medieval texts suggests
retention of the Latin difference between phrasal and clausal complements. Later, however, there has been confusion between the two, resulting
in a degree of redundancy, and differential development, with French,
Spanish and Rumanian reducing the redundancy most radically.

(d)   Pronouns / determiner forms

One simple example of exaptation in Romance is the specialization of
pronominal forms that were originally phonologically determined into different morphological categories. We have already seen (in 3.3) that the determiner systems of Romance were to a large extent developed out of the Latin
pronominal system. It is surprising that so much 'bricolage' (or 'do-it-your-
self') was applied to the Latin distal demonstrative pronoun ILLE set of
forms, while other sets were abandoned. In one and the same language – like
French – ILLE provides the stuff from which new categorial sets were tinkered.

Subject and object pronouns, the definite article and the demonstrative system, not to mention the word for 'yes', all have drawn on the one source.

The formal differences that are today associated with distinct functions can often be traced to phonological contextual variants: thus clitic person 3 subject and free-standing feminine pronoun *elle* and feminine clitic object and definite article *la* originate respectively as clause-initial, with a vowel onset, and proclitic, with initial vowel elision, variants of the same Latin form ILLA. In Italian the masculine singular definite article *il*, with vowel onset, still has a variant *lo*, identical with the object pronoun, used before *s*-clusters that require the support of a vowel to aid syllabification (see 7.2 for prosthetic vowels).

In Spanish the equivalent article form *el*, identical (except for a graphical accent) with the subject pronoun, is differentiated functionally from *lo*, the 'neuter' article, which in its turn is formally identical with the object pronoun. Although it can be claimed that the modern forms perpetuate a Latin case distinction, between ILLE and ILLUM/ILLUD, there is no evidence for direct line of descent, rather than the effects of phonological accident. In French and Italian person 3 subject pronouns *il* and *egli* remain distinct from the article forms and cannot be explained in terms of Latin case. The final [i] which subsists in Italian and must have had metaphonic effect in French can be accounted for only by postulating analogical influence from the interrogative/relative QUĪ.

The familiar story applies here. Whereas in early texts, phonological contextual forms of ILLE were not clearly functionally differentiated, by the early modern period they came to be assigned different roles and sight was lost of their phonological motivation. However, what would have become meaningless 'junk' was recycled in rather different ways by the diverse languages, in the formation of new systems unknown to Latin.

(e)   Past participle and adjective

Another example of exaptation is the way analogically regularized past participles have differentiated from inherited irregular forms semantically and categorially. This is most evident in Spanish, which has (like Portuguese) standardized its regular past participles into two conjugation types *-ado* and *-ido*. The earlier -ŪTU ending, which persists in other languages, has usually been replaced in the modern language by -ĪTU (to such an extent that it has been suggested that the *u* form was never truly Castilian, but an Occitanism, or a Leonese or Aragonese form):

(113)   Span. *tenido*, Ptg. *tido* / Cat. *tingut*, Ital. *tenuto*, French *tenu*, Rum. *tinut* (but Sard *tentu*).

Analogically reformed participles, used for instance in the compound past or the passive, exist alongside older 'strong' forms with only adjectival function:

(114)   Span. *suspenso* 'hanging' / *suspendido* 'hung', *confuso* 'confused' / *confundido* 'confounded', *junto/juntado* 'joined'.

In Portuguese, on the other hand, frequently both 'strong' and 'weak' forms survive as stylistic variants, though the former is less often used with verbal function:

(115)   *diviso/dividido*; *roto/rompido*; *surpreso/surprendido*; *junto/juntado*.

         Past participial doublets are not unknown in other languages, usually with some stylistic or regional variation:

(116)   Ital. *visto/veduto*; *perso/perduto*.

7.6   LEXICAL AND SEMANTIC DIFFERENTIATION

In chapter 2 we suggested that shared lexicon was what identified the Romance languages. This may be true at the level of basic lexicon; yet there is conscious perception of more subtle lexical differences within Romance: there are few Italians or Spaniards who have not sniggered over *burro* ('butter' in Italian, but 'donkey' in Spanish).

         *BŬRRICCU 'mule' (Classical BŬRRĪCU 'pony') rivals in the Iberian languages ASINU 'donkey'. In Latin America it has acquired a host of different meanings, relating to plants, perhaps via the Portuguese use to mean 'saw-bench' (Span. *caballete*). Daco-Rumanian uses for 'donkey' the 'substrate' word *măgar*, though Arumanian preserves *asin*. BŪTYRU, of Greek origin, entered Italian as *burro* probably via borrowing from French (see also *butirroso* 'buttery'). The Rumanian word for 'butter' *unt* (UNCTU 'ointment') is paralleled in standard Italian (as elsewhere) in the meaning 'grease', and in Northern varieties for 'butter'. Whereas Old Catalan used *bure* for 'butter', the modern language has borrowed *mantega* from Spanish (see 6.3).

Whereas phonological differentiation can be ignored or overcome, semantic or lexical differentiation is part of the conscious assertion of identity, of 'otherness', of a linguistic community. An analogy with wine is one most Romance speakers would appreciate. Slight variations in weather, soil, maturation, balance of grape varieties, or wine-making techniques can effect quite dramatic changes to the taste (and aroma) of the wine: yet the connoisseur can still identify its provenance, its personality, and attempt to analyse the impact of the variables on the final product. Study of lexical variation in Romance has something of the same fascination, and necessitates the same sort of meticulous attention to detail and to multiple causation. Lexicological and onomasiological studies are particularly popular among Romance scholars. 'Butterfly collection' it may be, from the point of view of the dedicated theorist, but the sheer wealth and wondrous variety of data cannot fail to hold in thrall those whose interest lies in languages as they are used in the real world.

Here we can only glance briefly at one or two examples of how different Romance languages have differentiated lexically. In each case the differentiation need not always hamper communication, as frequently the usual word in one language may be tagged by another form that differs only slightly in meaning, or prestige. We have already seen how the Romance languages have borrowed from substratum and superstratum languages, from each other and from Latin. In this section we shall consider a few examples of how Romance languages have called in different lexical forms to express similar meanings, and how they have assigned different meanings to formally similar lexical items. The illustrations are chosen by virtue of the complexity of their interaction and their emotive connotations. It will be noted that sometimes the etymology is uncertain and the semantic shifts obscure.

(a)   Verbs

The Romance languages provide rich material for the study of lexical and semantic fields and interaction between different forms referring to activities, events and sensations. The following list illustrates with the kind of examples frequently studied by Romanists.

Verbs: some differences between Romance forms

Killing: Latin INTERFICERE 'to do away with' did not survive into Romance, but
            OCCĪDERE 'to cut down' was current in the medieval languages and survives in
            Italian, Sard and Occitan as the normal word. NECARE is a general word for 'to

kill' in Rumanian dialects south of the Danube, but means 'to drown' in most Romance languages and 'to infest with plague' in some Italian dialects. French *tuer* deserves special mention. Until the seventeenth century, and still in regional varieties, it was used for putting out a fire. Its etymological origin (*TUTARE 'to take care of') suggests Mafia-like connotations. Some believe its modern meaning arose from damping down a fire (so as to stir it up later), others that it generalized from expressions like 'to slake (and thence to get rid of) thirst'. The Iberian *matar* words may derive from MACTARE 'to slay, smite' or from the Persian word that gives us '(check) mate', or perhaps *MATTU 'insane'. Rum. *a omorî* (/ *a ucide*) is of Slavonic origin.

Stopping, staying, closing, leaving: Latin (RE)MANERE,'to stay' is known in most languages, but by the seventeenth century Old French *remaindre* was replaced by the early Latinism *rester* < RESTARE 'to stand behind, stand still, be left' (also Ital. (*ar*)*restare*, French *arrêter* 'to stop'). A Latin derivative *QUIETARE 'to be quiet, to calm' (cf. Ital. *quietare*) gives Spanish *quedar* 'to stay' and French *quitter* 'to leave, take away'. PARARE 'to get ready' in Italian means 'to shield, block, stop, defend', in French 'to ward off' but in Spanish 'to stop'. The Italian normal word for 'to stop' is *fermare* from the Latin word 'to make firm', which becomes the French word for 'to close' (replacing *clore* < CLAUDERE in the seventeenth century). In Spanish the Latinism *firmar* means 'to sign', a development that can be paralleled semantically perhaps by Ptg. *fechar* 'to close', which seems to be related to the Spanish word for 'date', from the closing formula of medieval documents < FACTA ('things done', cf. modern Span. *hecho* 'done'). The normal Spanish word for 'to close' *cerrar* may be derived from SERA 'lock' (in Italian and French its cognates mean 'to squeeze in', with the related noun used for 'dyke' or 'greenhouse' etc.). CLAUDERE 'to close', known in nearly all the medieval languages, survives in Ital. *chiudere*, Rum. *a închide*, but Catalan and Occitan prefer *tancar*, which may relate to a form *STANTI-CARE, which in Occ., Cat., Span. *estancar* and French *étancher* primarily means 'to stem the flow of water' (cf. French *étang* 'pond').

Tricking and duping: DĒCIPERE 'to catch out, deceive' survives into some medieval languages, taking on the meaning 'to disappoint' in modern French. The more usual words, however, seem to come from *INGANNARE, implying 'mockery', formed from GANNIRE 'to yelp, snarl': Ital. *ingannare*, R-R (Engadine) *ingianare*, Occ. *inganar*, Cat. *enganyar*, Span. *engañar*, Ptg. *enganar*. French (and hence Occitan, Catalan) uses, from the fourteenth century a similar metaphor 'to make game of' from 'to play the trumpet' (*tromper*). Rum. *a înşela* may be derived from SELLA 'saddle' (the same form / *a inşaua*, means 'to saddle a horse'), using a different metaphor, though some seek its origin in Bulgarian.

Wanting, seeking, asking for, finding: *VOLERE 'to want' has been lost, and AMARE 'to love' has declined in Spanish and Portuguese, replaced by *querer* < QUAERERE 'to seek, ask for'. Logudorian Sard uses *kerrere* in the same way, borrowed perhaps during the Spanish occupation of Sardinia. QUAERERE supplies the usual Italian word for 'to ask' (*chiedere* apparently with dissimilation of intervocalic [r] to [d]), and the older French words for 'to seek' (*querre*, then *quérir*). 'Ask' is rendered in Spanish, Portuguese and Logudorian Sard by PERCONTARE (*preguntar(e)*, *perguntar*), and 'seek' in Spanish and Portuguese by *buscar*, apparently derived from a Germanic form for 'bush, wood'. The putative link with hunting is reflected also in the more widespread Romance word for 'to seek', or originally 'to search', which is derived from CIRCARE, used for 'to encircle' or 'to go round a place hunting for something'. In Italian it seems very early to have acquired the 'seek, fetch' connotations, but in French it did not definitively replace *quérir* until the early modern period. The modern French form *chercher*, with assimilation of the initial to the medial consonant, compared with the older form reflected by the English borrowing *search*, may owe something to the influence of Italian. Rum. *a căuta* may also be derived from hunting vocabulary (< CAPTARE?, which also supplies words for 'to seek' and 'to find' in varieties of north Italy). Other Romance words for 'to find as a result of seeking' may also linked to hunting metaphors: AFLARE 'to sniff out' seems to be at the root of Span. *hallar*, Portuguese *achar* and Rumanian *a afla*, whereas the rather mysterious French and Italian words *trouver*, *trovare* may originate as a fishing term, with TURBARE referring to stirring up the water (in Sard it means 'to urge on, to drive, beasts of burden'). Others, however, seek the origin in poetic invention via TROPARE, formed on the word for trope. 'To ask insistently, to beg, pray', derives in most modern languages from PRECARE, but ROGARE, which is known in most older languages, survives in Spanish and Portuguese (*rogar*), in Rumanian (*a ruga*) and in Rhaeto-Romance (Engadine *ruvar*).

Working: OPERARE has tended to specialize in the sense of artisanal achievement, whereas LABORARE 'to toil, suffer' (except in Italian) has moved over exclusively to agricultural activity, especially ploughing. (The Argentinian Spanish expression *Qué labura!* 'What a chore!' is borrowed from Italian.) The most widespread verb for 'to work' is derived from an instrument of torture with three spikes, TRIPALIUM: French *travailler*, Span. *trabajar*, etc. (in English the 'travail' is associated with moving around – 'travel'). Rum. *a lucra* < LUCRARE 'to gain, profit' is associated with reward, though the frequent but more restricted Slavonic word *a munci* has 'painful' as well as political connotations. In the same spirit of seeing work as painful we should perhaps note the specialization of French *chômer*, derived from the Greek CAUMA 'heat', originally 'to rest, to keep calm', in the sense of 'to be unemployed' (cf. the loanwords Rum. *şomer*, *şomaj* etc.). In Italian we have the transparent *disoccupato*, *senza lavoro* for 'unemployed', and the Iberian languages use the participial form of *parar* 'to stop'. The idea of withholding labour as a weapon against employers is a modern one, and it is not surprising that words for 'strike' differ: in nineteenth-century French, *grève*, in this sense, derives from the gravelly site on the banks of the Seine where workless labourers gathered in hope of being hired (Rum. *grevă* is borrowed). Catalan *vaga* comes from VACARE 'to be empty' (cf. Span., Ptg. *vagar* 'to be idle'). Span. *huelga*, Ptg. *folga,* derived ultimately from FOLLE 'bellows, windbag', suggest a similar semantic evolution; note that the Andalusian form *juerga* entered the standard in the nineteenth century in the sense of 'binge, spree'. Ital. *sciopero* (< *EXOPERARE 'to stop work') also has emotive overtones (cf. e.g. *scioperone* 'shirker, fool').

(b)   Nouns

There is less interaction between nouns in Romance, especially when they refer to concrete things. Often one Latin word has survived in a number of languages, but sometimes there is a maverick form in others. Here are a few examples from common concrete nouns.

Some everyday Romance nouns

Cheese:	CASEU gives most Romance words, but French *fromage* (borrowed as Ital. *formaggio*, Cat. *formatge*) refers to the shape (FORMA) of the cheese. Rum. *brînză* is of uncertain origin.
Dog:	CANE gives the usual Romance words, but the isolated Spanish *perro*, and Catalan *gos*, which has now obsolete parallels in several other languages, may be onomatopoeic.
House:	From CASA 'hut' nearly everywhere, but the French form *chez* has become syntactically restricted to locative prepositional status ('at the house of'; similar forms are found in north Italy) and is replaced by *maison* < MANSIONE 'stay', hence 'place one stays' (in other Romance varieties 'cattle-shed' etc.). DOMUS 'house, home' survives in the same sense in Sard, but Italian *duomo* has specialized as 'cathedral' (borrowed as French *dôme*).
Meat:	CARNE survives everywhere, but modern French *chair* means 'flesh' (cf. also *faire bonne chère* 'to eat well', which may involve CARA 'face' or CARNE 'meat'). From the early modern period, *viande* is used in French for edible meat, penetrating also to other languages. It derives probably from VIVENDA 'things necessary for life', which is used for a variety of foodstuffs in other Romance varieties (cf. Span. *vianda*, from the French, 'food' / *vivienda* 'house, dwelling'; Ital. *vivanda* 'dish of food').
Paper:	The Egyptian plant name PAPYRU supplies the most widespread Romance words (the Iberian forms are probably borrowed from French *papier*). Rum. *papură* 'bullrush', Span. *pabilo* 'candle-wick' are nearer the original meaning.

Greek CHARTA 'paper' is reflected in Ital. *carta*, but more widespread meanings are 'charter, letter' (French *carte* 'card' is a fourteenth-century Latinism). French *lettre* 'letter, written communication' derives from LITTERA 'letter', whereas the equivalent Rumanian word *scrisoăre* is a derivative of SCRIBERE 'to write'. Rum. *hîrtie* 'paper' is borrowed from a Slavonic word, itself probably borrowed from Greek CHARTA.

On the whole, parts of the body retain in Romance their Latin names (see page 91). However, popular shifts of meaning are frequent, resulting in some notable variation between the languages. The following list gives some examples.

Parts of the body

Belly: VENTER gives popular words everywhere, but PANTICE 'paunch' rivals it in most languages. Span., Ptg. *barriga* (from the fifteenth century) is from the word for 'barrel' (seventeenth-century *barrica* is borrowed from Gascon). Rum. *burtă* (/*pîntece*) is of unknown origin.

Face: ORE (also 'mouth') survives nowhere. FACIE ('form') remains a primary word in Italian and Rumanian (also in older French). VULTU ('appearance') gives Ital. *volto* 'countenance' (also older forms like Old French *vout*). Greek CARA is a widespread form (Span., Cat., Ptg. *cara*, Old French *chiere*, also in north Italy). VISU 'appearance' is also common: Old French *vis* was replaced by derivative *visage*, which in the modern language is rivalled by more popular *figure*. Span., Ptg. *rostro*, Cat. *rostre* is from ROSTRU 'beak' (words normally used for animals are often slangily used for the human face in other Romance languages). Rum. *chip* is from Hungarian.

Hand: MANUS nearly everywhere, but BRANCA 'paw' is also current in Rumanian, Sard and Rhaeto-Romance.

Head: CAPUT and its derivatives remain common, but in French *chef* retains only figurative meanings. TESTA 'egg-shell' became the usual word in French (borrowed as 'head' into numerous other varieties, and in others still meaning 'skull', 'nutshell', etc.).

Jaw: MAXILLA gives Ital. *mascella*, Cat. *maixella* 'jaw', Rum. *măsea* 'molar tooth' and Span. *mejilla* 'cheek'. Late twelfth-century French introduced the derivative *mâchoire* from *mâcher* < MASTICARE 'to chew', which ousted Old French *maisselle*. Ital. *ganascia* 'jaw' derives from the Greek. Ptg. *queixo* 'jaw, chin', Cat. *queix* 'cheek' ultimately derive from CAPSA 'box': Span. *quijada* is today used for an animal jaw, while the eighteenth-century Latinism *mandíbula* refers to humans. Rum. *falcă* 'jaw' is said to be from Latin FALCIS 'sickle' – a meaning shift that is apparently found also in Albanian.

Knee: GENUCULU, diminutive of GENU 'knee', is usual but medieval Span. *hinojo*

	(which had become identical with the reflex of FENUCULU 'fennel') was replaced by *rodilla* 'knee cap', a diminutive of ROTA 'wheel'.
Leg:	Latin CRURE does not survive. Span. *pierna*, Cat., Ptg. *perna* continue Latin PERNA 'ham', whereas elsewhere Greek CAMBA 'joint, leg' is preferred (Cat. *cama*, Occ., Sard *camba*, R-R (Engadine) *chamma*). Ital. *gamba*, French *jambe*, Rum. *gambă* ('shin'), R-R (Surselvan) *tgomba* derive from a variant GAMBA, attested in fourth-century Latin texts.
Shoulder:	HUMERU is widespread but French *épaule* derives from Greek SPATULA 'flat sword', which also gives Span. *espalda* 'back' and Ptg. *espadua* 'shoulder-blade'.

(c)   Adjectives

Common adjectives again usually are fairly uniform over the Romance area, but there are apparently random variations here as elsewhere, especially where emotive factors intervene.

Some adjectives

Colours (two examples):	*Yellow*: CROCEU 'saffron' survives only in Cat. *groc* and Sard *grogu* (cf. Old Ital. *gruogo*). Span. *amarillo*, Ptg. *amarelo* are derivatives of AMARU 'bitter'. GALBINU 'greenish-yellow' gives Rum. *galben*, Old French *jalne* (modern *jaune*), which was borrowed into other languages, notably Ital. *giallo*. *Red*: derivatives of RUBER give Sard *ruyu*, French *rouge*, Cat. *roig* (cf. Span. *rubio* 'blond'), RUFU gives Cat. *ruf* and RUSSU/RUSSEU Ital. *rosso*, Cat. *ros*, French *roux* / Rum. *roşu*, Span. *rojo*, Ptg. *roxo*. Cat. *vermell* etc. are from VER-MICULU 'grub' (which provides vermilion).
Dirty:	From SPURCU we have Rum. *spurcat*; Ital. *sporco* seems to be crossed with PORCU 'pig', which also gives Span. *puerco*, Ptg. *porco*. The other common word for 'dirty', Span. *sucio*, Ptg. *sujo*, Cat. *sutze*, is from *SUCIDU 'juicy' (cf. also Ital. *sucido*, a Latinism, 'grease' / *sudicio* 'dirty'/ *sozzo*, from Occitan, 'filthy' / Old *spurcido* crossed with *sporco*). French *sale* is of Germanic origin; older words were *put* < PUTIDU 'stinking' (cf. modern *putain* 'whore'), and *ord* < HORRIDU (cf. Ital. dial. (Tuscany) *ordo* 'dirty', modern French *ordure* 'garbage'). The usual Catalan word for 'dirty' is *brut* (cf. Ital. *brutto* 'ugly'). Rum. *murdar* is of Slavonic origin.
Mad:	INSANU, DEMENTE do not survive as popular words. FOLLE 'bellows' gives words in Italian, French, Occitan and Catalan, though Cat. *boig* < BALBIU 'stammering' is also current. For Ital. *matto*, cf. Span. *matar* 'to kill', and *pazzo* probably derives from PATIENS, which has in Latin the meaning 'stubborn'. Sard *mákku* seems to come from MACCU, a name for a clown, and Rum. *nebun* is derived from BONU 'good'. Other words are of more uncertain origin: Span. *loco*, Ptg. *louco*, for instance, have variously been derived from ULUCCU 'owl',

Thin: or the personal name GLAUCU.

MACRU is the usual word but more evaluative 'slim' in some languages derives from a word connected with MINUTU: French, Occ. *mince*, Cat. *minso*. Catalan and Occitan also use *prim* < PRIMU. In Rhaeto-Romance SUBTILU (Engadine *stigl*, Surselvan *satel*) is the preferred word. Ital. *snello*, also 'nimble', is from the Germanic word for 'quick' (cf. Old French *isnel*), while more elevated *esile* < EXILE is probably a Latinism.

Ugly: FOEDU survives in Sard *feu*, Span. *feo*, Ptg. *feio*. French *laid*, Cat. *lleig* are Germanic borrowings, Cat. *llord* (like French *lourd* 'heavy') is from LURIDU 'pale yellow, ghastly'. Modern French *vilain* was in the Middle Ages 'a peasant, a villein' from VILLANU 'inhabitant of a villa' (cf. also English *villain*). Ital. *brutto* is from BRUTU 'heavy, dull', and Rum. *urît* is a derivative of HORRERE 'to bristle, look frightful'.

Weak: DEBILE survives in learned and some dialect words. FLEBILE 'lamentable, tearful' is more general, with dissimilation of the first L in some languages: French *faible*, Span. Cat. *feble* (but Ital. *fievole*, R-R (Engadine) *flaivel*); and sometimes apparently crossed with FRAGILE or GRACILE. However, FLUXU 'lax' gives us more popular Span. *flojo*, Cat. *fluix*. FLACCU 'flabby' gives Ital. *fiacco* and Old French *flac* (from the seventeenth-century, *flasque*), as well as the Latinisms Span. *flaco*, Ptg. *fraco*. Rum. *slab* is of Slavonic, and *şubred* of unknown, origin.

7.7   CONSERVATISM IN ROMANCE

The conservative tendencies of one or other of the Romance languages have often been mentioned in the course of our exposition. Some would go further and talk about 'conservative languages', though what constitutes conservatism is not always specified. Sard is sometimes cited as ultraconservative, largely on the basis of a few features like the non-palatalization of velar consonants by following front vowels, the retention of final Latin -S, the failure to merge Latin short Ĭ and Ŭ with long Ē and Ō, and the derivation of the definite article from IPSE rather than ILLE. Yet Sard has undergone radical phonological transformations since the Latin era, including the opening and even loss of consonants in intervocalic sentence context and the change of lateral geminates [ll] to retroflex plosive [ɖ]. Those who maintain that the central Sardinian varieties are archaic in character argue that the island was early isolated from innovations in the later Latin period. But there is no clear evidence that the centre of the island was thoroughly Romanized in classical times. The putative conservative character may therefore be a reflection of a later introduction of an artificial learned version of Latin rather than a natural evolution of an inherited spoken Latin.

Portuguese is another so-called conservative language, allegedly owing to its geographical distance from the innovatory centres. It resisted innovative tendencies like diphthongization of tonic vowels, and the replacement of the simple past by a compound form, and preserved, however marginally, verb forms, like the Latin pluperfect and future perfect indicative. Yet at the phonological level Portuguese is far removed from the Romance stereotype, with vowel nasalization, reduction of unstressed vowels and loss of intervocalic L and N. An interesting example of the ambiguous position of Portuguese on the 'conservation' scale is its unique use of old Christian terms for days of the week, where other languages perpetuate pagan terms: e.g. for 'Monday', *segunda feira* < SECUNDA FERIA 'second festival (after Sunday "Lord's day")' rather than DIES LUNAE 'moon's day'.

Rumanian cannot qualify as a conservative language either, even though it is argued that its early isolation from the Western Latin world left it out on a limb. Its nominal case system and its 'neuter' gender seem, however, to be innovations rather than relics of the Latin equivalents. Its vocabulary is the least Latin-based of all the languages, and phonological and syntactic innovations are numerous.

Each Romance variety has apparently random conservative features. Even in French, probably in modern times the most innovative of all, the old language retained traces of the Latin case system. We may wish to designate as 'conservative' those varieties that, although they have undergone phonological transformations, have not radically refashioned their morphological systems by analogical processes, and have kept intact, by default, relics inherited from Latin. This would be most true of isolated local varieties, in southern Italy or in the Alpine region, for instance. The term 'conservative', on the other hand, may equally be applied to those varieties that have looked to Latin as their model, or have clung to traditions established in a prestigious past. This would embrace the standard languages, especially Italian.

That the languages should change at different rates and in divergent directions seems inevitable. How far these differences can be related to social factors is something we shall consider in the final chapter.

FURTHER READING

On change in general, Breivik & Jahr eds. (1989), Aitchison (1991), McMahon (1994). On sandhi, Andersen ed. (1986). On *ser/estar*, Stengaard (1991). On comparatives, Price (1990). On negation, Haegeman (1995), Schwegler (1990), Zanuttini (1997). On relatives, Schafroth (1993). On interrogation, Roberts (1993). On vocabulary, Rohlfs (1986).

8

Sociolinguistic factors

8.1   SOCIAL ASPECTS OF ROMANCE

In nearly all parts of the Romance world the most salient social feature is regional variation. The social perception of such variation differs in different areas, but speakers will almost always be more conscious of the geographical than of the social significance of language differences. However, educational status will also figure large in their evaluation of variants: on the whole there is still respect for traditional educational qualifications and for the types of language use these encourage. Moreover, there is often conflict between regional language varieties, which are identified with loyalty to a local community. Fear of loss of common cultural values, symbolized by language, has often focused on the need to preserve dying varieties and to discourage language shift. Support has thus been afforded to the dialectological studies and to the moves towards standardization of local varieties discussed in chapter 5. Much of this chapter will therefore be concerned with the interaction between different Romance varieties, as well as with neighbouring non-Romance languages.

8.2   SOCIOLINGUISTIC VARIATION

The sort of questions that preoccupy English-speaking sociolinguists are comparatively rarely discussed within Romance. It is mainly in those regions where geographical variation is limited that factors such as socio-economic status, age and sex loom large in variation studies. On the other hand, register and discourse-type differences are frequently studied, particularly with reference to lexical and stylistic variation. In general it is probably true that Romance sociolinguistic thinking is more firmly rooted in the conflictual tradition of Marx than in the consensus view associated with American theorists like Parsons.

American-style sociolinguistics (in the methodology associated with William Labov) flourishes most, within the Romance sphere, in Canada, where the use of extensive spoken language corpora is exploited, using the statistical techniques developed especially by David Sankoff in Montreal. Here so-called 'popular' features of French, some of which are often comparatively obsolescent in France, can be correlated clearly with socioeconomic and educational status, and more ambiguously with age and sex. As a methodological tool for investigation the Canadian sociolinguists substituted for the usual sociological measures the concept of 'linguistic market', which matches language use with the social and professional requirement of speakers to employ more or less prestigious variants. Those employed in service industries and liberal professions, who require to exercise 'communicational' or 'interpersonal' skills, would be expected to make more use of standard linguistic forms than others, while the young (especially males), the very old and the ideologically disaffected would prefer nonstandard forms, particularly in informal interactions.

A conclusion that may be tentatively drawn, from observation of nonprestigious variants in Canada, is that the dead hand of authoritarian purism has had less far-reaching effects there than in France. A possible explanation is that Canadian French usage to some degree has distanced itself from that of the Hexagon, even more than might be expected from the breaking of political links in the mid-eighteenth century. This certainly was so during the nineteenth century, especially in Republican periods and when France loosened its ties with the Church. Another explanation is that Canadian French had early reduced dialect diversity (by 'colonial levelling') and had established some sort of regional identity, which was buttressed by a common resistance to the incursion of English. Although there are remnants of a localized 'Acadian' French on the east coast, surviving or restored after the deportation of the Francophone population by the British in 1755, there seems to be rather little in the way of geographical variation in Canadian French, which in some respects appears archaic, even though there have been salient phonetic changes and extensive lexical borrowing from English.

> We should here note that sociolinguistic investigation of the Labovian type is exemplified also in other Romance-speaking American countries. In Argentina and Brazil, but especially among 'Chicano' populations in the United States,

there have been studies in this tradition. However, as in most parts of the Romance-speaking world, the question of interaction between different languages receives more attention than that of social variation within one and the same language.

In France, more recently than in Canada, there has been reduction of geographical linguistic diversity. This was achieved very largely by deliberate institutional discouragement of dialect use, from the time of the Revolution, but especially since the establishment of universal education (see chapter 5). Another important factor may have been the sluggish demographic growth in modern France, and transfer of population from countryside to town, as well as the sizeable immigration into France from other countries.

One unexpected effect of the imposition of the standard language on all Frenchmen has been the apparent development of a nationwide 'popular' variety that shadows the official language. 'Popular French' acquired covert prestige, especially in the first half of the twentieth century, as the idiom of the working class and of the young. The fact that some of the features of this 'popular' variety (like non-use of negative *ne*, of interrogative inversion, of the synthetic future or of prescribed auxiliary selection in the compound perfect) are also found in Canadian French suggests that they originate in older (seventeenth-century?) unprestigious usage, that remained underground, suppressed in the textual evidence by the weight of prescriptive authority.

Already in the nineteenth century the 'popular' language, associated first with the lower social strata of Paris, was described with affection and amusement: it was usually linked to underworld *argot* that had been known from the fifteenth century. It began to penetrate into literary texts especially during the First World War, mainly in reported conversational exchanges between *poilus* (non-commissioned ranks). Between the wars it acquired political significance and was seen by some linguists as foreshadowing changes in the French of the future, if oppressive authority could be prevented from blocking the creativity of the people. The 'language of revolt' was naturally vehemently condemned by traditionalists, who saw in it a threat to national culture, just as, later, traditionalists regarded the incursion of English loanwords. Since the Second World War, the 'popular' idiom has penetrated to more and more discourse types, and today, in some form or other, it is part of the linguistic repertoire of nearly all French speakers.

Sociolinguistic investigation in France is mainly concerned with use and distribution of 'popular' variants: as elsewhere, it is found that they are more current in disadvantaged, economically and educationally, sections of society and that they are favoured most by young males and least by elderly middle-class females. As elsewhere, among young people preference for nonstandard usage is so great that they are often seen as having their own secret language: language distortions like *verlan* 'back slang' are particularly favoured, as are swiftly changing fashionable lexical items. However, the idea that there is a 'popular language' distinct from French is challenged by linguists, who point out that deviant usage occurs in only a smallish proportion of any stretch of discourse.

The almost obsessive preoccupation of the French with their language has often been noted. This dates from the sixteenth century, when efforts for codification began, fortified in the seventeenth and eighteenth centuries with the insistence on the social and cultural importance of language standardization, and at the Revolution, which stressed the necessity for unifying the national language. The education system has always placed emphasis on the value of clear, elegant, concise and fluent expression, and on grammatical correctness and lexical precision. Newspapers continue to feature regular columns on language use and grammatical subtleties, and high-profile television programmes cover language matters alongside other cultural topics. The flip-side of this interest in language is the phenomenon of insecurity that besets those who feel disadvantaged linguistically, and so are reluctant to display their incompetence in public. Studies suggest that linguistic insecurity may be more prevalent in northern industrial areas, where local dialects are virtually dead, than in the south, where speakers may retain more sense of their regional linguistic identity, even though their Occitan dialects may be moribund.

8.3   LANGUAGE CONFLICT

The idea of language conflict was first fully developed within the Romance sphere, by Catalan activists protesting at the subjugation of their language to Castilian. This was a political issue especially during the Franco era, when language nationalism was identified with separatism and seen as a threat to the unity of the state, so that political moves were made to suppress the regional languages. Mussolini adopted a similar policy, but carried it out less thoroughly.

The belief, however, that language is a badge of cultural and ethnic identity dates further back and is associated with revolutionary ideas and with Romanticism. It was during the nineteenth century that minority languages within Romance sought to assert their worth and seek cultural, if not political, autonomy. The spread of standard languages, identified as the idiom of the state, began earlier, as we saw in chapter 5. From the sixteenth century already there were those, especially among the merchant classes, who perceived advantages in educating their children in a vernacular language that had wider currency than the local dialect. The decline of Latin as the language of transnational communication encouraged the adoption of codified and unified standards within each Romance-speaking country. The growth of literacy was bound to level out linguistic variation, at least in the written language.

This movement, however, had comparatively little effect on rural populations before the mid-nineteenth century, even in France, where ideologically the link between language and nationhood was most stressed. Educational surveys towards the end of the century suggested that a large proportion of French citizens had the perception that they were not speakers of French, but were conscious of having as their mother-tongue 'another language' – whether a Romance, Celtic or Germanic variety. One of the prime aims of universal education was to suppress these other languages, reducing them to subservient status and eventually eliminating them, so as to strengthen a feeling of unity, with participation in and loyalty to the French nation–state. Where the speakers were not so conscious of speaking 'another language' – that is, when they were users of Northern French nonstandard varieties – they were subject to similar pressures to 'purify' their own usage, by scorning local speech habits.

On the whole, the drive towards unification of French succeeded; though, as we have seen, it may have bred a 'popular' sub-culture, and a degree of linguistic insecurity among those who learned to distrust their own language competence. Although not completely eliminated, regional varieties have declined, leaving often only traces that are socially stigmatized. In the northern Picard old industrial areas, for instance, *chtimi* features, relics of older dialects, persist mainly in the speech of very old lower-class speakers (imitated sometimes especially by young dissident males), and in a few localities, usually in close contact with the Flemish that has lost ground steadily since the sixteenth century. In Belgium, dialect usage survived rather longer, especially in the eastern Walloon area wedged between German- and Flemish-speaking regions, but looks almost certain to die out in the near future. Similarly, Francoprovençal varieties have virtually perished in eastern France and in Switzerland, barely surviving in Alpine regions among the older generation.

Catalan, in Roussillon, and the Germanic dialect of Alsace persist better, probably because of the support they receive from neighbouring varieties across state frontiers (in Spain and Germany or Switzerland), but in the towns especially there is a growing proportion of monolingual French speakers, and middle-class speakers often discourage use of the language by their children, on the grounds that it may hamper their social and economic prospects.

In these latter regions, however, as in Brittany, Corsica and the Occitan areas, there is support for conservation of their own language. In Alsace and Roussillon, official encouragement usually takes the form of providing teaching in related standard languages – German and Catalan – rather than in developing local varieties, just as in Corsica some advocate the use of standard Italian, and in Galicia of standard Portuguese. For Breton and Occitan, on the other hand, where there is no obvious extraterritorial model to follow, standard languages have been elaborated, that purportedly serve as an umbrella for local varieties (see chapter 5). How far the decline of these languages can be halted, however, is open to doubt.

It is the fear of decline and death of local languages, usually via shift to a dominant state language, that prompts language activism, sometimes even with resort to violence (here the most obvious example today is of Basque militants). The phenomenon is not, of course, confined to the Romance world, and often the motivation is not primarily linguistic, except in so far as the language is perceived as the emblem of ethnicity and subjugation of the language is a sign of withdrawal of political and economic power from the community that uses it.

Language death is often an act of suicide rather than murder, as speakers (usually through their children) seek to desert a language that seems to offer no prospects of advancement. Usually in these circumstances bilingualism is perceived as a hindrance to prestigious use of the dominant language and there is resentment of imposed asymmetrical bilingualism, when the mother-tongue speakers of the dominant language are under no obligation to master the minority language.

One feature of Romance language conflict which is rather unusual is that in some cases the languages in competition are so similar to each other that speakers may not be fully aware in every case which language they are using. Here, as elsewhere, the social perception of language versus dialect status is all-important. I shall examine some questions relating to Romance–Romance bilingualism in the next section.

8.4   ROMANCE–ROMANCE BILINGUALISM AND DIGLOSSIA

The German term *Binnendiglossie* has been coined to describe use of two closely related languages in different social situations. The fifth volume of Posner & Green eds. (1980–93) fully covers this question for all Romance-speaking areas, so here I shall make only some general remarks about the contrast between France, Italy and Spain. In chapter 5 we saw that in France non-standard Romance varieties have largely given way to the national language: only in the Occitan region has this been a contentious issue. Although southerners often express general support for the revival of their language, it is noteworthy that champions are frequently not habitual users of Occitan varieties, while mother-tongue speakers, mainly in rural areas, tend to regard them as unprestigious and suitable for only intimate discourse. All speakers are bilingual and usage is diglossic in the classic senses of this term. Interpenetration of French and Occitan, producing a shifting 'francitan' interlect, is often seen as more a mark of southern identity than the codified standard Occitan. Frenchification of Occitan has been particularly evident from the sixteenth century, and Occitan (especially Gascon) use of French has long provoked amusement, tinged with condescending affection, on the part of northerners.

In Italy most of the population operates with at least two varieties, which are broadly labelled dialect and standard. At present about 65 per cent of the population claim to have Italian as their first language: this proportion has increased massively since the Second World War. Most Italians have little perception of regional varieties as lacking prestige. It is said that in the interwar years esteem for relatively affluent Italo-Americans may have helped to bolster speakers' favourable assessment of dialect: most immigrants to the United States were monolingual dialect speakers who had experienced no social pressure to shift to standard Italian.

The linguistic situation in Italy is, however, much more complex than often realized, not least because of internal migration in modern times, coupled with conspicuous territorial diversity. A commonly held simplification maintains that in the Industrial Triangle of the North (Turin–Genoa–Milan), koineization is general, whereas further south a mosaic of dialects persists. Certainly in Veneto, Lombardy and Piedmont, there have for centuries been written koineized 'dialects' (at earlier periods, alongside French), and these continue to be used (though more vigorously in the east than the west). On the other hand, in northerly Emilia Romagna each locality has its own idiom which is difficult to classify in terms of 'dialect', while Campania in the south has some degree of dialect standardization. In the industrial north, speakers often operate with a variety of 'dialect' forms that are more or less localized or koineized, as well as with a 'standard' that is usually heavily penetrated with regional features. Whereas middle-class speakers may claim lack of proficiency in the more dialectal forms, this does not seem to be true of the majority of speakers, who are often proud of their own regional varieties (while mocking, for instance, Roman, Sicilian or Tuscan usage).

Traditionally in Italy local nobility, as well as commoners, were said to use dialect, whereas 'rootless' Italian was favoured by the merchant classes, and in the Papal States. Note too that until recently university courses, in Padua for instance, could be delivered in dialect, and that today dialect features, like Florentine *gorgia toscana*, or Roman consonantal lenition, have acquired 'street credibility' in many quarters.

Dilalia has been suggested as a term to replace diglossia with reference to the Italian linguistic scene, which is characterized by overlapping of High and Low varieties, both being used in ordinary conversation, and by social stratification within the Low variety itself. The unifying thread of complex Italian usage seems to be the relationship of local varieties to the standard, with which they have interacted for centuries. The relationship has rarely been conflictual, though in the early modern period purism reigned with regard to the written code. Today most Italians, leaving aside the residue of Tuscan purists, are fairly relaxed about variation in the language, and it is usually claimed that there is no nationwide spoken standard.

One should mention, however, that propaganda of the northern Leagues proclaims the superiority of Northern culture and languages and thus antagonizes those who fear intolerance and extremism. It is an undoubted fact that economic prosperity differs widely between the Italian regions. Immigrants from the south, and from Sardinia, who seek work in the industrial north are clearly disadvantaged linguistically as well as socially, in having to adjust to a new complex dialectal situation. It is to be noted too that Swiss Italian speakers, while retaining affection for their parish-pump Tessin dialects, tend to distance themselves from nearby regional koines, and espouse more purist standard usage for serious discourse.

The position of Sardinia is more controversial, as some varieties there are distinct enough from the run of Italian dialects to merit classification as a different language. Here we should mention that some theorists believe that Sard falls together with Sicilian dialects, with which it shares some linguistic features as well as social problems, and that there is some resentment about the protection given to Sard as a 'minority language', while 'Italian dialects' are left to fend for themselves.

Sardinia has had a particularly chequered history and has always suffered from grave disadvantages, including disproportionate depopulation and emigration. At present, as an autonomous region, the island is attempting to counter the effects of dialectal diversity and linguistic self-deprecation, but there seems little prospect that linguistic conflict, and the related questions of communal identity, can easily be resolved.

Other separate Romance linguistic groups within Italy that should be mentioned are the Rhaeto-Romance speaking communities of the Dolomites and Friuli. The former area became (in the main) an autonomous region (Alto Adige / Süd Tirol), following a period of terrorist activity by local German-speaking activists. The Ladin speakers there have always identified socially more closely with their German-speaking neighbours than with Italy, to which the region was joined after the dismemberment of the Austro-Hungarian Empire. Although there are few moves towards unification of the disparate Rhaeto-Romance varieties of this area, they seem at present to be under no threat of extinction. The region now prospers, as a tourist playground, and linguistic conflict appears to be slight, although most Ladin speakers must be bi- or even trilingual (with German as well as Italian).

In Friuli the linguistic situation is less happy. The autonomy of the region and of the language is not recognized by the Italian state, even though Friulian has had a literary form for several centuries. Most Friulian speakers are bilingual or even trilingual (using Venetan as well as Italian), and although there is considerable language loyalty, there are indications that more privileged classes discourage their children from use of the language, as lacking social prestige.

In Spain, the question of linguistic conflict takes on a very different complexion. The comparatively early unification of the country, with reconquest from the Moors and resettlement of reconquered areas by newcomers, reduced linguistic diversity within the country. But more or less homogeneous dialect groupings that did persist in the north came into conflict with central government especially during the Franco era. In 1978, however, was instituted a new regional policy, allowing a degree of linguistic and political autonomy to the regions, though decreeing that Castilian should remain the national language. Catalan and, less positively, Galician profited from the new legislation to establish themselves as regional languages, distinct from Castilian. In other regions the separate identity of the regional idioms is disputed and there is wrangling about their status. In Aragon, for instance, the incursion of Castilian into the local language dates far back and some see the regional language as no more than a variant of the national one. In Asturias, local dialects clearly differ from Castilian, but also among themselves, and are referred to by the depreciative plural *bables*. Passions are aroused in rows about whether a standardized form should be elaborated as an umbrella for the local varieties. Further south, there is discord about whether, for instance, Valencian is merely a variant of Catalan or a language in its own right, or whether Murcian or Andalusian are anything other than regional Castilian. In all these quarrels, myths about separate ancestry play more part than linguistic classification. A discrete 'language', that can be promoted educationally and culturally, is an object of veneration, while 'dialect' implies subordination and decline, so that language figures high on the agenda of political activity in Spain, much more than in Italy.

8.5   ROMANCE INTERLECTS

Whereas, on the whole, Italians accept the consequences of interaction of dialect and standard as inevitable, purist attitudes, seeking to dictate language prototypes clearly differentiated from neighbouring varieties, are more widespread among Romance speakers. As we have seen, language legitimacy is often regarded as established by unilateral historical descent (though never from further back than Roman times). So more archaic features are seen as more authentic than modern 'bastard' usage. Similarly a narrowly locally limited dialect, especially in the mouths of those who have never left the village, may be more highly valued than a regional dialect koine.

As we have seen, though, linguists assume that, before standardization, there was catenate mutual intelligibility between Romance local varieties, which did not fit smoothly into discrete classificatory slots. Today a territorial linguistic continuum has been replaced largely by polarization of dialects towards regional centres. In the northern Iberian peninsula, however (also, but less so, in south-west France), it is still hard to draw a line between different dialect types. This is particularly striking when the dialect continuum bestrides a state frontier, as between Spain and Portugal, or between French Roussillon and Spanish Catalonia.

Here we should mention the well-attested existence of some more or less stable Romance interlects that have grown up in Latin America. One is the *fronterizo* of northern Uruguay, which lies somewhere between Spanish and Brazilian Portuguese, and the other is *cocoliche* of the River Plate region of Argentina, which originated with massive Italian immigration into this Spanish-speaking area. In both cases, the interpenetration of the two related languages is so intense that speakers cannot reliably distinguish them. Both varieties are regarded as socially unprestigious and are condemned by educational authorities. Yet they persist and appear to have emblematic value for the communities that use them. Descriptions of these varieties and their fluctuations appear in volume v of Posner & Green eds. (1980–93). It is suspected that similar, but less well-known, interlects survive in other Latin-American areas, where there has been close contact between different Romance varieties.

8.6   CONTACT WITH OTHER LANGUAGES

Within Europe, there seems today to be resistance to influence on Romance varieties from neighbouring non-Romance languages. All the languages, of course, make extensive borrowing of lexical items from English, especially in the 'Coca-Cola culture' and the 'computer-speak' sort of sphere. But in areas like Belgium and Switzerland, where Walloon or Francoprovençal and French are spoken hard up against Germanic languages, and where one assumes contact changes were frequent in earlier times, the Romance speakers today make little adjustment to their neighbours and linguistic frontiers have remained stable and virtually impermeable for at least a century. In Alsace, French has penetrated the Germanic dialect, rather than vice versa, so much so that the dialects spoken on each side of the Rhine have grown quite far apart.

In the Swiss Grisons, where the Rhaeto-Romance dialects are receding before Swiss German, the Germanic influence is much more conspicuous, affecting especially the more westerly and northerly varieties. Isolates like Istro-Rumanian in former Yugoslavia, which only marginally survive, are even more open to contact influence. Istro-Rumanian has incorporated into its grammar even totally alien Slavonic features like aspectual verb distinctions. I have suggested (2.7) that the 'Romanceness', or more probably the very survival, of such varieties is under threat.

Although Rumanian today does not appear very much subject to influence from neighbouring languages, its vocabulary, as we have seen, retains many earlier Slavonic, Magyar and Greek borrowings. Some features that distinguish it from other Romance languages are seen as 'Balkan', possibly deriving from a common substratum, as they are shared to some extent by other languages of the region, whether Slavonic, Greek or Albanian. Postposition of the definite article and reduction of use of the infinitive are among the features that have been explained in these terms.

Perhaps we should mention here too the contact of Southern Romance with Romany. This is greatest in Rumanian, where the Gipsy population is numerous (2–3 million). The Ceauşescu regime forbade nomadism, so Gipsies were settled, at least temporarily, within more stable communities, though many of them have since migrated further west. How far they retained their own language is not properly recorded, but it seems that many Gipsy words have penetrated into informal, slangy Rumanian. Resentment of the Gipsies seems acute in present-day Rumania: just recently there have been attempts to stop them being called *Romali* rather than the official name *Ţigani*, as it is feared that westerners equate Gipsy nomads with 'more respectable' Rumanians. Gipsy loanwords seem to have penetrated also into Spanish and Portuguese slang usage. Little is known, however, about what precisely the linguistic status of the Gipsy population is at the present time.

8.7   ROMANCE OVERSEAS

Romance languages are spoken all over the world, and it is not surprising that there are differences between them in far-flung regions. We have already discussed (5.7) the question of whether a distinction can be made between creole and overseas dialect. On the whole, where a language spread to an overseas territory as late as the nineteenth century, or when there remained contact and exchange of population with the metropolis, the overseas variety has not deviated greatly from the home standard. We can contrast here, for instance, Portuguese creoles on the Guinea coast and in India with the more standard forms of Mozambique or Angola. In creole-speaking areas where close contact with the metropolis remains, as in French DOMs, the sociolinguistic relationship between creole and standard has more the character of diglossia than of a creole continuum. In Brazil, on the other hand, more creolized forms are giving way to a standard that is based on local usage, rather than that of the European standard.

Latin-American usage has never been totally divorced from that of the Iberian peninsula, in spite of the independence struggles of the nineteenth century. Immigration by Europeans, especially but not exclusively from Iberia, has continued to the present day. Diversity within the vast American territory remains immense but interintelligibility has not normally been lost. It has often been suggested that conservative usage correlates closely with climate, assuming that European settlers were more at home in more temperate areas, but this does not adequately fit the facts. Rather, it would seem that coastal areas, with more contact with the outside world and which were often permanently settled rather late, display more linguistic homogeneity than inland districts, where Spanish colonial administrative centres tended to be established from the mid-sixteenth century.

Latin-American linguistic features have been mentioned throughout this book, so we shall not rehearse them again. On the whole, it can be claimed that many American features reflect sixteenth-century peninsular usage: for Spanish it is usually assumed that southern characteristics loom large and that the Canary Islands served as a funnel through which most of these reached America. More controversial is how far later divergences stem from the influence of indigenous languages. Clearly lexical borrowings, especially relating to locally produced items, were numerous; but penetration of Amerindian Spanish sociolects into the phonological and grammatical norm was more questionable, in the social climate that prevailed during most of the history of Latin America. In some parts, as in Paraguay, though, mixed marital unions were frequent and bilingual speech habits seem to have profoundly influenced the Spanish norm. In more modern times, popular political movements, as in Cuba, Bolivia or Nicaragua, have facilitated the social acceptance of lower-class speech patterns. It is not easy to point precisely to ways in which Latin American usage has clearly been influenced by indigenous languages or by the input of African slaves, especially as nearly always a parallel can be drawn with some European variety, but John Lipski has sought to link, for instance, the frequency of clitic doubling in American Spanish with such influence.

American French, on the other hand, shows little influence from Amerindian (for creoles see 5.7). The link with popular regional varieties of the seventeenth century is clear, though, as we have seen, 'colonial levelling' tended to iron out dialectal differences early. What is in question, though, is how far later development was influenced by contact with English. Although lexical borrowing is very frequent, other influences are not as incontrovertible as sometimes assumed: for instance, lowering of vowels in blocked syllables seems to be carrying to its logical conclusion a process initiated in early modern metropolitan French. In some cases, however, it is hard to deny that English must have made a mark: for instance, Prince Edward Island French uses preposition-stranding in a way totally unknown to other French varieties.

It is not possible here to survey all forms of 'emigrant' Romance, but Judeo-Spanish calls for particular comment. For most it is clearly basically a version of the language used in Spain in 1492 at the time of the expulsion of the Sephardic Jews. Some maintain, however, that Judeo-Romance had retained distinctive characteristics from Roman times, when Jews formed an important element in the Imperial population and spread to different parts of the Empire. Spanish, French and Italian documents written in Hebrew script are said to show similar features, but so far they have been inadequately studied.

The expelled Jews dispersed to the Maghreb, Italy and especially to the Ottoman Empire, where their services were much appreciated, at least until the seventeenth century. Undoubtedly Spain suffered a great loss from the emigration of skilled personnel: curiously Queen Isabella's own medical adviser was expelled, and the carpet which she presented to him on his departure still adorns the tiny synagogue in Dubrovnik (Ragusa). Some Jews converted (*marranos*), but not infrequently took an early opportunity to flee elsewhere – for instance, to Holland or Brazil. Their language survives precariously today, mostly in Israel and various African and American locations, although many speakers perished in the Holocaust, and others have been assimilated linguistically.

The Judeo-Spanish known as *ladino* was originally only a written language, used in Spain mainly for word-for-word translation of religious texts, for the benefit of those whose Hebrew was not up to scratch. It therefore has Hebrew syntactic features. The spoken language of the Sephardics was, however, known as *judezmo*, which began as a number of disparate archaic Spanish varieties (with, for instance, retention of initial [f] – see 6.3), spoken in scattered ghettos, where a Spanish life-style was not maintained. These varieties changed little, though naturally they took in loanwords, and there was some simplification of phonological and morphological structures which can be paralleled from other Spanish varieties (for instance, the *-se* past subjunctive was lost – see 7.5). From the mid-nineteenth century, with the educational endeavours of the Alliance Israélite Universelle, however, *judezmo* underwent koineization and substantial influence from French, and it came sometimes to be known as *ladino*. It was also adopted by more recent German Jewish immigrants to the Balkans, as a mark of Jewish identity. In western Europe it has disappeared, though Sephardic communities maintain prestige, exerting influence, for instance, on the Israeli pronunciation of Biblical Hebrew.

8.8 LANGUAGE ATTITUDES: IN PLACE OF A CONCLUSION

As I come to the end of this book, in which I am conscious of being able only to skim the surface of the rich linguistic material proffered by the Romance languages, I shall try to draw together some of the rather tangled threads of my earlier arguments. I have tried to show that in spite of all the diversity within Romance, there is nevertheless a degree of unity. That this depends to a large extent on common perceptions and attitudes I have tried to convey by my use of the catch-phrase 'Romance club'. Myths about identity are not usually founded on hard fact, but on construction of a historical record. For the Romance languages, the history is there for all to see: no-one denies that they occupy today much of the geographical space covered by the Roman Empire. Puzzles remain: like why Britain or the Maghreb are not still members of the Romance club, whereas Rumania is. What I have tried to emphasize is the fellow-feeling, based on the idea of continuity of tradition, which certainly survived in the Middle Ages and fuelled common enterprises like the Crusades.

What is more remarkable, perhaps, is that the unity of Romance was not shattered by the renewal, the 'born-again' jerk that came with the

Renaissance and the Reformation, followed by the expansion of the Romance domain far beyond Europe. There was, as I have tried to show, differentiation between the languages, as dialects polarized to form statewide standards. But there was also promotion of language attitudes that created a different, more conscious sense of unity, with a turn towards the linguistic and stylistic ideals that had characterized *Latinitas*. Romanceness is more a matter of cultural awareness than of ethnic or religious brotherhood. In the Middle Ages the languages drifted apart without any sense of direction, at the whim of random universal impulses. Speakers did not wholly realize what was happening, because Medieval Latin still provided the adhesive which held the edifice together.

In the early modern period, however, heralding an era of comparative linguistic stability, the languages were differentiated, but on fairly predictable lines. No unscalable barriers were imposed on easy acquisition of another Romance language by any Romance speaker. A recent prize contest in Bucharest asked competitors to execute translations between various Romance languages, including some in which they had no previous competence. This proved a feasible task, and competitors readily coined forms that would be recognized, by users of the other language, as conceivably acceptable, though not current in general use. An invented Romance interlanguage is not beyond the bounds of possibility, and indeed Esperanto to some degree represents such an interlanguage, as did the earlier lingua franca.

Until recently, most educated Romance speakers would, in any case, be familiar with Latin and would have acquired as their first foreign language another Romance tongue. Now, as English becomes the first foreign language for more and more countries, and as Latin descends further into its grave, some sense of the 'sameness' of the Romance languages may get lost. The same effect of 'distanciation' could be achieved by further 'democratization' of linguistic discourse: informal colloquial forms in each language are usually further removed from the common linguistic pool than are more stilted standard forms.

Perhaps then the Romance languages will move further apart, and the Romance club will put up its shutters. Only time will tell.

FURTHER READING

Posner & Green eds. (1980–93) vols. II, III and V give full cover of these questions. On Romance sociolinguistics in general, Dittmar & Schlieben-Lange eds.

(1982) and relevant sections of the triennial proceedings of the Société de Linguistique Romane. See also Green & Ayres- Bennett (1990). On contact studies, Thomason & Kaufman (1988), Fisiak ed. (1995). On European language questions, Parry, Davies & Temple eds. (1994). On language shift, Fishman (1991), Ureland ed. (1982). On 'Balkan linguistics', Solta (1981). On Latin American Spanish, Sala *et al.* (1982), Lipski (1994); on Canadian French, Sanders ed. (1993); on Judeo-Spanish, Sephiha (1986).

REFERENCES

Abel, F. (1971). *L'Adjectif démonstratif dans la langue de la Bible latine. Formation des systèmes déictiques et de l'article défini des langues romanes* (Tübingen: Niemeyer).

Adams, M. (1988) 'Old French, null subjects and verb-second phenomena'. Ph.D thesis, UCLA,

Agard, F. B. (1984) *A course in Romance linguistics*, 2 vols. (Georgetown University Press).

Aitchison, J. (1991) *Language change: progress or decay?* (Cambridge University Press).

Andersen, H., ed. (1986) *Sandhi phenomena in the languages of Europe* (Berlin: Mouton de Gruyter).

Andersen, H. L. & Skytte, G., eds. (1995) *La Subordination dans les langues romanes* (Copenhagen University Press).

Asher, R. E. & Simpson, J. M. Y., eds. (1994) *Encyclopedia of language and linguistics*, 10 vols. (Oxford and Aberdeen: Pergamon and Aberdeen University Press).

Auwera, J. van der (ed.) 1998 *Adverbial constructions in the languages of Europe* Berlin, Mouton de Gruyter.

Ayres-Bennett, W. 1996 *A History of the French Language through Texts.* London, Routledge.

Bahner, W. (1983) *Kontinuität und Diskontinuität in der Herausbildung der romanischen Sprachwissenschaft* (Berlin: Akademie).

Bal, W., Germain, J., Klein, J. & Swiggers, P. (1991) *Bibliographie sélective de linguistique romane et française* (Brussels: Duculot).

Barbarino, J. L. (1981) *Latin and Romance intervocalic stops: a quantitative and comparative study* (Potomac: Studia Humanistica).

Battye, A. & Hintze, M.-A. (1992) *The French language today* (London: Routledge).

Battye, A. and Roberts, I. (eds.) 1995 *Clause Structure and Language Change* New York-Oxford, Oxford University Press.

Bauer, B. L. M. (1992) *Du latin au français: le passage d'une langue SOV à une langue SVO* (The Hague: Gegevens).

Belletti, A. & Rizzi, L. (1994) *Parameters and functional heads: essays in comparative syntax* (London: Routledge).

Benincà, P., ed. (1989) *Dialect variation and the theory of grammar* (Dordrecht: Foris).

Bernini, G. (ed.) 1998 *Pragmatic organization of discourse in the languages of Europe* Berlin, Mouton de Gruyter

Bickerton, D. (1981) *Roots of language* (Ann Arbor: Karoma).

Blake, B. J. (1994) *Case* (Cambridge University Press).

Blasco-Ferrer, E. (1986) *La lingua sarda contemporanea: grammatica del logudorese e del campidanese. Norma e varietà del'uso: sintesi storica* (Cagliari: Ed. della Torre.)

(1995) *La lingua nel tempo: variazione e cambiamento in latino, italiano e sardo* (Cagliari: CUEC).

Borer, H. (1984) *Parametric syntax: case studies in Semitic and Romance languages* (Dordrecht: Foris).

ed. (1986) *The syntax of pronominal clitics* (Syntax and Semantics 19) (New York: Academic Press).

Bossong, G. (1990) *Sprachwissenschaft und Sprachphilosophie in der Romania. Von den Anfängen bis August Wilhelm Schlegel* (Tübingen: Narr).

Bourciez, E. (1910) *Eléments de linguistique romane* (Paris: Klincksieck).

Breivik, L. E. & Jahr, E. H., eds. (1989) *Language change: contributions to the study of its causes* (Berlin: Mouton de Gruyter).

Bright, W., ed. (1991) *International encyclopedia of linguistics*, 4 vols. (New York and Oxford: Oxford University Press).

Burke, P. & Porter, R., eds. (1991) *Language, self and society: a social history of language* (Oxford: Polity).

Burzio, L. (1986) *Italian syntax: a government binding approach* (Dordrecht: Kluwer).

Bybee, J. (1985) *Morphology: a study of the relation between meaning and form* (Amsterdam: Benjamins).

Calboli, G., ed. (1989) *Subordination and other topics in Latin: proceedings of the third colloquium on Latin linguistics* (Amsterdam: Benjamins).

ed. (1990) *Latin vulgaire – latin tardif II: actes du IIième Colloque*

International sur le latin vulgaire et tardif (*Bologne, du 29 août au 2 septembre, 1988*) (Tübingen: Niemeyer).

Carstairs, A. (1987) *Allomorphy in inflexion* (London: Croom Helm).

Comrie, B. (1985) *Tense* (Cambridge University Press).

Corbett, G. (1991) *Gender* (Cambridge University Press).

Coseriu, E. (1988) 'Der romanische Sprachtypus Versuch einer neuen Typologisierung der romanischen Sprachen', in *Energeia und Ergon: sprachliche Variation – Sprachgeschichte – Sprachtypologie. Studia in honorem Eugenio Coseriu*, ed. J. Albrecht, J. Lüdtke & H.Thun, vol. I: *Schriften von Eugenio Coseriu* (*1965-1987*) (Tübingen: Narr), pp. 207–24.

Croft, W. (1990) *Typology and universals* (Cambridge University Press)

Dahl, Ö. (ed.) 1998 *Tense and aspect in the languages of Europe* Berlin, Mouton de Gruyter.

Dahmen, W., Holtus, G., Kramer, J. & Metzeltin, M., eds. (1987) *Latein und Romanisch* (Tübingen: Narr).

Dardel, R. de (1983) *Esquisse structurale des subordonnants conjonctionnels en roman commun* (Geneva: Droz).

Dauses, A. (1981) *Das Imperfekt in den romanischen Sprachen: seine Bedeutung im Verhältnis zum Perfekt* (Wiesbaden: Steiner).

David, J. & Kleiber, G., eds. (1986) *Déterminants: syntaxe et sémantique* (Metz: Centre d'Analyse Syntaxique).

Diefenbach, L. (1831) *Über die jetzigen romanischen Schriftsprachen, die spanische, portugiesische, rhätoromanische* (*in der Schweiz*)*, französische, italienische und dakoromanische* (*in mehreren Ländern des östlichen Europa, mit: Vorbemerkungen über Entstehung, Verwandtschaft usw. dieses Sprachstammes*) (Leipzig: Ricker).

Diez, F. (1836–44, 2nd edition 1856–60, 3rd edition 1869–72, 4th edition 1876–77, 5th edition 1882) *Grammatik der romanischen Sprachen*, 3 vols. (Bonn: Weber).

Dittmar, N. & Schlieben-Lange, B., eds. (1982) *Die Soziolinguistik in romanischsprachigen Ländern* (Tübingen: Narr).

Drijkoningen, F. (1989) *The syntax of verbal affixation* (Tübingen: Niemeyer).

Eckert, G. (1986) *Sprachtypus und Geschichte: Untersuchungen zum typologischer Wandel des Französischen* (Tübingen: Narr).

Elcock, W.D. (1975) *The Romance languages* (revised, with new Introduction by John N. Green) (London: Faber).

Embleton, S. M. (1986) *Statistics in historical linguistics* (Bochum: Brockmeyer).

Ernst, G., M.-D. Glessgen, C. Schmitt and W. Scheichard (eds.) (In preparation) *Romanische Sprachgeschichte: Histoire des langues romanes. Ein internationales Handbuch zur Geschichte der romanischen Sprachen und ihrer Erforschung: Manuel international d'histoire linguistique de la Romania.* Berlin-New York. Walter de Gruyter.

Everaert, M. (1986) *The syntax of reflexivization* (Dordrecht: Foris).

Fagan, S. M. B. (1992) *The syntax and semantics of middle constructions: a study with special reference to German* (Cambridge University Press).

Farkas, D. F. (1982) *Intensionality and Romance subjunctive* (Bloomington: Indiana Linguistics Club).

Feuillet, J. (ed.) 1997 *Actance et Valence dans les langues de l'Europe* Berlin, Mouton de Gruyter.

Fishman, J. A. (1991) *Reversing language shift: theoretical and empirical foundations of assistance to threatened languages* (Clevedon: Multilingual Matters).

Fisiak, J., ed. (1980) *Historical morphology* (The Hague: Mouton).

ed. (1988), *Historical dialectology: regional and social variation* (Berlin: Mouton de Gruyter).

ed. (1990) *Historical linguistics and philology* (Berlin: Mouton de Gruyter).

ed. (1995) *Linguistic change under contact conditions* (Berlin: Mouton de Gruyter).

Fleischman, S. (1982) *The future in thought and language* (Cambridge University Press).

Fleischman, S. & Waugh, L. R., eds. (1991) *Discourse pragmatics and the verb: the evidence from Romance* (London: Routledge).

Gaeng, P. A. (1984) *Collapse and reorganization of the Latin nominal flexion as reflected in epigraphical sources* (Potomac: Scripta Humanistica).

Geisler, H. (1992) *Akzent und Lautwandel in der Romania* (Tübingen: Narr).

Giorgio, A. & Longobardi, G. (1991) *The syntax of noun phrases: configuration, parameters and empty categories* (Cambridge University Press).

Goebl, H. (1984) *Dialektometrische Studien: Anhand italoromanischer, rätoromanischer und galloromanischer Sprachmaterialien aus AIS und ALF*, 3 vols. (Tübingen: Niemeyer).

Green, J. N. & Ayres-Bennett, W. (1990) *Variation and change in French* (London: Routledge).

Gröber, G., ed. (1888) *Grundriss der romanischen Philologie,* vol. I (Strasburg, Trübner).

Gsell, O. & Wandruszka, U. (1986) *Der romanische Konjunktiv* (Tübingen: Niemeyer).

Guillet, A. & La Fauci, N., eds. (1984) *Lexique-grammaire des langues romanes* (Amsterdam: Benjamins).

Haegeman, L. (1995) *The syntax of negation* (Cambridge University Press).

Haiman, J. & Benincà, P. (1992) *The Rhaeto-Romance languages* (London: Routledge).

Hajek, J. 1997 *Universals of sound-change in nasalization* Oxford, Blackwell.

Hall, R. A., Jr (1974) *External history of the Romance languages* (New York: Elsevier).

(1976) *Proto-Romance phonology* (New York: Elsevier).

(1983) *Proto-Romance morphology* (Amsterdam: Benjamins).

Harré, C. E. (1991) Tener + *past participle: a case study in linguistic description* (London: Routledge).

Harris, M. & Ramat, P., eds. (1987) *Historical development of auxiliaries* (Berlin: Mouton de Gruyter).

Harris, M. & Vincent, N., eds. (1988) *The Romance languages* (London: Croom Helm).

Harris, T. K., ed. (1982) *Sociology of Judezmo: the language of the Eastern Sephardim* (*International Journal of the Sociology of Language* 37).

Haudricourt, A. G. & Juilland, A. (1949) *Essai pour une histoire structurale du phonétisme français* (Paris: Klincksieck).

Heine, B. (1994) *Auxiliaries: cognitive forces and grammaticalization* (London: Routledge).

Herman, J., ed. (1987) *Latin vulgaire – latin tardif: actes du Ier colloque international sur le latin vulgaire et tardif* (*Pécs, 2–5 septembre 1985*) (Tübingen: Niemeyer).

(1990), *Du latin aux langues romanes: études de linguistique historique* (Tübingen: Niemeyer).

Holm, J. (1988-9) *Pidgins and creoles*, 2 vols. (Cambridge University Press).

Holtus, G., Metzeltin, M. & Schmitt, C., eds. (1988–) *Lexikon der romanistischen Linguistik,* 7 vols. (Tübingen: Niemeyer).

Hopper, P. J. & Traugott, E. C. (1993) *Grammaticalization* (Cambridge University Press).

Hualde, J. C. (1992) *Catalan* (London: Routledge).

Hulst, H. van der (ed.) 1998 *Word prosodic systems in the languages of Europe* Berlin, Mouton de Gruyter.

Iliescu, M. & Mourin, L. (1991) *Typologie de la morphologie verbale romane*, vol. I: *Vue synchronique* (Innsbruck: AMOE).

Iliescu, M. & Slusanski, D. (1991) *Du latin aux langues romanes: choix de textes traduits et commentés (du IIe siècle avant J.C. jusqu'au Xe siècle après J. C.)* (Wilhelmsfeld: Egert).

Iliescu, M. & Marxgut, W., eds. (1992) *Latin vulgaire – latin tardif III: actes du IIIème colloque international sur le latin vulgaire et tardif (Innsbruck, 2–5 septembre 1991)* (Tübingen: Niemeyer).

Iordan, I., Orr. J. & Posner, R. (1970) *Introduction to Romance linguistics: its schools and its scholars* (Oxford: Blackwell).

Jaeggli, O. (1981) *Topics in Romance syntax* (Dordrecht: Foris).

Jaeggli, O. & Safir, K., eds. (1989) *The null subject parameter* (Dordrecht: Kluwer).

Jenkyns, R., ed. (1992) *The legacy of Rome: a new appraisal* (Oxford University Press).

Jones, M. A. (1993) *Sardinian syntax* (London: Routledge).
   (1996), *Foundations of French syntax* (Cambridge University Press).

Joseph, B. D. (1983) *The synchrony and diachrony of the Balkan infinitive: a study in areal, general and historical linguistics* (Cambridge University Press).

Karlsson, K. E. (1981) *Syntax and affixation: the evolution of* MENTE *in Latin and Romance* (Tübingen: Niemeyer).

Klaiman, M. H. (1991) *Grammatical voice* (Cambridge University Press).

Klingebiel, K. (1989) *Noun–verb compounding in Western Romance* (Berkeley: University of California).

Kok, A. de (1985) *La Place du pronom personnel conjoint en français: une étude diachronique* (Amsterdam: Rodopi).

Kontzi, R., ed. (1982) *Substrate und Superstrate in den romanischen Sprachen*, (Darmstadt: Wissenschaftliche Buchgesellschaft).

Körner, K.-H. (1987) *Korrelative Sprachtypologie; die zwei Typen romanischer Syntax* (Wiesbaden and Stuttgart: Steiner).

Kursschildgen, E. (1983) *Untersuchungen zu Funktionsveränderung bei Suffixen im Lateinischen und Romanischen* (Bonn: Becker).

Labov, W. (1994) *Principles of linguistic change*, vol. I: *Internal factors* (Oxford: Blackwell).

Lamiroy, B. (1983) *Les Verbes de mouvement en français et en espagnol* (Amsterdam: Benjamins).

Lang, J. (1982) *Sprache im Raum: zu den theoretischen Grundlagen der Mundartforschung. Unter Berücksichtigung des Rätoromanischen und Leonesischen* (Tübingen: Niemeyer).

Lausberg, H. (1956–62) *Romanische Sprachwissenschaft*, 3 vols. (Berlin: Gruyter).

Leonard, C. S., Jr (1978) *Umlaut in Romance: an essay in linguistic archaeology* (Grossen-Linden: Hoffmann).

Lepschy, A. L. & Lepschy, G. (1989) *The Italian language today* (London: Routledge).

Lightfoot, D. (1991) *How to set parameters: arguments from linguistic change* (Cambridge, Mass.: MIT Press).

Lipski, J. (1994) *Latin American Spanish* (London: Longman).

Lodge, A. R. (1993) *French: from dialect to standard* (London: Routledge).

Maiden, M. (1991) *Interactive morphology: metaphony in Italy* (London: Routledge).

(1995) *A linguistic history of Italian* (London and New York: Longman).

Malkiel, Y. (1989) *Theory and practice of Romance etymology: studies in language, culture and history* (London: Variorum).

(1992) *Diachronic studies in lexicology, affixation, phonology: edita and inedita, 1979–1988* (Amsterdam: Benjamins).

(1993) *Etymology* (Cambridge University Press).

Mallinson, G. (1986) *Rumanian* (London: Croom Helm).

Mańczak, W. (1991) *La Classification des langues romanes* (Krakov: Universitas).

Manoliu-Manea, M. (1971) *Romanică, tipologie şi istoria* (Bucharest: Universitatea).

(1985) *Tipología e historia: elementos de sintaxis comparada románica* (Madrid: Gredos).

Matthews, P. H. (1991) *Morphology* (Cambridge University Press).

Mayerthaler, E. (1982) *Unbetonter Vokalismus und Silbenstruktur im Romanischen* (Tübingen: Niemeyer).

McMahon, A. M. S. (1994) *Understanding linguistic change* (Cambridge University Press).

Meyer-Lübke, W. (1890–1902) *Grammatik der romanischen Sprachen*, 4 vols. (Leipzig: Fues).

Muljačić, Ž. (1991) *Scaffale italiano: avviamento bibliografico allo studio della lingua italiana* (Florence: La Nuova Italia).

Muller, H. F. (1929) *A chronology of Vulgar Latin* (Halle: Niemeyer).

Nevis, J., Joseph, B., Wanner, D. & Zwicky, A. M. (1994) *Clitics: a comprehensive bibliography* (Amsterdam: Benjamins).

Niederehe, H.-J. & Schlieben-Lange, B. (1987) *Die Frühgeschichte der romanischen Philologie von Dante bis Diez* (Tübingen: Niemeyer).

Ouhalla, J. (1991) *Functional categories and parametric variation* (London: Routledge).

Palmer, F. R. (1986) *Mood and modality* (Cambridge University Press).

(1994) *Grammatical roles and relations* (Cambridge University Press).

Panhuis, D. G. J. (1982) *The communicative perspective in the sentence: a study of Latin word order* (Amsterdam: Benjamins).

Parry, M. M., Davies, W. V. & Temple, R. A. M., eds. (1994) *The changing voices of Europe: social and political changes and their linguistic repercussions, past, present and future* (Cardiff: University of Wales).

Pearce, E. (1990) *Parameters in Old French syntax: infinitival complements* (Dordrecht: Kluwer).

Penny, R. (1991) *A history of the Spanish language* (Cambridge University Press).

Pinkster, H. (1990) *Latin syntax and semantics* (London: Routledge).

Plank, F., ed. (1991) *Paradigms: the economy of inflection* (Berlin: Mouton de Gruyter).

Polomé, E. C. & Winter, W., eds. (1992) *Reconstructing languages and culture* (Berlin: Mouton de Gruyter).

Posner, R. (1966) *The Romance languages: a linguistic introduction* (New York: Doubleday).

Posner, R. & Green, J. N., eds. (1980–93) *Trends in Romance linguistics and philology*, 5 vols (Berlin: Mouton de Gruyter).

Pountain, C. J. (1983) *Structures and transformations: the Romance verb* (London: Croom Helm).

Price, S. (1990) *Comparative constructions in Spanish and French syntax* (London: Routledge).

Pulgram, E. (1975) *Latin–Romance phonology: prosodics and metrics* (Munich: Fink).

Raible, W., ed. (1989) *Romanistik, Sprachtypologie und Universalienforschung* (Tübingen: Narr).

Raynouard, F.-J. (1816–21). *Choix des poésies originales des Troubadours*, 6 vols. (Paris: Firmin Didot).

Rizzi, L. (1982) *Issues in Italian syntax* (Dordrecht: Foris).

Roberge, Y. & Vinet, M.-T. (1989) *La Variation dialectale en grammaire universelle* (Montreal University Press).

Roberts, I. (1993) *Verbs and diachronic syntax: a comparative history of English and French* (Dordrecht: Kluwer).

Rohlfs, G. (1983) *Romanische Lehnübersetzungen aus germanischer Grundlage* (*Materia romana, spirito germano*) (Munich: Sitzungsberichte der Bayerische Akademie der Wissenschaft).

  (1984) *Vom Rom zur Romania: Aspekte und Probleme romanischer Sprachgeschichte* (Tübingen: Narr).

  (1986) *Panorama delle lingue neolatine: piccolo atlante linguistico panromanzo* (Tübingen: Narr).

Sala, M. ed. (1988) *Vocabularul representativă al limbilor romanice* (Bucharest: Editura Ştiinţifică şi Enciclopedică).

  (1989) *Enciclopedia limbilor romanice* (Bucharest: Editura Ştiinţifică şi Enciclopedică).

Sala, M., Munteanu, D., Neagu, V. & Şandru-Olteanu, T. (1982) *El español de America*, vol. I: *Léxico* (Mexico: Academia Mexicana; Bucharest: Academiei Române).

Sanders, C., ed. (1993) *French today: language in its social context* (Cambridge University Press).

Sankoff, D., ed. (1986) *Diversity and diachrony* (Amsterdam: Benjamins).

Saussure, F. de (1916) *Cours de linguistique générale* (Paris: Payot).

Schafroth, E. (1993) *Zur Entstehung und vergleichenden Typologie der Relativpronomina in den romanischen Sprachen* (Tübingen: Niemeyer).

Schøsler, L. (1984) *La Déclinaison bicasuelle de l'ancien français: son rôle dans la syntaxe de la phrase, les causes de sa disparition* (Odense University Press).

Schuchardt, H. (1866–8) *Der Vokalismus des Vulgärlateins*, 3 vols. (Leipzig: Teubner).

Schwegler, A. (1990) *Analyticity and syntheticity: a diachronic perspective with special reference to Romance languages* (Berlin: Mouton de Gruyter).

Seklaoui, D. R. (1989) *Change and compensation: parallel weakening of /s/ in Italian, French and Spanish* (New York: Lang).

Sephiha, H. V. (1986) *Le Judéo-espagnol* (Paris: Entente).

Solta, G. R. (1980) *Einführung in die Balkanlinguistik mit besonderer*

Berücksichtung des Substrats und des Balkanlateinischen (Darmstadt: Wissenschaft Buchgesellschaft).

Stengaard, B. (1991) *Vida y muerte de un campo semántico: un estudio de la evolución semántica de los verbos latinos* STARE, SEDERE, e IACERE *de latín al romance del s. XIII* (Tübingen: Niemeyer).

Tagliavini, C. (1949) *Le origini delle lingue neolatine: introduzione alla filologia romanza* (Bologna: Pàtron).

Teyssier, P. (1984) *Manuel de langue portugaise (Portugal–Brésil)* (Paris: Klincksieck).

Thomason, S. G. & Kaufman, T. (1988) *Language contact, creolization and genetic linguistics* (Berkeley: University of California).

Trager, G. L. (1932) *The use of Latin demonstratives (especially* ILLE *and* IPSE*) up to 600 as the source of the Romance article* (New York: Institute of French Studies).

Tranel, B. (1981) *Concreteness in generative phonology* (Los Angeles: University of California Press).

Ureland, P. S., ed. (1982) *Die Leistung der Strataforschung und der Kreolistik: typologische Aspekte der Sprachkontakte. Akten des 6. Symposions über Sprachkontakt in Europa, Mannheim* (Tübingen: Niemeyer).

Väänänen,V. (1981) *Recherches et récréations latino-romanes* (Naples: Bibliopolis).

    (1987) *Le Journal-Epitre d'Egérie: étude linguistique* (Helsinki: Suomalainen Tiedeakatemia).

Vance, B. (1988) 'Null subjects and syntactic change in Medieval French' (Ph.D thesis, Cornell University).

Vernay, H. (1991–) *Dictionnaire onomasiologique des langues romanes* (Tübingen: Niemeyer).

Vincent, N. & Harris, M., eds. (1982) *Studies in the Romance verb* (London: Croom Helm).

Wanner, D. (1987) *The development of Romance clitic pronouns from Latin to Old Romance* (Berlin: Mouton de Gruyter).

Wartburg, W. von (1950) *Die Ausgliederung der romanischen Sprachräume* (Bern: Francke).

Wright, R. (1982) *Late Latin and early Romance* (Liverpool: Cairns).

    ed. (1991) *Late Latin and the Romance languages in the early Middle Ages* (London and New York: Routledge).

Zimmer, R. (1992) *Morphologie des italienischen, spanischen und portugiesischen Verbs* (Tübingen: Niemeyer).

INDEX OF NAMES

Abel, F. 154, 346
Adams, M. 70, 346
Agard, F. B. 6, 199, 346
Aitchison, J. 328, 346
Albrecht, J. 70, 348
Alcuin of York 153
Alonso, A. 38
Andersen, H. L. 186, 328, 346
Ascoli, G. I. 4, 192–3, 194, 196, 202
Asher, R. E. 30, 346
Augustus, Octavius Caesar (Roman Emperor) 99, 116
Ayres-Bennett, W. 349

Bahner, W. 31, 346
Bal, W. 30, 346
Barbarino, J. L. 281, 346
Bartsch, K. 247, 248, 289
Battye, A. 226, 346
Bauer, B. L. M. 154, 346
Belletti, A. 70, 346
Bello, A. 209
Bembo, Pietro (Cardinal) 212
Benincà, P. 226, 347, 349
Benveniste, E. 19
Bickerton, D. 224, 347
Blake, B. J. 154, 347
Blasco-Ferrer, E. 226, 347
Bloomfield, L. 6
Bocaccio, Giovanni 212
Borer, H. 7, 186, 347
Bossong, G. 31, 347
Bourciez, E. L. 5, 347
Breivik, L. E. 328, 347
Bright, William 30, 347
Burke, P. 254, 347
Burzio, L. 7, 19, 30, 347
Bybee, J. (Hooper) 70, 347

Calboli, G. 154, 186, 347

Calvin, Jean 211
Camões, Luis de 209
Carstairs, A. 154, 347
Ceauşescu, N. (Rumanian communist leader) 340
Charlemagne (Holy Roman Emperor) 152, 191, 232
Chomsky, N. A. 6
Comrie, B. 154,347
Contreras, H. 200
Corbett, G. 70, 347
Coseriu, E. 6, 36–38, 70, 115, 347–8
Croft, W. 70, 348
Cyril, Saint 139

Dahmen, W. 154, 348
Dante (Alghieri) 2, 141, 149, 212, 227, 241
Dardel, R. 186, 348
Dauses, A. 154, 348
David, J. 281, 348
Davies, W. V. 345, 352
Diefenbach, Lorenz 3, 348
Diez, Friedrich 3, 4, 168, 191, 348
Dittmar, N. 345, 348
Drijkoningen, F. 70, 348

Eckert, G. 281, 348
Edmont, E. 203
Elcock, W. D. 5, 348
Embleton, S. M. 226, 348
Erasmus, Desiderius 153
Everaert, M. 186, 348

Fagan, S. M. B. 186, 348
Farkas, D. F. 154, 348
Fishman, J. A. 345, 348
Fisiak, J. 70, 226, 349
Fleischman, S. 154, 349
Franco, Francisco (Spanish dictator) 209, 215, 332, 338

François I (King of France) 210
Fredegar 177

Gaeng, P. A. 154, 349
Germain, J. 346
Gilliéron, J. 203
Giorgio, A. 186, 349
Goebl, H. 205, 226, 349
Goethe, Johann Wolfgang von 191
Green, J. N. xi, xiii, xiv, 30, 96, 154, 186, 226,
    281, 335, 339, 345, 348, 349, 353
Greenberg, J. 200
Grégoire (Abbé) 203
Grimes, J. 199
Gröber, G. 4, 349
Gsell, O. 154, 349
Guillet, A. 70, 349
Guiter, H. 205

Haegeman, L. 154, 328, 349
Haiman, J. 226, 349
Hall, R. A. Jr 6, 70, 197, 349
Harré, C. E. 154, 349
Harris, M. xiii, 30, 226, 350
Harris, T. K. 154, 186, 350
Haudricourt, A.-G. 239, 350
Heine, B. 154, 350
Herman, J. 154, 350
Hintze, M.-A. 226, 346
Hitler, Adolf (German dictator) 192
Holm, J. 96 , 350
Holtus, G. xi, xiii, 30, 348, 350
Hope, T. E. 186
Hopper, P. J. 70, 350
Hualde, J. C. 226, 350

Iliescu, M. 70, 350
Iordan, I. 5, 30, 350
Isabel (Queen of Spain) 208, 342

Jaberg, K. 203
Jaeggli, O. 7, 70, 186, 350
Jahr, E. H. 328, 347
Jakobson, R. 108
Jenkyns, R. 154, 350
Jones, M. A. 226, 350
Joseph B. D. 185, 351, 352
Jud, J. 203
Juilland, A. 239, 240, 350
Justinian I, (Byzantine Emperor) 177

Karlsson, K. E. 96, 351
Kaufman, T. 345, 354
Kayne, R. 7
Klaiman, M. H. 186, 351

Kleiber, G. 281, 348
Klein, J. 346
Klingebiel, K. 96, 351
Kok, A. de 186, 351
Kontzi, R. 281, 351
Körner, K.-H. 201, 226, 351
Kramer, J. 348
Kursschildgen, K. 96

La Fauci, N. 70, 349
Labov, W. 157, 161, 330, 351
Lamiroy, B. 186, 351
Lang, J. 226, 351
Lass, R. xiv, 283, 310
Lausberg, H. 5, 6, 351
Leonard, C. S. Jr. 154, 198, 351
Lepschy, A. L. 226, 351
Lepschy, G. 226, 351
Lightfoot, D. 70, 351
Lipski, J. 226, 342, 345, 351
Lodge, A. R. 226, 351
Longobardi, G. 186, 349
Louis XIV (King of France) 211
Lucchesi, V. xiv
Lüdtke, J. 348
Luther, Martin 211

Maiden, M. 154, 226, 351
Malkiel, Y. xiv, 96, 352
Mallinson, G. 226, 352
Mańczak, W. 226, 352
Manoliu-Manea, M. 6, 70, 352
Martinet, A. 294
Marx, Karl 330
Marxgut, W. 350
Matthews, P. H. 70, 352
Maurer, T. H. 38
Mayerthaler, E. 154, 352
McMahon, A. M. S. 328, 352
Metzeltin, M. xi, xiii, 30, 348, 350
Meyer-(Lübke), W. 4, 352
Mistral, F. 191
Montaigne, Michel de 153
Mourin, L. 70, 350
Muljačić, Ž. 199, 226, 352
Muller, H. F. 154, 352
Munteanu, D. 353
Mussafia, A. 170
Mussolini, Benito (Italian dictator) 192, 194,
    332

Neagu, V. 353
Nevis, J. 185, 352
Niederehe, H.-J. 31, 352

Orr, J. 5, 30, 350
Ouhalla, J. 70, 352

Palmer F. R. 154, 352
Palsgrave, John 238
Panhuis, D. G. J. 154, 352
Paris, G. 4
Parry, M. M. 345, 352
Parsons, T. 330
Pearce, E. 186, 352
Pei, M. 199
Pellegrini, G. 200
Penny, R. 226, 353
Perlmutter, R. 19
Petrarch, Francesco 212
Petronius, Caius Arbiter 102
Pinkster, H. 154, 353
Pisarro, Camille 222
Plank, F. 70, 353
Pollock, J.-Y. 7
Polomé, E. C. 96, 353
Porter, R. 154, 353
Posner, R. xi, 30, 96, 154, 186, 226, 281, 335, 339, 345, 353,
Postal, P. 19
Pountain, C. J. 154, 353
Price, S. 328, 353
Pulgram, E. 154, 353
Purschinky, J. 186

Raible, W. 70, 226, 353
Ramat, P. 154, 186, 350
Raynouard, François-Juste 3, 191, 353
Rivero, M.-L. 7
Rizzi, L. 7, 70, 154, 346, 353
Roberge, Y. 226, 353
Roberts, I. 328, 353
Rohlfs, G. 96, 154, 203, 281, 328, 353

Safir, K. 70, 186, 350
Sala, M. 30, 96, 353
Sanders, C. 345, 354
Şandru-Olteanu, T. 353
Sankoff, D. 226, 330, 354
Sapir, E. 38
Saussure, Ferdinand de 5
Schafroth, E. 328, 353
Schlegel, August W. von 3
Schlieben-Lange, B. L. M. 31, 345, 348
Schmitt, C. xi, xiii, 30, 350
Schøsler, L. 154, 354
Schuchardt, H. 4, 38, 90, 158–9, 198, 202

Schwegler, A. 154, 328, 354
Séguy, J. 205
Seklaoui, D. R. 281, 354
Sephiha, H. V. 345, 354
Simpson, J. M. Y. 30, 346
Skytte, G. 186, 346
Slusanski, D. 350
Smith, Adam 156
Solta, G. R. 345, 354
Stengaard, B. 328, 354
Suetonius, Gaius Tranquilius 116
Swadesh, M. 90–1
Swiggers, P. 346

Tagliavini, C. 5, 354
Temple, R. A. M. 345, 352
Terentianus Claudius Maurus 102–3
Teyssier, P. 236, 354
Thomason, S. G. 354
Thun, H. 348
Tobler, A. 170
Trager, George L. 154, 197, 354
Tranel, B. 31, 354
Traugott, E. C. 70, 350
Tuttle, E. xiv

Ureland, P. S. 354–5

Väänänen, V. 154, 355
Valdman, A. 224, 355
Vance, B. 70, 355
Varro, Marcus Terentius 132
Vergnaud, J.-R. 7
Vernay, H. 96, 355
Vicente, Gil 209
Vincent, N. xiii, 30, 154, 226, 350, 355
Vinet, M.-T. 226, 353
Voltaire, F.-M. Arouet 288

Wackernagel, J. 170
Wagner, M. L. 203
Wandruszka, U. 154, 349
Wanner, D. 186, 281, 352, 355
Wartburg, W. von 194, 198, 228–9, 234, 355
Waugh, L. R. 154, 349
Wheeler, M. xiv
Wilson, Woodrow (U.S. President) 214
Winter, W. 96, 353
Wright, R. xiv, 153–4, 355

Zimmer, R. 70, 355
Zwicky, A. M. 352

INDEX OF LANGUAGES

Classification of some languages is disputed, so cross-references are given. Main headwords are roman, subheadings are italicized.

Abruzzese, Abruzzian *see* Italian: *Abruzzo*
Acadian *see* French: Canada
African 6, 35, 73, 74, 93, 108, 183, 220, 225, 342
   Bambara 219
   Bantu 78
   Kimbundu 88
African Portuguese *see* Creole: *Portuguese*
Afro-Hispanic *see* Creole: *Spanish*
Afro-Lusitanian *see* Creole: *Portuguese*
Ajaccio *see* Corsican
Albanian 35, 91–2, 96, 233, 245, 324, 340
Algherese *see* Catalan: *Alghero*
Alpine Romance 63, 117, 119, 194, 245, 327
Alsatian (Alsace) 206, 334, 339
American creoles *see* Creoles
American English *see* English
American Italian *see* Italian
American Spanish *see* Spanish
Amerindian 183, 341, 342
   Quechuan 269
Andalusian *see* Spanish
Angolan *see* Portuguese
Angolar *see* Creole
Antilles *see* Creole
Arabic 183, 233, 240, 250–2
   Spanish 104
Aragonese *see* Spanish
Aramaic 104
Aranese *see* Occitan
Argentinian *see* Spanish
Argot *see* French
Arumanian *see* Rumanian
Asian creoles *see* creoles
Asturian *see* Spanish
Bables *see* Spanish: *Asturian*
Balkan Romance 6, 217, 340
Bantu *see* African
Basque 35, 107, 168, 205, 208, 237, 243, 245, 295, 334

Bastia *see* Corsican
Bearnese *see* Occitan
Belgian *see* French: *Walloon, Gaumais*
Bellunese *see* Italian
Berber 35
Bivian *see* Romansh
Bolivian *see* Spanish
Bonifacio *see* Corsican
Bonorvese *see* Sardinian
Bozal *see* Creole
Brava *see* Creole
Brazilian *see* Portuguese
Bregaglian *see* Romansh
Breton, Brittany 238, 334
Bulgarian 17, 91, 321

Cajun *see* French
Calabria(n) *see* Italian
Campidanese / Campidanian *see* Sard
Canadian French *see* French
Cape Verde *see* Creole
Caribbean *see* Creole
Castilian *see* Spanish
Catalan 12–15, 18, 37, 42, 56–7, 77–8, 81–6, 89, 93, 95, 100, 109, 112–14, 120–2, 129–32, 134, 138–40, 142–5, 148, 160, 171, 176, 178, 180, 183, 190, 197, 199, 200–1, 205, 208, 214–15, 216, 226, 229, 234–5, 247, 257–8, 261, 266–7, 268, 272, 275–9, 290–3, 297–300, 303, 306, 312–13, 316, 319, 321, 323–6, 332, 334, 338, 339
   Alghero, Algherese 191, 300
   Balearics 16, 191, 258; *Majorca* 122
   Barcelona 214
   Capcir 18
   Central 43
   Gerona 18
   Old 191, 311, 319
   Roussillon 191, 205, 334, 339

Standard 258, 260, 268, 306, 311
Valencian 191, 215, 311, 338
Western 43
Caviteño *see* Creole: *Philippines*
Celtic 3, 4, 29, 89, 100, 234–5, 237–8, 239, 244, 333
  Gaulish 238
Chabacano *see* Creole: *Philippines*
Chicano, Mexican-American *see* Spanish
Chtimi *see* French
Cocoliche *see* Spanish, Italian
Colombia(n) *see* Spanish
Corsica(n): 122, 195, 216, 290, 334
  Bastia 260
Creole: 219, 221, 224–5, 341
  African (Portuguese) 35, 73, 78, 220, 341
  American 35
  Angolar (Portuguese), *see* Gulf of Guinea
  Antilles (French), *see* also Guadeloupe, Grenada, Martinique, St Lucia 73, 75: *St Barth* 73, 221; *St Thomas* 73, 222
  Asian 35, 74, 77, 220
  Batticoloa see Sri Lanka Portuguese
  Brava (Portuguese), *see* Cape Verde
  Cape Verde, crioulo (Portuguese) 73, 74, 75, 77, 78, 93, 220
  Caribbean (French) *see* also Antilles 219, 220–1
  Colombia see Palenquero
  Congo see Palenquero
  Curaçao see Papiamento
  Djoe-tongo 90, 93, 95, 225
  Forro see Principe
  French 72–3, 75, 78, 80, 220–2, 303, 341
  Grenada (French) 221
  Guadeloupe (French) 68, 77, 221–2
  Guinea-Bissau, Guinea coast, crioulo (Portuguese) 73, 74, 84, 220, 341
  Gulf of Guinea (Portuguese) 74, 221; *Angolar* 88, 90, 95, 225; *Annobon* 225; *Principe* 68, 80, 220; *São Tomé* 68, 73, 74, 77, 78, 80, 88, 93, 220, 225
  Guyana (French) 80
  Haiti (French) 77, 78, 80, 91–2, 220, 223, 225
  India (Portuguese) 341
  Indian Ocean (French) 46, 68, 72–4
  Kristang (Portuguese) 73, 122
  Louisiana (French, *see* also *Cajun*) 48, 73–5, 91, 95, 219, 223, 225; *Avoyelles* 223; *Lafayette* 223; *St Martin* 75, 223; *Vacherie* (*St James*) 223
  Malacca (Portuguese) 73
  Martinique (French) 221

Mauritius (French) 72, 77, 80, 85, 91, 222
Moncó see São Tomé
New World 68, 220–1
Palenquero (Spanish) 75, 219
Papiamento, papiamentu 74, 75, 85, 90, 93, 219
Philippines, Chabacano (Spanish) 74
Port au Prince see Haiti
Portuguese (Afro-Lusitanian, Lusocreole, Indo-Portuguese) 73, 74, 75, 95, 219
Réunion (French) 74, 222, 225
São Tomé (Portuguese), *see* Gulf of Guinea
Samaraccan see Djoe-tongo
Senegal (French) 84
Seychelles (French) 72, 84
Spanish (Afro-Hispanic) 75, 219
Sri Lanka 74
St Lucia (French) 85, 221
Surinam see Djoe-tongo
Trinidad (French) 221
Croatian *see* Serbo-Croat
Cuba *see* Spanish

Dacian 245
Daco-Rumanian *see* Rumanian
Dalmatian 16, 95, 104, 113, 195, 197, 229, 292
  Istrian Peninsula 196
  Ragusa 195
  Veglia 12, 14, 16, 81, 91, 113–14, 159, 196, 229
Djoe-tongo *see* Creole
Dolomites *see* Rhaeto-Romance: *Ladin*
Dutch (*see* also Flemish) 14, 90, 93

East Romance 107, 197, 252
Egyptian 323
Engadine/Engadinish/Engadinian *see* Rhaeto-Romance
English 36, 79, 81, 90–1, 95, 104, 145, 182, 189, 214, 221, 223, 238–9, 290, 314, 329, 330, 331, 342
Etruscan 202, 235, 241–2

Fassa *see* Rhaeto-Romance: *Ladin*
Flemish 333, 334
Florentine *see* Italian: *Florence*
Francoprovençal 18, 25, 46, 116, 123, 142, 147, 176, 194, 198–9, 200, 204, 238, 240, 246, 262, 334, 339
  Alpine 118, 127, 176, 334; *Saint Martin de la Porte* (Maurienne) 118; *Valais* 128; *Val d'Aosta* (valdôtain) 194; *Vaud* 297
  Guardia Piemontese (*Calabria*) 176

Jura Vermes 22
Old 240
Frankish 105, 138–9, 233
French (Oïl) 1, 4–6, 12–13, 19–21, 23–9, 35,
    37–8, 43, 45–7, 51, 53–8, 60, 67–70, 75,
    77, 80–7, 89–95, 99–101, 104–6, 108–17,
    119–20, 122–7, 131–2, 135, 137–41,
    143–7, 149–50, 158–65, 167–9, 171–2,
    175–84, 189–94, 197–205, 210–12,
    215–16, 218, 220–6, 229–30, 233–5,
    237–40, 243–50, 255, 257, 261, 264–9,
    273–8, 285–6, 288–94, 297–312, 314–19,
    321–27, 330–1, 333–5, 339, 342
Acadia, see Canada
Alps 194
American (*see* also Canada, Louisiana)
    48–9, 222, 342; *Missouri* (Old Mines), 48
Argot 331
Belgian see Walloon
Cajun 48, 223–4
Canada 25, 27, 84, 175, 189, 223, 309, 330,
    331; *Acadian* 25, 330; *Prince Edward
    Island* 342
Central 209, 287–8, 306
Champagne 209
chtimi (Picard) 333
Creole see Creole
Demuin (Picard) 46
Dominica see Creole
East see Francoprovençal
England (Anglo-Norman) 256
Gaumais (Lorraine)
Guadeloupe see Creole
Haiti see Creole
Ile de France 210
Louisiana see cajun, Creole
Martinique see Creole
Mauritius see Creole
Medieval see Old
Middle 17, 256, 286
Missouri (Old Mines) *see* American
Modern 45, 53, 134, 173–4, 240, 248,
    259–60, 274, 276, 279, 286–7, 289, 307,
    310
Monaco see Occitan
Nice see Occitan
Norman 209, 221: *Old* (*see* also England,
    Anglo-Norman) 13
Northern 113, 134, 147, 166, 179, 204, 206,
    209, 211–12, 232–3, 238–9, 246, 247, 333
North-East 287–9
Old 12, 14, 21, 29, 36, 45, 47, 53, 56, 57,
    59, 69, 92, 100, 108–10, 112, 114, 116,
    123–5, 127–8, 139–40, 142, 147, 158,
    162–3, 173, 175, 230, 240, 246–7, 248–9,

252, 256, 267, 276, 279, 285, 287–90,
    292, 307–9, 313, 315, 321, 324, 326
Paris 189, 210, 288, 294, 331
Picardy 46, 48, 68, 204, 209, 286, 333
Popular 331, 332
Quebec see Canada
Réunion see Creole
Saintonge 246
Seychelles see Creole
South 133–4, 204, 206, 215, 246, 256,
    304
South-East 190, 194
South-West 50, 339
Standard 17, 45, 84, 89, 137, 206, 224, 259,
    262, 304–5
Swiss (*Suisse Romande*) 89, 189, 303
Trinidad and Tobago see Creole
verlan 332
Walloon 13, 89, 105, 189, 204, 333, 339;
    East 238; *Liège* 205; *Old* 204
Western 117, 123, 204, 246
Forro *see* Creole: *Principe*
Friulian, Friulan, Frioulian *see* Rhaeto-
    Romance: *Friuli*
Fronterizo/Fronteiriço *see* Portuguese

Gadera *see* Rhaeto-Romance: *Ladin*
Galego-Portuguese 191
Galician, Gallego 28, 79, 95, 122, 125, 142,
    165–6, 170, 175, 191, 194, 207, 215, 231,
    252, 256, 265, 334, 338
Gallo-Italian *see* Italian
Gallo-Roman (*see* also Latin) 197
Galluran *see* Sard
Gardena *see* Rhaeto- Romance: *Ladin*
Gascon *see* Occitan
Gaumais *see* French
Genoese *see* Italian: *Genoa*
German 4, 5, 14, 15, 17, 20, 79, 95, 112, 118,
    192, 193, 206, 214, 233, 238, 240,
    247–50, 273, 304, 334, 337, 343
    Swiss 193, 340
Germanic 8, 14, 36, 63, 81, 92, 98, 102,
    104–5, 117, 139, 157–8, 167, 200, 206,
    211, 232, 233, 238, 245–50, 256, 291,
    303, 322, 325, 326, 333–4, 339, 340
Greek 3, 13, 14, 84, 99, 108, 126, 131–3,
    139–40, 144, 147, 150, 165, 171, 175,
    228, 233, 237–8, 239, 319, 324, 325,
    340
    Byzantine 65
Gypsy, Romany 340
Grenadian *see* Creole: *Grenada*
Guadeloupe *see* French, Creole
Guineense *see* Creole: *Guinea-Bissau*

Haitian *see* Creole: *Haiti*
Hebrew 251, 342, 343
  Biblical 343
Hungarian *see* Magyar

Iberian 133, 143–4, 149, 166, 191, 199, 208,
    242–3, 245, 290, 312–13, 314, 321, 322,
    323, 339, 341
  Northern 251
  Western 132, 136–7, 209
  Proto-Ibero-Romance 197
Indian Ocean *see* Creole
Indo-European 36, 75, 156, 179, 185, 200,
    234, 299–300
Istriot 196
Istro-Rumanian *see* Rumanian
Italian 3, 6, 12, 14–15, 19–21, 23, 38, 40–5,
    47–50, 53, 55–7, 62–7, 77–87, 89–95,
    99–102, 105, 107, 109–15, 117, 120–5,
    127–8, 130–1, 133, 135, 138–9, 140–5,
    148–50, 158–60, 162–3, 167–70, 171,
    175–6, 177, 179–84, 189–90, 195, 197–8,
    200–4, 212–13, 216, 229, 234–7, 240,
    245–6, 250, 256–7, 259, 261–2, 264–72,
    275–9, 286, 290–4, 297–301, 303–4,
    306–7, 309, 312, 316–23, 325–7, 334–6
  Abruzzo 13–14, 23–4, 61, 62, 64, 77, 79,
    101, 119, 160, 198; *Sulmona* 62; *Western*
    61, 64
  Apulia 198
  American 335
  Asolano 21
  Bari 61
  Bologna see Romagna
  Bormio 24
  Calabria 18, 83
  Campania 57, 336
  Carpignano 18
  Central 101, 120, 122, 129, 148, 149, 246,
    267, ?92
  Chieti
  Cocoliche (⌣   ınish, Argentina)
    339
  Cori (*see* Latium)
  Corsica (*see* Corsican)
  Cremona 50, 257
  Emilia Romagna 13–14, 17, 81, 336
  Florence see Tuscany
  Gallo-Italian 217
  Genoa 18, 48, 53, 291, 336
  Greek-speaking areas 233
  Imola 25
  Ischia 160
  Liguria 17–18, 50, 190, 213
  Latium (*Lazio*) 18; *Cori* 18

  La Spezia 198, 229
  Livorno 241
  Lombardy 13–14, 17, 52, 192, 291, 336
  Lucania (*Basilicata*) 6, 61, 62, 83, 120,
    200, 297
  Lucca 241
  Marche (Marchigiano, Marsian)
    Servigliano, Ascoli Piceno 18, 62
  Medieval see Old
  Milan 17, 24–5, 336
  Monaco (Monégasque) *see* Occitan
  Naples (Neapolitan) 18
  Nice (Niçois) *see* Occitan
  Northern 17, 41, 45–6, 48, 51–4, 77, 79, 88,
    104, 120, 122, 132, 137, 149, 178, 192,
    201, 206, 213, 217, 230, 232, 236, 238,
    241, 244–5, 247, 256, 257, 267, 277, 291,
    299, 303–4, 305, 310, 336
  North-eastern 196, 198
  Novara 18
  Old 18, 21, 79, 100, 112, 149, 298, 309,
    313–14, 325
  Padua 336
  Papal States 204, 336
  Piedmont 17, 24, 297, 336
  Pugliese see Apulia
  Rimini 198, 229
  Romagna 17, 81
  Rome 213, 236, 336
  Salento 64, 237
  San Marino 190
  San Tommaso 23
  Sardinia see Sard
  Sicily 18, 24, 64, 91, 122, 133, 183, 237,
    256, 336, 337
  Siena 42
  South 18, 41, 48, 57, 61, 63–4, 77, 79, 88,
    101, 105, 112, 120, 122, 131–2, 134,
    136–7, 149, 164–5, 197, 217, 229, 233–4,
    236–7, 243, 246, 286, 292, 311
  South-Central 64, 120, 165, 236
  Standard 7, 37, 38, 41, 104, 136, 148,
    160, 234, 236, 258–9, 276, 278, 290,
    292, 303
  Swiss (Tessin, Ticino) 18, 46, 190, 202, 337
  Trevi 120
  Tridentine 30
  Turin 303, 336
  Tuscany 17, 24, 41–2, 49, 64, 66, 77, 124,
    195, 202, 212, 216, 234–5, 241, 256, 261,
    268, 272, 290, 325, 336; *North* 235; *Old*
    50, 311
  Umbria 120
  Veneto (Venetan) 18, 21, 41, 52, 82, 192,
    194, 336, 337; *Central* 53

Venice (Venetian) 17, 24, 52, 53, 88, 195, 196, 198
Italic 98, 202, 228

Judeo-Romance 342
Judeo-Spanish, Sefardí, Sephardic *see* Spanish
Jugoslavia *see* Yugoslavia

Ladino, Ladin *see* Spanish, Rhaeto-Romance, Dalmatian
Languedoc *see* Occitan
Latin 1–3, 7, 9, 12, 21, 36–40, 43, 47, 55–61, 63, 65, 67, 69–70, 75, 76, 78, 79, 80, 83–118, 120–6, 129–33, 135, 138–45, 147–54, 157–8, 160–3, 166–7, 170, 175, 177–81, 183–5, 197–8, 199, 201–3, 207, 211, 218, 227–9, 231–3, 235, 238–40, 242–4, 248, 250–2, 254–5, 262, 275–80, 286–7, 291–2, 294–5, 298–302, 305–7, 309–12, 314, 317–18, 320–1, 323–7, 333
Christian 126
Church 104
Classical 36, 81, 177
Gallo-Roman 238–9
Imperial 232
Late 99, 102–3, 111, 113–14, 129, 135, 144, 154, 158, 177, 179, 229, 231, 235, 314
Medieval 104, 153, 344
Neo-Latin 104
Popular 38, 98
Vulgar 4, 6, 98, 102–3, 197
Western 327
Latin American 41, 83, 136, 169, 319, 341–2
Latium *see* Italian
Leonese *see* Spanish
Ligurian *see* Italian
Limousin *see* Occitan
lingua franca 181
Livinallonga *see* Rhaeto-Romance: *Ladin*
Logudorese, Logudorian *see* Sardinian
Lombard *see* Italian: *Lombardy*
Louisiana *see* Creole and French: *Cajun*
Lucanian *see* Italian

Macedo-Rumanian *see* Rumanian
Madinka 84
Magyar (Hungarian) 253, 254, 324, 340
Malaccan *see* Creole: Malacca
Maltese 35
Marches, Marsian *see* Italian: *Marche*
Martinique *see* Creole
Mauritian *see* Creole: *Mauritius*
Megleno-Rumanian *see* Rumanian

Mexican *see* Spanish
Milanese *see* Italian: *Milan*
Moldavian, Moldovan *see* Rumanian
Moncó *see* Creole: *São Tomé*
Monégasque *see* Occitan: *Monaco*
Mozarabic *see* Spanish
Murcian *see* Spanish

Neapolitan *see* Italian: *Naples*
Niçois *see* Occitan: *Nice*
Nidwaldisch *see* Rhaeto-Romance: *Romansh*
Norse 239
Nuorese-Bittese *see* Sard

Oberhalbsteinisch *see* Rhaeto-Romance: *Romansh*
Oberwaldisch *see* Rhaeto-Romance: *Romansh*
Occitan, Oc 12–14, 37, 42–3, 56–7, 79, 81–2, 84, 87, 91, 93, 95, 100, 105–6, 113–14, 117, 120, 123, 125, 132, 134, 137–8, 139, 161, 171, 178, 183, 190, 194, 197–8, 200, 204, 206, 229–30, 239–47, 261, 267, 270, 272, 278–90, 292, 294, 302–3, 311, 313, 319, 320, 321, 325, 326, 332, 334–5
Aranés/Aranese see Val d'Aran, Vall d'Aran
Bearnese 122, 130, 133, 190, 206, 237
Biarritz 205
Foix 20
Gascony 122, 205–6, 230, 260, 265, 310, 313, 324, 335
Gévaudan 303
Languedoc, Western 258
Limousin 105
Menton 205
Monaco, Monégasque 190
Nice, Niçois 190, 213
Old 3, 57, 82, 89, 116, 135, 190–1, 239
Provence, Provençal 3, 43, 105, 216
Pyrenees 190–1, 205–4
South-west 174
Standard 216
Val d'Aran 190
Western 122, 176

Palenquero *see* Creole
Paninarese *see* Italian
Papiamento *see* Creole
Parisian *see* French: *Paris*
Persian 321
Philippine Spanish *see* Creole
Picard *see* French: *Picardy*
Piedmontese *see* Italian: *Piedmont*

Portuguese 6, 12–16, 25, 27–9, 35, 40–2, 47–9,
56–9, 67, 77, 79–91, 93–4, 100, 109–14,
120, 124–5, 127–8, 131, 134–6, 138–9,
140–5, 148–50, 160–1, 165–6, 169–70,
171–2, 177–84, 189, 191, 197–201,
208–9, 215, 218, 220, 224, 229, 231,
234–5, 237, 239, 243–6, 250–3, 257–8,
261–2, 264, 266, 269–72, 275, 279, 290,
292, 294, 297–304, 306–7, 309–13, 316,
318, 319, 321, 323–7, 334, 339, 340
  Angolar see Creole
  Asian 220
  Brazil 42, 49, 51, 55, 144, 166–7, 170,
  172–6, 209–10, 220, 231, 243, 262, 264,
  330, 341, 339; *Rio* 231
  Cape Verde see Creole
  Creole see Creole
  European 170, 175–6, 209, 231, 243–4,
  262, 264
  Fronteiriço / Fronterizo 339
  Guinea-Bissau see Creole
  Lisbon 42, 209
  Macau 220
  Malacca see Creole
  Mozambique 341
  Old 82, 122, 170, 178, 244, 261, 309
  Northern 28
  São Tomé see Creole
  Sri Lanka 74, 220; *Batticoloa* 220
  Standard 141, 170, 252
Principe *see* Creole
Provençal *see* Occitan
Puter *see* Rhaeto-Romance: *Ladin*

Québécois *see* French: *Canada*
Quechuan *see* Amerindian

Réunion *see* Creole
Rhaeto-Romance 22, 44, 57, 117–18, 122–3,
192–3, 194, 200, 260, 277, 290, 303, 310,
324, 326, 337, 340
  Engadine Engadinish/Engadinian/Ladin
  13–15, 77, 81, 86, 88–9, 91–2, 104,
  113–14, 122–3, 128, 131, 180, 193,
  196–7, 200–1, 217, 226, 229, 245–6, 247,
  260, 277, 278–9, 291, 299–300, 306–7,
  311, 321, 322, 325, 326; *Inn Valley* 193;
  Lower (Vallader) 44, 193, 260; *Remus*
  44; *Santa Maria* 44; *Mustair, Val* 88,
  193; *Upper (Puter)* 44, 193, *Zernez* 44;
  Zuoz 44
  Friuli (Friulian, Friulan, Frioulian) 12–14,
  15, 21, 27, 45, 48, 50, 78, 79, 82, 130, 133,
  169, 193–4, 197, 200, 218, 261, 302, 337
  Italy (*see* also Dolomites, Friuli) 117

Ladin, Dolomites 15, 45, 82, 87, 104, 200,
337; *Alto Adige* 337; *Ampezzo* 45; *Fassa*
(Val di) 200; *Gardena* 82, 87; *Pàdola*
(Comelico) 45
Romansh Romontsch, Roumanche,
Roumantsch-Grischun, Upper Rhine
44, 95, 105; *Surmeiran* Surmeirish,
Oberhalbsteinisch, Unterhalbsteinisch
44, 63, 127, 193; *Surselvan, Sursilvan*
Surselvisch, Oberwaldisch, Churwälsch
17, 21, 23, 44, 54, 55, 77, 79, 81, 84, 86,
88, 105, 117–19, 123, 159, 167, 176, 180,
193, 217, 249, 277, 279, 291, 303–4, 325,
326; *Brigels* 44; *Old* 64; *Tavetsch* 44;
Sutselvan, Sutsilvan (Sutselvisch,
Nidwaldisch) 193
Switzerland (Graubunden, Grisons) (*see*
also Romansh, Engadine) 36, 63, 88,
117, 125, 127, 131, 180, 192, 216–17,
239, 278, 309, 340
Roman *see* Italian: *Rome*
Romany *see* Gipsy
Rumanian/Romanian 4, 6, 8, 12–15, 29,
36–8, 43, 48–9, 57, 63, 65–7, 69, 77,
79–84, 86–95, 100–1, 105, 107, 109–15,
120, 122–4, 127, 130, 132–4, 137–44,
147–8, 150, 157–9, 161, 164–6, 169,
171–2, 176, 179, 181–3, 185, 189, 194–5,
197–201, 207, 213–14, 217–18, 225,
229–30, 233–5, 243, 245–7, 250, 252–4,
256, 261, 263–4, 266–7, 275, 277–92,
297, 300, 302, 306–7, 309, 311–12, 314,
316, 317, 319, 321–7
  Albania 217, 233
  Arumanian (Macedo-Rumanian) 89, 217,
  302, 319
  Banat 171
  Bucharest 213
  Daco-Rumanian 16, 28, 88, 91–2, 122, 139,
  171, 196, 207, 213, 217–18, 319; *Old* 16
  Danube, South of 16, 89, 122, 165, 207,
  243, 250, 253, 321
  Danube delta 194
  Istro-Rumanian 43, 88–9, 93, 95, 196, 218,
  233, 340
  Macedo-Rumanian (Arumanian) 217, 233
  Megleno-Rumanian 92, 217
  Moldavian (Moldovan) 139, 169
  Old 309
  Oltenian 137
  Standard see Daco-Rumanian
  Translyvania 169

São Tomense *see* Creole: *São Tomé*
Sard(inia) 13, 20, 24, 36, 38, 42, 57, 79–81,

86–95, 100, 107, 113–15, 120, 122–3,
127–31, 135, 148, 157–8, 165, 174–5,
179, 183, 185, 195, 197, 199, 200–3, 217,
226, 229–30, 235, 246, 261, 266, 268,
275–9, 286, 290–3, 300, 302, 306,
309–11, 316, 317, 323, 324, 326, 336–7
Bitti 235
Campidanese, Campidanian 13–14, 25, 42,
85, 195, 236, 292–3, 309
Gallurese, Galluran 195
Logudorese, Logudorian 12–14, 42, 82,85,
86, 229, 239, 290, 309, 322
Northern 195
Nuorese-Bittese (Nuoro) 81, 84, 85, 128,
174, 235
Proto-Sardinian 197
Sarrabus 25
Sassarese (Sassari) 195
Sassarese *see* Sardinian
Scottish 238
Sefardí, Sephardic *see* Spanish
Serbo-Croat 93, 195
Seychellois *see* Creole: *Seychelles*
Sicilian *see* Italian: *Sicily*
Slavonic 17, 29, 65, 83, 88–9, 93, 96, 123,
171–2, 181, 213, 243, 252–4, 256, 290,
321, 324, 325, 326, 340
Slovenian 193
Spanish 12–16, 35, 40, 42, 47, 55–9, 63,
66–7, 77–85, 87, 89–91, 93–4, 100,
104, 109–14, 119–22, 124–5, 127–8,
131, 134–6, 138–40, 142–6, 148–50,
158–60, 162–3, 165–6, 168–70, 171,
175–80, 182–4, 189, 191, 197–202,
207–9, 215, 219, 226, 229–32, 234–5,
237, 240, 242–3, 245–6, 250–1, 256–8,
261–72, 275, 277–9, 286–7, 289, 292–5,
297–303, 306–7, 309–19, 321–4, 326,
335, 338–41
Amazon, Peruvian 242
American 48, 50, 78, 208–9, 218, 226, 230,
252, 262, 310, 341, 342
Andalusia(n), Andalucia 25, 49, 230,
251–2, 323, 338
Andes 137
Aragon(ese) 50, 130, 133, 191, 207, 215,
237, 261, 319, 338
Argentina River Plate, (*see* also Cocoliche)
49, 78, 322, 330, 339
Asturias, bables 50, 60–3, 101, 119–20,
159–60, 207, 215, 338
Bolivia 341
Canary Islands 252, 341
Castilian, Castile 122, 133, 139–40, 148,
198, 208–9, 215, 242, 251, 256, 258, 295,

310–12, 319, 332, 338
Old Castile, Castillo Viejo 242
Chicano Mexican-American 330
Chile 49
Cocoliche see Argentina, also Italian
Colombia (*see* also *Palenquero*) 74, 231
Costa Rica 67
Creole see Creole
Cuba 341
Ecuador 262
European 184, 209
Fronterizo see Portuguese: *Fronteiriço*
Judeo-Spanish see Sefardí
Judezmo see Sefardí
Galician, Gallego see Galician
Ladino see Sefardí, American
Leon(ese) 50, 207–8, 319
Madrid 263
Medieval see Old
Mexico (*see* also *Chicano*) 25
Mozarabic 207–8
Murcia(n) 207–8
Nicaragua 341
North of Spain 50, 262, 263
North America 50
Old 16, 56, 59, 79, 82, 109, 121, 139, 159,
178–9, 231, 245, 252, 261, 268, 275, 293,
296, 299, 309–10, 313, 324
Palenquero see Creole
Paraguay 262, 341
Peru 67
Philippines (*see* also Creole) 74, 93
Puerto Rico 67
San Domingo (Dominican Republic) 51
Sefardí, Sephardic, Judeo-Spanish 95, 218,
233, 342–3
Seville 252, 311
Southern Spain 208
Standard 141, 311
Toledo 208
Uruguay 339
Sursilvan, Surselvisch *see* Rhaeto-Romance:
Romansh
Sutsilvan, Sutselvisch *see* Rhaeto-Romance:
Romansh
Swedish 239

Tessinese, Tessin, Ticino see Italian: *Swiss*
Thracian 245
Thraco-Dacian 92, 243
Trinidad *see* Creole
Turkish 96, 254

Uruguayan *see* Spanish: *Uruguay* and
Portuguese: *fronteiriço*

Valencian *see* Catalan
Vallader Ladin *see* Rhaeto-Romance: *Ladin*
Venetan *see* Italian: *Veneto*
Venetian *see* Italian: *Venice*
Walloon *see* French
Welsh 105, 238

West Romance 38, 107, 119, 171, 177, 181,
    197, 213, 234–5, 237, 244

Yugoslavia 340

Zamboangueño *see* Creole: *Philippines*

SUBJECT INDEX

ablative 81
abstract *see* noun
'abstract' analysis 26
Abstand ('stand-off') language 206–7
accent, accentuation 40, 47, 79, 99, 100,
    108–11, 154, 157, 235, 285–7
  placement 108
  stress 174, 246
  tonal 108
accommodation 206, 218
accusative, acc. *see* case
accusative + infinitive 143–6, 163
actualization 37
adjectival article 148
adjective placement 36, 146–7, 201
adjectives 36, 55, 58, 59, 60, 62, 67, 81, 83,
    86, 90, 105, 118, 123, 128, 146, 277, 279,
    325–6,
  adnominal ('epithet' or 'attributive')
    117–18, 129
  determining 146
  nominalized, substantivized 59
  predicative (i.e. post-copular) 257, 277
adstratum 232–3
adverbs, adverbializer 74, 81–3, 90
affective 146, 147
affix, affixation 81–7, 130–1, 174, 178
  inflectional 174
affricate, *see* consonant
agent 19, 179
agglutination 22, 74, 75, 84, 123, 178, 200
agreement 23, 36, 48, 63, 64, 68, 135, 141,
    143, 148, 168, 201, 257–61, 269–71,
    286
  verb 270–4
Albigensian crusade 190
Alliance Israelite Universelle 343
allophone, allophonic 241, 287, 295
ambigeneous *see* gender
analogy 57, 134, 297–301, 313, 319

analytic 37, 136, 156, 177, 185, 200, 314
anaphoric 126, 129, 167
anaptyxis 99, 109
animate 55, 58, 66, 69, 121, 262–3
apheresis 290
apocopation, apocope 50
apophony 162, 297–8
Appendix Probi 12, 15, 102
approximant 242, 289
archetype 37
argot 331
argument 52, 129, 168, 257, 267
article (*see* also definite, indefinite, partitive)
    59, 61, 64, 87, 123, 126–7, 128, 173,
    277
articulation
  apical 113
  dental 113
  laminal 113
aspect, *see* marker, TAM, perfect, imperfect,
    progressive
aspectual forms 75, 134, 156, 175–6, 339
  periphrastic 156
assibilation 140
assimilation 110, 112, 115, 156, 234, 236,
    248, 268, 287, 322
  regressive 27, 291, 293
assonance 27, 29, 159, 287
atlas, linguistic 202–5
atonic 15, 29, 36, 44, 100
attitudes 343–4
attrition, phonetic 52
augmentatives 84
Ausbau ('built-up') language 206, 207
auxiliary 7, 15–24, 36, 75, 130, 135–6, 154
  modal 166
  perfect 257–61
auxiliary selection 15–24, 257–8, 331
    BE 16, 20, 180
    HAVE 20, 257

bables 338
back slang, *verlan* 332
backing 288
Balkanization 207
Bartsch's Law 247–8, 289
bilingualism 232, 282, 335–8, 341
    asymmetrical 334
Binnendiglossie see diglossia
bioprogramme 224
bleaching 6, 18
borrowing 85, 93, 151, 185, 244–5, 250, 325,
    235, 330, 339, 341
bound forms 40
Bourbon 208
breaking (*see* also Bartsch's Law) 159
bricolage 317

cajun 223
Carolingian reforms 152–3, 231
case 12, 115–20, 122–4, 127, 140, 154, 155,
    199, 230 263, 327
    ablative 314
    accusative 12, 54, 61, 63, 119, 122, 124–5,
        127, 129, 229, 259, 262, 286, 305–6; per-
        sonal, prepositional (PA) 121–3
    dative 21, 78, 121, 124–5, 127, 169, 201,
        306; ethic 125, 266
    direct 123
    genitive 123, 275, 278, 314
    nominative 78, 115–20, 123–4, 127, 273
    oblique 115–20, 123–4
    vocative 123
case marker 275
case vide see chain-shift 161
causative, factitive 7, 144–5, 164, 201, 266
ceceo 252
cedilla 140
centralization, vowel 140, 243–4, 252
chain-shift 161, 237
    drag-chain 161, 239
    push-chain 161, 239, 240
chtimi 333
circumflex 140
classification 71, 196–206
    genetic 196–200
    historical / synchronic 199–200
    quantitative 199
    subgrouping 197
    typological 200
clause
    complement, completive 144, 149, 163
    finite 144–5
    main, matrix 163, 248
    subordinate 142–5
clause union or matiness 263

clefting 286
clitic, cliticization 21, 36, 52, 54, 77, 78, 79,
    121, 125, 170, 186, 281, 303, 305
    adverbial 20, 169, 251, 261–2, 267, 268–9
    array, cluster 167, 266–9
    climbing 21, 263–6
    doubling, copying 122, 168, 201, 253, 265,
        341
    enclisis 44, 45, 50, 127, 169, 170, 174, 267,
        310
    neuter 169
    object 36, 45, 103, 121, 127–8, 129, 167–74
        phonological 51
    proclisis 46, 52, 169, 174, 185, 265, 267
    reflexive 78, 264, 266
    subject 46, 47, 52, 70, 202
    syntactic 51
cluster, consonantal 107, 291–4
    medial 15, 101, 112, 113
    word-initial 112
coda, syllable-final 42, 66, 108, 160, 287, 290
code-switching 221, 223
codifiers, codification 58, 210, 214, 255, 267,
    283, 335
CODOFIL 223
cognate 11, 12, 85, 273, 311, 313
cognate object 24
cognitive structure 6
collective 88, 275
comparative construction 314–17
comparativist, comparison 11, 71, 97, 149,
    181
compensatory lengthening 108, 160
complement 313, 316
complement clause, complementation 144,
    163, 186, 203, 304, 314, 317
complementizer 141, 149, 307, 315
    prepositional 163
    QU- 145 163, 307, 317
complex nucleus 161
compound, compounding, compound
    words 15, 23, 81, 200, 310
compound tenses (*see* perfect, pluperfect,
    surcomposé) 132, 137, 154, 156, 201,
    257–61
conative 265
concrete 27, 61, 66
conditional (*see also* tense, future in the
    past) 16, 133
conflict 330, 332–5, 337
conjugation *see* verb
conjugation-class 130–1, 318
conservatism 326–7
consonant 62, 65, 69, 99, 110, 113, 197
    affricate 12, 139, 193, 240

apical 294
back 112
continuant 242
dental 113, 139, 240, 251, 294
flap 294
fricative 113, 251, 294, 295
front 111, 113
interdental 295
intervocalic 26, 27, 234–7, 281, 327
labial 289
lateral 326
long (geminate) 106, 111, 112, 140, 199,
234–7, 290, 292, 293, 294, 326
nasal 25–9, 42, 247
obstruent 247, 290, 292–3
palatal, palatalized 110, 111, 289
palato-alveolar, postalveolar 12, 113
plosive, stop 113, 241, 281, 295
retroflex 244, 326
sibilant 113, 234, 251–2, 281, 295–6; apical 231, 251; dental 12, 294
syllable-final *see* coda
velar 111, 112, 115, 239, 294, 295, 298, 326
voiced 114, 295
voiceless (surds) 199, 241
consonantal clusters 43, 111
contact 345
contamination 82
continuous *see* progressive
continuum
creole 221
Romance 94–6, 163, 223, 339
control constructions 163
convergence 155–86
copula 179, 257, 312, 313
core languages 92
corpora, language 330
corpus planning *see* planning
Council of Tours (813) 152
count noun 63
creole 25, 35, 36, 39, 51, 54, 55, 68–75, 80,
90, 92, 156, 166, 175–6, 185, 219–26,
340, 341, 342
creolization 3, 93, 96, 167
Crusades 172, 255, 343
cultismos see Latinisms
cursus 286
cycle, cyclical 176
Cyrillic script 28, 139, 190

Dark Ages 103, 227, 251
dative *see* pronoun, case
declension *see* noun
decreolization 75, 76
default 291

definite article 36, 59–61, 66, 68, 123, 126–7,
129, 154, 199, 275–6, 286, 306, 318, 326,
340
definiteness 121, 168, 269
deixis *see* demonstrative
delayed release 240
delinking 161, 239
democratization 344
demonstrative, deictic 47, 59, 68, 126,
279–80, 286, 318
distal 125–6, 129, 278–9, 317
middle distance 279
neuter 279–80
proximal 279
denasalization 27, 28
dental *see* consonant
depreciative 89
derivation 58, 84, 85, 91, 97, 101, 200, 254,
309
derived subject 24
determiner 123, 201, 274–81, 286, 317–18
zero, non-overt 275, 276
devoicing 247, 252, 295–6
diachronic 11, 27, 38, 70
diacritic 139
dialect 11, 21, 39, 40, 41, 45, 46, 49, 53, 57,
61, 62, 64, 68, 75, 78, 92, 101, 121, 184,
190, 192, 194–5, 202–6, 210, 226, 241,
283, 305, 331, 333, 337, 340
dialectalization 227
dialectology 226, 329
dialectometry 202–6, 226
differentiation *see* dissimilation
diglossia 153, 184, 232, 335–8, 341
Binnendiglossie 335
dilalia 336
digraph 158
dilalia *see* diglossia
diminutive 37, 58, 67, 84, 101, 111, 324
diphthong 13, 25–7, 161–2, 230, 238–9, 241,
285, 288–9
falling 158, 247
heavy or light 159–61
levelling, fusion, resolution 160, 285–6,
288
nasal 25, 42
rising 158
upgliding 158
diphthongization 9, 102, 108, 157–9, 186,
236, 247–8, 253, 276, 287–9, 298, 327
conditioned 159
spontaneous 158
direct object *see* object dissimilation
disjunctive 51, 52, 54, 79, 124–5, 278
dislocation 286

left 46, 129, 168, 201
  right 129
dissimilation 134, 158, 248, 292, 322
DOMs (*Départements d'Outre-Mer*) 341
doublet 66, 288, 294, 319
doubling *see* consonant, long
doubling, syntactic 62
drag-chain *see* chain-shift
drift 155, 176

e instable, *e caduc*, mute *e* 27, 173, 292
'Each word has its own history' 203
ellipsis 54, 314, 315, 318
enclisis *see* clitic
epenthesis 28, 286, 291–4
Equi-NP *see* control constructions
ergative 20
ethnicity 192
etymology, etymon 13, 44, 73, 96, 100, 108,
  118, 127, 244, 250, 263, 298, 305, 321
Eurotype 200
exaptation 119, 310–19
experiencer 19
expletive 46, 52, 168, 304, 314
extrametrical 27

factitive, causative 7, 144–5
family, language 38–9, 71, 96
family tree 197
feature splitting 242, 287
feminine *see* gender
filter 267
finite *see* verb
fission 239
flipflop 160
forclusif 303, 305
fortition 234, 285
français avancé 156, 220
français fondamental 151
francitan 335
Franco-Prussian war (1870–1) 5
Franks 245
free form 83
French Revolution (1789) 203, 211, 288
frequency 90
fricative *see* consonant
fronterizo 339
fronting 237–41, 259, 296
functional load 161
function class 80
function words 9, 72
future 77, 103, 177–9, 186
  GO-future 176
  synthetic 177–9
  stem 178–9

Gallicism 183
geminate *see* consonant, long
gemination, doubling 234–7
gender 14, 36, 55–69, 70, 83, 96, 119, 125,
  141, 169, 246, 253, 278, 286
  ambigeneous 63–6
  assignment 69
  classes 55
  feminine 14, 44, 55, 56, 57, 58, 63, 64, 65,
    66, 67, 68, 88, 123
  fluctuating 56, 58
  function 66
  masculine 55, 56, 57, 58, 59, 60, 61, 62, 64,
    65, 66, 69, 117–18, 119, 127–8
  neuter 55, 56, 58, 59, 60, 64, 65, 70, 83, 87,
    88, 101, 327; abstract 60; article 61–2,
    318; collective 61–2; *neutro de materia*
    60
generative grammar 6, 19, 27, 45
  'classic' 26
generic meaning 275
gerund(ive) 75, 174, 175
genitive *see* case
Gipsy 213, 340
glide, palatal 43, 45, 111, 113, 159, 230, 287
glottalization 231
Golden Age 156, 183, 228
gorgia toscana *see* spirantization
Graeco-Latin tradition 140
grammar 115, 140–1, 157, 171, 208, 220,
  280, 284, 341
grammarians 126, 128, 140
grammaticalization 6–7, 18, 70, 76, 121–2,
  135–6, 258, 268, 273
graphy *see* spelling
grasseyé (*see* uvular *r*) 294

hardening 45, 114, 298
harǧa's 251
heterosyllabic 292
hiatus 289
historiography 10
homonyms, homonymy, homophony 45, 47,
  66, 67, 286
honorifics 48, 49, 53, 78
hypercharacterization 305–19
hypercorrection, hyperurbanism 44, 117,
  265, 291

iconocity 156
Idealism 5, 6
idiolect 189
imperfect *see* tense
imparisyllabic 117
imperative 132, 142, 143, 173

imperfect endings 133–5
imperfective 93
impersonal (*see* also indeterminate agent)
22, 24, 46, 53, 118
inanimate 65, 69, 262–3, 306
inceptive 299
inchoative 131
incorporation 147
indefinite article 59, 68, 87, 275, 276
indeterminate agent, impersonal 268–74
indicative *see* tense
indirect speech 133
infectum and perfectum 132, 179
infinitive 75, 130, 144, 163–6, 175–6, 186,
201, 263–5, 340
conjugated, inflected, personal 41, 132,
142, 145, 165–6, 209
historical 163
prolative 163
substantivized 164–5, 173
inflection 7, 40, 45, 51, 52, 109, 115, 118,
122–4, 130
ending 49, 50
personal 40, 52
verb 36
inherent pronominal *see* pronominal verb
insecurity, linguistic 332
intensive affix 84–5
interdental *see* consonant
interlanguage 282, 344
interlects 38, 335, 339
'internal'/'external' relationships 115
interrogative 143, 249, 306–10, 318
intervocalic 26, 27, 94, 234–7, 281, 294
intransitive 19, 136
inversion 309
complex 249, 309
interrogative 249, 331
stylistic 308
subject 20
invisible hand 156
irregular 130, 133, 134, 296, 300, 313
isogloss 202, 204, 246
iterative 85

Jacobin 211
jodization 103, 111, 253
jota 251

koine, koinai 38, 202, 204, 206, 210, 217, 338
koineization 206, 208, 336

labial 115
labio-velar 162
laminalization 231

language acquisition device 152
language community 71
language death 93, 334
language loyalty 337
language names 104
language nationalism 332
language of revolt 331
langue romane 3, 191, 246
Latinisms, learned word, *cultismo* 138–9,
150–1
Latinitas 344
lax 295
leísmo 263, 285
lenition 234–7, 285, 336
lexicalization 20, 22, 28, 29, 161, 236, 288
lexicochronology 197–8, 226
lexicology 320
lexicon, vocabulary 9, 11, 35, 37, 39, 70, 71,
80, 87–94, 96, 97, 100, 102, 106, 110,
138–9, 150–1, 181–4, 209, 220, 224, 244,
250, 253, 280, 284, 319–26
lexifier languages 35, 72, 80, 90
liaison 26
lingua franca 181, 255, 344
lingua do preto 219
linguistic atlas *see* atlas
linguistic market 330
literacy 211, 333
literary language 36, 42, 43, 45, 94, 136, 184,
190–1, 215
loan-translation (calque) 253
loanwords, borrowings 69, 83, 93, 150,
182–3, 238, 241, 243, 250, 252, 253, 322
locational adverbial 126
locational goal 124
locative 261, 323
Loi des Trois Consonnes 293

manner 27
marker 27, 58, 66, 73, 74, 122, 134
dative 121
feminine 55, 64
gender 66–8, 126
graphical 55
partitive 124
person 39, 51, 53, 54, 72, 79, 202, 230, 286
tense/aspect/modal (*TAM*) 72–6, 115;
ANTERIOR 76; *CONDITIONAL* 73; *COMPLE-
TIVE* 73; *FUTURE* 72, 73, 74, 76; *HABITU-
AL* 73, 74, 76; *IMPERFECTIVE* 74;
IRREAL(IS) 74, 76; *ITERATIVE* 74; *NEGA-
TIVE* 74; *NON-PUNCTUAL* 74, 76; *PAST* 72,
76; *PERFECTIVE* 72, 74; *PROGRESSIVE* 73
maroon 90, 219
marranos 342

mass-noun *see* noun, non-count; mass
matiness *see* clause union
matrix clause *see* clause, main
mechanization 6
medial cluster 15
metalanguage 10, 140
metaphony, umlaut 60, 159–61, 253, 300
metaphor 321
metarule 155
metathesis 14
metric 119
middle 20
minimal pair 106, 180, 186, 243, 289, 295
minority language 333, 337
modal, modality 36, 72, 75, 266
monophthong, monophthongization 161–2, 287
mood (*see* tense, indicative; imperative; subjunctive) 141, 143
mora 106, 108, 158–9, 288
moriscos 251
morpheme 76, 84, 95, 108
    structure 9
morphologization 6, 9, 29, 159–60
morphology 9, 27, 35–6, 39, 47, 49, 53–6, 59, 60, 70–1, 90, 115–16, 121, 126, 129, 131–4, 136, 140–1, 154–5, 164, 176–7, 246, 280, 284, 296–302
    case 140
    verb 130–2
morphophonology 65
morphosyntax 9, 11, 35, 39, 69, 72, 248–50
mozarabic, musta'ribun 251
multiple causation 284
mute *e, see e instable*
mutual intelligibility 254, 339
muwaššah poems 251

nasalization, nasality 8, 9, 24–9, 42, 119, 140, 199, 235, 292–3, 327
    nasal hardening 28
    nasal occlusion 28
    nasal vowels 24–6, 29; height 28
nation–state 211–14
nationhood 214–17, 283
negation 148–9, 154, 302–5, 315
    expletive negative 149, 315
    negative attraction, concord 148–9
    negative incorporation 148
    negative operator 304–5
    negative polarity 148, 302, 316
    partial 149
    reinforcer 303–5
Neogrammarian 4, 150, 203
neuter *see* gender

nominal 36, 37, 45, 79, 96, 115–17, 123
nominalization 132
nominative, nom. *see* case
nominativus pendens 201
non-count *see* noun, non-count; mass
non-standard usage 21, 22, 51, 66, 68, 184, 202–3, 254, 262, 280, 296–7, 308, 310–11, 330, 333
non-pro-drop *see* pro-drop
norm, normative 2, 58, 182
normalization 215
normativization 215, 255
noun 36, 45, 46, 56, 58, 60, 61, 65, 67, 68, 69, 73, 77, 80, 116–18, 120, 123, 126, 128–9, 323–5
    abstract 55, 58, 61, 66, 126
    agentive 85
    ambigenous 63, 65, 66
    collective 122
    concrete 323
    count 118
    declension; first 55, 123; fourth 57; second 55–6, 119, 123; third 56, 57, 64, 68, 120
    inherited 73
    instrumental 85
    non-count, mass 60, 61, 62, 63, 66, 118, 120
NP (noun phrase) 129–30, 186, 259
nuclear vowel, nucleus *see* vowel
    complex 161
null subject *see* pro-drop
number, noun 37, 126, 141, 229
    plural 45, 48–9, 56–8, 61, 63–7, 116–18, 122–3, 125–6, 230
numeral 59, 87–9, 253

object 58, 121, 124, 129
    direct 19, 23, 259
object pronouns, 'atonic' *see* pronoun
objective conjugation 168
obligative 177
oblique *see* case
obstruent *see* consonant
onomasiology 320
onomatopoeia 323
onset 158–9, 287, 318
optative 142
orthography *see* spelling
Ottoman 196, 207
oxytonic 14

palatal, palatalization 9, 110–15, 150, 229, 231, 239–41, 252, 291, 293, 298
panchronic 12, 14–15, 43
paradigm 120, 131, 135, 297–301

paradigmatic 37
paragogic 42, 290–1, 300
parameter setting *see* Principles and
  Parameters
paroxytone 109, 237
participle 135
  passive 179, 258
  participial adjective 179, 258
  past 16, 22, 62–3, 75, 135–6, 147, 201,
    257–61, 318–19
particle 128
  adnominal 129
  identifying 128–9
  invariable 53
partitive 201, 262, 273–6
  prepositional 274
  pseudo-partitive 273
passato remoto, passé historique, passé défini,
  see tense preterite
passive, passivization 18, 20, 23, 103, 124,
  132–3, 135, 179–81
  BE-passive 180, 272, 313
  SE-passive 180-1, 269–74, 313
  periphrastic 36
past *see* tense
patois 216, 219
Peregrinatio Aetheriae 103
perfect 23, 132, 136, 177
  active 16
  BE-perfect *see* auxiliary
  compound 23, 62, 133–7, 257–61, 299
  future 132
  HAVE-perfect *see* auxiliary
  historic 132
  indefinite past 135
  indicative 16
  periphrastic 36
  present 132, 179, 299
  subjunctive 16, 17
perfective 93, 299
peripheral 8, 155–6
periphrastic 36, 72, 73, 76, 88, 89, 156, 175,
  177, 179, 300, 308
  passive 36
  perfect 36
  progressive 72
person, person markers 22, 39–55, 127
  first and second plural 47–51
personal infinitive *see* infinitive
philology *see* comparativist 39
phonemes, phonemic 26, 50, 68, 106, 162,
  173, 243
phonetics 35, 35, 39, 43, 68, 71, 87, 94, 95,
  110, 111, 240, 285
phonologization 29, 241

phonology 9, 11, 27, 35, 50, 51, 60, 61, 71,
  78, 97, 102, 105–6, 108, 110, 111, 126–7,
  130, 150, 155, 197, 199, 209–10, 232,
  240, 280, 285–96, 341
  generative 26, 45
phonotactic 290
phrasal 317
pidgin 224
pivot, link particle 314, 316
place (phonology) 27
planning
  corpus 215, 255
  status 215
pleonastic 44, 46, 314
plosive *see* consonant
pluperfect 137, 311
plural *see* number
polar questions 249, 308, 310
polite form *see* honorific
polynomic standard 211, 216
Pompeii 100, 234
popular 22, 49, 83, 85, 100–1, 102, 138, 150,
  325, 331, 333
possessive 59, 68, 77, 84, 118, 124, 126, 136,
  276–8
  adjectival 129, 276–8
  reflexive 278
  strong 129, 276–8
  weak 129, 276–8
potential 142
pragmatics 8, 146
predicative 18
predicative relative *see* tensed complement
prefix 74, 75, 84, 267, 290, 302
preposition 115–16, 123–4, 127, 144, 323
preposition stranding 342
prepositional accusative (PA) 121–3, 168,
  200, 201
prepositional phrase (PP) 261
prescriptive 297
present indicative *see* tense
preterite *see* tense
Principles and Parameters 2, 7, 10, 20, 51,
  70, 76, 167, 201
Principle of Least Effort 285
pro-adjective 315
proclitic *see* clitic
pro-drop, null subject 51, 53–4, 70, 201, 274,
  307
progressive *see* aspect
promotion raising 20, 265
pronominal *see* pronoun
pronominalization 315
pronominal verb 20–3, 36, 51, 59, 124, 129
  impersonal 181, 269–74

inherent 20, 21, 22, 274
middle 23, 180, 269
passive 21, 23, 180, 269–74
reciprocal 20, 21
reflexive 21–3, 49, 125, 181, 253, 269–74
pronoun (*see* also clitic) 45–54, 59, 116, 121,
   124–5, 127–8, 173, 317–18
adverbial 259
anaphoric 47, 167
clitic (q.v.) 20, 41, 45, 46, 52, 53, 122, 125
conjunctive 167
copying *see* clitic doubling
dative of interest 169
definite 59
deictic (*see* demonstrative) 47, 126
discourse 47, 167
disjunctive, tonic 45, 57, 125, 127, 167,
   262, 265
object 21, 36, 258, 318; atonic 36
personal 41, 51, 76, 79, 90, 122; tonic 122
pleonastic 44
possessive 76
postposed vestigial 52
post prepositional 78
preposed 49
reflexive 264
subject 37, 40, 41, 43, 45, 46, 51, 53, 54,
   73, 79, 145, 170, 248, 262, 318
third person 125, 129
proparoxytone 108–9
prosthetic 289–91
proto-language 11, 14, 97, 199
prototype 115
pseudo-adjective 147
punctual 299, 311
purism 214, 330, 336, 338
push-chain *see* chain-shift

quality, vowel 107
quantifier 275
quantity, vowel (*see also* vowel, long) 107, 158
QU- (WH-) conjunction, complementizer
   145, 164, 309, 314, 317
   question marker 307–10
questionnaire, dialect 203

rafforzamento sintattico 236–7, 286
raising *see* promotion; vowel
reciprocal *see* pronominal verb
reconstruction, reconstructionism 4, 11–15
Reconquest 208, 215
redundancy 317
reflex 13, 56, 57, 85, 114, 123, 229, 262
reflexive (*see* pronominal) 186
reform, spelling 240

Reformation 211, 344
regular 40, 99, 300
regularist 4
Relational Grammar 19
relative clause, restrictive 146
   non-restrictive 146
relative pronoun, relativizer 305–6, 317–18
Renaissance 152, 207, 227, 344
Republican 330
restrictive *see* relative clause
resultative 313
retraction 244
retroflex 294
Rhaetian 192
rhotacism 28
rhyme, rime 25, 29
rhythmic group 110, 286
Risorgimento 212
Roman Empire 152, 227, 231, 245, 343
Romany, Romali *see* Gipsy
Romania continua 38
Romanticism 333
roofing language 206, 217–18, 256
root 130
rounding 288

sandhi 9, 285–7
schwa 27, 173, 291
scriptorium 210
sdrucciole 99, 100, 293
segment, segmental 25, 40, 108
   tier 161
semantics 10, 18, 48, 60, 90, 92, 94, 96, 115,
   129, 133, 135–6, 154, 156, 284, 319–26
   patterns 55
semi-cultismos 150
sentence roles 122
servitude grammaticale 143
seseo 252
sex-gender marking *see* gender
sibilant, *see* consonant
simplification 310–19
sinalefa 286
singular 22, 56, 57, 61, 64, 65, 66, 67, 68,
   116, 118–20, 123, 125, 128
skeletal tier 161
slang 340
small nation 214–18
social variation 100
sociolect 228, 341
sociolinguistics 54, 221, 232, 329–45
solidarity pronoun 169
sound-change 120, 150, 255, 301
sound-law 203
specific 275

spelling, orthography 26, 27, 119, 139, 151,
   209, 210, 230, 236, 237, 240, 243, 247,
   283, 286, 287
spirant *see* consonant
spirantization, gorgia toscana 235, 241–3
Stammbaum (*see* family tree) 196–7
standard theory *see* generative
standardization, standard 21, 23, 27, 37, 47,
   51, 54, 121–2, 136, 141, 143, 149–50,
   168, 178, 205, 215, 256, 276, 280,
   329–34
   regional 202, 218, 254, 284, 295–6, 299,
   338
standardology 196, 206–17
stative 19, 313
stem (*see also* future) 44, 45, 62, 120, 132,
   162, 297
stem alternation 117, 297–9
stem-stressed, rhizotonic 45, 51, 297–9
Strasburg Oaths (842) 177, 273
stress (*see also* accentuation), 50, 54, 99, 100,
   108, 111, 131
   antepenultimate 100
   pattern 108–9
   rhythmic group 110
style, stylistics 8, 10, 133, 147, 310, 319, 329
subject 19, 20, 22, 45, 46, 62, 74, 83, 124,
   129, 145
subjunctive 132, 141–4, 149, 154, 164, 298,
   304, 314, 315
   future 132, 142, 209
   imperfect, past 132, 142, 310–11
   perfect 132, 142
   pluperfect 132, 142
   present 142, 300
subordination (*see also* clause) 186, 315
substratum 152, 202, 232–45, 281, 320, 340
suffix, suffixation 44–5, 64, 69, 74, 84–7, 99,
   111, 133, 147, 309
   bound 83
   derivational 85–7, 254
superstratum 232–3, 245–54, 281, 320
supine 144
suppletion 131–2, 296, 313
surcomposé 137
surds *see* consonants, voiceless
surface ordering 201
SVO, SOV *see* word order
syllabicity 288
syllable 13, 108–9, 119, 131
   accented, stressed, tonic 101, 107–8, 160,
   162, 239, 246
   antepenultimate 41, 99, 109
   atonic, unstressed 99, 107, 109, 162, 246
   blocked, checked, closed 239

final 109, 246
free, open 40, 158, 160, 239
length 248
penultimate 40, 99, 107, 109
pretonic 239
weight 107; light 108; heavy 109
synchronic 10, 26, 38, 96
syncope, syncopation 15, 99, 100, 102, 111,
   292
syncretism 116, 141
synonym 92, 255
syntagma 59, 81, 126
syntagmatic 37
syntax, syntactic 10, 35, 37, 62, 103, 115,
   129–30, 154, 176–7, 254–80, 284, 302–10
synthetic 156, 176–8, 185, 200–1, 331

TAM (tense–aspect–mood) *see* marker
tautosyllabic 27, 108
template 298–9, 313
tense *see* lax
tense (*see also* subjunctive; perfect) 37
   aorist 15, 179, 299
   future 177–9, 185, 331
   future in the past 16, 177–9
   future subjunctive 327
   GO-past 300
   imperfect 41, 44, 50, 74, 75
   indicative 39, 42
   pluperfect 327
   present 39, 40, 42–3, 45, 47
   preterite, simple past, remote past, past
      definite, past historic 299–301, 313, 327
tensed complement, predicative relative,
   attributive relative, pseudo-relative 201
thematic vowel 44, 50, 297, 300
theme, thematic 19–20
theta role 19
Tigani *see* Gipsy
tilde 25, 140
timbre 55
tmesis 178
Tobler-Mussafia Law 170
tonic *see* vowel, syllable
topic, topicalization 46, 126, 201, 248–9,
   275, 286
transitive 21–2
transparency 156
Tre Corone 212
triphthong 161
troubadours 190–1
truncation 26, 99, 286
type, typology 2, 6, 70, 226
   'holistic' 36
   'integral' 36

umlaut, metaphony 101–2, 118–19, 154, 159–60
unaccusative 19–24, 52, 62, 135, 259
   unaccusative/ergative hypothesis 20
unergative 20
Universal Grammar (UG), 283
universals 6
Ursprache *see* proto-language
uvular *r* 244, 294–5

Vatican Council (1962) 152, 154
velar, velarizing 12, 243, 294–300
verb-first (V1), verb-second (V2) *see* word order
verb phrase (VP) 53
verbs, verbals 36, 44, 35, 36, 51, 52, 53, 54, 71, 73, 80, 83, 93, 128, 131, 133, 135, 320–2
   conjugation 41, 42, 47, 130–2, 133–4, 177, 300
   finite 135
   inflections 36, 39, 46, 52
   intransitive 15, 16, 17, 18, 20, 83, 135
   irregular 130, 134
   lexical 36, 134
   paradigm 60
   perception, *see* VERBA SENTIENDI
   pronominal 36
   regular 96, 130, 177
   system 39, 115, 140
   transitive 18, 23. 63
   volition 143–4
   voluntative 142
VERBA DECLARANDI, verbs of saying 144
VERBA SENTIENDI, verbs of perception 144, 264, 266
verbi servili 17
verlan see back slang
Villers-Cotterêts (Edict, 1539) 210
Vlach, 105, 207
vocabulary *see* lexicon
vocalization 292–3
voice *see* passive
voiceless stops, intervocalic 94
voicing (*see* also lenition) 231, 232
volgare illustre 141

VOS (Verb–Subject–Object), *see* word order
vowel 55–6, 61–2, 65, 68–9, 99, 106–8, 111, 113, 119, 197
   back 240
   central, centralization 140, 243–4
   front, fronting 112, 240, 244, 298
   high, height 28, 157, 243, 253
   high-tone 99
   intertonic 111
   lax 157
   long, length 13–14, 106–8, 157, 244, 253
   low 28
   lowering 253, 288
   low-tone 99
   mid 158, 231, 240
   nasal *see* nasalization
   non-peripheral 157
   peripheral 157
   raising 161, 288
   round, rounded, rounding 241, 288
   schwa-type 99
   short 99, 106–7, 109, 111, 157
   theme, stem-vowel 40, 42–3, 130, 135
   tonic, accented 44, 99, 199
   unaccented, atonic 292
vowel harmony (*see also* umlaut) 160
Vulgar Latin 102–3

Wackernagel's Law 170
weather verbs 23–4, 53
WH- *see* QU-
word formation 9, 80
word order 53, 117, 202
   noun–adjective 36
   surface 36, 146
   SVO (subject–verb–object) 36, 61, 146, 202, 248, 271, 304
   verb-first ordering, VOS (V1) 36, 52
   verb-last (SOV) ordering 103, 146, 167, 178, 202, 304
   verb-second order (V2) 53, 54, 248–50, 304
word stress 246

zero marker 40, 45